Recent Trends in
Mortality Analysis

This is a volume in

STUDIES IN POPULATION

A complete list of titles in this series appears at the end of this volume.

# RECENT TRENDS IN
# MORTALITY ANALYSIS

*Kenneth G. Manton*
*Eric Stallard*
CENTER FOR DEMOGRAPHIC STUDIES
DUKE UNIVERSITY
DURHAM, NORTH CAROLINA

 1984

ACADEMIC PRESS, INC.
(Harcourt Brace Jovanovich, Publishers)
Orlando   San Diego   New York   London
Toronto   Montreal   Sydney   Tokyo

ACADEMIC PRESS, INC.
Orlando, Florida 32887

*United Kingdom Edition published by*
ACADEMIC PRESS, INC. (LONDON) LTD.
24/28 Oval Road, London NW1 7DX

Library of Congress Cataloging in Publication Data

Manton, Kenneth G.
    Recent trends in mortality analysis.

    (Studies in population)
    Includes index.
    1. Mortality. 2. Death--Causes. 3. Mortality--
Tables. I. Stallard, Eric. II. Title. III. Series.
HB1321.M36   1984      304.6'4'072      83-11736
ISBN 0-12-470020-9

PRINTED IN THE UNITED STATES OF AMERICA

84 85 86 87      9 8 7 6 5 4 3 2 1

# Contents

v

**Chapter 4**   A Conceptual Framework for Mortality Analysis

**Chapter 5**   Life Table Methods for the Analysis
of Underlying- and Multiple-Cause Mortality Data

**Chapter 6**   Life Tables for Heterogeneous Populations:
Cohort versus Period Life Table Computations,
an Examination of the Black–White Mortality Crossover

**Chapter 7**  Ecological Models of Cause-Specific Mortality Differentials

**Chapter 8**  Projection and Estimates of the National State of Health: Disease-Specific Compartment Models of Mortality Time Series

# Preface

In this book we present a series of demographic models designed to investigate the effects of morbidity and mortality processes on human populations. In developing these models we have attempted to fulfill two criteria. The first criterion is that the models be biologically realistic: By developing models whose structures realistically portray the biological mechanisms of mortality and morbidity, we hope to be able to project future health status changes more accurately and to achieve better estimates of the effects of possible interventions in morbid and mortal processes. The second criterion in developing population models of health is that our models be consistent with both macro- and microlevel changes. That is, population models are often developed that lead to inconsistent results at the level of the individual. If there were inconsistency between the implications of model results at the population and individual levels, the model would be of little use in developing plans of action and formulating public health policy.

Developing biologically realistic models of population health requires a comprehensive approach to modeling in which results from a broad range of disciplines must be integrated into the production of models. For example, the development of models of morbidity and mortality must be informed by concepts and data developed by clinicians, epidemiologists, biomedical scientists, and biostatisticians as well as demographers and actuaries. Clearly, such a multidisciplinary effort is difficult, but it is the only way in which truly useful models can be developed. The need for a multidisciplinary perspective extends beyond the range of substantive areas involved. Very often, demographic models have been developed that pay inadequate attention to the principle of inference and to existing mathematical models of stochastic processes and time series analysis.

In our investigation we have focused on the role of chronic degenerative diseases and their interaction with physiological aging. This focus emerged both because we have a substantive interest in population aging changes and because modeling chronic diseases involves special methodological problems. Specifically, modeling the impact of chronic diseases on the population requires us to develop, in effect, models of the operation of processes operating within processes. That is, in addition to modeling the age dependency of total mortality risks, one must generate models of how chronic disease processes operate within the individual to determine the age dependency of total mortality. For two reasons, we believe that now is a particularly appropriate time for such methodological and substantive studies. First, demographic changes have rapidly accelerated the absolute and relative growth of our elderly population. Indeed, the extremely elderly (i.e., those over 85 years of age) are projected to be one of the fastest-growing components of the U.S. population. Second, we have apparently entered a hitherto unanticipated stage of what has been called the "epidemiological transition." Specifically, we have recently observed increases in life expectancy at advanced ages and major declines in the mortality risks of chronic diseases. It is challenging to attempt to forecast the future course of mortality and life expectancy changes because we do not yet understand well the precise causes of such changes. It is also exciting to develop models that can immediately draw on new scientific understanding garnered from ongoing biomedical and epidemiological studies of chronic disease incidence, progression, and management and of basic changes in aging.

Finally, in our modeling efforts we have attempted to pay attention to the assessment of the societal and health service implications of the results of our models. That is, if the modeling of population health changes is to be useful in planning and guiding health programs and policy, the outputs of the models have to be translatable into quantities that are meaningful for policy questions. We have endeavored to develop procedures by which our models of morbid and mortal processes can be used for such evaluation.

We wish to acknowledge the support of the National Institute on Aging, which was essential to the analyses and methodological developments reported herein. This research benefited greatly from collaboration with Max A. Woodbury, H. Dennis Tolley, and George C. Myers. Research facilities were provided by the Center for Demographic Studies, Duke University. Special thanks go to Elaine McMichael, Betsy Smith, Janice Yuwiler, Michael Carney, and Barbara Priboth for assistance in the preparation of this monograph.

**Chapter 1** | Trends in Mortality
Analysis: An Overview
of the Need and the Approach

## 1   The Need for New Methods for Assessing Population Health Characteristics

There are many federal and state programs mandated to respond to the health needs of the state and national populations. The Health Care Financing Administration (HCFA) requires estimates of the need for medical services among the elderly in order to administrate and manage the Medicare program. Various components of the National Institutes of Health (NIH) require detailed evaluations of national health needs both to assign priorities for research and to assess the impact of medical research and clinical innovations on the population's health. The Environmental Protection Agency (EPA) is required to establish national standards for ambient air quality based on the likely health impact of various pollutants on susceptible portions of the U.S. population. The Center for Disease Control (CDC) is charged with monitoring the health state of the national population. Not only do governmental agencies need accurate estimates and forecasts of the health status of the particular populations they intend to serve, but also the private sector needs accurate data if it is to play an increasing role in certain areas of health service delivery. For example, a number of strategies have been proposed to use prospective reimbursement as the basis for greater involvement of the private sector in the provision of acute care medical services to elderly populations. For such strategies to be effective, accurate estimates of the expected costs of medical services to an aging population must be made.

A variety of data and strategies is employed by governmental and health agencies to assess the health characteristics of the U.S. population.

1

Each of these has certain limitations, however, in evaluating population health. For example, HCFA maintains files on a 20% sample of hospitalizations funded under Medicare. They also maintain other files that reflect aspects of health service utilization for persons who are entitled under the Medicare system. However, sometimes the level of utilization of health services is not well coordinated with the need for such services. Consequently, HCFA's assessment of the need for health services may sometimes be strongly confounded with the peculiar characteristics of the medical services market.

A second approach to conducting an assessment of population health characteristics is to utilize population health surveys. Although useful, these surveys have certain limitations. A survey such as the Health Interview Survey (HIS), conducted by the National Center for Health Statistics (NCHS), is restricted in scope to those conditions that can be accurately reported and described by the members of the general population. Studies show that many chronic illnesses (NCHS, 1965, 1973) and illnesses with strong psychological implications (e.g., cancer; see Chambers *et al.*, 1976) are often poorly reported when compared with medical and hospital records. Difficulties are also frequently encountered when surveying special populations (such as the very elderly) or when studying rare disorders. As a response to some of these difficulties, NCHS also conducts the Health and Nutrition Examination Survey (HANES). The HANES differs from the HIS in that physical examination and measurements are actually performed. With actual physical examination, far more reliable and specific measurements of health can be made. The HANES strategy is more expensive, however, so that far fewer persons are examined in the HANES than are surveyed in the HIS, making it more difficult to adequately represent the full geographic and demographic variability of the health state of the U.S. population.

A third approach to assessing population health is through clinical studies, such as those conducted by the EPA. In essence, such clinical studies are carefully controlled human experiments conducted under laboratory conditions. These studies have the advantages of controlled experiments but the disadvantage that only highly selected components of the population can be included in the experimental protocol. Thus, although invaluable in studying the basis of individual human physiological response to various pollutants, such studies by themselves cannot yield insight into aggregate health risks because the population mixture of human characteristics affecting such health risks is abstracted from such studies by the logic of the experimental protocol. These studies also have ethical restrictions that preclude the study of severe health effects or the study of highly susceptible population groups.

Such ethical restrictions on human experimentation are sometimes dealt with by augmenting the available experimental and epidemiological data on humans with results from controlled animal studies. A much broader range of effects can be studied with animals, although the results must always be qualified by extrapolation across species from the animal model to humans. In addition, animal studies are often conducted by using an accelerated-life testing principle in which the suspected agent is applied at abnormally high doses (with respect to its likely level in the human environment). This permits the experimenter to obtain results in a more limited time span and with a more limited group of animals, although interpretation of the results involves additional qualifications due to the need to extrapolate from high to low doses.

Finally, a critically important source of data for studying the health of human populations is derived from various types of epidemiological studies (Fleiss, 1973). These studies can be classified by the type of population examined or surveyed. For example, one type of population studied is the *clinical population*. Studies of clinical populations are useful because detailed medical evidence is available about the disease process and because one deals directly with a group of individuals possessing the disease of interest. Difficulties arise, however, when one attempts to relate results from a specific clinical population to any other external population; that is, there is considerable potential for bias in dealing only with persons who become clinically identified as having the disease (Berkson, 1946). For this reason, clinical studies are generally more useful for generating hypotheses about the natural history of disease, and disease and risk factor associations, than for confirming those observations and associations within a population.

To evaluate the actual health risks of a population, two other types of epidemiological studies are performed. One type involves retrospective studies of *populations of convenience*. That is, populations are examined that have experienced a "natural experiment" such as an accidental exposure to a health risk of interest. An example would be an occupational group such as the Portsmouth Naval Shipyard population, which was chronically exposed to low-dose radiation. One difficulty with such studies is that they are subject to biases arising because the health outcome is known before the search for the cause is initiated.

Another important type of epidemiological study is the truly prospective cohort or population study in which special populations characterized only by exposure to serious risk factors are followed longitudinally to determine the prospective incidence of disease. Although the opportunities for bias are reduced because the outcomes are not known, such studies are expensive in terms of both time and money; usually, these studies are restricted in scope to one or a small group of communities so that often the phenomenon of interest cannot be totally unconfounded from other health characteristics unique to the community populations in question. As a result, one is left with the difficult task of extrapolating from the specific community (e.g., Evans County or Framingham; see Kessler and Levin, 1970) to more general populations. Finally, population-based epidemiological studies are sometimes merged with the experimental logic of controlled intervention programs in which specific health service changes are instituted in community trial programs to determine their effect on population health.

Another important source of data is broad-scope monitoring systems such as the pneumonia–influenza epidemic surveillance system conducted by the CDC in 123 U.S. cities. In this system, weekly mortality data from the cities in the system are compared with a model of seasonal influenza activity to determine whether influenza activity is above normal for a long enough period of time to indicate that influenza activity is epidemic. Although this population-monitoring system carefully indexes changes in population health status, the data collected are extremely limited; the most important information is the time series variation of the mortality indices. Monitoring systems of a different type exist for chronic diseases. The National Cancer Institute (NCI) monitors a series of population-based tumor registries to assess time trends in national cancer incidence (Pollack and Horm, 1980) and to determine changes in the patterns of treatment and clinical management of cancer. Indeed, data from this system have led to suggestions that cancer incidence has recently begun to increase after a long period of stability (Smith, 1980). A number of methodological critiques has been made of the system, primarily focusing on changes in the identity and number of population-based tumor registries in the system, changes in the system over time, and difficulties in determining time of incidence for tumors reported in the system. One other frequently used source of health data derives from insured populations (Singer and Levinson, 1976). Such data are useful because they are extensive and often represent a long-term follow-up of the morbidity–mortality experience of the insured population; however, the difficulty with such data is that insured populations are generally selected on the basis of socioeconomic and health status.

Finally, a data source that is nationally representative and that has been compiled for a long period of time is the mortality registration system maintained by NCHS. From this system, cause-specific mortality data are made available for all deaths occurring in the United States. The strengths of this system are (1) the large numbers of events recorded, making it possible to study rare events, (2) the existence of a lengthy time series (at least back to 1962 for total mortality and 1950 for cancer mortality, with special cause-specific reports existing back to 1900), and (3) the existence of geographic detail to the county level. Although extensive in terms of the population covered, the amount of medical information collected on each person in the system is limited. Furthermore, there are a number of questions that are frequently raised about the quality of diagnostic information in the system.

In the preceding we have briefly listed some of the possible sources of data that could be utilized to assess the health characteristics of general populations. Although each type of data is important for understanding some dimension of the health status of the population, no data set is sufficient in its own right to study all aspects of population health. Given the tremendous investment in the collection of the various types of data listed, it would seem to be highly cost effective and hence desirable to integrate these various types of data in a comprehensive model of population health. This book examines more realistic demographic models of population health characteristics that use the types of data discussed in the preceding. Such models might be of value to policy makers to facilitate consideration of scientific and survey data in a more coordinated fashion.

Furthermore, these models can have a significant impact on the private sector, say, by allowing more accurate forecasts of the expected medical costs for elderly populations covered under prospective reimbursement plans or by allowing private insurance or pension programs to predict more accurately future changes in life expectancy.

## 2  Medical Demography: An Amalgam of Disciplines via a Common Methodology

In the preceding section we saw that there is a tremendous variety of data on the health status of the U.S. population but that no single source was adequate by itself to evaluate the health status of the U.S. population. This suggests the need for an approach that can integrate a variety of data sources and analytic results. The recognition of the need for such integration is evident in that a variety of strategies for policy analysis, consensus-generating conferences, meta-analysis, etc., have been developed. However, what has not received adequate attention is the specialized development of formal mechanisms to accomplish the integration of multiple sources of health data in the analysis of the health status of general populations. Formal efforts to organize such diverse data sources into a concrete model of the nation's health might be conveniently labeled *medical demography*. We select this term because the study is intrinsically a study of population characteristics and because the population model developed to examine those population characteristics must be based on and consistent with biomedical data and theory. It should be emphasized that the intent of such a modeling strategy is *not* to replace clinical, epidemiological, and experimental studies. The results of these studies figure prominently in the development of a formal model structure. Rather, the intent of medical demography is to provide an integrating structure for the various types of data and on the basis of that input and the model structure to provide specific quantitative estimates of population health characteristics.

The necessity for developing and implementing specialized models for medical demography is due to the need to discriminate, both conceptually and operationally, between health characteristics as manifest on a population or aggregate level and on the level of the individual organism. Specifically, biomedical models must abstract, from aggregate-level data, disease processes and health risk factors as they affect individuals, because interventions will be applied at an individual level. At the population level, there are many confounding or mixing factors that affect our perception of health in the aggregate. In order to translate with precision between the individual and population levels, analyses must take into account the population dynamics that cause the confounding or mixing. Thus, the purpose of medical demography is to integrate the best available biomedical knowledge and data into a model of population dynamics so that accurate quantitative assessments of population health and health change may be made—assessments that are in every way possible consistent with biomedical science.

The proposal for the development of tools for medical demography is a very general one, and it is appropriate to state explicitly certain organizing principles that might guide the development of the "bioactuarial" models (Clarke, 1950) that will be the primary task of medical demography.

First, the bioactuarial models to be developed must be *process oriented* on the individual level. That is, previous demographic and actuarial models of human mortality and morbidity have often dealt with disease and death as "shock" processes in which the phenomena of interest are manifest instantaneously. The implications of assuming a shock model of disease and death are great—both computationally and for the biomedical plausibility of the model. If diseases can be modeled as shocks, then they cannot occur simultaneously nor can an individual manifest a multiplicity of conditions. Although it might be argued that such shock models are useful approximations for acute disease processes, they are inappropriate for the analysis of chronic degenerative diseases and mortality—especially in elderly populations. Indeed, it seems likely that even infectious diseases should *not* be modeled as shock processes because chronic factors, such as nutrition, could greatly affect the risks of contracting and succumbing to the infectious disease process. In effect, we are suggesting that bioactuarial models must take into account the natural history of disease processes, including such factors as disease and disease–host interaction and dependency.

Second, the bioactuarial models to be developed must be process oriented on the aggregate level. That is, there are a number of population dynamics that can affect a translation of individual level health effects to what is observed at an aggregate level. Two mechanisms that are critical to these modeling efforts are mortality (or morbidity) selection and the competing risk effect. The need to adjust for *mortality selection* arises because individuals in a population are usually quite heterogeneous in their susceptibility to disease processes. Thus, as a population is subjected over time to disease or mortality risks, the most susceptible persons will have the highest likelihood of being "selected." If there is a high level of selection (such as might be manifest in very elderly populations), then the residual population will have a relatively lower average susceptibility (conditional on age-determined change in susceptibility) to the disease. Thus, high rates of selection may cause the age trajectory of aggregate risks to deviate from the age trajectory of individual risks. Therefore, in devising a model to translate the biological mechanisms operating at the individual level to risks operating at the aggregate levels, one must ensure that the model structure can be adjusted for selection phenomena.

The *competing risk* effect refers to the interaction between the cause-specific mortality rates when the causes of death are classified into two or more categories. Mention of this effect frequently occurs in the demographic and actuarial literature in discussions of multiple-decrement and cause-elimination life-table models. In these models, the elimination of a given mortality risk affects not only the mortality rate for that risk but also the mortality rates for all of the remaining active risks. This effect occurs despite the assumption that the risks are independent. In bioactuarial modeling of certain individual-level health effects, it may be more realistic to work with a weaker conditional independence assumption in which the dependence of a pair of diseases is represented as emanating from a common risk factor that varies over individuals in the population. Here, there is a direct connection between the mortality selection dynamics and the competing risk dynamics because both are modeled as effects of population heterogeneity. Naturally, because any derived estimates of the effect of a given health status intervention–modification program will be sensitive to the representation of risk dependency and risk factor heterogeneity, it is important to develop models that permit assessment of the extent of this sensitivity.

A third mechanism that must be represented in a successful bioactuarial model is the effects of aging on health—effects that are independent of, but may interact with, specific disease processes. Basically, this requires that we recognize that the risk of death for a human organism is, in part, determined by species-specific laws of biological senescence. The degree to which biological senescence is confounded with chronic degenerative diseases is not presently known, and the possibility exists that, as biomedical knowledge advances, more and more of the effects of senescence may be attributed to specific morbid states. Given the present state of knowledge, however, we are required to deal with the effects of an age-dependent increase in chronic disease risks attributable to basic aging processes in the host organism. Operationally, this requires that we can parametrically model the age trajectories of morbidity and mortality risks. It is critical that the models of the age trajectory of these risks be consistent with biomedical knowledge.

The bioactuarial models we develop should be adequate to represent time, age, and space variation in the health characteristics that we wish to describe. Furthermore, because we wish our models to be scientifically verifiable, it will be necessary that such models be fit to data with appropriate characteristics. The source of data that appears most capable of fulfilling these requirements is the cause-specific mortality statistics produced by NCHS from the national death registration system. This type of data has the breadth of coverage necessary to be used in a national monitoring system. Although these data have the necessary scope to form the basis of a monitoring system, they lack necessary in-depth information on disease behavior. Thus, it will be required that the logical structure of our bioactuarial model permits the inclusion of both objective and subjective input to elaborate the model's structure so that after the model is fit to mortality data, it can then be used to generate quantitative estimates of particular aspects of the disease process in the population. In accomplishing this task, any ancillary data or expert judgment input to the model should be explicitly identified in the model structure so that this input is reviewable. This is because the results of a bioactuarial modeling effort can be no better and no worse than the sum total of the information built into the bioactuarial model. This last point is critical to an understanding of the goals of medical demography. Specifically, the function of medical demography is not to supplant clinical, epidemiological, or laboratory research on human health; rather, the intent is to integrate that knowledge into a coherent model so that quantitative estimates of the parameters of the nation's health can be generated. In this context, an important byproduct of the modeling effort is an organized review of the biomedical science base from which areas of deficiencies, as well as strengths, might be identified. This effort might provide useful input into the process by which priorities in biomedical research are set. Thus, medical demography should be viewed as an evolutionary process whereby state-of-the-art bioactuarial models can be updated as biomedical knowledge is expanded. As the bioactuarial models are replaced, we would have measures of the rate of expansion of biomedical knowledge, at least in terms of its potential for producing measures of national health.

## 3  The Organization of This Book

In the preceding two sections of this chapter, we delineated the subject area for a new discipline, medical demography, and identified some of the organizing principles that might provide an operational basis for that discipline. Although no single comprehensive model of the nation's health yet exists, there have been several recent attempts to provide operational models and illustrative examples of the type of analyses proposed for the discipline of medical demography. It is ironic that in some ways the principles espoused in the preceding section were manifest more in the classical works of demographers and actuaries such as Gompertz and Makeham than they have been in the recent past. In the remainder of this book we shall briefly outline certain trends and developments in mortality analysis that might represent an initial although somewhat piecemeal approach to providing an operational basis for medical demography.

In Chapter 2 we shall examine the characteristics of mortality data— the primary data source that we believe will underlie the bioactuarial approach to be taken in medical demography. We shall examine various concepts such as the cause of death, the data-collection instrument, and the medical nomenclature system used to categorize health effects; and we shall review a range of studies of the reliability of death certificate data.

In Chapter 3 we shall discuss and examine multiple-cause-of-death mortality data—data in which all medical conditions listed on the death certificate are provided. The impact of multiple-cause data on our perception of the relative health significance of various conditions will be discussed, as well as the potential uses of this information.

In Chapter 4 we shall examine illness–death models and their specializations. The bioactuarial models developed in this chapter are variants of basic illness–death models. Also in this chapter we shall introduce *stochastic compartment methodology*, which will help suggest strategies to estimate indirectly various types of health-state-transition-rate parameters.

In Chapter 5 we shall examine major race–sex mortality differentials of chronic diseases in the U.S. population. We shall examine several variants of common life table procedures that reflect on aspects of individual survival not usually represented in standard actuarial models.

In Chapter 6 we shall present life-table models for representing the effects of heterogeneity in survival analysis. Cohort life table models will be presented for studying the age trajectory of mortality rates in individuals, and period life table models will be presented for adjusting period life table parameters to be consistent with the individual level mortality rates derived for that period from the cross section of living cohorts. The phenomenon of the black–white mortality crossover will be examined because it illustrates the substantive effects of population heterogeneity in the comparison of the mortality experience of different population groups. This example will also lead us to examine the implications of population estimates for our evaluation of population health characteristics.

In Chapter 7 several procedures will be presented for dealing with the geographic variability of health effects. Issues involved in estimation of the health characteristics of small areas will be discussed and various analytic approaches to deal with those problems will be presented.

In Chapter 8 we shall illustrate the use of a bioactuarial model for assessing the underlying health states of the population from information on categorical disease designations. The example uses mortality data for lung cancer in the United States from 1950 to 1977 to estimate the transition-rate parameters of a stochastic compartment model with one unobserved health-state transition.

## References

Berkson, J. 1946. Limitations of the application of fourfold table analysis in hospital data. *Biometrics Bulletin* **2**.

Chambers, L. W., Spitzer, W. O., Hill, G. B., and Helliwell, B. E. 1976. Underreporting of cancer in medical surveys: A source of systematic error in cancer research. *American Journal of Epidemiology* **104**:141–145.

Clarke, R. D. 1950. A Bio-actuarial approach to forecasting rates of mortality. *Proceedings of the Centenary Assembly of the Institute of Actuaries*, Vol. 2, p. 12. Cambridge: Cambridge University Press.

Fleiss, J. L. 1973. *Statistical methods for rates and proportions*. New York: Wiley.

Kessler, I. I., and Levin, M. L. (eds.). 1970. *The community as an epidemiologic laboratory: A casebook of community studies*. Baltimore: Johns Hopkins Press.

NCHS (National Center for Health Statistics). 1965. Health interview responses compared with medical records. U.S. Department of Health, Education and Welfare Pub. No. 1000, series 2, No. 7, Washington, D.C.

NCHS (National Center for Health Statistics). 1973. Net differences in interview data on chronic conditions and information derived from medical records. U.S. Department of Health, Education and Welfare Pub. No. (HSM) 73-1331, Rockville, Maryland.

Pollack, E. S., and Horm, J. 1980. Trends in cancer incidence and mortality in the United States, 1969–76. *Journal of the National Cancer Institute* **64**:1091–1103.

Singer, R. B., and Levinson, L. 1976. *Medical risks: Patterns of mortality survival*. Lexington, Massachusetts: D. C. Heath.

Smith, R. J. 1980. Government says cancer rate is increasing. *Science* **209**:998–1002.

# Chapter 2 | Mortality Data: Concepts and Data Quality Issues

## 1 Introduction

Cause-specific mortality statistics are often employed in epidemiological investigations of the health consequences of chronic diseases such as cancer (Pollack and Horm, 1980) and cardiovascular disease (Kuller *et al.,* 1969a–d). These statistics are also frequently used in the determination of priorities for the allocation of research funds in health fields (Abramson, 1974; Kleinman, 1977) and in the evaluation of the cost effectiveness of health projects or agencies (Colburn and Baker, 1974; Ortey and Parker, 1977; Todd, 1972) at the state as well as national level (Linder, 1976; U.S. National Committee on Vital and Health Statistics, 1975; WHO, 1974). Despite the range and importance of the roles that cause-specific mortality statistics fulfill, the researchers and policy analysts who employ these statistics often pay inadequate attention to their measurement and conceptual characteristics.

In this chapter we review a range of analyses and studies of the measurement characteristics of death certificates, especially the nature and quality of medical diagnostic information listed on death certificates. Although much of this information is dated because death certification studies are conducted infrequently and although the studies represent a variety of different designs, it is important to review this information as a preliminary to the design and interpretation of cause-specific mortality studies. Such information can indicate the degree of diagnostic specificity that is likely to be reliable for major classes of disease and can identify the direction of biases of specific diagnoses over such important demographic variables as age or sex.

In this chapter we shall examine in some detail the measurement characteristics of death statistics. This will involve reviewing

(1)   the concept of the cause of death and the relation of the cause of death concept to the death certificate;
(2)   selected studies of the reliability of death certificate diagnoses; and
(3)   the International Classification of Diseases (ICD), and other medical nomenclature systems used to represent cause of death, and the effects of changes in these systems over time.

## 2   The Concept of the Cause of Death

The term *cause-specific mortality statistics* refers to data on human mortality that are derived from a very specific model of human death—the underlying-cause-of-death model of human mortality. The premise of the underlying-cause model of human mortality is that death is a unidimensional process. This implies that a single disease or medical condition can be designated as the underlying cause of death when it is the disease or medical condition that initiated the sequence of morbid events that resulted in death. The underlying-cause model was developed when the primary public health problems were infectious disease epidemics and infant mortality (Moriyama, 1965; Peery, 1975); when death occurred its cause could be usually abstracted as a single condition occurring simultaneously with death. The underlying-cause concept was usefully employed for many years because it simplified the tabulation of cause-specific mortality frequencies and greatly simplified actuarial calculations. Increasingly, however, the primary public health problems have shifted to chronic and degenerative diseases—a shift labeled by Omran (1971) as the "epidemiological transition." As the U.S. population aged and the public health implications of chronic degenerative diseases increased, the significance of the deficiencies in the underlying-cause model has also increased. At present, it is critical that the underlying-cause concept be replaced by a concept of human mortality sufficiently general to

(1)   permit the possibility that any death may have *more* than a single cause,
(2)   allow the cause of death to operate over a period of time, and
(3)   reflect the possibility that diseases may interact in various ways or interact with the characteristics of the host, especially its aging characteristics (Kohn, 1982).

Each of these conditions suggests that the underlying-cause concept ought to be replaced with a more realistic model of death as being caused by multiple conditions.

Two basic multiple-cause-of-death models have been proposed, each of which leads to a variety of different analytic formulations. The first multiple-cause formulation can be designated as an extended underlying-cause model. Here the notion is retained that an underlying cause of death can be selected for each decedent but that it is also possible that associated and contributory causes of death can modify the behavior of the underlying cause of death. The second multiple-cause concept is the pattern-of-failure model of human mortality (Manton *et al.*, 1976). In this model of human mortality, all medical conditions noted at the time of death are assumed to contribute to death but no effort is made to disentangle the causal sequence from the conditions listed on the death certificate.

To understand how these various concepts of human mortality relate to the U.S. standardized death certificate, consider the death certificate reproduced in Fig. 1. Note that a variety of demographic information—age, race, and sex as well as geographic and occupational information—is elicited on the death certificate form. For the present, our attention is directed to the medical conditions (items 19 and 20a). It is apparent that the medical conditions are divided into two parts. In item 19 (Part I), the certifier (who may not be a physician) lists the morbid conditions in causal sequence on three lines. The condition on the last line used is designated as the underlying cause of death. Because the death certificate is often not appropriately filled out (e.g., multiple conditions are listed on one line or lines are skipped), NCHS has been using a computer program, the Automated Classification of Medical Entities (ACME), since 1968 to select an underlying cause of death. The empirical implications of this selection mechanism will be explored in a later chapter. The conditions listed on the two lines above the underlying cause of death are often called the immediate and intermediate causes of death, respectively. The conditions listed in item 20a (Part II) are designated as associated or contributory causes of death; these conditions are assumed to contribute to death but are assumed *not* to be involved in the causal sequence implied in item 19 of the death certificate.

To illustrate the implications of the structure of the death certificate further, let us consider the simple example illustrated in Fig. 1. On line (c) of item 19, we find that lung cancer (ICDA-8, 162.1; ICDA-8 denotes the eighth revision ICD, adapted for use in the United States) has been listed. This is the certifier's selection of the underlying cause of death. On line (b) of the death certificate, we find that pneumonia (ICDA-8, 486) has been listed as the intermediate cause of death. The assumption is that the

**Fig. 1.** Example of standard North Carolina death certificate with lung cancer coded as the underlying cause of death and septicemia as the immediate cause of death. (Forms for other states may vary slightly.)

pneumonia was caused by, and would not have occurred in the absence of, the lung cancer. On line (a), we find septicemia (ICDA-8, 038.9), which is presumed to be a consequence of the pneumonia. In item 20a, we find that diabetes mellitus has been listed as a contributory cause. It is assumed that diabetes mellitus was not a result of the lung cancer but was an independent condition that had an adverse effect on the patient's ability to survive the lung cancer. Note that it would be inappropriate if a "mode of dying" were listed on the death certificate. For example, cardiac arrest would generally be considered a mode of dying and hence not a legitimate cause of death.

NORTH CAROLINA DEPARTMENT OF HUMAN RESOURCES
DIVISION OF HEALTH SERVICES – VITAL RECORDS BRANCH

**CERTIFICATE OF DEATH**

Registration
District No._____ Local No. _____

| | | |
|---|---|---|
| Type, or print in permanent black ink | **Name of Deceased** First / Middle / Last — SAMPLE | Sex / Date of Death (Month, Day, Year) |
| | 1. | 2. / 3. |
| **DECEASED** | Color or Race / State of Birth (If not U.S.A., give Country) / County of Birth / Date of Birth | Age (In Years, Last Birthday) / If under 1 year Months Days / If under 24 hours Hours Min. |
| | 4. / 5a. / 5b. / 6. | 7. |
| | Place of Death-County / City or Town / Name of Hospital or Institution (If not in either, give street and number) | If Hosp. or Inst. (Specify DOA, Emer Rm, Inpatient/OP) / Inside City Limits (Yes or No) |
| | 8a. / 8b. / 8c. | 8d. / 8e. |
| | Residence - State / County / City or Town / Street and Number or R.F.D. & Box No. | Inside City Limits (Yes or No) |
| | 9a. / 9b. / 9c. / 9d. | 9e. |
| | Citizen of What Country? / Married, Never Married, Widowed, Divorced (Specify) / Surviving Spouse (If Wife, Give Maiden Name) | |
| | 10. / 11. / 12. | |
| | Social Security Number / Usual Occupation (Kind of work done during most of life, even if retired) / Kind of Business or Industry / Was Decedent Ever in U.S. Armed Forces?(Yes or No) | |
| | 13. / 14a. / 14b. / 15. | |
| **PARENTS** | Father's Name / Mother's Maiden Name | |
| | 16. / 17. | |
| | Informant's Name and Address / Relation to Deceased | |
| | 18a. / 18b. | |

**PART I.** DEATH CAUSED BY: ENTER ONLY ONE CAUSE PER LINE FOR (a), (b), (c) — Approximate Interval Between Onset and Death

Conditions, if any which gave rise to immediate cause (a), stating the underlying cause last.

(a) Immediate Cause: Stroke

(b) Due to, or as a consequence of: Acute Myocardial Infarction

**CAUSE** 19. (c) Due to, or as a consequence of: Generalized Arteriosclerosis

PART II. Other Significant Conditions Contributing to Death but not related to cause given in Part I(a).

20a. Diabetes Mellitus

| Autopsy? (Yes or No) | If yes, were findings considered in determining cause of death | Was case referred to Medical Examiner (Yes or No) | Time of Death |
|---|---|---|---|
| 20b. | 20c. | 21. | 22. M. |

NOTICE: STATE LAW REQUIRES THAT ALL DEATHS DUE TO TRAUMA, ACCIDENT, HOMICIDE, SUICIDE, OR UNDER SUSPICIOUS, UNUSUAL, OR UNNATURAL CIRCUMSTANCES BE REPORTED TO, AND CERTIFIED BY A MEDICAL EXAMINER ON A MEDICAL EXAMINER'S CERTIFICATE OF DEATH. ANY DEATHS FALLING INTO THESE CATEGORIES IS WITHIN THE MEDICAL EXAMINER'S JURISDICTION REGARDLESS OF THE LENGTH OF SURVIVAL FOLLOWING THE UNDERLYING INJURY.

| | Name and Title of Certifier (Type or Print) / Address | |
|---|---|---|
| **CERTIFIER** Sign with permanent black ink. | 23a. / 23b. | |
| | Signature of Certifier / Date Signed | |
| | 23c. / 23d. | |
| | Burial, Cremation, Other (Specify) / Date / Name of Cemetery or Crematory / Location (City, Town or County) / (State) | |
| | 24a. / 24b. / 24c. / 24d. | |
| **BURIAL** | Funeral Home Name / Address / Signature of Funeral Director / License No. | |
| | 25. / 26. | |
| DHS 1872 FORM 8 REV. 7/79 | Date Rec'd by Local Reg. / Signature of Registrar / Signature of Embalmer (If embalmed) / License No. | |
| | 27a. / 27b. / 28. | |

**Fig. 2.** Example of standard North Carolina death certificate illustrating unclear causal sequence of diseases. (Forms for other states may vary slightly.)

This example is straightforward in terms of assigning a causal sequence. Unfortunately, this does not always occur. Consider the medical conditions presented in Fig. 2.

Here we see that generalized arteriosclerosis (ICDA-8, 440.9) is listed on line (c), acute myocardial infarction (ICDA-8, 410.9) on line (b), stroke (ICDA-8, 436.8) on line (a), and diabetes mellitus (ICDA-8, 250.9) on 20a. Here the causal sequence is not clear. Both acute myocardial infarction and stroke may be due to generalized arteriosclerosis. They may also be due to conditions other than generalized arteriosclerosis (e.g., hypertension). Indeed, stroke may be produced by the stress of a myocardial infarction and vice versa. The assignment of generalized arteriosclerosis as the underlying cause, although biomedically plausible, involves assuming that a disease process that almost universally affects white males to some degree and that may have begun 30 (or more) years before death is a meaningful designation of the underlying cause of death. In fact, by application of the "linkage" provisions of ICDA-8, the underlying-cause code selected by ACME is 410.9, not 440.9 as intended by the certifier. Thus, the underlying cause is assigned as if line (b) reads "acute arteriosclerotic heart disease" and the stroke is assumed to be due to the stress of the myocardial infarction.

The occurrence of diabetes mellitus listed in item 20a is also problematic in this case, because diabetes may have accelerated death by compromising peripheral circulation and, consequently, the general viability of the host or accelerated generalized arteriosclerosis.

Clearly, in the example in Fig. 1, the full set of circumstances surrounding death can be adequately described by an extended underlying-cause model because a relatively unambiguous underlying cause is designated by the certifier and accepted by ACME. It is frequently necessary to use the extended underlying-cause model because if only the underlying cause of death is used to represent the medical conditions, a considerable amount of information is lost. The example presented in Fig. 2 is quite different because the linking of generalized arteriosclerosis with acute myocardial infarction means that the specific role of generalized arteriosclerosis is not recognized as an underlying cause. In this case, the pattern-of-failure model, which makes no assumptions about the causal ordering of conditions or the possible effects of diabetes mellitus on any of the three conditions in item 19, is probably more appropriate.

The existence of two multiple-cause models means that each death can be described in two ways. With the extended underlying-cause model, one can use the entity axis multiple-cause data on the NCHS public use computer tapes to describe each death. These data are the ICDA-8 codings (up to 1978; ICDA-9 for 1979 and beyond) that best describe each medical diagnostic term or condition on the death certificate and represent not only the medical term or condition but also its placement on line (a), (b), or (c) of item 19 or on item 20a of the certification. These are the data from which the usual underlying-cause codes are selected, although, as already noted, modification may occur in the interest of obtaining more meaningful designations of the underlying cause of death.

With the pattern-of-failure model, one can use the record axis multiple-cause data on the NCHS public use computer tapes to describe each death. These data are the ICDA-8 codings that best describe the diseases present at the time of death and (should) always include the underlying-cause code. Note that the record axis data are obtained from the entity axis data through a process called axis translation (Chamblee and Evans, 1982). The logic of this system is based on the premise that the best coding of each medical diagnostic term is not necessarily the coding that best describes the diseases present at the time of death. This is because many ICDA-8 codes are linkage or combination codes in which the fourth digit gives additional detail about the disease. For example, under axis translation the entity axis codes 401 (hypertension) and 412.4 (heart disease without mention of hypertension) would appear in the record axis data as 412.2 (hypertensive heart disease). Indeed, the entity axis code 412.4 cannot be interpreted as implying that the person was not hypertensive, only that the adjective "hypertensive" was not used in the medical diagnostic term. Thus, the pattern-of-failure model may be easier to use because the record axis data remove certain "contradictions" and ambiguities found in the entity axis data.

## 3   Studies of the Reliability of Death Certificate Diagnoses

In this section we shall present an overview of selected studies of the reliability of death certificate diagnoses. Studies were selected for review to represent a wide variety of diseases, methodologies, and analytic purposes. In particular, because the studies span many years, various ICD revisions are evaluated in the individual studies. Specific characteristics of the ICDA-8 and other medical nomenclature systems will be discussed in the next section of this chapter.

### *Stroke*

In the past decade, intensive analysis has been made of death certificate data on cerebrovascular and cardiovascular mortality. Stroke has received perhaps the most intensive treatment due at least in part to a series of articles on the results of the Nationwide Cerebrovascular Disease Mortality Study (Kuller *et al.*, 1969a–d). These studies represent perhaps the most complete analysis of the reliability of the certification of death due to a specific disease. The studies examined whether certain striking geographic differentials in stroke mortality could be explained by (1) certification customs (i.e., the variation of physicians' habits in listing stroke as an underlying or associated cause of death), (2) inconsistency between clinical records and death certificates, or (3) inaccuracy of the clinical diagnosis of cerebrovascular disease. Kuller and associates studied 6314 death certificates, of which 1960 mentioned stroke (66.8% listed stroke as the underlying cause of death). The core finding of the study was that no combination of certification factors could explain the striking geographic differentials (a ratio of 3:1 from highest to lowest) in stroke mortality. Approximately 90% of stroke deaths occurring in hospitals (about 75% of the total) could be validated by either autopsy, arteriogram, hemorrhagic spinal fluid, hemiplegia, or recognition on admission of coma not obviously due to other disease causes. Attempts to be more specific in diagnosis, such as attempts to determine the type of stroke from the death certificate, proved to be less fruitful. Kuller *et al.* (1969d) found a great variation in the evidence supporting specific stroke diagnoses: 88% of diagnoses of subarachnoid hemorrhage, 40.7% of diagnoses of cerebral hemorrhage, and 47% of diagnoses of cerebral thrombosis could be verified by either autopsy, arteriogram, craniotomy, or spinal puncture. Acheson *et al.* (1973) studied 1164 stroke deaths and 2854 nonstroke deaths among U.S. veterans in Georgia and five western states to determine whether the differential stroke mortality between Georgia and the western states could be attributed to certification error. Their results confirmed those of Kuller *et al.* in that although there were differences in autopsy rates and the amount of diagnostic evidence in the two areas, neither differences in standards of medical care nor in rates of certification error explained the geographic differentials.

Florey conducted two studies of cases in which stroke was mentioned on the death certificate. In the first (Florey *et al.*, 1967), the study population comprised all New Haven, Connecticut, residents older than 15 years of age who died from 1959 to 1964 and who had vascular lesions of the brain mentioned on the death certificate ($N = 1426$). In comparing the total number of death certificates in which stroke is mentioned versus the number of times it occurred in government tabulations as the underlying cause of death, the authors found that 27% of the certificates with stroke mentioned were tabulated under other ICD rubrics. Thus, government statistics missed 27% of the cases in which stroke was a factor in causing death. In an investigation that compared the demographic characteristics of persons who had stroke listed as the underlying cause of death with the demographic characteristics of those for whom it was an associated condition, it was not possible to detect any biases. Thus, although the certificates do not accurately reflect the absolute mortality risks of stroke, it is possible to compare the ratio of mortality risks among age, sex, and racial groups because of the similar bias of the mentions of stroke over these variables. Hence, one can obtain unbiased estimates of relative risks of stroke from the distribution of stroke deaths by age, sex, and race. When one further stratifies these distributions by subdiagnoses of stroke, however, significant bias is introduced into these relative risks. The authors attributed this bias to two factors: (1) the natural history of the disease and (2) coding conventions. In the first case, discrepancies were found in the greater enumeration of cerebral embolism as an associated condition due to the logical necessity for a prior pathological event to produce an embolus. In the second case, vagueness on the part of the certifier necessitates the imposition of an artificial nosological coding convention. Thus, when a physician entered CVA or stroke on the certificate, the seventh revision of the ICD coding rule required that it be coded as cerebral hemorrhage (ICD-7, 330). Because the most probable alternative diagnosis is cerebral thrombosis, the artificial application of the rule leads to an underestimate of the frequency of this condition. [Under the eighth revision of ICD, the entries CVA and stroke were coded to the new category acute but ill-defined cerebrovascular disease (ICDA-8, 436.9). Thus, the uncertainty in diagnosis between cerebral hemorrhage and cerebral thrombosis was resolved in the ICD-8 by defining a new code to reflect this uncertainty.] Florey et al. compared the New Haven results on stroke mortality with those from other sections of the country. They found that there were few differences in terms of rates based on underlying-cause statistics. When, however, the multiple-cause data were analyzed, certain clear and basic differences arose, which are illustrated in Table 1.

The discrepancies for diabetes (approximately 2½-fold) could be due to sampling in the national study or to differences in the natural history of the disease. However, Florey et al. believe that the most likely explanation is a higher standard of certification in the New Haven study, that is, the probable effect of a large university medical center in a medium-sized city.

Florey et al. (1969) studied 620 cases of New Haven residents who died of stroke in 1962 to 1964. In this study a comparison was made of the

**Table 1**

Percentage of All Certificates Mentioning CVA as a Secondary Cause of Death

| Survey | Underlying causes of death (%) | | |
| --- | --- | --- | --- |
| | Diabetes | ASHD, MI, myocardial degeneration | Hypertension |
| New Haven | 12.6 | 45.4 | 16.8 |
| United States | 5.3 | 34.9 | 26.6 |

Source: Florey et al., 1967, p. 160, Table 10.

diagnoses found in the autopsy report, clinical record, and death certificate and a computer evaluation of the clinical results. It was found that the autopsy results agreed with clinical records most often (identical and similar, 79%), with the computer evaluations next often (77%), and with the death certificates least often (65%). The most striking finding of the study was that the hemorrhage–thrombosis ratio from death certificate data was 2.7 : 1, whereas from autopsy and clinical data it was 0.78 : 1.

The findings from the analysis of stroke mortality seem to indicate that death certificate data are adequate to assess broad mortality differentials for coarse diagnostic categories across age, sex, and race. Specific diagnoses of the type of stroke are poorly determined on the death certificate. In general, it was found that multiple-cause analysis and interpretation of the death certificate data yielded considerable additional insight into stroke mortality and that underlying-cause analyses tended to distort the true magnitude of stroke as a health risk. Nosological coding conventions seemed to have the greatest impact when ambiguous verbal descriptions were entered on the death certificate, and an "unfair" assignment rule was employed to select nosologically precise categories. Interestingly, Acheson et al. (1973) found that when stroke was listed as an associated condition, it often played a specific role in clinical treatment.

### Cardiovascular Disease

Moriyama et al. (1971) performed an extensive study of cardiovascular mortality in the United States by using vital statistics data. They found that specific cardiopulmonary events listed on the death certificate could be confirmed about 80% of the time although the error confirmation rate was highly dependent on the fineness of the diagnostic categories employed. This study is interesting because of Moriyama's basic concern with disease representation on the death certificate. In other words, he was concerned with the difficulties in describing complex cardiovascular syndromes by using the death certificate and its underlying-cause structure. Moriyama argued that there is great difficulty in making fine distinctions between individual cardiopulmonary pathological events and even greater difficulty in trying to assess the causal linkage of such events. Weiner et al. (1955) discussed certain analytic strategies to alleviate the problems engendered by representing cardiovascular–renal deaths by a single underlying cause of death by reclassifying cardiovascular deaths into more reasonable multiple-cause categories. They found that if multiple-cause information were available, all but about 1% of the certificates could be classified into etiologic and site-specific disease patterns on the basis of clinical and biological insights. If only a single cardiovascular category was coded on the death certificate, about 13.5% could not be classified according to site involvement and etiology. Thus, if multiple-cause information were available (as it was for over 60% of cardiovascular–renal deaths), then some reasonable determination of the nature of the disease process would be possible. If only the underlying-cause category were available (precisely the information available in present mortality statistics), then the ability to characterize the course of the morbid process would suffer.

Beadenkopf *et al.* (1963) examined the sensitivity (i.e., probability of a positive test response in the presence of a given disease) and specificity (i.e., probability of the presence of the disease given a positive test response) of diagnosed arteriosclerotic heart disease on 611 consecutively autopsied individuals 45 years and older who had died from any cause at Albany Medical Center Hospital. A comparison of autopsy findings and death certificates suggested that death certificate data were insensitive to arteriosclerotic heart disease because the death certificate reflected only 50% of the individuals with infarct or thrombosis noted at autopsy. The specificity of the death certificate data was much better with 82% of arteriosclerotic deaths confirmed at autopsy. Cancer deaths, on the other hand, enjoyed an overall specificity of 98% and a sensitivity of 82% (differential by age). It was concluded that although it was reasonable to make determinations about the prevalence at death of cancer from death certificates, it was probably inappropriate to do so for arteriosclerotic heart disease. Note that this study avoided the complex conceptual issues in selecting underlying causes of death by viewing the notion as inappropriate for the study of chronic disease and by emphasizing disease prevalence at death.

Cardiovascular events, which are often acute episodes, represent a major component of sudden deaths. Moriyama *et al.* (1966) studied the certification of deaths by all types of certifiers and found that there were few discernible differences in error rates for particular diseases falling in the sudden-death category by certifier type (i.e., physician, medical examiner, or coroner).

Kuller *et al.* (1969a) found that in 1857 nontraumatic deaths of Baltimore residents aged 20 to 64 years the diagnosis of arteriosclerotic heart disease as the underlying cause of death was often based on meager evidence. Of deaths attributed to arteriosclerotic heart disease, almost 60% were sudden and only 19% in the study survived longer than 24 hours in the hospital. Hence, most of these diagnoses were based only on a previous history of arteriosclerotic heart disease and the rapidity of death and not on firm diagnostic evidence. It seems likely that this created a positive bias toward arteriosclerotic heart disease as a cause of death, with the consequence of negative bias in the mortality rate for stroke, pulmonary embolism, or ruptured abdominal aneurysm.

### Pulmonary Embolism

In a study of 6385 death certificates filed for a single month (April 1973) in New York City, Rossman (1974) found in the process of coding death certificates that there occurred a sizable reduction in the number of cases attributable to pulmonary embolisms. Thus, far fewer deaths were attributed to pulmonary embolism in the vital statistics data than were attributed by the certifier of the death certificate as being due to pulmonary embolism.

Specifically, Rossman found that 207 certificates (3.2%) listed pulmonary embolism as a major or contributory cause of death, with the peak incidence (4.1%) occurring at ages 50 to 59 and with incidence being about 4% from ages 40 to 79. In 182 cases (2.8%), death was directly ascribed to pulmonary embolism on the certificate. Coding procedures (reduction of verbal descriptions to ICD nomenclature) led to a reduction of deaths due to pulmonary embolism from 182 to 31, with more than half of the 151 cases reassigned to cancer (34), chronic ischemic heart disease (31), and acute myocardial infarct (13). Thus, in five of six deaths in which the certifier believed pulmonary infarct to be the underlying cause of death, Rossman found that the deaths were assigned to other categories during the coding procedure. Consequently, in the mortality statistics the importance of pulmonary embolism as a cause of death will be reduced by about 83%. This problem is further confounded by the fact that there may be additional underreporting at the clinical level; that is, that for death certificates for which autopsies were not performed, the diagnosis of pulmonary embolism as a cause of death may be frequently missed. Evidence of such underreporting is found in mortality statistics (after coding) in which the incidence of pulmonary embolism is greater for certificates when an autopsy is performed than for certificates when it is not. Consequently, Rossman concluded that the health risk represented by pulmonary embolism was inaccurately reflected in mortality statistics due to both coding procedures and high false-negative rates (i.e., high probabilities of having a given disease in the presence of a negative test response) in clinical data when autopsies were not performed. Additionally, it was suggested that underreporting for pulmonary embolism necessarily implied overreporting for other diseases—especially those in which clinical diagnosis should be easily made, for example, breast or prostate cancers. Rossman suggested that one approach to relieve such problems is to utilize multiple-cause information.

## Cancer

Cancer is often cited as the disease that is most accurately reflected in death certificate data. In the following discussion, we shall show that there are many sources of error in the diagnosis and subsequent reporting of cancer deaths and that there exists legitimate concern over the *validity* of the ability of underlying-cause statistics to reflect major changes in cancer mortality.

Dorn and Horn (1941) studied 13,524 deaths due to cancer in 10 U.S. metropolitan areas during 1938 to 1940. For each death, the death certificate was obtained and a case report developed by means of a questionnaire mailed to every physician, hospital, and clinic in the study area. Information from those who failed to return the questionnaire was obtained by an interview. All hospitals and clinics responded, and 98% of the physicians responded. The case reports indicated the primary tumor site, any other sites involved, the type of cancer, and whether or not the diagnosis was confirmed by histological examination.

When the cases were grouped by primary tumor site into nine broad categories (buccal cavity, digestive tract, respiratory system, genitourinary system, breast, skin, brain, bones, and other), 84.5% of the death certificates had a primary tumor site that fell into the primary tumor site category determined from the case report (see Table 2). The best agreement was found for digestive cancers (92.6%) and the worst for skin, brain, bones, and other (42.6, 46.3, 51.5, and 51.5%, respectively). Part of the discrepancy for skin and brain tumors was due to the frequency with which the case reports settled on a nonmalignant cause of death (10.7 and 48.5%). The discrepancy for brain tumors was also attributed to coding procedures in which the diagnosis of malignancies was not made specific by the physician.

Coding of tumors by site reduced the overall correspondence of case reports and death certificates to 77.3%. Surprisingly, it was found that in 3390 cases in which histological data were available, confirmation rates (i.e., the probability of having a given disease in the presence of a specific test response) were only marginally higher (86.2%). The percentage of deaths with a case report of a nonmalignant cause of death is a little smaller with histological evidence (3.2%) than without (4.8%). Much of the discrepancy between case reports and death certificates was attrib-

**Table 2**

Comparison of the Primary Site of Cancer Reported in Survey with That Recorded on Death Certificates

| Primary site on death certificate | Primary site reported in survey | | | | | | | | | |
|---|---|---|---|---|---|---|---|---|---|---|
| | Buccal cavity | Digestive tract | Respiratory system | Genitourinary system | Breast | Skin | Brain | Bones | All others | Total |
| Buccal cavity | 463 | 12 | 20 | 1 | — | 48 | — | 10 | 12 | 566 |
| Digestive tract | 22 | 5,194 | 29 | 1,127 | 43 | 19 | — | 8 | 128 | 5,570 |
| Respiratory system | 14 | 26 | 816 | 24 | 33 | 7 | 1 | 7 | 35 | 963 |
| Genitourinary system | 3 | 75 | 11 | 3,046 | 16 | 8 | 2 | 6 | 76 | 3,243 |
| Breast | — | 8 | 3 | 28 | 1,166 | 2 | — | 2 | 16 | 1,225 |
| Skin | 20 | 1 | 3 | 4 | 1 | 144 | — | 4 | 19 | 196 |
| Brain | 1 | 1 | 1 | — | 1 | 3 | 90 | — | 7 | 104 |
| Bones | 3 | 3 | 3 | 1 | 6 | 5 | 2 | 101 | 30 | 154 |
| Other malignant | 35 | 115 | 24 | 101 | 55 | 66 | 5 | 49 | 408 | 858 |
| Total malignant | 561 | 5,435 | 910 | 3,332 | 1,321 | 302 | 100 | 187 | 731 | 12,879 |
| Nonmalignant | 22 | 174 | 55 | 156 | 38 | 36 | 94 | 9 | 61 | 645 |
| | 583 | 5,609 | 965 | 3,488 | 1,359 | 338 | 194 | 196 | 792 | 13,524 |

Source: Dorn and Horn, 1941.

uted to coding difficulties when multiple-cause information was provided on the certificate and imprecise wording of diagnoses by physicians.

Pohlen and Emerson (1942) studied 3462 cases in which some form of malignancy was listed as the primary cause of death in an autopsy summary. These cases were selected from 4051 deaths (out of a total of 20,000 deaths surveyed) in which a tumor was mentioned either on autopsy reports or in clinical records. The authors evaluated the rate of correspondence of death certificates and autopsies on two criteria: (1) topographic or site accuracy and (2) etiologic accuracy. They found that two-thirds of the death certificates were accurate in both ways, 77% were etiologically correct, and 77% were anatomically correct. The confirmation rates are provided in Table 3.

From the table, we can see that the number of entirely correct diagnoses ranges from 96% (breast tumors) to 26% (liver tumors). Tumors with marked and early clinical signs were, not surprisingly, most accurately diagnosed. More than 80% accuracy of diagnoses was found for cancers of the breast, rectum, cervix, pharynx and larynx, and esophagus; below 50% accuracy was found for cancers of the liver, small intestine, brain, and bile duct.

Pohlen and Emerson correctly point out that the usual cause-specific mortality statistics report *only* the underlying cause of death and neglect all contributory information. They suggest that because of the selection of a single, underlying cause of death, biases are generated in mortality statistics: "In cases where a malignant neoplasm occurs coincidentally with another disease, preference is usually given in registration practice to the neoplasms" (Pohlen and Emerson, 1942, p. 256). They also point out that at autopsy it is not unusual to find small, early neoplasms that cannot properly be considered as a primary cause of death because they were clinically silent. Clinically silent neoplasms are frequently found in the small intestine, prostate, kidney, and thyroid. Clinically silent neoplasms are seldom found in bones, lymph nodes, esophagus, and pharynx and larynx. In addition to these findings, 148 cases (4.2%) of the death certificates showing a malignant neoplasm as the cause of death were found to be due to nonmalignant causes.

By using a methodology pretested in Moriyama *et al.* (1958), study was made of the relation of lung cancer mortality to residence and smoking histories (Haenszel and Taeuber, 1964; Haenszel *et al.*, 1962). This methodology employed a follow-back survey of death certificates collected in a nationwide 10% sample to confirm the diagnosis of lung cancer by histologic type. The basic mechanism used to confirm diagnosis was a questionnaire mailed to the certifying physician (see Sirken *et al.*, 1960). It was found that the percentage of "well-established" certificates fell off rapidly

**Table 3**

Rates of Correspondence by Site for Cancers Reported in Survey and Recorded on
Death Certificates

|  | Both topographic and etiologic statement (%) | Topographic statements (%) | Etiologic statements (%) |
|---|---|---|---|
| Breast | 96 | 96 | 97 |
| Pharynx, larynx | 84 | 86 | 95 |
| Lung | 62 | 77 | 70 |
| Esophagus | 82 | 86 | 90 |
| Stomach | 72 | 77 | 85 |
| Small intestine | 29 | 29 | 50 |
| Cecum, appendix | 49 | 51 | 71 |
| Colon | 71 | 75 | 80 |
| Sigmoid, sigmoid-colon | 72 | 76 | 83 |
| Rectum, recto-sigmoid | 88 | 89 | 90 |
| Pancreas | 57 | 60 | 79 |
| Brain | 30 | 91 | 31 |
| Liver | 26 | 66 | 44 |
| Gallbladder | 49 | 55 | 87 |
| Bile ducts | 37 | 53 | 70 |
| Kidney | 55 | 68 | 64 |
| Urinary bladder | 78 | 81 | 85 |
| Prostate | 74 | 81 | 81 |
| Uterus-corpus | 65 | 71 | 77 |
| Cervix | 86 | 86 | 95 |
| Ovaries | 70 | 75 | 86 |
| Thyroid | 76 | 80 | 84 |
| Bones | 71 | 74 | 75 |
| Lymphnodes (lymphosar-comatosis) | 58 | 70 | 65 |
| Other sites | 55 | 65 | 68 |
|  | 67 | 77 | 77 |

Source: Pohlen and Emerson, 1942.

with age: 86% at 35 to 44 years, 86.5% at 45 to 54, 84.4% at 55 to 64, 71.2% at 65 to 74, and 48.5% at ages 75 and older. The percentage of well-established diagnoses also varied by metropolitan status, size of place, and farm or nonfarm residence. Stratification by histologic type revealed that the ratio of adenocarcinoma to epidermoid and undifferentiated carcinoma also varied along these dimensions.

Griffith (1976) reviewed several studies to ascertain the appropriate-

**Table 4**

Deaths at Ages 15 to 74 Certified to Malignant Neoplasms and Percentage Changes after Review of
Diagnostic Evidence, in 12 Cities, 1962–1964

| Site and ICD category 1955 revision | Number certified | Number after review as percentage of number certified | | | | |
|---|---|---|---|---|---|---|
| | | Total | Confirmed | Eliminated[a] | Added[b] | Net change |
| All sites (140–205) | 8423 | 100 | 96 | 4 | 9 | +5 |
| Oesophagus (150) | 264 | 100 | 85 | 15 | 16 | +1 |
| Stomach (151) | 1465 | 100 | 87 | 13 | 18 | +6 |
| Intestines (152, 153) | 388 | 100 | 79 | 21 | 16 | −5 |
| Rectum (154) | 227 | 100 | 89 | 11 | 23 | +11 |
| Other digestive system (155–159) | 999 | 100 | 80 | 20 | 18 | −2 |
| Larynx (161) | 115 | 100 | 88 | 12 | 27 | +15 |
| Lung (162, 163) | 1073 | 100 | 92 | 8 | 12 | +5 |
| Other respiratory system (160, 164, 165) | 60 | 100 | 69 | 32 | 48 | +17 |
| Breast (170) | 624 | 100 | 98 | 2 | 13 | +11 |
| Cervix uteri (171) | 472 | 100 | 98 | 2 | 76 | +74 |
| Corpus uteri (172) | 55 | 100 | 91 | 9 | 142 | ±133 |
| Other uterus (173, 174) | 354 | 100 | 12 | 88 | 5 | −83 |
| Urinary bladder (181:0) | 194 | 100 | 89 | 11 | 20 | +9 |
| Other genito-urinary system (175–180, 181:7) | 568 | 100 | 85 | 15 | 25 | +10 |
| Lymphoma (200–203, 205) | 316 | 100 | 90 | 10 | 27 | +17 |
| Leukaemia (204) | 282 | 100 | 89 | 11 | 11 | +1 |
| Other and unspecified sites (remainder) | 967 | 100 | 66 | 34 | 24 | −9 |

Source: Griffith, 1976.
[a]Assigned on review to a different site or to a nonmalignant cause.
[b]Originally certified to a different site or to a nonmalignant cause.

ness of mortality data as a cancer surveillance device. He created a table
(shown as Table 4 here) from 8423 autopsied deaths originally certified as
due to cancer from the Inter-American Investigation of Mortality [a representative sample of all deaths (42,000) at ages 15–74 years in 10 Latin
American cities, San Francisco, and Bristol, England, from 1962 to 1964
(Puffer and Griffith, 1967)].

Overall, the table suggests that cancer mortality is underrreported by
5%—results that are consistent with the findings of Dorn and Cutler
(1959; 6%) and Heasman and Lipworth (1966; 4%). Griffith makes four
deductions about the use of the death certificate data (1976, p. 71):

1. The death rate based on the original certificates would have been accurate to within about 10% for seven of the 17 sites and groups of sites listed.

2. The diagnosis on the original certificates was confirmed for 85% or more of deaths due to 13 of 17 sites.

3. The percentage transferred either to another site of cancer or to a non-malignant cause was substantial (15% or more) in respect to several sites.

4. Reliance on death certificates alone to identify all cases of cancer of a given site among a set of deaths from all causes would lead to serious underestimates, e.g., in this material, 16% of esophagus cancers would have been missed.

Griffith also discussed certain problems with specificity of coding that detract from the usefulness of death certificates and the problems of studying trends due to changes in the ICD. This latter problem was illustrated with an example (bronchus and lung cancer) from the seventh and eighth revisions of the ICD.

In two autopsy studies of cancer patients (Bauer *et al.*, 1973; Bauer and Robbins, 1972), it was found that there was considerable error in clinical diagnoses of cancers as compared with autopsy results. Of 2734 patients autopsied at Boston City Hospital between 1955 and 1965 (about 25% of all autopsies at that facility), when cancer was diagnosed at autopsy, it was found that about 40% of the clinical diagnoses were in error (Bauer and Robbins, 1972). Of all patients reviewed, 26% had clinically undiagnosed cancer (of which 45% was lethal), and of cancer patients, 24% succumbed to nonmalignant cause of death. These results suggest a minimal level of error for death certificate diagnoses based only on clinical records. The distribution of error by site is consistent with previously cited studies in that "deep-seated" tumors were most often misdiagnosed. Bauer *et al.* (1973) found that the accuracy of cancer diagnosis was a function of the number and duration of hospital visits. Furthermore, they suggested that their results were partly a product of socioeconomic factors. Again, the conclusion is that the factors that affect clinical diagnoses also affect the accuracy of death certificates when autopsies are not performed. Because the national autopsy rate is about 15–16%, such factors represent major constraints on the accuracy of death certificate diagnoses.

A recent study of the accuracy of the diagnosis of malignant neoplasms and vascular diseases was conducted on 257 autopsied cases collected at a short-stay hospital (Engel *et al.*, 1980). This study produced an estimate of the reliability of death certificate diagnosis of cancer by having a pathologist prepare clinicopathologic cause-of-death certificates. The study found that cancer at death may be underreported by as much as 10%, that 28% of cancers had to be reclassified as to type or primary site, and that the accuracy of diagnosis was related to the ease of diagnosis.

Percy *et al.* (1974) discuss in detail the effects of the changeover from the seventh to eighth revision of the ICD on cancer mortality trends in the period 1967–1968. Between 1963 and 1967, lung cancer deaths increased 5.7% annually. In 1968 the rate of increase was 9.6%, with a concomitant decrease in malignant neoplasms of thoracic organs, specified as secondary (62%), and malignant neoplasms of other and unspecified sites (8%). It was determined that the 9.6% increase in lung cancer was a product of changes in coding rules and not a real increase (determined by coding a sample of 2752 deaths according to both seventh and eighth revisions of ICD rules).

In a study of multiple-cause reporting of cancer prepared by Manton and Myers (1983), it was found that the total cancer occurrence at death might be underreported by 15%. It was also found that the rate of underreporting (1) increased with age and (2) was correlated with the median survival time of the tumor type. It was also found (Myers and Manton, 1983) that the correspondence between hospital record reports of cancer during the terminal hospital stay and the reporting of cancer anywhere on the death certificate was quite high.

### *Studies of All Causes of Death*

In studies of all causes of death, we find that many of the principles found in the studies discussed in the preceding are applicable. Three studies that are representative of these findings are a study of all 1889 autopsied deaths in 12 hospitals in Albany, New York, in 1951–1952 (James *et al.*, 1955), a study of a 10% sample of deaths among Pennsylvania residents in 1956 (Moriyama *et al.*, 1958), and a British study of 1216 deaths contained in the Oxford Record Linkage Study (Alderson and Meade, 1967).

James *et al.* (1955) evaluated the adequacy of the certification of deaths by comparing the original death certificate with death certificates filled out by specially trained certifiers with access to complete autopsy results. In this study no attempt was made to isolate physicians' errors in recording antemortem data from errors due to a lack of information, although a methodological study conducted at a large teaching hospital showed that a sizable portion of the error in the original certificate was due to a lack of certain facts found in autopsy. It was decided that the primary deficiencies of the original death certificate were (1) that they were often incomplete (i.e., that certain significant medical facts uncovered by autopsy were not disclosed on the original death certificate) and (2) that some deaths could not reasonably be represented by an underlying cause of death (i.e., that pathologists could not select a *single* explanatory factor to explain death). Additionally, it was suggested that the elderly and those who died of arteriosclerotic types of diseases were underautopsied (possibly due to a correlation of age and the incidence of arteriosclerotic causes of death). It was found that of the causes of death malignant neoplasms were relatively the most accurately reported (91% of individual cases confirmed by autopsy), although compensating errors could make total rates correspond even more closely.

Moriyama *et al.* (1958) assessed the quality of supporting diagnostic information for a sample of 1837 deaths occurring in Pennsylvania in 1956. On the basis of a well-defined set of rules, the "reasonableness" of the death certificate diagnosis was assessed on (1) the quality (amount and kind) of diagnostic data, (2) the consistency of medical certification with diagnostic evidence, and (3) the reviewer's opinion of the certitude of diagnosis.

Moriyama *et al.* rated the quality of diagnostic information by using four classes: (1) very good, (2) good, (3) sketchy, and (4) no report. Cancer deaths were by far the best-supported diagnoses, with 68.4% having very good evidence and 12.9% having good evidence (the criterion for these qualitative distinctions is not clear in the report). Ischemic heart disease, among other diseases, was frequently diagnosed on the basis of sketchy evidence (49.0% of the time). The consistency of the diagnosis with medical evidence was broken into four categories: (1) most probable diagnosis, (2) another diagnosis equally probable, (3) another diagnosis preferred, and (4) no diagnostic information. Again, cancer diagnoses were among the best supported, being most probable 86% of the time and equiprobable 5% of the time. The reviewer's evaluation of the diagnostic support for certification was classified as (1) solidly established, (2) reasonable, (3) in doubt, and (4) probably wrong. About 68% of cancer deaths were viewed as solidly established and 14% as reasonable. Approximately 7% of cancer deaths were viewed as in error, but this was largely a product of error in diagnosing cancers of the digestive system. Additionally, it was found that the accuracy of cancer diagnosis tended to fall off after age 65.

This study represents the first extensive test of the use of survey techniques to augment the information collected in death certificates and other vital statistics (Sirken, 1962, 1963; Sirken *et al.*, 1960; Sirken and Dunn, 1958). This methodology is contrasted with the majority of studies that compare the death certificate data with clinical and autopsy records in the following.

Alderson and Meade (1967) compared the accuracy of diagnosis and death certificates with that found in medical records. Using the WHO's list B disease categories, they discovered that the correspondence of the principal condition treated in the hospital and the underlying cause of death varied tremendously, with a correspondence of 89% for cancer and 45% for pneumonia. They found that discrepancies were positively correlated with age, with certain medical specialties, and with increasing length of stay but were unrelated to autopsy, sex, social class, and marital status.

## Cancer and Associated Conditions

In reviewing the papers on the reliability of death certificate diagnoses of cancer presented in the preceding, one can see that there was only limited discussion of multiple-cause coding and problems of the representation of the medical characteristics of cancer deaths by a single underlying cause. It could even be argued that the basic concept of an underlying cause of death is inappropriate for chronic diseases such as cancer in which the condition and age of the patient interact with multiple disease processes to determine the time of death (see Dorn, 1966; Krueger, 1966). Such an argument is consistent with the clinical findings of the cause-of-death studies performed for cerebrovascular and cardiovascular diseases. To explore this issue we shall review studies of the basic nature of cancer as a disease entity, its natural history, its integration with related morbid processes leading to death, and the possible use of multiple-cause mortality data and models to elucidate such relations. We shall review the first two studies (Abramson and Ehrlich) in the simple terms of cancer's prevalence at death—an epidemiological strategy developed to measure the total contribution of a disease to mortality without getting involved in the complication of establishing its linkage with other conditions (Markush and Seigel, 1968). The studies by Hersh and Inagaki deal with a conceptually more advanced model of cancer mortality in that the natural history of cancer is evaluated in terms of its association with other conditions. Finally, in West's study explicit attention is paid to the timing of events in the natural history of cancer.

Abramson *et al.* (1971) analyzed the confirmation rates (CRs), sensitivity rates (Ss), false-positive rates (this is the probability of a positive test response in the absence of a given disease), and case/certificate ratios (ccrs) between conditions found at autopsy and underlying-cause mentions of a disease on the death certificate. The results for all diseases and cancer specifically are shown in the tabulation on p. 32.

The data indicate, at least for this series (500 consecutive autopsies during 1963–1968 at Hadassah University Hospital, Israel), that cancer deaths reported on the certificate are largely reliable, though there is some

| Parameter | All diseases (%) | Cancers (%)* |
|-----------|------------------|--------------|
| CR | 80 | 98 (95) |
| S | 80 | 80 (85) |
| f+ | 6 | 1 (2.6) |
| ccr | Between 1.2 and 1.9 | 1.2 (1.1) |

*Parenthesized rates refer to conditions specified as underlying or contributory causes of death.

lack of sensitivity [results similar to those of Beadenkopf et al. (1963), who were also studying the prevalence at death of chronic diseases].

It should be noted that these results indicate a best-possible case because they involve certification at a medical center and that a lack of reliability in making site-specific cancer diagnoses causes the confirmation rates to drop to about 60%. Cancer sensitivity dropped with age but was unaffected by sex. Again, biases toward reporting heart disease, stroke, and cancer as the underlying causes of death were noted; the case/certificate ratio for pulmonary embolism is large (42:1) but more reasonable for all mentions (2.6:1).

Ehrlich et al. (1975) reviewed all 1212 autopsies over a 2-year period (1968–1969) for deaths at Chaim Sheba Medical Center in Israel. The false-positive rate was 16% (based only on clinical data) and the false-negative rate was 11% (based on autopsy diagnoses). Misdiagnosis rates were found to be correlated with age (false positives increased at age 50 and beyond; false negatives increased at age 70 and beyond) and lack of clinical data. Again, these figures represent a best-possible case estimate, although it was suggested that error rates may be inflated because solidly established cancer diagnoses were less likely to be autopsied.

These results, although of interest because they indicate something of the nature of the reliability of cancer diagnosis for prevalence at death studies, do not yield sufficient insight into the association of morbid processes leading to death to sufficiently assess variation in the natural history of the disease and thus to assess the validity of its representation by underlying-cause statistics. Investigations of this type require more information than is likely to be on death certificates; therefore, we shall review two studies of the causes of death for clinical series of cancer patients (Inagaki et al., 1974; and Hersh et al., 1965).

Hersh et al. (1965) studied the medical records of all 414 NCI patients who died of acute leukemia from 1953 to 1964. The authors concluded that "recent advances in the therapy of patients with acute leukemia have altered the natural history of this disease." Additionally, they suggested that "analysis of the cause of death points out areas where further research on supportive care in malignant diseases is needed'' (Hersh *et al.*, 1965, p. 105). What we shall show from both studies is that (1) even if some neoplasms can be accurately determined to be the initiating morbid event leading to death, changes in treatment may so alter the course of the disease process (associated condition or complication) that a simple count of neoplasms hides basic changes in the natural history of the disease and that (2) with advances in treatment and increased survival time, cancer patients may die of independent pathological events or after long periods of remission—in either case, underlying-cause mortality statistics reflect few such changes.

Of the 414 patients in the Hersh study, 60% suffered from lymphocytic leukemia, 38% from myelogenous, 1% from monocytic, and 1% from stem cell. In the accompanying tabulation (abstracted from Hersh *et al.*, 1965, p. 101, Table 3), we show the changing pattern of causes of death for the 354 patients who were autopsied (out of a total of 366) and for whom a definite cause of death could be identified.

| Diagnosis | Percentage by cause of death | |
|---|---|---|
| | 1954–1959 | 1960–1963 |
| Infection (alone) | 24.4 | 44.0 |
| Infection and hemorrhage | 40.0 | 23.0 |
| Hemorrhage (alone) | 21.8 | 13.7 |
| Other causes (alone) | 5.4 | 7.1 |
| Other causes and infection | 2.7 | 4.4 |
| Other causes and hemorrhage | 4.9 | 0.5 |
| Other causes, hemorrhage, and infection | 0 | 0.5 |
| $N$ | 184 | 170 |

Source: Data from Hersh *et al.*, 1965.

The major changes reflected in the table are the decline in the number of deaths due to hemorrhage (either alone or with infection) and the increase in the number dying of infection alone. The explanation of these changes is to be found in the perfection of platelet transfusion methods in about 1960–1961 and the use of modified penicillin to control certain types of infection. We find that the most striking change underlying the changes noted is in the types of infectious processes that proved lethal. Pseudomonas septicemia and fungal infections have increased in incidence and compensate for a decrease in deaths due to other organisms. It is interesting to note that a reduction in host defenses led to increased susceptibility to both fungal and staphylococcal infections–even though staphylococcal infections have generally proved treatable by the use of methicillin. With the further observation that the changes in the mode of failure for cancer patients usually are also associated with increased survival time, we can see that mortality statistics that fail to differentiate between the pattern of conditions associated with cancer and the changes in these patterns are functioning to hide progress in the control of the disease. Thus, progress can reasonably be claimed for a treatment protocol even if survival time is not markedly increased if it serves to control some pathological concomitants of cancer.

Inagaki *et al.* (1974) studied the causes of death for 816 autopsied patients (of a total of 1230 patients with malignancies other than leukemias, lymphomas, and myelomas) who died at M. D. Anderson Hospital and Tumor Institute during 1968–1970. The primary causes of death are shown in the accompanying tabulation (from Inagaki *et al.*, 1974, p. 569, Table 2).

| Primary cause | Percentage |
| --- | --- |
| Infection | 47 |
| Organ failure | 25 |
| Infarction | 11 |
| Hemorrhage | 7 |
| Carcinomatosis | 10 |
| N | 816 |

Source: Inagaki *et al.*, 1974.

The most striking result shown is that only 10% of cancer patients die without major complicating factors. Thus, 90% of cancer deaths would require multiple-cause information for the accurate characterization of the events surrounding death. Indeed, even in the 10% of cases dying of carcinomatosis, patients had extreme degrees of debilitation, malnutrition, and electrolyte imbalance; the diagnoses actually represent a failure to isolate particular causes of death.

There were three basic mechanisms underlying the infections causing death in 47% of cases ($N = 380$): (1) necrotic or ulcerated tumors or tumor masses that compressed or obstructed urinary, alimentary, or respiratory tracts (67%), (2) neutropenia (below 1000 neutrophils/mm$^3$) resulting from chemical or radiologic therapy (14%), and (3) mucositis, necrosis, perforations, or adhesions due to radiotherapy or wound dehiscence and peritonitis due to surgery (19%). The dominant infectious organisms were gram-negative bacteria (68% of cases in which organisms were identified). Other types of infectious diseases that were implicated included gram-positive organisms (10%) and mixed gram-negative and gram-positive organisms (15%), with fungal infections occurring infrequently.

The second major cause of death, organ failure, broke down as shown in the accompanying tabulation (from Inagaki *et al.*, 1974, p. 571, Table 7). What is important to note from this table is that 16% of deaths due to organ failure were due to non-tumor-related pathology, for example, primarily arteriosclerotic diseases, especially of the heart (23 of 42 cases).

| Type of failure | Organ failure (%) | Tumor (%) | Other (%) |
|---|---|---|---|
| Respiratory | 41.3 | 100 | — |
| Cardiac | 20.9 | 45 | 55 |
| Hepatic | 19.4 | 87 | 13 |
| Central nervous system | 10.9 | 100 | — |
| Renal | 7.5 | 67 | 33 |
| N | 201 | 169 | 32 |

Source: Inagaki *et al.*, 1974.

Infarction caused death in 11% of the cases distributed by site as follows (from Inagaki *et al.*, 1974, p. 571, Table 8).

| Site | Infarcts (%) | Tumor (%) | Other (%) |
|---|---|---|---|
| Lungs | 57 | 55 | 45 |
| Heart | 37 | 9 | 91 |
| Other | 6 | 50 | 50 |
| N | 90 | 32 | 58 |

Source: Inagaki *et al.*, 1974.

Among patients dying of lung infarct not due to tumor, distal venous thrombosis resulting in embolization was the major cause. Arteriosclerosis was the cause of infarct in the other cases not due to tumor.

Of the 62 patients who died of hemorrhage, 24% hemorrhaged due to factors not related to the tumor (peptic ulcer, 4 cases; postsurgery, 8 cases; postirradiation, 1 case; and arteriosclerosis, 2 cases).

From this study we see that (1) solid tumors, as well as leukemias, have varied patterns of associated conditions that cannot be represented by a single underlying-cause diagnosis and that (2) a sizable proportion of cancer patients, patients for whom cancer is a medically significant factor, die of pathological events unrelated to tumor load or invasiveness.

The previous studies assay the conditions associated with cancer morbidity and death. They emphasize that some cancer patients die of diseases unrelated to cancer and that the pattern of conditions associated with a particular type of neoplasm varies considerably. What is missing from these studies is a detailed recognition of the effects of survival time and patient age on the course of cancer morbidity leading to death. To summarize some of these issues, we shall consider West's (1977) discussion of deaths due to cervical cancer.

West (1977) found that the mean survival time of patients diagnosed at stage I of tumor development (average age at registration was 51 years; estimated age at death, 66) was greater than those diagnosed at stage IV (average age at registration, 59; estimated age at death, 61). However, much of the difference in mean survival time was due to the later ages at which stage IV tumors were diagnosed. As West suggests, "Crude survival rates exaggerate the mortality of treated cancer particularly after 10 or 15 years, because a 'normal' (or non-cancer) population also dies." Hence, the greater the age of a patient at diagnosis, the greater are the forces of mortality due to all other causes of death. Consequently, in order to reflect accurately the effectiveness of cancer therapy, the age-specific scheduling of deaths due to all causes must be taken into account to ascertain whether a tumor was successfully managed by therapy. A further ramification of this necessary analytic consideration is its impact on possible misreporting of deaths, that is, the known bias toward recording cancer as the cause of death even though it is in remission or not advanced to a clinically significant stage.

Related to West's concerns about the proper analysis and interpretation of cancer patients' survival times are Neyman's (1975) admonitions about the analysis and interpretation of mortality data to demonstrate an increase in environmental hazards and cancer mortality. Neyman suggests that the recent declines in mortality due to cardiovascular disease and stroke (NCHS, 1977, 1976, 1975a, 1974a–c) may have contributed significantly to the apparent increase in cancer mortality. Specifically, because cardiovascular and stroke deaths comprise a major proportion of all deaths, a reduction in the mortality impact of these two diseases may lead to an increased mortality impact of other less frequent causes of death, such as cancer. Specifically, the logic of such an argument is simply that (1) every person must die at some time of some disease, (2) every person is endowed with a theoretical time to die of each disease, and (3) if a person's time to die of some disease is somehow bypassed, then he or she is "saved" to die of the next disease at the second hypothetical time to die. Consequently, if the force of mortality due to cardiovascular disease and stroke is reduced (and therefore certain persons are saved from their first time to die), then the probability of cancer death will necessarily increase if the force of mortality of cancer is unaltered (i.e., since some proportion of persons saved from cardiovascular disease and stroke will die of cancer at their second time to die if that time is unaltered by treatment of the other diseases). Note that a number of technical difficulties have to be resolved in estimating the actual effects of mortality reduction because of the possibility that the times to die of the target disease groups are not independent across individuals.

## 4  Medical Nomenclature Systems

In addition to the lack of reliability of death certificates, one of the important aspects of mortality data that must be kept in mind by the analyst is the implication of the system used to categorize medical conditions. The nosological system that is presently used is the ninth revision of the ICD (ICD-9). Considerable debate has emerged over the aspects of the new revision (Kurtzke, 1979) because it deviates substantially in some ways from the eighth revision and because it has become more symptom oriented. The ICD-9 illustrates the difficulties of trying to describe in a single-dimension system all disease categories. By single-dimension system we mean a classification system that links together in a single code all the characteristic elements of a disease entity. Thus, for example, the ICD has no way of directly specifying the type of microorganism that causes an infection of a specific organism such as pneumonia. Difficulties also arise in specifying certain chronic diseases as causes of circulatory failure. For example, hypertension is often only found linked in combination with a specific circulatory event as a fourth digit code. Therefore, to determine the role of hypertension in causing death, a detailed *decoding* operation is required (see Wing and Manton, 1981). Even more problematic for the analysis of cancer mortality is the lack of provision within the ICD to indicate the histological type of tumor. To appreciate these difficulties it is useful to review briefly other standard medical nomenclatures that resolve these issues in various ways.

The ICDO (ICD for oncology) is a special version of the ICD that has been modified so that two codes—T for topography and M for morphology—are assigned to each cancer diagnosis. The T codes are quite similar to the cancer site code provided in the ICD. The morphology code is added to specify the histologic type. Thus, to represent adenocarcinoma of the stomach, the ICD code would be 151.9 and the ICDO code would be T-151.9, M-8140/3.

A second medical nomenclature system that is frequently employed is the Systematized Nomenclature of Pathology (SNOP) system. Developed by the College of American Pathologists, this system allows a medical condition to be classified in up to four dimensions: (1) *topography*, the part of the body affected; (2) *morphology*, the structural changes that are manifest, ranging from gross observations to intracellular ultrastructural changes; (3) *etiology*, including physical agents, chemicals, and injury; and (4) *function*, representing physiological or chemical disorders or alterations as well as including a list of complex disease entities. By coding the various manifestations of disease along one or more of these dimensions, it is hoped that retrieval of case records, tissue slides, photographs, and other medical artifacts can be made efficient.

Although both the ICDO and SNOP have the capability for more precise specification of the medical conditions surrounding death, they are not necessarily superior to the ICD as a mortality classification system. This is because the ICD is designed to facilitate *statistical analyses* of disease phenomena. From this perspective, the use of two or more dimensions of classification found in the ICDO and SNOP represents a distinct disadvantage, especially given that these dimensions are interdependent in the sense that the specific codes frequently need to be interpreted jointly. With its single-dimension classification system, the ICD titles refer to groups of separate but usually related morbid conditions. Only when the frequency of its occurrence or its importance as a morbid condition warrant it is a specific disease entity isolated as a separate category of the ICD. The single dimension of classification facilitates statistical analysis by making it easy to construct a limited number of aggregate categories that encompass the entire range of morbid conditions. This is the case because adjacent codes in the ICD usually refer to related disease groups so that a new aggregate category may be formed from a range of ICD codes.

In time series analysis of mortality data, two additional problems are likely to be encountered. The first problem arises due to the discontinuity that is associated with the revision of the ICD about every 10 years to reflect the current level of medical knowledge. In the United States, causes of death for the period 1949 to 1957 were coded according to the sixth revision of the ICD; for 1958 to 1967, according to the seventh revision; for 1968 to 1978, according to the eighth revision; and for 1979 onward, according to the ninth revision. The main problem with these revisions is the changes in the component diseases that define the various ICD categories. A related problem has to do with changes in the rules by which a given category is assigned as the underlying cause of death. To assist researchers in dealing with these issues, the NCHS conducts comparability studies (NCHS, 1963, 1964, 1965, 1975b, 1980) of the revisions in which a sample of deaths are coded according to each of two revisions so that the underlying-cause assignments can be compared.

A second problem in time-series analysis has to do with coding changes that occur within the tenure of a given revision of the ICD. For example, under the eighth revision the mortality rate for asthma, bronchitis, and emphysema (ICDA-8, 490-493) dropped 6.5% from 1974 to 1975. However, the mortality rate for chronic obstructive lung disease (ICDA-8, 519.3) increased so that the combined category of 490 to 493 *and* 519.3 increased 2.1%. It appeared that the decrease in mortality due to asthma, bronchitis, and emphysema was not real but due to changes in the practices of certifiers who at increasing rates selected the more general categorization of chronic obstructive lung disease.

Adjusting cause-specific mortality analyses for within-revision changes of the type reported in the preceding is not as easy as making adjustments for the between-revision changes because such change may be identified at any time and not simply as a result of the special comparability studies. In fact, one could anticipate some changes of this type based on the information contained in Appendix C of the NCHS's documentation for the 1968–1978 multicause mortality data (NTIS, 1980). The reader should note that the coding used in these data is actually the eighth revision of the ICD adapted for use in the United States (ICDA-8), not ICD-8. These data differ from ICD-8 data primarily in their handling of ICD-8 codes 412.0 and 412.9 for chronic IHD and in the use of the new code 519.3 for chronic obstructive lung disease.

# References

Abramson H. A. 1974. Editorial: Fifteen leading causes of death. *Journal of Asthma Research* **11**:139–140.

Abramson, J. M., Sacks, E., and Kahana, E. 1971. Death certificate data as an indicator of the presence of certain common diseases at death. *Journal of Chronic Disease* **24**:417–432.

Acheson, R. M., Nefzger, M. D., and Heyman, A. 1973. Mortality from stroke among U.S. veterans in Georgia and five western states: II. Quality of death certification and clinical records. *Journal of Chronic Disease* **26**:405–413.

Alderson, M. R., and Meade, T. W. 1967. Accuracy of diagnosis on death certificates compared with that in hospital records. *British Journal of Preventive and Social Medicine* **21**:2–29.

Bauer, F. W., and Robbins, S. L. 1972. An autopsy study of cancer patients: I. Accuracy of clinical diagnoses (1955 to 1965), Boston City Hospital. *Journal of the American Medical Association* **211**:1471–1474.

Bauer, R. W., Robbins, S. L., and Berg, J. W. 1973. An autopsy study of cancer patients: II. Hospitalization and accuracy of diagnoses (1955 to 1965), Boston City Hospital. *Journal of the American Medical Association* **223**:299–301.

Beadenkopf, W., Abrams, M., Daoud, A. and Marks, R. 1963. An assessment of certain medical aspects of death certificate data for an epidemiological study of arteriosclerotic heart disease. *Journal of Chronic Disease* **16**:249–262.

Colburn, H. N., and Baker, P. M. 1974. The use of mortality data in setting priorities for disease prevention. *Canadian Medical Association Journal* **110**:679–681.

Chamblee, R. F., and Evans, M. C. 1982. New dimensions in cause of death statistics. *American Journal of Public Health* **72**:1265–1270.

Dorn, H. F. 1966. Underlying and contributory causes of death. In *Epidemiological approaches to the study of cancer and other chronic diseases,* ed. W. Haenszel. National Cancer Institute Monograph No. 19, pp. 421–430. Washington, D.C.: Public Health Service.

Dorn, H. F., and Cutler, S. J. 1959. Morbidity from cancer in the United States. Public Health Monograph No. 56. Washington, D.C.: U.S. Government Printing Office.

Dorn, H. F., and Horn, J. I. 1941. Reliability of certificates of death from cancer. *American Journal of Hygiene* **34**:12–24.

Ehrlich, D., Li-Sik, M., and Modan, B. 1975. Some factors affecting the accuracy of cancer diagnosis. *Journal of Chronic Disease* **28**:359–364.

Engel, L. W., Straucher, J. A., Chiazze, L., and Heid, M. 1980. Accuracy of death certification in an autopsied population with specific attention to malignant neoplasms and vascular diseases. *American Journal of Epidemiology* **111**:99–112.

Florey, C., Senter, M. G., and Acheson, R. M. 1967. A study of the validity of the diagnosis of stroke in mortality data: I. Certificate analysis. *Yale Journal of Biology and Medicine* **40**:148–163.

Florey, C., Senter, M. G., and Acheson, R. M. 1969. A study of the validity of the diagnosis of stroke in mortality data: II. Comparisons by computer of autopsy and clinical records with death certificates. *American Journal of Epidemiology* **89**:15–24.

Griffith, G. 1976. Cancer surveillance with particular reference to the uses of mortality data. *International Journal of Epidemiology* **5**:69–76.

Haenszel, W., Loveland, D. B., and Sirken, M. G. 1962. Lung cancer mortality as related to residence and smoking histories: I. White males. *Journal of the National Cancer Institute* **28**:974–1001.

Haenszel, W., and Taeuber, K. E. 1964. Lung cancer mortality as related to residence and smoking histories: II. White females. *Journal of the National Cancer Institute* **32**:803–838.

Heasman, M., and Lipworth, L. 1966. Accuracy of certification of causes of death. Studies of Medical and Population Subjects No. 20, General Register Office of England and Wales, London.

Hersh, E. M., Bodey, G. P., Nies, B. A., and Freireich, E. J. 1965. Causes of death in acute leukemia—A ten-year study of 414 patients from 1954–1963. *Journal of the American Medical Association* **193**:105–109.

Inagaki, J., Rodriquez, V., and Bodey, G. P. 1974. Causes of death in cancer patients. *Cancer* **33**:568–573.

James, G., Patton, R. E., and Heslin, A. S. 1955. Accuracy of cause of death statements on death certificates. *Public Health Reports* **70**:39–51.

Kleinman, J. C. 1977. Mortality, statistical notes for health planners. National Center for Health Statistics. Washington, D.C.: U.S. Government Printing Office.

Kohn, R. R. 1982. Cause of death in very old people. *Journal of the American Medical Association* **20**:2793–2797.

Krueger, D. E. 1966. New numerators for old denominators: Multiple causes of death. In *Epidemiological approaches to the study of cancer and other chronic diseases,* ed. W. Haenszel. National Cancer Institute Monograph No. 19, pp. 431–443. Washington, D.C.: Public Health Service.

Kuller, L. H., Bolker, A., Saslaw, M., Paegel, B., Sisk, C., Borhani, N., Wray, J., Anderson, H., Peterson, D., Winkelstein, W., Cassel, J., Spiers, P., Robinson, A., Curry, H., Lilienfeld, A., and Seltser, R. 1969a. Nationwide cerebrovascular disease mortality study: I. Methods and analysis of death certificates. *American Journal of Epidemiology* **90**:536–544.

Kuller, L. H., Bolker, A., Saslaw, M., Paegel, B., Sisk, C., Borhani, N., Wray, J., Anderson, H., Peterson, D., Winkelstein, W., Cassel, J., Spiers, P., Robinson, A., Curry, H., Lilienfeld, A., and Seltser, R. 1969b. Nationwide cerebrovascular disease mortality study: II. Comparison of clinical records and death certificates. *American Journal of Epidemiology* **90**:545–555.

Kuller, L. H., Bolker, A., Saslaw, M., Paegel, B., Sisk, C., Borhani, N., Wray, J., Anderson, H., Peterson, D., Winkelstein, W., Cassel, J., Spiers, P., Robinson, A., Curry, H., Lilienfeld, A., and Seltser, R. 1969c. Nationwide cerebrovascular disease mortality study: III. Accuracy of the clinical diagnosis of cerebrovascular disease. *American Journal of Epidemiology* **90**:556–566.

Kuller, L. H., Bolker, A., Saslaw, M., Paegel, B., Sisk, C., Borhani, N., Wray, J., Anderson, H., Peterson, D., Winkelstein, W., Cassel, J., Spiers, P., Robinson, A., Curry, H., Lilienfeld, A., and Seltser, R. 1969d. Nationwide cerebrovascular disease mortality study: IV. Comparison of different clinical types of cerebrovascular disease. *American Journal of Epidemiology* **90**:567–578.

Kurtzke, J. F. 1979. ICD-9: A regression. *American Journal of Epidemiology* **109**:383–393.

Linder, F. E. 1976. Recent trends in health statistics. *World Health Organization Chronicle* **30**:58–63.

Manton, K. G., and Myers, G. C. 1983. National patterns of reporting of cancer on death certificates. Unpublished manuscript.

Manton, K. G., Tolley, H. D., and Poss, S. S. 1976. Life table techniques for multiple-cause mortality. *Demography* **13**:541–564.

Markush, R., and Seigel, D. 1968. Prevalence of death: Methodological considerations for use in mortality studies. *American Journal of Public Health* **53**:544–557.

Moriyama, I. M. 1965. Development of the present concept of cause of death. *American Journal of Public Health* **46**:55–69.

Moriyama, I. M., Baum, W., Haensel, W., and Mattison, B. 1958. Inquiry into diagnostic evidence supporting medical certifications of death. *American Journal of Public Health* **48**:1376–1387.

Moriyama, I. M., Dawber, T. R., and Kannel, W. B. 1966. Evaluation of diagnostic information supporting medical certification of deaths from cardiovascular disease. National Cancer Institute Monograph No. 19, pp. 405–419. Washington, D.C.: Public Health Service.

Moriyama, I. M., Krueger, D. E., and Stamler, J. 1971. *Cardiovascular diseases in the United States*. Cambridge, Massachusetts: Harvard University Press.

Myers, G. C., and Manton, K. G. 1983. Accuracy of death certification. Paper presented at the 1983 Joint Meetings of the American Statistical Association, the North American Regions of the Biometric Society, and the Statistical Society of Canada, Toronto, Canada, August 1983.

NCHS (National Center for Health Statistics). 1963. Comparability of mortality statistics for the fifth and sixth revisions: United States, 1950. Vital Statistics—Special Reports, Vol. 51, No. 2. Washington, D.C.: Public Health Service.

NCHS. 1964. Comparability ratios based on mortality statistics for the fifth and sixth revisions: United States, 1950. Vital Statistics—Special Reports, Vol. 51, No. 3. Washington, D.C.: Public Health Service.

NCHS. 1965. Comparability of mortality statistics for the sixth and seventh revisions: United States, 1958. Vital Statistics—Special Reports, Vol. 51, No. 4. Washington, D.C.: Public Health Service.

NCHS. 1974a. Summary report, final mortality statistics, Part II—Cause of death statistics, 1972. (HRA) 75-1120, 23:8, supplement.

NCHS. 1974b. Summary report, final mortality statistics, Part II—Cause of death statistics, 1971. (HRA) 74-1120, 23:3, supplement.

NCHS. 1974c. Summary report, final mortality statistics, Part II—Cause of death statistics, 1970. (HRA) 74-1120, 22:11, supplement.

NCHS. 1975a. Summary report, final mortality statistics, 1973. (HRA) 75-1120, 23:11, supplement.

NCHS. 1975b. Comparability of mortality statistics for the seventh and eighth revisions of the International Classification of Diseases, United States. U.S. Department of Health, Education and Welfare Pub. No. (HRA) 76-1340, Series No. 66, Rockville, Maryland.

NCHS. 1976. Final mortality statistics, 1974, advance report. (HRA) 77-1120, 24:11, supplement.

NCHS. 1977. Final mortality statistics, 1975, advance report. (HRA) 77-1120, 25:11.

NCHS. 1980. Estimates of selected comparability ratios based on dual coding of 1976 certificates by the eighth and ninth revisions of the International Classification of Diseases. U.S. Department of Health, Education and Welfare Pub. No. (PHS) 80-1120. *Monthly Vital Statistics Report* **28**:1–18.

Neyman, J. 1975. Assessing the chain: Energy crises, pollution and health. *International Statistical Review* **43**:253–267.

NTIS (National Technical Information Service). 1980. Multiple causes of death public use tape: ICDA-8 (1968–1978). Hyattsville, Maryland: U.S. Department of Commerce, National Center for Health Statistics.

Omran, A. R. 1971. The epidemiologic transition: A theory of the epidemiology of population change. *Milbank Memorial Fund Quarterly* **49**:509–538.

Ortey, J., and Parker, R. 1977. A birth-life-death model for planning and evaluation of health sciences programs. *Health Sciences Research* **6**:120–143.

Peery, T. M. 1975. The new and old diseases. *American Journal of Clinical Pathology* **63**:453–474.

Percy, C., Garfinkle, L., Krueger, D. E., and Dolman, A. B. 1974. Apparent changes in cancer mortality, 1968: A study of the effects of the introduction of the eighth revision International Classification of Diseases. *Public Health Reports* **89**:418–428.

Pohlen, K., and Emerson, H. 1942. Errors in clinical statements of causes of death. *American Journal of Public Health* **32**:251–260.

Pollack, E. S., and Horm, J. 1980. Trends in cancer incidence and mortality in the United States, 1969–76. *Journal of the National Cancer Institute* **64**:1091–1103.

Puffer, R., and Griffith, G. 1967. Patterns of urban mortality. Pan American Health Organization publication No. 151. Washington, D.C.

Rossman, I. 1974. True incidence of embolization and vital statistics. *Journal of the American Medical Association* **230**:1677–1679.

Sirken, M. G. 1962. Sampling survey programs of the National Vital Statistics Division. *Proceedings of the 9th national meeting public health conference of records and statistics,* PCHRS, document No. 574, pp. 39–41.

Sirken, M. G. 1963. Research uses of vital records in vital statistics surveys. *Milbank Memorial Fund Quarterly* **41**:309–316.

Sirken, M. G., and Dunn, H. L. 1958. Expanding and improving vital statistics. *Public Health Reports* **73**:537–540.

Sirken, M. G., Pifer, J. W., and Brown, M. L. 1960. Survey procedures for supplementing mortality statistics. *American Journal of Public Health* **50**:1753–1764.

Todd, M. C. 1972. Vital statistics reporting. *American Journal of Public Health* **62**:133–135.

U.S. National Committee on Vital and Health Statistics. 1975. The analytical potential of NCHS data for health care systems. *Vital and Health Statistics* 4:1–26.

Weiner, L., Bellous, M., McAvoy, G, and Cohen, E. 1955. Uses of multiple causes in the classification of deaths from cardiovascular and renal disease. *American Journal of Public Health* **45**:492–501.

West, R. R. 1977. Cervical cancer: Age at registration and age at death. *British Journal of Cancer* **35**:236–241.

Wing, S., and Manton, K. G., 1981. A multiple cause of death analysis of hypertension-related mortality in North Carolina, 1968–1977. *American Journal of Public Health* **71**:823–830.

WHO (World Health Organization). 1974. Second International Conference on National Committees on Vital and Health Statistics: New approaches in health statistics. WHO Technical Report, Series 559, pp. 1–40.

# Chapter 3 | Empirical Methods for Examining the Information Content of Multiple-Cause Mortality Data

## 1  Introduction

In Chapter 2 we reviewed available evidence on the reliability of cause-specific diagnoses on death certificates. We also examined the implications of various concepts of human mortality for the assessment of population health characteristics using mortality data. In this chapter we shall examine the empirical characteristics of the source of cause-specific mortality statistics—the entity axis multiple-cause data, that is, the computerized abstract of the set of medical conditions coded in items 19 and 20a of the North Carolina standard death certificate. In particular, by using the 1969 multiple-cause mortality tapes for the entire United States, we shall attempt to contrast underlying-cause-of-death information, which is familiar to demographers in the form of cause-specific mortality statistics, with multiple-cause-of-death information, a data form with which demographers are less familiar. Because multiple-cause data are a novel data form, we shall present several examples of ways in which these data can be organized for analysis. We shall also examine the particular implications of the various organizations of multiple-cause data for demographic analyses—and interpretations of analyses. We shall examine multiple-cause data forms in six different ways. First, we shall discuss the amount of multiple-cause information for individuals with specified demographic characteristics. Second, we shall examine how the medical conditions are structurally distributed on the death certificate. Third, we shall evaluate the implications of using the total occurrence of a disease, rather than only its occurrence as the underlying cause of death, for one very common measure of the public health significance of a disease—the rank ordering of the frequency of the occurrence of the disease at death. Fourth, we shall examine the relative magnitude of multiple-cause versus underlying-cause reporting for specific chronic degenerative diseases and the variation of that relative magnitude over demographic variables. Fifth, we shall examine several diseases and their joint occurrence in the *pattern-of-failure* representation of multiple-cause death. Finally, we shall examine the joint occurrence of various diseases in terms of their *cause-structured* patterns and the effects of the ICDA-8 rules for selection of the underlying cause of death for measurements of the structural dependency of two diseases.

## 2 Multiple-Cause Counts

Before attempting to examine detailed, cause-specific analyses of multiple-cause data, we shall first determine the number of conditions appearing on death certificates for different demographic groups. In Table 1 we present the mean number of medical conditions listed on death certificates specific to racial, age, and sex categories for all deaths in the United States in 1969 as well as the percentage distributions of the number of conditions coded on each death certificate.

**Table 1**

Percentage Distribution of Deaths by Number of Conditions Coded per Death Certificate by Race, Age, and Sex

| | Mean number of conditions | Total deaths | Percentage distribution of deaths by number of conditions coded | | | | | | |
|---|---|---|---|---|---|---|---|---|---|
| | | | Total | 1 | 2 | 3 | 4 | 5 | 6+ |
| *White males* | | | | | | | | | |
| All ages | 2.69 | 944,617 | 100.0 | 18.6 | 32.3 | 25.7 | 13.6 | 5.9 | 3.7 |
| Under 1 year | 2.22 | 32,079 | 100.0 | 28.5 | 38.4 | 21.4 | 7.7 | 2.7 | 1.4 |
| 1–14 | 2.74 | 13,591 | 100.0 | 12.9 | 39.6 | 25.0 | 12.7 | 5.9 | 3.9 |
| 15–44 | 2.78 | 79,795 | 100.0 | 14.0 | 37.3 | 24.8 | 12.9 | 6.1 | 4.9 |
| 45–64 | 2.51 | 263,270 | 100.0 | 23.8 | 33.5 | 23.2 | 11.4 | 4.9 | 3.1 |
| 65–84 | 2.78 | 466,018 | 100.0 | 17.0 | 30.5 | 26.9 | 15.0 | 6.6 | 4.0 |
| 85+ | 2.85 | 89,575 | 100.0 | 13.3 | 30.9 | 29.2 | 16.1 | 6.7 | 3.0 |
| Age unknown | 2.35 | 289 | 100.0 | 26.6 | 38.1 | 19.7 | 10.0 | 2.8 | 2.8 |

*(Continued)*

**Table 1** (*Continued*)

| | Mean number of conditions | Total deaths | Percentage distribution of deaths by number of conditions coded | | | | | | |
|---|---|---|---|---|---|---|---|---|---|
| | | | Total | 1 | 2 | 3 | 4 | 5 | 6+ |
| *White females* | | | | | | | | | |
| All ages | 2.78 | 737,756 | 100.0 | 15.6 | 31.8 | 27.6 | 14.9 | 6.4 | 3.7 |
| Under 1 year | 2.22 | 22,905 | 100.0 | 28.3 | 38.8 | 21.3 | 7.6 | 2.6 | 1.4 |
| 1–14 | 2.74 | 9,416 | 100.0 | 14.6 | 37.6 | 24.2 | 13.7 | 5.0 | 4.0 |
| 15–44 | 2.74 | 39,106 | 100.0 | 16.5 | 35.0 | 24.7 | 13.2 | 6.0 | 4.6 |
| 45–64 | 2.65 | 136,477 | 100.0 | 19.6 | 33.2 | 24.9 | 13.0 | 5.8 | 3.6 |
| 65–84 | 2.84 | 387,385 | 100.0 | 14.4 | 30.4 | 28.5 | 15.9 | 6.8 | 3.9 |
| 85+ | 2.83 | 142,291 | 100.0 | 12.9 | 31.8 | 29.8 | 15.6 | 6.5 | 3.4 |
| Age unknown | 2.51 | 176 | 100.0 | 21.0 | 31.8 | 29.5 | 11.9 | 4.5 | 1.1 |
| *Nonwhite males* | | | | | | | | | |
| All ages | 2.53 | 135,070 | 100.0 | 24.7 | 32.2 | 23.0 | 11.5 | 5.2 | 3.4 |
| Under 1 year | 2.01 | 11,018 | 100.0 | 37.8 | 36.1 | 17.4 | 5.7 | 2.1 | 0.9 |
| 1–14 | 2.57 | 3,904 | 100.0 | 16.8 | 41.9 | 22.8 | 10.5 | 4.8 | 3.3 |
| 15–44 | 2.73 | 24,841 | 100.0 | 17.0 | 34.7 | 25.0 | 12.7 | 6.0 | 4.6 |
| 45–64 | 2.46 | 43,447 | 100.0 | 27.5 | 31.5 | 22.0 | 10.8 | 4.9 | 3.2 |
| 65–84 | 2.59 | 45,566 | 100.0 | 24.1 | 29.9 | 24.1 | 12.7 | 5.7 | 3.6 |
| 85+ | 2.64 | 6,187 | 100.0 | 22.2 | 30.2 | 24.8 | 13.1 | 6.1 | 3.6 |
| Age unknown | 2.10 | 107 | 100.0 | 30.8 | 43.0 | 16.8 | 4.7 | 3.7 | 0.9 |
| *Nonwhite females* | | | | | | | | | |
| All ages | 2.53 | 102,454 | 100.0 | 24.4 | 31.5 | 23.7 | 12.1 | 5.2 | 3.2 |
| Under 1 year | 2.00 | 8,749 | 100.0 | 38.8 | 35.6 | 17.0 | 6.0 | 1.8 | 0.8 |
| 1–14 | 2.56 | 2,759 | 100.0 | 18.9 | 38.6 | 23.1 | 11.5 | 5.0 | 2.9 |
| 15–44 | 2.57 | 13,767 | 100.0 | 22.8 | 33.4 | 22.9 | 11.7 | 5.6 | 3.6 |
| 45–64 | 2.54 | 30,314 | 100.0 | 24.9 | 30.8 | 23.7 | 12.0 | 5.3 | 3.2 |
| 65–84 | 2.63 | 38,971 | 100.0 | 22.4 | 29.7 | 25.2 | 13.6 | 5.7 | 3.5 |
| 85+ | 2.59 | 7,817 | 100.0 | 21.6 | 32.4 | 25.2 | 12.3 | 5.3 | 3.2 |
| Age unknown | 2.36 | 77 | 100.0 | 26.0 | 33.8 | 24.7 | 10.4 | 3.9 | 1.3 |

Source: Pitts, 1976. Note that this tabulation excludes component codes.

One can see from the table that whites have, on average, more conditions coded on their death certificates (2.69 and 2.78 for males and females, respectively) than nonwhites (2.53 for both sexes). The age pattern of the mean number of conditions is similar for all four race–sex groups; that is, the mean number of conditions increases from birth to age

44, drops slightly for ages 45–64, and increases to ages 85 and over, except for a slight decrease for nonwhite females.

The increase to age 44 probably represents the fact that deaths due to external causes (accidents, poisonings, and violence) have relatively many conditions coded (they must have at least an external-cause and nature-of-injury code) and that the proportion of externally caused deaths is high for young adults. Thus, the slight decline in the number of conditions coded for deaths in the age range 45–64 is probably due to a decrease in the relative frequency of deaths due to external causes. The increase in the number of conditions at advanced ages is due to the high prevalence of chronic degenerative diseases at those ages and their increasing importance in causing death.

## 3  Line Density: The Structural Distribution of Medical Information on the Death Certificate

Although age changes in the mean number of conditions used on death certificates seem consistent with a high relative frequency of externally caused deaths at the younger ages followed by transition to a high relative frequency of deaths induced by chronic degenerative disease at older ages, these statistics yield no insight into an important feature of the information content of the death certificate, that is, the line and part placement of medical conditions. For example, even if the average number of conditions coded on the death certificate were constant over age, the complexity of that information might change, for example, by the physician using more lines of item 19 of the death certificate to indicate more morbid stages in the mortality process. To examine the information content implicit in the structural placement of conditions on the death certificate, we shall examine three types of plots. First, in Fig. 1 we plot the change with age of the probability that each of the three lines of item 19 of the death certificate is the line on which the underlying cause has presumably been coded, that is, the last in item 19 filled in. This plot displays age changes in the "complexity" of the mortality process for various race–sex groups. Second, in Fig. 2 we plot the change with age in the probability that the lowest used line in item 19 has more than a single medical condition coded on it. This represents one aspect of the "line density" information. Third, in Fig. 3 we plot the probability that an "inner line" (a line above the lowest used line in item 19) has more than a single condition. This represents a second aspect of the line density information.

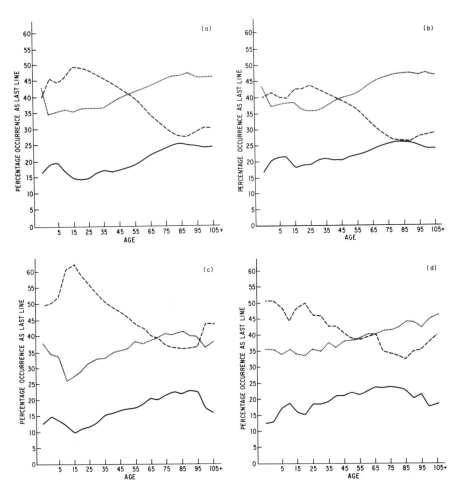

**Fig. 1.** Age-specific proportion of deaths for (a) white males, (b) white females, (c) black males, and (d) black females with one (------), two (·····), or three (——) lines used in item 19 of the North Carolina standard certificate of death. (From Special Tabulation of 1969 Multiple Cause of Death Data Files. Note that this tabulation excludes component codes.)

In Fig. 1 we plot the change with age of the number of lines used. This is different from the data in Table 1, which displays the change with age of the probability of a given number of codes listed on the death certificate because it relates to information in item 19 only and reflects the number of lines used rather than the number of conditions reported. By examining a measure of the number of lines used, one controls for certain artifacts in coding, such as the use of multiple ICDA-8 codes to describe a single disease state on a prior line of the death certificate. Thus, the number of

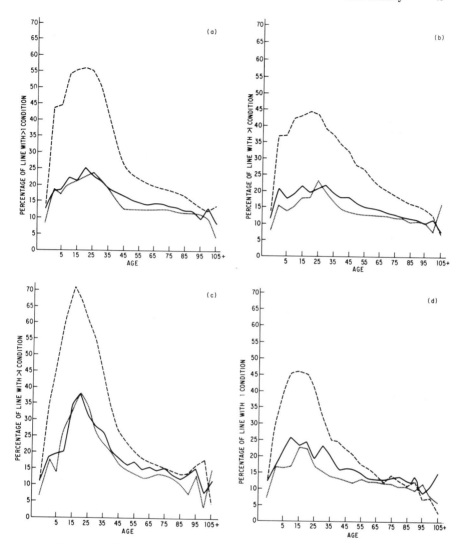

**Fig. 2.** Age-specific probability for (a) white males, (b) white females, (c) black males, and (d) black females that the lowest used line in item 19 contains more than one coded medical diagnostic term. ------ denotes the proportion of certificates with more than one code on line (a) when line (a) is the lowest used line in item 19; ······ denotes the proportion of certificates with more than one code on line (b) when line (b) is the lowest used line in item 19; —— denotes the proportion of certificates with more than one code on line (c) when line (c) is the lowest used line in item 19. (From Special Tabulation of 1969 Multiple Cause of Death Data Files. Note that this tabulation excludes component codes.)

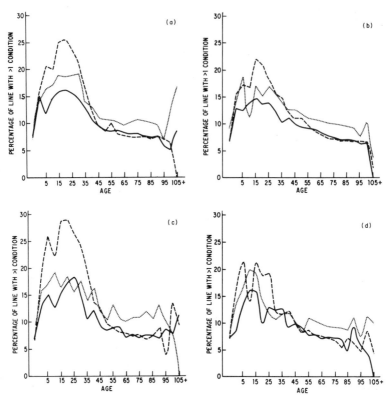

**Fig. 3.** Age-specific probability for (a) white males, (b) white females, (c) black males, and (d) black females that the immediate and intermediate cause lines contain more than one coded medical diagnostic term. ------ denotes the proportion of certificates with more than one code on line (a) when line (b) is the lowest used line in item 19; —— denotes the proportion of certificates with more than one code on line (a) when line (c) is the lowest used line in item 19; ⋯⋯ denotes the proportion of certificates with more than one code on line (b) when line (c) is the lowest used line in item 19. (From Special Tabulation of 1969 Multiple Cause of Death Data Files. Note that this tabulation excludes component codes.)

lines used may be a better measure of the amount of information on the death certificate. Also, by considering only item 19 information, our attention is focused on the detail in which the primary death process was described because information on contributory chronic conditions is generally reported in item 20a of the death certificate. That is, the number of lines used in item 19 reflects the number (up to three) of morbid stages that the physician identified in the mortality process.

During the first year, a large percentage of white male deaths (43%) is indicated on the death certificate on both lines (a) and (b) of item 19 (as shown by ⋯⋯ on Fig. 1a); for ages 1–30, the percentage of death certificates with two lines used drops with a compensatory increase in the proportion with only one line used in item 19 (shown by ------). Apparently, many of the white male deaths in this 1–30-year age category can be described by a one-step death process. After age 30, however, this trend reverses and the relative proportion of certificates with two and three lines used increases, and at approximately the same age rate—about 1% every 5 years. Naturally, these increases are accompanied by a decrease in the proportion of death certificates with only line 19(a) used. At advanced ages, for example, over 90, these trends reverse somewhat. The dominant trend is an increase with age from age 30 in the complexity of the death process as indicated by the number of lines used in item 19 of the death certificate. Thus, both the mean number of medical conditions and the complexity of the mortality process increase with age for white males.

The same general age patterns in the number of lines used in item 19 of the death certificate are also found for white females (see Fig. 1b). The major difference is that the number of certificates with only a single line used never reaches as high a percentage (44% at age 25) as it does for white males (49% at age 15). This is probably due to the higher risk of externally caused deaths at young ages for white males as compared to white females. Thus, the most significant feature of the plot is the repetition of the white males' pattern of a gradual and parallel increase in the percentage of death certificates with two and three lines filled out.

As one can readily see, major differences occur between the plots for black males (Fig. 1c) and the plots for the two white sex-groups in terms of the very high percentage of black male death certificates with only line 19(a) used (up to 62% at age 15). Despite these differences, however, the general form of age change of the plots shows structural similarities. That is, for a high percentage of deaths under 1 year of age, two lines are used, but with increasing age this percentage rapidly drops off, whereas the percentage of death certificates with exactly one line used increases. In addition, the gradual and parallel rise of the proportion of death certificates with two or three lines used is found for black males, whereas the proportion of certificates with two or three lines used drops off somewhat after age 90.

The graph for black females (Fig. 1d) shows the same structural characteristics as the other three graphs (i.e., a gradual and parallel increase with age of the proportion of death certificates with two and three lines used). There are, however, several interesting differences. First, unlike the plots for black males, there is no initial rapid increase in the proportion of death certificates with one line used. Second, the increase over white females in the proportion of certificates with only a single line used is offset by a decrease in the proportion with three lines used. The conclusion to be reached from Fig. 1 is that all four race–sex-groups exhibit an increase in the complexity of the mortality process with age—at least as indicated by the number of morbid stages identified by the physician. Within this general pattern, death certificates for whites tend to be somewhat more complex than for blacks and death certificates for females tend to be somewhat more complex than for males.

As suggested, an examination of the number of lines used in item 19 is only a partial representation of the structural placement of conditions on the death certificate. A second component of the structural distribution of conditions is the relative frequency with which more than one condition is placed on a given line of item 19 of the death certificate. We shall discuss these structural factors in two parts: (1) in Fig. 2 we shall examine the age-specific probability that the lowest used line of item 19 contains more than one condition and (2) in Fig. 3 we shall examine the proportion of death certificates in which any line above the lowest used line contains more than a single condition specific to age, race, and sex.

The density of information on the lowest used line is of interest analytically because the underlying cause of death is, in general, supposed to be listed on the lowest used line in item 19. Hence, a high proportion of death certificates in which the lowest used line of item 19 contains more than a single condition implies a large proportion of deaths for which the physician's selection of an underlying cause of death was ambiguous.

Figure 2 shows that when only one line is used (as shown by ------ in Fig. 2) on the death certificate, it frequently has more than one condition. For example, at about age 20–24, 55% of certificates for white males (Fig. 2a) with only line 19(a) used have more than a single condition on line (a). This proportion drops off rapidly with age so that by age 55 years the probability of more than one condition on line (a) approaches that for lines (b) and (c). The plots for black males (Fig. 2c) are quite different at young ages, indicating a much higher probability that the lowest used lines will contain more than a single condition. Line density peaks at about age 15–19, with line (a) having the highest probability of containing more than one condition when it is the lowest used line.

For white females (Fig. 2b), a peak in the proportion of certificates with the lowest used line having more than a single condition occurs in the early adult years, though the age change of this proportion is somewhat different than was observed for either of the male groups. In contrast, black females (Fig. 2d) show an age pattern that is more similar in form to that of the two male groups, with a sharp peak in line density for young adults and with the highest density for line (a) when it is the only line used.

Taken together, Figs. 1 and 2 indicate that death certificates for blacks use fewer lines but that more conditions are reported on the lowest line used than on death certificates for whites. For all groups the density of conditions on the lowest used line depends strongly on which line is the lowest used line.

On certificates on which line 19(b) or (c) is the lowest used line, there exist inner lines (i.e., lines that are not the lowest used line). In Fig. 3 we present the age-specific probability that these inner lines contain more than a single coded medical condition. The figure identifies two structurally distinct age domains in a manner consistent with a transition from externally caused deaths at younger ages to deaths induced by chronic degenerative disease at older ages. Above age 55, the plots for line (a) are virtually identical regardless of whether the lowest used line is line (b) (indicated by ------) or line (c) (indicated by ———). For all four race–sex-groups, the immediate cause of death will be a single ICDA-8 code in 90–95% of these death certificates. When line (a) is the only line used, the probability of a single ICDA-8 code is as low as 80% in this age range (see Fig. 2). The plots for line (b) (······ in Fig. 3) are distinctly higher than the plots for line (a) and much more closely resemble the line (b) plot (------) in Fig. 2. Thus, above age 55, the density for line (b) seems to be independent of whether line (c) is used.

At most younger ages, the plot denoted by ------ in Fig. 3 is the highest and the plots denoted by ——— in Fig. 3 is the lowest with the largest differences occurring for black males, the smallest for black females, and with white males and white females falling in between. This suggests that the use of line (a) in this age range with line (c) as the lowest used line might characterize a different morbid process than when line (b) is the lowest used line. The plots in Figs. 1–3 suggest that demographic categories with similar levels of multiple-cause reporting (average number of conditions; see Table 1) exhibit substantial variation with respect to both the line density of information and the complexity of the lethal morbid processes. This suggests that the differences between death certificates for whites and blacks are a function of a variety of medically relevant differences in the morbid processes that lead to death as well as possible differences in the care with which the death certificates are filled out. For example, the higher likelihood of death at younger ages for black males may be primarily a result of greater exposure to external causes.

## 4 Relative Ranking of Major Causes of Death

The ranking of the frequency of various diseases as underlying causes of death has often been used as a general measure of the population health significance of those diseases. Nonetheless, the ranking of the frequency of the underlying-cause occurrences of a disease is determined in part by the rules by which the underlying causes of death are selected from all the medical conditions on a death certificate. The ranking also ignores the information contained in the multiple medical conditions reported on the death certificate as other than the underlying cause of death. To illustrate the effects of multiple-cause reporting on the frequency ranking of various conditions, we present Table 2, which contains race-, sex-, and age-specific ranking of both the underlying cause and total mentions of 10 major medical conditions.

Table 2 shows that both the underlying-cause and total-mention ranking change over a variety of demographic variables. For example, cancer, accidents, and cirrhosis tend to decrease in significance as causes of death with age. In contrast, stroke and generalized arteriosclerosis (GA) increase in significance with age. Diabetes mellitus (DM) and nephritis and nephrosis appear to be more significant as causes of death for blacks, whereas the chronic respiratory diseases bronchitis, emphysema, and asthma seem to be more significant for whites. Diabetes mellitus is more significant for females, whereas chronic respiratory disease is more significant for males. These variations suggest that attempting to determine the significance of a disease according to its overall ranking as a cause of death is potentially misleading because of important variations in rankings across age, race, and sex.

In addition to demographic variability in the ranking of conditions, the rankings are dependent on whether conditions are ranked on their underlying-cause or total-mention frequencies. For example, the total-mention ranking of both cancer and accidents is often lower than their underlying-cause ranking. On the other hand, generalized arteriosclerosis has a much higher ranking in terms of its total occurrence on the death certificate than as an underlying cause of death.

To help understand the shifts in relative ranking in Table 2 between the underlying-cause and total-mention rankings, we find it useful to examine ratios of the total occurrence of each condition to its underlying-cause occurrence. These ratios have a simple interpretation as the sum of the odds against a given mention of a disease being selected as the underlying cause of death. For example, a ratio of 1.44 indicates the odds are 0.44 to 1.00 that the disease will not be selected as the underlying cause of death. These are relatively low odds. In contrast, the ratio 22.45 represents odds of 21.45 to 1.00.

Table 3 illustrates these ratios of total occurrence by showing the race- and sex-specific ratios for the 10 major diseases examined in Table 2.

**Table 2**

Race–Sex-Specific Underlying-Cause and Total-Mention Rankings of 10 Major Causes of Death[a]

| | Disease | White males <65 UCD | <65 TM | 65-84 UCD | 65-84 TM | 85+ UCD | 85+ TM | Black males <65 UCD | <65 TM | 65-84 UCD | 65-84 TM | 85+ UCD | 85+ TM | White females <65 UCD | <65 TM | 65-84 UCD | 65-84 TM | 85+ UCD | 85+ TM | Black females <65 UCD | <65 TM | 65-84 UCD | 65-84 TM | 85+ UCD | 85+ TM |
|---|---|---|---|---|---|---|---|---|---|---|---|---|---|---|---|---|---|---|---|---|---|---|---|---|---|
| 410–414 | Heart disease | 1 | 1 | 1 | 1 | 1 | 1 | 1 | 1 | 1 | 1 | 1 | 1 | 2 | 1 | 1 | 1 | 1 | 1 | 1 | 1 | 1 | 1 | 1 | 1 |
| 140–199 | Cancer | 2 | 2 | 2 | 2 | 3 | 5 | 3 | 3 | 2 | 3 | 3 | 5 | 1 | 2 | 3 | 4 | 3 | 5 | 2 | 2 | 2 | 4 | 3 | 5 |
| 430–438 | Stroke | 4 | 5 | 3 | 4 | 2 | 3 | 4 | 5 | 3 | 2 | 2 | 3 | 4 | 5 | 2 | 2 | 2 | 3 | 3 | 3 | 3 | 2 | 2 | 2 |
| E800–E949 | Accidents | 3 | 3 | 6 | 8 | 6 | 8 | 2 | 2 | 5 | 7 | 6 | 7 | 3 | 3 | 7 | 7 | 6 | 7 | 4 | 5 | 7 | 7 | 6 | 7 |
| 470–474 480–486 | Pneumonia and influenza | 6 | 4 | 4 | 5 | 4 | 4 | 5 | 4 | 4 | 5 | 4 | 4 | 5 | 4 | 4 | 5 | 5 | 4 | 5 | 4 | 5 | 6 | 5 | 4 |
| 250 | Diabetes mellitus | 8 | 8 | 8 | 7 | 8 | 7 | 7 | 7 | 7 | 6 | 7 | 6 | 7 | 6 | 6 | 6 | 7 | 6 | 6 | 6 | 4 | 5 | 7 | 6 |
| 440 | Generalized arteriosclerosis | 10 | 7 | 7 | 3 | 5 | 2 | 10 | 8 | 6 | 4 | 5 | 2 | 10 | 8 | 5 | 3 | 4 | 2 | 10 | 8 | 6 | 3 | 4 | 3 |
| 490–493 519.3 | Bronchitus, emphysema, and asthma | 7 | 9 | 5 | 6 | 7 | 6 | 8 | 9 | 8 | 8 | 9 | 8 | 8 | 9 | 8 | 8 | 8 | 8 | 9 | 10 | 10 | 9 | 9 | 9 |
| 571 | Cirrhosis of liver | 5 | 6 | 9 | 9 | 10 | 10 | 6 | 6 | 10 | 10 | 10 | 10 | 6 | 7 | 9 | 10 | 10 | 10 | 7 | 7 | 9 | 10 | 10 | 10 |
| 580–584 | Nephritis and nephrosis | 9 | 10 | 10 | 10 | 9 | 9 | 9 | 10 | 9 | 9 | 8 | 9 | 9 | 10 | 10 | 9 | 9 | 9 | 8 | 9 | 8 | 8 | 8 | 8 |

Source: Special Tabulation of 1969 Multiple Cause of Death Data Files.

[a] UCD = Underlying-cause definition; TM = total mentions.

**Table 3**

Race–Sex-Specific Ratios of Underlying Causes to Total Mentions of 10 Major Causes of Death

| Disease | White males | | | Black males | | | White females | | | Black females | | |
|---|---|---|---|---|---|---|---|---|---|---|---|---|
| | <65 | 65–84 | 85+ | <65 | 65–84 | 85+ | <65 | 65–84 | 85+ | <65 | 65–84 | 85+ |
| Heart disease | 1.44 | 1.58 | 1.58 | 1.62 | 1.55 | 1.54 | 1.72 | 1.66 | 1.58 | 1.65 | 1.55 | 1.49 |
| Cancer | 1.07 | 1.22 | 1.42 | 1.07 | 1.16 | 1.29 | 1.05 | 1.18 | 1.34 | 1.07 | 1.15 | 1.25 |
| Stroke | 1.71 | 1.57 | 1.48 | 1.57 | 1.50 | 1.44 | 1.61 | 1.54 | 1.46 | 1.56 | 1.52 | 1.46 |
| Accidents | 1.15 | 1.82 | 1.64 | 1.14 | 1.63 | 1.51 | 1.29 | 1.79 | 1.64 | 1.30 | 1.63 | 1.34 |
| Pneumonia and influenza | 3.16 | 3.65 | 3.08 | 2.19 | 2.96 | 2.54 | 2.86 | 3.41 | 3.04 | 2.06 | 2.98 | 2.60 |
| Diabetes mellitus | 3.36 | 4.10 | 3.93 | 2.30 | 2.87 | 2.81 | 2.87 | 3.66 | 3.66 | 2.26 | 2.66 | 3.00 |
| Generalized arterio-sclerosis | 22.45 | 8.88 | 5.93 | 13.20 | 7.97 | 5.51 | 16.91 | 7.64 | 5.68 | 15.08 | 8.07 | 5.63 |
| Bronchitus, emphysema, and asthma | 2.23 | 2.77 | 3.39 | 2.04 | 2.69 | 3.30 | 1.98 | 3.24 | 3.70 | 1.67 | 3.10 | 3.11 |
| Cirrhosis of liver | 1.39 | 1.91 | 2.32 | 1.42 | 1.69 | 1.71 | 1.34 | 1.82 | 2.75 | 1.33 | 1.70 | 2.00 |
| Nephritis and nephrosis | 2.05 | 2.66 | 2.80 | 1.73 | 2.13 | 2.27 | 2.08 | 2.50 | 2.56 | 1.84 | 2.28 | 2.17 |

In Table 3 we see that the diseases can be grouped into one of three categories on the basis of the change in the ratio of total mentions to underlying-cause occurrences of the disease. The first group—heart disease, stroke, and generalized arteriosclerosis—has ratios that decrease with age. This suggests that these might be diseases whose severity increases with age—an interpretation supported by the fact that the total occurrences of these diseases increase with age (see Chapter 5). The second group of medical conditions—cancer, chronic respiratory diseases, cirrhosis, and nephritis and nephrosis—are characterized by increasing ratios. Increasing ratios might imply that the severity of these conditions decreases with age. The third set of conditions—accidents, pneumonia and influenza, and diabetes—increases from ages 64 and below to ages 65–84 and then decreases at ages 85 and above. This age variability in the ratios suggests that these diseases and conditions interact with other conditions at different ages in different ways. Ratios also vary over sex (females generally having higher ratios) and race (whites generally having higher ratios).

In Table 3 we see that the highest ratios are obtained for generalized arteriosclerosis (up to 22.45) and the lowest for cancer (down to 1.05). These ratios can also be interpreted as conversion factors to be applied to published underlying-cause death rates to obtain estimates of multiple-cause death rates. Note that it is the wide range of these ratios over diseases that accounts for the changes in relative ranking between the UCD and TM rankings observed in Table 2.

## 5   Pattern-of-Failure Representations of Mortality

In Chapter 2 we discussed two models of multiple-cause mortality that gave rise to the entity axis versus record axis description of each death. Although the record axis data are the basic data of the pattern-of-failure model, we can also obtain those data directly from the entity axis data. This is done by defining $2^k - 1$ distinct *patterns* representing all the possible combinations of $k$ diseases of interest. To illustrate what this means computationally, let us define $k$ binary variables that take the value of 1 if that condition is found on the death certificate and a 0 if it is not found on the death certificate. For example, to develop the pattern of failure for six diseases and a residual, we use the binary codes based on the index $i$ in the tabulation on p. 58.

These diseases were selected because they were significant in the recent changes in U.S. mortality patterns and levels. For example, IHD, stroke, and generalized arteriosclerosis are important components of cir-

| $i$ | Description | ICDA-8 | Binary code = $2^i$ |
|---|---|---|---|
| 0 | Residual, not listed below | | 0000001 |
| 1 | Infectious diseases | 480–486, 038 | 0000010 |
| 2 | Cancer | 140–209 | 0000100 |
| 3 | Diabetes mellitus | 250 | 0001000 |
| 4 | Ischemic heart disease (IHD) | 410–414 | 0010000 |
| 5 | Stroke | 430–438 | 0100000 |
| 6 | Generalized arteriosclerosis | 440 | 1000000 |

culatory disease deaths that have been declining in the United States. Cancer is a major disease category whose mortality risk has been rising in the United States. Diabetes mellitus is a chronic degenerative disease that (1) is a significant risk factor for circulatory diseases, (2) has a high prevalence, and (3) is often reported as a contributory condition on item 20a of the death certificate. The particular infections were selected for group one because they are frequently complicating and lethal conditions in many elderly persons with chronic degenerative diseases. In addition to these six conditions, a seventh category was created to record the occurrence of any medical condition other than the six described in the tabulation. Thus, for the six diseases and one residual category, seven binary variables need to be coded for each death. This string of binary codes is used to represent the medical condition of the decedent. For example, given that our binary variables are ordered from right to left—residual diseases, infectious disease, cancer, diabetes mellitus, IHD, stroke, and generalized arteriosclerosis—then the sequence 0000001 represents a death with none of the six criterion diseases reported and 1000000 represents a death with generalized arteriosclerosis. The pattern 0001110 represents a death with infectious disease, cancer, and diabetes mellitus. There are 127 such patterns. To get an impression of how much information is provided on the death certificate, in Table 4 we present the 127 patterns and their frequency of occurrence for the 945,081 white male deaths in 1969.

In Table 4 only one pattern (1111110) is not represented. Naturally, the structure of such a pattern representation is dependent on the categories selected. However, Table 4 does show that very complex medical conditions are reported on the death certificate.

To understand how this pattern-of-failure information is distributed over age, race, and sex, we have selected certain patterns for study in more detail. All of these patterns involve IHD, and we shall express their rate of occurrence in terms of the proportion of all IHD deaths (specific to age, race, and sex categories) that they represent.

**Table 4**

Frequencies of 127 Disease Patterns for White Males, Total Deaths

| Disease pattern | Frequency | Disease pattern | Frequency | Disease pattern | Frequency |
|---|---|---|---|---|---|
| 0000001 | 212,090 | 0101100 | 78 | 1010111 | 97 |
| 0000010 | 6,948 | 0101101 | 82 | 1011000 | 2,245 |
| 0000011 | 36,663 | 0101110 | 15 | 1011001 | 2,440 |
| 0000100 | 72,501 | 0101111 | 21 | 1011010 | 64 |
| 0000101 | 52,275 | 0110000 | 9,381 | 1011011 | 183 |
| 0000110 | 9,519 | 0110001 | 12,672 | 1011100 | 74 |
| 0000111 | 8,992 | 0110010 | 1,278 | 1011101 | 83 |
| 0001000 | 411 | 0110011 | 2,272 | 1011110 | 1 |
| 0001001 | 5,380 | 0110100 | 494 | 1011111 | 5 |
| 0001010 | 345 | 0110101 | 571 | 1100000 | 11,358 |
| 0001011 | 1,662 | 0110110 | 40 | 1100001 | 11,742 |
| 0001100 | 1,298 | 0110111 | 86 | 1100010 | 1,577 |
| 0001101 | 1,302 | 0111000 | 1,159 | 1100011 | 1,765 |
| 0001110 | 165 | 0111001 | 1,377 | 1100100 | 650 |
| 0001111 | 221 | 0111010 | 109 | 1100101 | 432 |
| 0010000 | 136,458 | 0111011 | 205 | 1100110 | 53 |
| 0010001 | 121,670 | 0111100 | 40 | 1100111 | 58 |
| 0010010 | 3,880 | 0111101 | 40 | 1101000 | 1,401 |
| 0010011 | 12,579 | 0111110 | 4 | 1101001 | 1,114 |
| 0010100 | 7,652 | 0111111 | 6 | 1101010 | 142 |
| 0010101 | 9,714 | 1000000 | 1,988 | 1101011 | 137 |
| 0010110 | 693 | 1000001 | 18,615 | 1101100 | 53 |
| 0010111 | 1,119 | 1000010 | 1,687 | 1101101 | 26 |
| 0011000 | 8,877 | 1000011 | 4,801 | 1101110 | 4 |
| 0011001 | 11,593 | 1000100 | 1,346 | 1101111 | 4 |
| 0011010 | 368 | 1000101 | 2,186 | 1110000 | 3,093 |
| 0011011 | 1,016 | 1000110 | 240 | 1110001 | 4,276 |
| 0011100 | 614 | 1000111 | 339 | 1110010 | 255 |
| 0011101 | 639 | 1001000 | 226 | 1110011 | 613 |
| 0011110 | 50 | 1001001 | 1,587 | 1110100 | 108 |
| 0011111 | 83 | 1001010 | 158 | 1110101 | 128 |
| 0100000 | 19,402 | 1001011 | 385 | 1110110 | 9 |
| 0100001 | 22,817 | 1001100 | 101 | 1110111 | 18 |
| 0100010 | 3,696 | 1001101 | 117 | 1111000 | 355 |
| 0100011 | 5,863 | 1001110 | 14 | 1111001 | 478 |
| 0100100 | 2,442 | 1001111 | 14 | 1111010 | 27 |
| 0100101 | 1,965 | 1010000 | 19,992 | 1111011 | 50 |
| 0100110 | 297 | 1010001 | 23,880 | 1111100 | 9 |
| 0100111 | 318 | 1010010 | 905 | 1111101 | 11 |
| 0101000 | 1,378 | 1010011 | 1,957 | 1111110 | 0 |
| 0101001 | 1,751 | 1010100 | 977 | 1111111 | 1 |
| 0101010 | 288 | 1010101 | 1,073 | | |
| 0101011 | 376 | 1010110 | 54 | | |

In Table 5 for each race–sex-group and for each of three broad age categories (0–64, 65–74, 75+), we present the proportions of all IHD deaths at that age that occur jointly with diabetes mellitus, stroke, or generalized arteriosclerosis. For example, for white males aged 0–64, we see that 47.7% of IHD deaths at that age occur with no other condition mentioned. We selected IHD for these comparisons because it is a highly lethal condition that would be sufficient to cause death by itself.

We see from Table 5 that males have a higher proportion of IHD deaths with no other condition mentioned than do females. We can also see that the percentage of IHD deaths with no other condition mentioned declines with age for all race–sex-groups.

What is most significant about this table is the frequency with which IHD appears with these various other conditions. For example, 14.0% of white males who die with IHD above age 75 also have generalized arteriosclerosis. Nearly 2.8% of white males over age 75 who die with IHD also have stroke and generalized arteriosclerosis listed on the death certificate. For white females who die with IHD over age 75, 3.8% also have stroke and generalized arteriosclerosis. This observation suggests that as the population ages, the most significant public health problems will involve the management of multiple, chronic degenerative diseases. It also suggests that there has been some success in the long-term medical management of a variety of chronic degenerative diseases because it appears that a significant proportion of the population lives long enough after the acquisition of a "first" chronic degenerative disease to acquire one or more other chronic diseases. These observations seem to support the argument made by Schatzkin (1980) that calculations of life-expectancy changes due to the elimination of a given cause of death may understate the actual change experienced because (1) many chronic degenerative diseases have a high frequency as a contributory cause of death and (2) the control of many risk factors (e.g., smoking, cholesterol, and hypertension) may reduce the mortality risks of several chronic degenerative conditions.

The table also shows some interesting race-specific mortality differentials. First, both white groups have higher proportions of IHD-associated deaths with diabetes mellitus or generalized arteriosclerosis either singly or in combinations than do blacks. On the other hand, blacks generally have higher proportions of IHD deaths with stroke even if diabetes mellitus or generalized arteriosclerosis are also associated. This suggests different underlying degenerative etiological mechanisms leading to circulatory disease death. For blacks the higher frequency of IHD associated with stroke suggests that hypertension is a more profound mortality risk factor in blacks (Wing and Manton, 1981). On the other hand, the higher frequency of diabetes mellitus and generalized arteriosclerosis implies these degenerative processes are stronger risk factors for whites.

**Table 5**

Frequencies (F) and Percentages (%) of Deaths Occurring for Three Age-Groups with Ischemic Heart Disease with Complications

| Age | Total | Alone | | Diabetes mellitus | | Stroke | | Generalized arteriosclerosis | | Diabetes and stroke | | Diabetes and arteriosclerosis | | Stroke and arteriosclerosis | |
|---|---|---|---|---|---|---|---|---|---|---|---|---|---|---|---|
| | | F | % | F | % | F | % | F | % | F | % | F | % | F | % |
| **White males** | | | | | | | | | | | | | | | |
| 0–64 | 128,912 | 61,433 | 47.7 | 7,030 | 5.5 | 3,684 | 2.9 | 9,285 | 7.2 | 512 | 0.4 | 1,155 | 0.9 | 759 | 0.6 |
| 65–74 | 118,455 | 39,091 | 33.0 | 6,913 | 5.8 | 6,233 | 5.3 | 11,815 | 10.0 | 894 | 0.8 | 1,527 | 1.3 | 2,006 | 1.7 |
| 75+ | 162,833 | 35,934 | 22.1 | 6,527 | 4.0 | 12,131 | 7.4 | 22,772 | 14.0 | 1,130 | 0.7 | 2,003 | 1.2 | 4,604 | 2.8 |
| Total | 410,200 | 136,458 | 33.3 | 20,470 | 5.0 | 22,048 | 5.4 | 43,872 | 10.7 | 2,536 | 0.6 | 4,685 | 1.1 | 7,369 | 1.8 |
| **White females** | | | | | | | | | | | | | | | |
| 0–64 | 39,038 | 12,953 | 33.1 | 4,845 | 12.4 | 2,007 | 5.1 | 2,495 | 6.4 | 500 | 1.3 | 862 | 2.2 | 343 | 0.9 |
| 65–74 | 72,690 | 18,168 | 25.0 | 8,317 | 11.4 | 5,192 | 7.1 | 6,712 | 9.2 | 1,341 | 1.8 | 1,843 | 2.5 | 1,507 | 2.1 |
| 75+ | 192,948 | 35,170 | 18.2 | 10,562 | 5.5 | 18,705 | 9.7 | 28,862 | 15.0 | 2,398 | 1.2 | 3,312 | 1.7 | 7,258 | 3.8 |
| Total | 304,676 | 66,291 | 21.8 | 23,724 | 7.8 | 25,904 | 8.5 | 38,069 | 12.5 | 4,239 | 1.4 | 6,017 | 2.0 | 9,108 | 3.0 |
| **Black males** | | | | | | | | | | | | | | | |
| 0–64 | 15,091 | 6,656 | 44.1 | 681 | 4.5 | 1,131 | 7.5 | 698 | 4.6 | 114 | 0.8 | 71 | 0.5 | 113 | 0.7 |
| 65–74 | 10,348 | 3,387 | 32.7 | 434 | 4.2 | 964 | 9.3 | 811 | 7.8 | 86 | 0.8 | 87 | 0.8 | 238 | 2.3 |
| 75+ | 9,102 | 2,457 | 27.0 | 252 | 2.8 | 865 | 9.5 | 1,042 | 11.4 | 68 | 0.7 | 65 | 0.7 | 271 | 3.0 |
| Total | 34,541 | 12,500 | 36.2 | 1,367 | 4.0 | 2,960 | 8.6 | 2,551 | 7.4 | 268 | 0.8 | 223 | 0.6 | 622 | 1.8 |
| **Black females** | | | | | | | | | | | | | | | |
| 0–64 | 10,397 | 3,590 | 34.5 | 1,107 | 10.6 | 992 | 9.5 | 431 | 4.1 | 188 | 1.8 | 145 | 1.4 | 124 | 1.2 |
| 65–74 | 9,385 | 2,529 | 26.9 | 905 | 9.6 | 1,099 | 11.7 | 718 | 7.7 | 244 | 2.6 | 181 | 1.9 | 198 | 2.1 |
| 75+ | 10,361 | 2,480 | 23.9 | 507 | 4.9 | 1,238 | 11.9 | 1,349 | 13.0 | 148 | 1.4 | 134 | 1.3 | 323 | 3.1 |
| Total | 30,143 | 8,599 | 28.5 | 2,519 | 8.4 | 3,329 | 11.0 | 2,498 | 8.3 | 580 | 1.9 | 460 | 1.5 | 645 | 2.1 |

## 6   Structured Disease Dependency

In Section 5 we briefly examined the joint occurrence of four chronic diseases—IHD, diabetes mellitus, stroke, and generalized arteriosclerosis—and the variation of that joint occurrence over race, sex, and age. The presentation did not attempt to identify causal relations between the various diseases. In this section we shall examine another type of multiple-cause data form that attempts to make such distinctions. In Table 6 we present a set of 21 possible patterns of joint occurrence of two diseases (labeled $x$ and $y$), where one of the conditions is identified as the underlying cause of death and where the placement of the nonunderlying-cause occurrence of the conditions is identified as occurring on either item 19 or 20a of the death certificate.

From Table 6 we see that these 21 patterns capture a wide variety of disease interrelations among two diseases $(x, y)$ and a residual category

**Table 6**

Cause-Structured Patterns of the Joint Occurrence of a Disease Pair
with Items 19 and 20a Occurrence Identified

| Pattern number | Underlying cause | Item 19 occurrence | Item 20a occurrence | Items 19 and 20a occurrence |
|:---:|:---:|:---:|:---:|:---:|
| 1 | $x$ | | | |
| 2 | $x$ | | | $o$ |
| 3 | $x$ | $y$ | | |
| 4 | $x$ | $y$ | | $o$ |
| 5 | $x$ | | $y$ | |
| 6 | $x$ | | $y$ | $o$ |
| 7 | $y$ | | | |
| 8 | $y$ | | | $o$ |
| 9 | $y$ | $x$ | | |
| 10 | $y$ | $x$ | | $o$ |
| 11 | $y$ | | $x$ | |
| 12 | $y$ | | $x$ | $o$ |
| 13 | $o$ | | | |
| 14 | $o$ | $x$ | | |
| 15 | $o$ | $y$ | | |
| 16 | $o$ | $x + y$ | | |
| 17 | $o$ | $x$ | $y$ | |
| 18 | $o$ | $y$ | $x$ | |
| 19 | $o$ | | $x$ | |
| 20 | $o$ | | $y$ | |
| 21 | $o$ | | $x + y$ | |

(*o*) of all other causes. For example, pattern 1 represents all deaths for which disease *x* was the underlying cause of death but no other condition appeared on the certificate. Pattern 2 also represents deaths for which disease *x* was the underlying cause without an occurrence of *y* but for which a disease in the residual category appeared somewhere on the death certificate. Pattern 3 represents deaths in which disease *x* was the underlying cause and disease *y* appeared in item 19 of the certificate—implying, given the rationale of item 19, that *x* caused *y*. Pattern 4 represents the same disease relation as that for pattern 3 but with some other disease present. Pattern 5 represents deaths in which disease *x* was the underlying cause but in which condition *y* appeared in item 20a of the death certificate. Because we know that diseases that contribute to death but are not part of the causal sequence initiated by *x* are reported in item 20a, this pattern represents a different disease relation than patterns 3 or 4. To illustrate the causal dependency suggested by pattern 3, one might examine cancer as the underlying cause and septicemia as the immediate cause of death. Under these conditions, the presumption might be made that either the neoplastic disease process or the complications of therapy lead to the individual being immuno-compromised and then to increased risk of infection (Hersh *et al.*, 1965; Inagaki *et al.*, 1974). Pattern 5 might be illustrated by a death in which IHD was selected as the underlying cause with diabetes mellitus showing in item 20a of the certificate. In this case, one would have to decide whether the pattern should be interpreted as representing either (1) that peripheral circulatory degeneration due to diabetes mellitus decreased the ability of the individual to resist the stress of IHD or (2) that diabetes was a long-term risk factor for IHD. Although, strictly speaking, the second interpretation is inconsistent with the logic of the death certificate (i.e., diabetes should be placed in item 19 as the underlying cause of death), this second interpretation seems to be the most plausible. Indeed, the coding of long-term chronic degenerative diseases on the death certificate is perhaps the most difficult problem facing the certifier in representing the medical facts surrounding death.

An examination of patterns 7–12 shows that they are simply the mirror image of the patterns 1–6, with the roles of the diseases reversed. Patterns 13–21 have some underlying cause other than *x* and *y* but are included to exhaust the possibilities of their non-underlying-cause occurrence and placements on the death certificate.

It is apparent that the definition of these 21 patterns is dependent on the ICDA-8 rules for the selection of the underlying cause of death. On the death certificate this is supposed to be the single condition on the lowest used line of item 19. Unfortunately, as was illustrated in Chapter 2, not all death certificates are properly filled out, so that the NCHS is required to

**Table 7**

ACME- and Physician-Coded Underlying Cause of Death for White Males for 21 Disease Patterns: Ischemic Heart Disease versus Generalized Arteriosclerosis[a]

| Disease pattern | Age | | | | | | | | | | Unknown | Total |
|---|---|---|---|---|---|---|---|---|---|---|---|---|
| | 0–9 | 10–19 | 20–29 | 30–39 | 40–49 | 50–59 | 60–69 | 70–79 | 80–89 | 90–99 | | |
| | ACME-coded underlying cause of death | | | | | | | | | | | |
| 1 | 9 | 14 | 131 | 1,818 | 11,619 | 28,298 | 39,461 | 35,541 | 17,042 | 2,412 | 54 | 136,399 |
| 2 | 8 | 18 | 117 | 990 | 6,465 | 19,669 | 38,395 | 52,500 | 36,711 | 6,452 | 130 | 161,455 |
| 3 | 1 | 0 | 9 | 81 | 622 | 2,097 | 4,253 | 5,937 | 4,692 | 1,041 | 19 | 18,752 |
| 4 | 1 | 1 | 4 | 86 | 548 | 2,219 | 5,854 | 11,111 | 10,453 | 2,211 | 53 | 32,541 |
| 5 | 0 | 0 | 0 | 2 | 24 | 99 | 264 | 416 | 365 | 68 | 2 | 1,240 |
| 6 | 0 | 0 | 0 | 5 | 58 | 248 | 758 | 1,508 | 1,417 | 301 | 4 | 4,299 |
| 7 | 0 | 0 | 1 | 1 | 6 | 34 | 128 | 539 | 896 | 370 | 13 | 1,987 |
| 8 | 0 | 1 | 0 | 6 | 44 | 258 | 1,127 | 3,242 | 4,940 | 1,517 | 54 | 11,190 |
| 9 | 0 | 0 | 0 | 0 | 0 | 0 | 0 | 0 | 0 | 0 | 0 | 0 |
| 10 | 0 | 0 | 0 | 0 | 0 | 0 | 0 | 2 | 0 | 0 | 0 | 2 |
| 11 | 0 | 0 | 0 | 0 | 0 | 0 | 0 | 0 | 0 | 0 | 0 | 0 |
| 12 | 0 | 0 | 0 | 0 | 0 | 0 | 0 | 0 | 0 | 0 | 0 | 0 |
| 13 | 41,343 | 16,563 | 22,987 | 18,404 | 37,389 | 69,366 | 99,792 | 101,043 | 54,813 | 8,296 | 192 | 470,188 |
| 14 | 33 | 24 | 81 | 192 | 874 | 2,391 | 5,149 | 6,378 | 3,685 | 476 | 6 | 19,289 |
| 15 | 5 | 1 | 6 | 22 | 225 | 1,410 | 5,905 | 13,567 | 13,434 | 2,727 | 48 | 37,350 |
| 16 | 0 | 0 | 4 | 9 | 76 | 218 | 588 | 812 | 589 | 101 | 1 | 2,398 |
| 17 | 0 | 0 | 0 | 1 | 10 | 42 | 90 | 176 | 137 | 15 | 0 | 471 |
| 18 | 0 | 0 | 0 | 2 | 20 | 153 | 684 | 1,338 | 1,109 | 177 | 4 | 3,487 |
| 19 | 6 | 4 | 28 | 102 | 508 | 2,284 | 6,316 | 11,260 | 7,775 | 1,157 | 26 | 29,466 |
| 20 | 0 | 2 | 4 | 14 | 86 | 411 | 1,804 | 4,522 | 4,526 | 944 | 22 | 12,335 |
| 21 | 0 | 0 | 0 | 2 | 11 | 88 | 241 | 647 | 622 | 108 | 5 | 1,724 |
| Total | 41,406 | 16,628 | 23,372 | 21,737 | 58,585 | 129,285 | 210,809 | 250,539 | 163,206 | 28,373 | 633 | 944,573 |

64

Physician-coded underlying cause of death

| | | | | | | | | | | | | |
|---|---|---|---|---|---|---|---|---|---|---|---|---|
| 1 | 9 | 14 | 131 | 1,818 | 11,619 | 28,298 | 39,461 | 35,541 | 17,042 | 2,412 | 54 | 136,399 |
| 2 | 9 | 7 | 91 | 818 | 5,546 | 16,996 | 33,455 | 45,782 | 31,590 | 5,385 | 100 | 139,779 |
| 3 | 0 | 0 | 0 | 2 | 32 | 60 | 192 | 205 | 161 | 34 | 0 | 686 |
| 4 | 0 | 0 | 0 | 7 | 43 | 166 | 424 | 773 | 784 | 157 | 5 | 2,359 |
| 5 | 0 | 0 | 0 | 2 | 24 | 99 | 264 | 416 | 365 | 68 | 2 | 1,240 |
| 6 | 0 | 0 | 0 | 4 | 51 | 217 | 674 | 1,279 | 1,189 | 252 | 4 | 3,670 |
| 7 | 0 | 2 | 0 | 1 | 6 | 34 | 128 | 539 | 896 | 370 | 13 | 1,987 |
| 8 | 2 | 0 | 3 | 20 | 202 | 1,345 | 5,987 | 14,422 | 15,927 | 3,641 | 84 | 41,635 |
| 9 | 1 | 1 | 9 | 79 | 590 | 2,036 | 4,061 | 5,723 | 4,513 | 997 | 19 | 18,028 |
| 10 | 1 | 0 | 4 | 72 | 471 | 1,852 | 4,871 | 9,027 | 8,032 | 1,623 | 33 | 25,987 |
| 11 | 0 | 0 | 0 | 0 | 0 | 1 | 0 | 9 | 18 | 10 | 0 | 38 |
| 12 | 0 | 0 | 0 | 3 | 27 | 153 | 708 | 1,412 | 1,205 | 210 | 6 | 3,724 |
| 13 | 41,343 | 16,563 | 22,987 | 18,404 | 37,389 | 69,366 | 99,792 | 101,043 | 54,813 | 8,296 | 192 | 470,188 |
| 14 | 32 | 35 | 106 | 353 | 1,752 | 4,923 | 9,827 | 12,660 | 8,446 | 1,473 | 32 | 39,639 |
| 15 | 3 | 0 | 4 | 9 | 68 | 341 | 1,158 | 2,712 | 3,037 | 766 | 24 | 8,122 |
| 16 | 0 | 0 | 4 | 14 | 101 | 367 | 913 | 1,535 | 1,342 | 284 | 7 | 4,567 |
| 17 | 0 | 0 | 0 | 2 | 14 | 65 | 149 | 349 | 284 | 47 | 0 | 910 |
| 18 | 0 | 0 | 0 | 0 | 1 | 27 | 80 | 153 | 138 | 24 | 0 | 423 |
| 19 | 6 | 4 | 29 | 113 | 549 | 2,425 | 6,578 | 11,696 | 8,135 | 1,227 | 30 | 30,792 |
| 20 | 0 | 2 | 4 | 14 | 88 | 420 | 1,826 | 4,581 | 4,629 | 984 | 23 | 12,571 |
| 21 | 0 | 0 | 0 | 2 | 12 | 94 | 261 | 682 | 660 | 113 | 5 | 1,829 |

[a] Definitions of these 21 patterns are given in Table 6, with the substitutions $x$ = IHD, $y$ = generalized arteriosclerosis, and $o$ = all other conditions.

use a computer program (ACME), which implements a wide range of nosological rules to make this selection. In Table 7 we present the frequency of occurrence of deaths due to IHD ($x$), generalized arteriosclerosis ($y$), or with some other condition ($o$) by using either (1) the left-most condition (when more than one was listed) on the lowest used line of item 19 (designated as the physician-coded underlying cause of death) or (2) the computer-selected underlying cause of death. This second type of selection represents the medical condition that is reported as the underlying cause of death in the standard cause-specific mortality statistics released from the NCHS.

From Table 7 we see that a total of 470,188 of 944,573 white male deaths, or only 49.7% have neither IHD nor generalized arteriosclerosis mentioned on their death certificates (pattern 13). Ischemic heart disease is represented by $x$ (i.e., it is the underlying cause in patterns 1–6) and generalized arteriosclerosis by $y$.

One important comparison to be made between the two parts of Table 7 is to contrast the differences in the frequencies between the underlying cause selections of IHD and generalized arteriosclerosis by the physician and ACME. In the ACME-coded section we see that IHD was the underlying cause 354,686 times (total count for patterns 1–6) and generalized arteriosclerosis the underlying cause 13,179 times (total count for patterns 7–12). Ischemic heart disease was an associated cause of death 56,837 times (total count for patterns 9–12, 14, 16–19, and 21) and generalized arteriosclerosis an associated cause of death 114,597 times (total count for patterns 3–6, 15–18, 20, and 21). In the physician-coded section we see a very different situation. Here, IHD is mentioned as an underlying cause of death 284,133 times (patterns 1–6) and generalized arteriosclerosis 91,399 times (patterns 7–12). This suggests a net decrease of 70,549 occurrences of IHD as an underlying cause of death and a net increase of 78,220 occurrences of generalized arteriosclerosis as an underlying cause of death. These numbers reflect the considerable effect of ACME's reassignment of the underlying cause of death. To understand where at least part of the reassignment occurred, we should examine patterns 9–12. Patterns 9 and 10 represent a causal sequence of generalized arteriosclerosis leading to IHD. These patterns were observed 44,015 times on the death certificate, but ACME only permitted two underlying-cause assignments. Patterns 11 and 12 represent deaths in which the physician listed generalized arteriosclerosis as the underlying cause of death and IHD on item 20a, that is, as a condition contributing to death but not resulting causally from the generalized arteriosclerosis. These patterns occurred only 3762 times in the physician coding but did not occur at all in the ACME coding.

Thus, 47,777 deaths in which generalized arteriosclerosis was reported as the underlying cause of death were assigned to other underlying causes of death. In particular, ACME reassignments of generalized arteriosclerosis deaths to IHD could account for up to 68% of the decrease in mentions of IHD as the underlying cause of death in the physician selections.

Table 7 also reports the age-specific frequencies of occurrence of each of the 21 patterns. For example, in the physician-coded section of the table, we find that there are few occurrences of patterns 9 and 10 (generalized arteriosclerosis leading to IHD) for white males until age 30. Then, from ages 30 to 39, for which these patterns constitute 0.7% of the deaths,

**Table 8**

Frequencies and Percentages of 21 Disease Patterns: Ischemic Heart Disease versus Diabetes Mellitus[a]

| Disease pattern | White males Frequency | % | Black males Frequency | % | White females Frequency | % | Black females Frequency | % |
|---|---|---|---|---|---|---|---|---|
| 1 | 410 | 0.043 | 172 | 0.136 | 488 | 0.012 | 292 | 0.297 |
| 2 | 5,919 | 0.627 | 1,085 | 0.855 | 8,878 | 1.203 | 2,053 | 2.901 |
| 3 | 2,164 | 0.229 | 198 | 0.156 | 2,385 | 0.323 | 352 | 0.358 |
| 4 | 4,462 | 0.472 | 373 | 0.294 | 6,360 | 0.862 | 785 | 0.799 |
| 5 | 54 | 0.006 | 5 | 0.004 | 73 | 0.010 | 18 | 0.018 |
| 6 | 569 | 0.060 | 67 | 0.053 | 858 | 0.116 | 145 | 0.148 |
| 7 | 136,399 | 14.440 | 12,494 | 9.847 | 66,250 | 8.980 | 8,593 | 8.750 |
| 8 | 196,690 | 20.823 | 16,148 | 12.726 | 164,659 | 22.319 | 14,596 | 14.863 |
| 9 | 145 | 0.015 | 25 | 0.020 | 158 | 0.021 | 32 | 0.033 |
| 10 | 738 | 0.078 | 49 | 0.039 | 988 | 0.134 | 139 | 0.142 |
| 11 | 6,495 | 0.688 | 345 | 0.272 | 6,603 | 0.895 | 578 | 0.588 |
| 12 | 14,219 | 1.505 | 846 | 0.667 | 17,876 | 2.423 | 1,594 | 1.623 |
| 13 | 512,857 | 54.295 | 89,550 | 70.574 | 404,333 | 54.805 | 62,997 | 64.150 |
| 14 | 1,143 | 0.121 | 172 | 0.136 | 1,449 | 0.196 | 311 | 0.317 |
| 15 | 14,739 | 1.560 | 1,418 | 1.118 | 10,743 | 1.456 | 1,164 | 1.185 |
| 16 | 258 | 0.027 | 19 | 0.015 | 287 | 0.039 | 42 | 0.043 |
| 17 | 65 | 0.007 | 6 | 0.005 | 83 | 0.011 | 9 | 0.009 |
| 18 | 537 | 0.057 | 32 | 0.025 | 628 | 0.085 | 64 | 0.065 |
| 19 | 12,721 | 1.347 | 1,288 | 1.010 | 16,031 | 2.173 | 2,264 | 2.305 |
| 20 | 31,462 | 3.331 | 2,424 | 1.910 | 25,609 | 3.471 | 1,855 | 1.889 |
| 21 | 2,500 | 0.265 | 179 | 0.141 | 3,022 | 0.410 | 319 | 0.325 |
| Total | 944,573 | | 126,888 | | 737,761 | | 98,202 | |

[a]Definitions of these 21 patterns are given in Table 6, with the substitutions $x$ = diabetes mellitus, $y$ = IHD, and $o$ = all other conditions.

these patterns increase in relative frequency all the way to the last age category, in which they represent 9.2% of all white male deaths over age 90.

In order to understand how the frequency of these patterns varies across race–sex-groups, we present Table 8, in which we have collapsed the age detail and present the joint occurrence of IHD ($y$ in Table 6) and diabetes mellitus ($x$ in Table 6) for deaths to these four groups in 1969.

From Table 8 we can see that there are sizable race–sex differences in the proportion of total deaths for each pattern. For example, patterns 3 and 4 represent diabetes as the ACME-selected underlying cause of death leading to IHD (with or without an associated condition). We see that the proportion of the total deaths for both white and black males assigned to these patterns (0.701 and 0.450% for white and black males, respectively) is much less than the proportion of total deaths determined by these patterns for females (1.185 and 1.157% for white and black females, respectively). Patterns 11 and 12 represent deaths in which IHD has been selected by ACME as the underlying cause and diabetes mellitus was listed in item 20a of the death certificates. These are deaths in which diabetes mellitus may have served as a long-term risk factor. Here we see that, within race, females are far more likely to have diabetes mellitus as a contributory cause to IHD than are males (51% more likely for whites and 135% more likely for blacks). Furthermore, within sex, whites are far more likely to have diabetes mellitus as a contributory factor to IHD than are blacks (133% more likely for males and 50% more likely for females). It can be seen that a large amount of information on the pattern of disease interrelations can be derived by examining the cause-structured patterns. The one major difficulty with the cause-structured patterns is the selection of an underlying cause of death, which, as we have seen from Table 7, can vary depending on the criterion for selection.

## 7  Summary

In this chapter we have examined in some detail various strategies for representing the distribution and joint occurrences of medical conditions at death. We have presented a number of measures, each of which is designed to represent different aspects of this multiple-cause information. We have seen that considerable insight into population health characteristics can be derived from the mortality statistics. Some of these insights are substantive, some suggest the need for methodological variation, and some suggest various data characteristics that need to be examined before cause-specific analysis can be conducted.

# References

Hersh, E. M., Bodey, G. P., Nies, B. A., and Freireich, E. J. 1965. Causes of death in acute leukemia: A ten-year study of 414 patients from 1954–1963. *Journal of the American Medical Association* **193**:105–109.

Inagaki, J., Rodriguez, V., and Bodey, G. P. 1974. Causes of death in cancer patients. *Cancer* **33**:568–578.

Pitts, A. M. 1976. Some notes on the collection of U.S. multiple cause of death data with illustrative multiple cause tabulations for 1969. Paper presented at the Multiple Cause of Death Statistical Data Development Conference, Washington, D.C., November 9 and 10, 1976.

Schatzkin, A. 1980. How long can we live? A more optimistic view of potential gains in life expectancy. *American Journal of Public Health* **70**:1199–1200.

Wing, S., and Manton, K. G. (1981). A multiple cause of death analysis of hypertension-related mortality in North Carolina. *American Journal of Public Health* **71**:823–830.

# Chapter 4 | A Conceptual Framework for Mortality Analysis

## 1 Introduction

In Chapter 1 we argued (1) that it was necessary to utilize multiple data sources to analyze effectively the health state of a population and (2) that national mortality data are the most appropriate data to employ in models designed to monitor population health because these data enumerate the total deaths in the national population and cover a lengthy time span. These two propositions motivate our effort to develop bioactuarial models to fit the national mortality data time series—models that can include other data forms, theoretical concepts, and judgmental inputs. In this chapter we shall present a conceptual basis for such bioactuarial models. The underlying principle that will guide this effort is that the bioactuarial models used to monitor human mortality data must be biologically plausible, biomedically accurate, and sufficiently detailed, so that information on the behavior of chronic and acute diseases in individuals within the population can represented.

## 2 Stochastic Process Models

Many modes of mortality analysis have been based on one or another form of stochastic process. For example, the standard cause-elimination life table is, in effect, a discrete-state–discrete-time stochastic process model of human mortality. The term *stochastic process* refers to a family of random variables $\{Y_t\}$ that describe an empirical process that typically develops over time in a manner governed by probabilistic laws. For a general variate $Y_t$, we use $y_t$ to denote a random observed value of the variate at time $t$, where $t$ (in years, unless stated otherwise) is considered fixed. Hence, a *continuous-time* stochastic process can be defined on $\{y_t\}$ because $t$ may take on any real value. Alternatively, if we restrict the values of $t$ to just the nonnegative integers 0, 1, 2, ..., then we may define a discrete-time stochastic process on $\{y_t\}$. In our applications, the time $t$ will refer to either age (denoted by $a$ or $x$, depending on the context) or to time elapsed since some significant event (such as cancer being diagnosed). In both cases, time is fundamentally a continuous measure, so that when we wish to specify a discrete-time stochastic process, we shall do so by restricting our consideration of the range of $t$ in a continuous process to just the set of nonnegative integers. This will ensure that our discrete-time models are consistent with an underlying continuous-time stochastic process model. Without going through this form of model specification, one cannot be confident of such consistency, thereby opening the possibility that the results of an analysis are dependent on the specific age and time intervals employed therein. Attaining such consistency is not without cost, however, and the cost is basically that one must learn to develop the analytic models in a continuous-time framework but to estimate the model parameters in a discrete-time framework. In most of this chapter we shall present the mathematical specifications for both the continuous-time and discrete-time formulations of several general stochastic process models of morbidity and mortality.

In the development of these models we also wish to establish a consistency between continuous-state and discrete-state stochastic process models. Here we use the term *state* to mean health state so that a *continuous-state model* implies the availability of a set of physiological variables relevant to survival, at least one of which can take on any real value within its range. In contrast, a *discrete-state model* is defined for a finite number of health states so that the only physiological variable of relevance to survival is the categorical variable designating each individual's health state. Examples of physiological variables used in continuous-state models are blood pressure level and serum cholesterol concentration; in discrete-state models, designation as a diabetic or as a cancer patient.

The bioactuarial models that we shall present are classified as discrete-state–continuous-time stochastic process models of morbidity and mortality. In these models the variate $Y_t$ will denote a discrete quantity such as the number of deaths in a time interval $(t, t + 1)$ or the number of survivors in a cohort at a time $t$ years beyond initial observation. These bioactuarial models are special cases of *stochastic compartmental systems*, which are stochastic process models in which the total amount of material in a system (e.g., $Y_t$ in continuous or discrete form) is contained in some finite number of states or compartments and in which the transfer of material between compartments is probabilistic. Stochastic compartment models were developed in the biological sciences (Jacquez, 1972) as models of complex biological systems that could not be decomposed for study. Consequently, the only information available for the analysis of such systems was the identity of, and rate and timing of, material introduced into the system and the identity of, and rate and timing of, material exiting the system. No information is generally available on the identity of, and the rates of transfers between, states internal to the system. It is possible, however, by specifying the identity of the internal states and by imposing certain conditions on the rates of transfers between these and the external states to produce quantitative estimates of the transition rates involving internal compartments. Some general conditions on the amount of auxiliary information necessary to make such estimates unique can be found in Woodbury and Manton (1982).

We draw on results from the literature on stochastic compartmental systems because an analogous analytic situation arises in the investigation of the health state of the population. Specifically, we can usually identify the rate of entry of the persons into the population by assuming that they enter a hypothetical disease-free state at birth. Hence, by noting the age at death, the medical conditions present at death, and the number of persons alive at each age, it is possible to determine the rate of exit to identifiable absorbing "death" states. The information that is missing is any knowledge as to the timing of the acquisition of the medical conditions present at death. As noted, however, if one is capable and willing to make certain assumptions, then he or she can employ the stochastic compartment methodology to estimate the rates of transition to these morbid states and to make inferences about the timing of the onset of these medical conditions.

A discrete-state–continuous-time model of human morbidity and mortality will be biologically plausible and biomedically accurate if it is consistent with an underlying continuous-state–continuous-time representation of the same phenomena. Attainment of such consistency, however, is not easy, especially given the data restrictions usually associated with use of a discrete-state model. To see why this might be the case, it will be instructive to consider one continuous-state model—the random walk model of human mortality and aging (Woodbury and Manton, 1977).

In its most general form, this model represents population aging processes as a continuous-state–continuous-time stochastic process. Specifically, it describes how the distribution of a population on selected physiological variables changes with age or time as a function of

(1)  *drift*, or the shift in the mean values of each of the physiological variables of the population with age as a function of the prior values of the full set of physiological variables,

(2)  *regression*, or the random return of persons at extremes to more moderate values of the physiological variables,

(3)  *diffusion*, or the random movement of persons to more extreme values of the physiological variables, the "random walk" component of the model, and

(4)  *mortality selection*, or the *probabilistic removal* of persons from the population conditional on the values of their physiological variables.

Because the random walk model requires that physiological measurements are available for persons in the population, this model is most appropriate for the analysis of epidemiological data. Even so, for the model to be estimable from the type of information that is generally available in epidemiological studies, it is necessary to simplify the general model. By assuming that the temporal changes in physiological variables are linear and that the force of mortality or of selection is a quadratic function of the physiological variables, one can develop estimable equations based on maximum likelihood procedures. With these assumptions, the likelihood function for the change of the population distribution over a given time interval on physiological variables can be factored into two components—one involving only the survivors at the end of the interval and the other involving both the survivors and nonsurvivors. Thus, the estimation of the equations describing the change with age of physiological values can be conducted independently of the estimation of the relation of risk of death to an individual's set of values of physiological variables. This model was applied to data on cardiovascular disease risk in the Framingham study (Woodbury *et al.*, 1979; Manton *et al.*, 1979). By modeling the age dynamics of the physiological variables, it was possible to represent the underlying development of chronic and degenerative diseases in the population—a factor that generally had been ignored in other epidemiological analyses. The quadratic form of the force of selection also turns out to be a biologically meaningful type of selection or risk because it represents increased risk at both high and low physiological variable values and designates a range of physiological variable values as "optimum" in the sense of survival. Thus, it is a selection mechanism that helps to keep the predicted values of physiological variables within a biologically plausible range and in equilibrium as the population ages.

From the preceding description, it follows that a discrete-state model will be *consistent* with a continuous-state model when the forces of mortality or of selection are assumed to be distributed over individuals at each time $t$ in a manner consistent with the distribution of the physiological variables at each time $t$ in that population. Practically, since we use discrete-state models because of the unavailability of the physiological measurements required in continuous-state models, the assumed distribution of the force of mortality or of selection will not be verifiable, so that the consistency between the two types of models will be, at best, only approximate. Discussions of discrete-state models of this type will form the basis of the latter part of this chapter and much of the remainder of the book.

## 3  Models of Total Mortality

### The Life Table

With the possible exception of the direct analysis of age-specific death rates, it is likely that the most frequently used method of mortality analysis is the life table model. Indeed, the first modern life table was published over 320 years ago in 1662 by John Graunt in his famous *Bills of Mortality*. Life tables are published by the NCHS for the 3-year periods centered on each census year for the entire United States back to the 1910 census and for the triennium 1900–1902. Life tables for a variety of select and general populations have been in widespread use among actuaries concerned with insurance and pension plans. The use of life table methods is now commonplace in a variety of fields such as demography, epidemiology, economics, sociology, public health, and biostatistics. This section introduces the basic life table parameters and discusses their various interrelationships. Discussion of life table construction will be deferred to Chapters 5 and 6.

The standard life table consists of a number of columns, each of which displays a specific aspect of the mortality risks in given population at each age $x$, where $x$ is measured in whole units of years. For an example, see Table 1 of Chapter 5. At this point, we are interested in only three of these columns—the $q_x$, $l_x$, and $d_x$ columns. The age-specific entries in the $q_x$ and $d_x$ columns are actually defined for the age interval $(x, x + n)$ where $n$ is typically equal to 1 or 5 (years), depending on whether the life table is *complete* or *abridged*.

$q_x$ *Column*   The entries in the $q_x$ column, denoted as $_nq_x$, represent the probability that an individual alive at exact age $x$ will die prior to age $x + n$. For $n = 1$, we shall use the simpler notation $q_x$ rather than $_1q_x$. Note that $q_x$ is often called the age-specific probability of death or the age-specific mortality rate (but not death rate).

$l_x$ *Column* The entries in the $l_x$ column, denoted as $l_x$, represent the number of individuals in the life table population who will survive from birth to at least age $x$. Thus, the first entry in this column, $l_0$, is always equal to the initial number of persons in the birth cohort. It is common practice, however, in life table presentations to rescale each $l_x$ value to correspond to an initial birth cohort size, or *radix* value, of 100,000 persons, which implies that the *printed* $l_x$'s represents the number of persons who survive to exact age $x$ in a birth cohort of 100,000 persons. Because of this practice, it is possible for some confusion to arise. For example, if the radix value is arbitrarily set to 1.0 instead of 100,000, then the interpretation of $l_x$ may change from the *number* of persons who survive to age $x$ to the *probability* that a randomly chosen individual survives to age $x$. To avoid such ambiguities, we shall define $_np_x$ to be the probability that an individual alive at exact age $x$ survives to (at least) exact age $x + n$. For $n = 1$, we shall use the simpler notation $p_x$ rather than $_1p_x$. Thus, in general,

$$_np_x = l_{x+n}/l_x,\qquad (4.3.1)$$

and, in particular,

$$_xp_0 = l_x/l_0\qquad (4.3.2)$$

is the probability that an individual just born will survive to his or her $x$th birthday. For the $l_x$ persons alive at age $x$, we can specify two mutually exclusive possibilities: death before age $x + n$ or death after age $x + n$. The probabilities of each outcome sum to unity, that is,

$$1 = {}_nq_x + {}_np_x.\qquad (4.3.3)$$

From (4.3.3) we obtain the following relationship between $q_x$ and $l_x$:

$$_nq_x = 1 - {}_np_x\qquad (4.3.4a)$$

$$= 1 - l_{x+n}/l_x.\qquad (4.3.4b)$$

Equation (4.3.4b) shows that the $q_x$ column is completely determined by the $l_x$ column. Conversely, manipulation of Eq. (4.3.1), (4.3.2), and (4.3.4b) yielding

$$l_x = l_0 \prod_{i=0}^{x-1} (1 - q_i),\qquad (4.3.5)$$

where $\prod$ is used to denote cumulative multiplication, shows that the $l_x$ column is completely determined by the $q_x$ column.

$d_x$ *Column* The entries in the $d_x$ column, denoted as $_nd_x$, represent the number of individuals just born who will die in the age interval $(x, x + n)$. For $n = 1$, we shall use the simpler notation $d_x$ rather than $_1d_x$. The $d_x$ column may be derived from both the $l_x$ and $q_x$ columns; that is,

$$_nd_x = l_x \, _nq_x \tag{4.3.6}$$

and

$$_nd_x = l_x - l_{x+n}. \tag{4.3.7}$$

From (4.3.7) it is apparent that the $l_x$ column is completely determined by the $d_x$ column because the total number of persons who die beyond age $x$ is the number who were alive at age $x$:

$$l_x = \sum_{i=x}^{\omega} d_i, \tag{4.3.8}$$

where $\omega$ represents the final age category in the life table. By solving (4.3.6) for $_nq_x$, that is,

$$_nq_x = _nd_x/l_x \tag{4.3.9a}$$

$$= _nd_x \Big/ \left( \sum_{i=x}^{\omega} d_i \right), \tag{4.3.9b}$$

we also see that the $q_x$ column is completely determined by the $d_x$ column. Note that if the $l_x$ column is rescaled to a given radix value for printing, then the $d_x$ column must also be rescaled to the same radix value in order for (4.3.6)–(4.3.9) to hold. In this case, $_nd_x$ would represent the number of persons who die in the age interval $(x, x + n)$ in a birth cohort of, for example, 100,000 persons.

The preceding relationships indicate that the information in the $q_x$, $l_x$, and $d_x$ columns is redundant in the sense that possession of any one column is sufficient to reproduce the remaining two columns.

## A Stochastic Compartment Model of Total Mortality

With its assumption that age $x$ is measured in whole units of years, the standard life table model is obviously a discrete-time model. Nonetheless, its widespread acceptance is due in part to its consistency with an underlying continuous-time stochastic process model of total mortality. In this section we shall examine the properties of such a model and show how this basic consistency arises.

Consider the continuous-time stochastic process model represented in Fig. 1. This is a simple two-compartment model in which a transition rate $\mu(x)$ governs the rate of the transfer of individuals from the alive state to the dead state. The transition rate $\mu(x)$ is the force of mortality and is assumed to be a function only of the age $x$ of an individual. In the figure

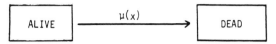

**Fig. 1.** States and transitions of a two-compartment system with one absorbing state.

the boxes are used to denote the health states or compartments and the arrows are used to denote the transfers permitted in the model. Hence, specification of a given model via a diagram such as in Fig. 1 is straightforward and usually can be made unambiguously.

Because this model is formulated in continuous time, it is possible to define a continuous survival function $S(x)$ that represents the probability that an individual just born will survive to age $x$. This is essentially the same as the definition of $_xp_0$ in (4.3.2) except that $S(x)$ is defined for all positive real values of $x$, not just for the set of nonnegative integers. An obvious initial condition is that $S(0) = 1$. An important second condition is that $S(x) \geq S(x')$ if $x < x'$, which means that $S(x)$ is a monotone decreasing (actually nonincreasing) function of age. The continuous decreases in $S(x)$ over age are due to the continuous transfer of the probability mass $S(x)$ over age from the alive state to the dead state. This suggests that $\mu(x)$ and $S(x)$ are functionally related.

The force of mortality $\mu(x)$ is frequently defined as the limiting form of the age-specific probability of death, or

$$\mu(x) = \lim_{\Delta x \to 0} \frac{1}{\Delta x} \Pr[\text{dead in age interval } (x, x + \Delta x), \text{ given survival to age } x]. \tag{4.3.10}$$

In terms of the survival function $S(x)$, this definition is equivalently expressed as the limiting form of the relative rate of decrease in $S(x)$:

$$\mu(x) = \lim_{\Delta x \to 0} \frac{1}{\Delta x} \left( \frac{S(x) - S(x + \Delta x)}{S(x)} \right)$$

$$= \frac{-1}{S(x)} \lim_{\Delta x \to 0} \left( \frac{S(x + \Delta x) - S(x)}{\Delta x} \right). \tag{4.3.11}$$

By observing that the limiting form of the final bracketed term in (4.3.11) is simply the time derivative of $S(x)$, we obtain the *hazard rate* form of $\mu(x)$:

$$\mu(x) = - \frac{1}{S(x)} \frac{d}{dx} S(x) = - \frac{d}{dx} \ln S(x). \tag{4.3.12}$$

From the final expression in (4.3.12), we find that the force of mortality is equal to the negative derivative of the natural logarithm of the survival function. Conversely, the survival function is an exponential function of the negative integral of the force of mortality over the inverval $(0, x)$. To see this, integrate (4.3.12) to obtain

$$\int_0^x \mu(a)\, da = \int_0^x -\frac{d}{da} \ln S(a)\, da = \ln S(0) - \ln S(x). \quad (4.3.13)$$

Exponentiation of (4.3.13) with a change of sign then yields the result

$$S(x) = S(0) \exp\left[-\int_0^x \mu(a)\, da\right] = \exp\left[-\int_0^x \mu(a)\, da\right] \quad (4.3.14)$$

because $S(0) = 1$ by assumption.

Some insight into this relationship between $\mu(x)$ and $S(x)$ can be gained by examination of the middle expression in (4.3.12). Specifically, by isolating the derivative term we find

$$\frac{d}{dx} S(x) = -\mu(x)S(x). \quad (4.3.15)$$

The rate of change in the survival function is expressed as the product of two independent factors: (1) the force of mortality acting on those persons alive at age $x$ and (2) the survival function value at age $x$. Furthermore, if we replace $S(x)$ with its value in (4.3.14), we obtain the relationship

$$\frac{d}{dx} S(x) = -\mu(x) \exp\left[-\int_0^x \mu(a)\, da\right], \quad (4.3.16)$$

which expresses the rate of change in the survival function as a function of the force of mortality at age $x$ and at all prior ages. These results demonstrate that specification of the functional form of $\mu(x)$ is sufficient to determine the functional form of the survival function and its derivative.

A discrete-time model can be formed by restricting our consideration of the survival function to its values only at nonnegative integer values of $x$. Because $x$ appears in the upper limit of the integral expressions in (4.3.13) and (4.3.14), we can facilitate discussion of this conversion to discrete time by defining a *cumulative force of mortality* for the age interval $(x, x + n)$. Following standard notational convention, we denote this cumulative force of mortality as $_nh_x$, defined as

$$_nh_x = \int_x^{x+n} \mu(a)\, da, \quad (4.3.17)$$

where for $n = 1$ we use the simpler notation $h_x$ rather than $_1h_x$. With this notation, Eq. (4.3.14) becomes

$$S(x) = \exp(-_xh_0). \quad (4.3.18)$$

The life table model will be consistent with the continuous-time model if the number of survivors $l_x$ at age $x$ is computed as the product of the initial radix $l_0$ and the probability that an individual just born will survive to age $x$. In other words, the following equation must be satisfied:

$$l_x = l_0 S(x). \tag{4.3.19}$$

By solving (4.3.19) for $S(x)$ and using (4.3.2) to introduce $_x p_0$, we find it must also be true that

$$S(x) = l_x/l_0 = {_x p_0}, \tag{4.3.20}$$

in which case we have

$$_x p_0 = \exp(-_x h_0), \tag{4.3.21}$$

which, in view of (4.3.1), implies the general formula

$$_n p_x = \exp(-_n h_x); \tag{4.3.22}$$

and because $_n p_x = 1 - {_n q_x}$,

$$_n q_x = 1 - \exp(-_n h_x). \tag{4.3.23}$$

To validate the consistency of the life table model, we successively modify (4.3.19) by using the implied relationships in (4.3.20)–(4.3.23):

$$l_x = l_0\, {_x p_0} = l_0 \exp(-_x h_0) = l_0 \prod_{i=0}^{x-1} \exp(-h_i)$$

$$= l_0 \prod_{i=0}^{x-1} p_i = l_0 \prod_{i=0}^{x-1} (1 - q_i), \tag{4.3.24}$$

where the final expression in (4.3.24) is the standard life table computational formula discussed in Eq. (4.3.5). Thus, the temporal consistency of the life table model with a continuous-time stochastic process is demonstrated.

Given the preceding demonstration that the age-specific probabilities of death in a temporally consistent discrete-time model satisfy the relationship stated in (4.3.23), it is apparent that we can define an $h_x$ column for the life table that uniquely determines the $q_x$ column, as well as both the $l_x$ and $d_x$ columns. Conversely, from a standard life table, we can obtain the $h_x$ column entries by using

$$_n h_x = -\ln(1 - {_n q_x}) = -\ln {_n p_x}. \tag{4.3.25}$$

These relationships are derived by solving (4.3.23) and (4.3.22) for $_n h_x$. They differ from the definition in (4.3.17) in that they permit determination of $_n h_x$ in cases in which the functional form of the force of mortality $\mu(x)$ is not known.

Even when one is not explicitly dealing with a continuous-time model, the relationships in (4.3.25) can still be of value because the cumulative force of mortality behaves in an additive manner whereas the survival probabilities behave multiplicatively. We implicitly used this property in manipulating (4.3.24), but it is important enough to give it explicit consideration. For example, we know that the probability that an individual just born will survive to age $x + n$ must be equal to the product of the probability that an individual just born will survive to age $x$ times the probability that an individual alive at age $x$ will survive to age $x + n$. Thus, we have

$$_{x+n}p_0 = {}_xp_0\, {}_np_x = \frac{l_x}{l_0}\frac{l_{x+n}}{l_x} = \frac{l_{x+n}}{l_0},\qquad(4.3.26)$$

as it should in view of (4.3.1) and (4.3.2). We can generalize this property to express $_np_x$ as the product of $n$ probabilities governing survival over the 1-year period following each of $n$ ages $x, x + 1, \ldots, x + n - 1$:

$$_np_x = \prod_{i=x}^{x+n-1} p_i.\qquad(4.3.27)$$

By taking the logarithmic transform of (4.3.27), we can transform the multiplication in (4.3.27) to addition; that is

$$\ln\, {}_np_x = \sum_{i=x}^{x+n-1} \ln p_i,\qquad(4.3.28)$$

which, in view of (4.3.22), can be rewritten with a change of sign as

$$_nh_x = \sum_{i=x}^{x+n-1} h_i.\qquad(4.3.29)$$

Thus, the additivity of the $h_x$'s implied by the definition (4.3.17) is maintained even when one is not dealing with a model in which $\mu(x)$ is explicitly specified. This property will be very useful in later sections of this chapter in which the separate effects of each of several causes of death are represented as additive contributions to the total force of mortality and hence to $h_x$.

### The Distribution of the Age at Death

Implicit in the two forms of the stochastic process model discussed in the preceding section is the notion that the death of any given individual is a probabilistic event. These models tend to restrict their consideration of this probabilistic element, represented by $q_x$ or $\mu(x)$, to a cohort of persons alive at age $x$. Thus, using the symbol $(x)$ to denote a typical member of such a cohort, we found that $q_x$ gives the probability that $(x)$ will die before age $x + 1$ and that $\mu(x)$ gives the instantaneous force of mortality exerted on $(x)$. An alternative representation of this probabilistic element regards the age at death as a random variable.

Following standard statistical practice, we use the symbol $X$ to denote the variate age at death and $x$ to denote an element of the range $R_X$ of $X$. We consider the following sampling scheme for the assignment of values of $X$. At birth each individual is assigned a time to die. Prior to the death of the individual, the value of $X$ will be unknown. However, when the individual dies, his or her age at death is recorded in the vital statistics data and is available to us for use in constructing an empirical distribution of age at death.

We define the distribution function $F(x)$ as the probability that an individual just born will die at or before age $x$:

$$F(x) = \Pr(X \le x), \qquad (4.3.30)$$

where $X \le x$ means that the value realized by the variate $X$ is less than or equal to $x$. In the continuous-time model the probability density or frequency function $f(x)$ of $X$ is defined by the derivative of $F(x)$ as follows:

$$f(x) = \frac{d}{dx} F(x), \qquad (4.3.31)$$

from which we obtain by integration the well-known relationship

$$F(x) = \int_0^x f(a)\, da. \qquad (4.3.32)$$

Note that (4.3.30) defines $F(0) = 0$, which is consistent with the initial value of $F(0)$ obtained by using (4.3.32).

The survival function $S(x)$ is the probability that an individual just born will survive to at least age $x$. Hence, with $F(x)$ defined as in (4.3.30), we have

$$S(x) = \Pr(X > x) = 1 - F(x) = \int_x^{\infty} f(a)\, da, \qquad (4.3.33)$$

in which case the age derivative of $S(x)$ is easily obtained as

$$\frac{d}{dx} S(x) = -f(x). \qquad (4.3.34)$$

Equating the right-hand sides of (4.3.15), (4.3.16), and (4.3.34), we establish the fundamental relationships between the two approaches to stochastic modeling of total mortality:

$$f(x) = \mu(x)S(x) = \mu(x) \exp\left[-\int_0^x \mu(a)\, da\right] \qquad (4.3.35)$$

and

$$\mu(x) = f(x)/S(x) = -\frac{d}{dx}\ln\left[\int_x^\infty f(a)\, da\right]. \qquad (4.3.36)$$

The description of total mortality in terms of random transitions governed by $\mu(x)$ is completely equivalent to the description of total mortality in terms of the distribution $F(x)$ of age at death. This result is of great practical importance because of the occurrence of situations in which data for only one or the other form of description is available.

It needs to be stressed that this equivalence is only mathematical: the two descriptions are not equivalent conceptually. On reviewing various theories of mortality, Sacher and Trucco (1962) found that such theories fell into two classes, predestination theories and process theories, and that with few exceptions the former were written in terms of the distribution $F(x)$ of age at death whereas the latter were written in terms of the force of mortality $\mu(x)$. However, with predestination theories soundly refuted by life table analyses of genetically uniform inbred animals (Sacher and Trucco, 1962), recent theoretical efforts have focused almost exclusively on process theories of mortality (Economos, 1982). Thus, our description of morbidity and mortality as a process is in concordance with current biological theories of mortality and represents the appropriate conceptual framework for bioactuarial models of morbidity and mortality. It is the mathematical equivalence of the two descriptions, however, that permits the distribution of age at death to be explained by a process theory of mortality.

The discrete-time life table model is related to the distribution of age at death in a simple way. The deaths that occur between ages $x$ and $x + n$ are defined by

$$_n d_x = l_0[F(x + n) - F(x)] \qquad (4.3.37a)$$

$$= l_0 \int_x^{x+n} f(a)\, da. \qquad (4.3.37b)$$

The number of survivors to exact age $x$ is defined by

$$l_x = l_0 S(x) = l_0 \exp\left[-\int_0^x \mu(a)\, da\right]$$

$$= l_0[1 - F(x)] = l_0 \int_x^\infty f(a)\, da. \qquad (4.3.38)$$

The probability of death in the interval $(x, x + n)$ given survival to age $x$ is defined by

$$_nq_x = {_nd_x}/l_x = [F(x + n) - F(x)]/[1 - F(x)]$$

$$= \int_x^{x+n} f(a) \, da \bigg/ \int_x^\infty f(a) \, da. \qquad (4.3.39)$$

Here we see that each of the three life table columns can be determined once the functional form of $f(x)$ or of $F(x)$ is specified. Again, the temporal consistency of the life table model is demonstrated, this time in terms of the continuous distribution of age at death.

Some further insight into the connection of the discrete- and continuous-time models can be gained from manipulation of the preceding relationships. Specifically, by replacing $f(a)$ in (4.3.37) with the appropriately modified form of (4.3.35), we obtain

$$_nd_x = l_0 \int_x^{x+n} \mu(a) \exp\left[-\int_0^a \mu(w) \, dw\right] da. \qquad (4.3.40)$$

Then, by bringing $l_0$ under the integral and combining it with the exponential term as in (4.3.38), we obtain

$$_nd_x = \int_x^{x+n} \mu(a) l_a \, da. \qquad (4.3.41)$$

From the basic definitions we know that $l_a$ is the number of persons alive at age $a$ and at risk of death at this age so that the product $\mu(a) l_a$ is the "instantaneous density" of deaths in the cohort at age $a$. Equation (4.3.41) shows that the observable number of deaths in the interval $(x, x + n)$ is obtained as the integral of this product.

An alternative manipulation of (4.3.40) separates the exponential term under the integral into two factors $\exp[-\int_0^x \mu(w) \, dw]$ and $\exp[-\int_x^a \mu(w) \, dw]$ and combines the first factor with $l_0$ as in (4.3.38) to yield

$$_nd_x = l_x \int_x^{x+n} \mu(a) \exp\left[-\int_x^a \mu(w) \, dw\right] da. \qquad (4.3.42)$$

As in (4.3.9a), division by $l_x$ yields $_nq_x$ in the form

$$_nq_x = \int_x^{x+n} \mu(a) \exp\left[-\int_x^a \mu(w) \, dw\right] da. \qquad (4.3.43)$$

The exponential term represents the conditional probability of surviving from age $x$ to age $a$, while $\mu(a)$ is the force of mortality faced by those who are alive at age $a$. Hence, the product of these two terms is a form of probability density whose integral defines the age-specific probability of death.

## 4  Models of Cause-Specific Mortality

### *Basic Concepts*

We can generalize the concepts developed in the preceding section to the situation in which deaths are classified into disjoint groups based on the medical conditions reported on the death certificate. Historically, such classification has been restricted to groups defined solely on the basis of the assigned underlying cause of death. With multiple-cause data now available, the criteria for such classification can be extended. Nonetheless, the classification process itself leads to consideration of some finite number of "death states," or causes of death, so that the compartment model method is conceptually appropriate as a stochastic process representation of such data. Furthermore, as we shall show shortly, this method has wide applicability because it requires only the classification of deaths into two causes: (1) the disease or set of medical conditions of particular interest and (2) the residual classification of deaths due to all other causes. Chiang (1968) notes that, after death has occurred, what is termed the *cause* is, before death, more properly termed a *risk*. This may be relevant if an individual is viewed as being exposed to several competing risks of death because only one risk can ultimately be the cause of death.

Figure 2 displays a simple three-compartment stochastic process model of cause-specific mortality in which the transition rate $\mu(x)$ is de-

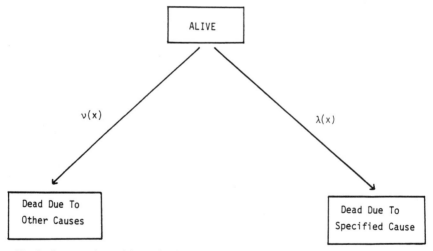

**Fig. 2.** States and transitions of a three-compartment system with two absorbing states.

composed into two component rates: $\lambda(x)$, which governs the transition from the well-state compartment to the death-state compartment that represents the mortality risk defined by the disease or set of medical conditions of interest, and $\nu(x)$, which governs the transition to the complementary death-state compartment that represents the mortality risk defined by all other causes of death.

The *transition rates* $\lambda(x)$ and $\nu(x)$ are defined as the limiting forms of the age-specific, cause-specific probabilities of death:

$$\lambda(x) = \lim_{\Delta x \to 0} \frac{1}{\Delta x} \text{Pr[dead due to cause } \lambda$$
$$\text{in age interval } (x, x + \Delta x),$$
$$\text{given survival to age } x], \qquad (4.4.1)$$

$$\nu(x) = \lim_{\Delta x \to 0} \frac{1}{\Delta x} \text{Pr[dead due to cause } \nu$$
$$\text{in age interval } (x, x + \Delta x),$$
$$\text{given survival to age } x]. \qquad (4.4.2)$$

We use the terms *cause* $\lambda$ and *risk* $\lambda$ to refer to the death state whose transition rate is the function $\lambda(x)$. A similar interpretation applies to the terms *cause* $\nu$ and *risk* $\nu$. Furthermore, because cause $\nu$ is the complement of cause $\lambda$, we have the identity

Pr[dead in age interval $(x, x + \Delta x)$, given survival to age $x$]

$\quad$ = Pr[dead due to cause $\lambda$ in age interval $(x, x + \Delta x)$,
$\qquad$ given survival to age $x$]

$\qquad$ + Pr[dead due to cause $\nu$ in age interval $(x, x + \Delta x)$,
$\qquad$ given survival to age $x$]. $\qquad (4.4.3)$

If one replaces the probability expression in (4.3.10) with the equivalent form on the right-hand side of (4.4.3), then it is possible to separate the resulting expression into the sum of the two limiting forms in the right-hand sides of (4.4.1) and (4.4.2). The implication of this manipulation is that the total of the cause-specific forces of mortality yields the total force of mortality, or

$$\mu(x) = \lambda(x) + \nu(x). \qquad (4.4.4)$$

This suggests that the cause-specific forces of mortality may be given a physical interpretation as components of the total force of mortality in much the same manner as forces in physics are represented as sums of component forces acting along the $x$, $y$, or $z$ coordinates. Additionally, this property of additivity may be reapplied to decompose $\nu(x)$ into its component death-state transition rates, with the sum of the component forces of mortality yielding $\nu(x)$. However, because this more detailed specification would not affect $\lambda(x)$, such a specification is unnecessary for the analysis of risk $\lambda$. That is, cause-specific mortality analyses via the model in Fig. 2 can be conducted separately for each disease or set of medical conditions with $\lambda(x)$ representing in each analysis the force of mortality for the specified mortality risk.

Three standard life table models can be derived from the simple three-compartment stochastic process model in this section. They are the multiple-decrement life table (Preston *et al.*, 1972; Jordan, 1975), the independent competing-risk cause-elimination life table (Chiang, 1968), and the lethal-defect pattern-of-failure life table (Manton *et al.*, 1976). In each application it is required that the risks $\lambda$ and $\nu$ be defined in a manner appropriate to the goals of the analysis. Hence, in one analysis, risk $\lambda$ might be cancer whereas in a second analysis it might be heart disease. The specific substantive issues addressed by the multiple-decrement life table relate to the analysis of the observed distributions of death by cause and are of obvious importance in actuarial computations. Although the multiple-decrement life table computations can be developed directly from a generalization of the life table for total mortality, the development from the stochastic process model in Fig. 2 yields greater insight into the connection between the multiple-decrement life table model and the more complex bioactuarial models that are developed to analyze the same set of death rates. Indeed, one of the fundamental problems in specifying a complex bioactuarial model of morbidity and mortality is the problem of specifying the manner in which the bioactuarial model gives rise to the associated multiple-decrement life table for the disease or set of diseases under analysis.

The substantive issues addressed by the other two models relate to the potential change in mortality patterns that would occur if a given mortality risk were eliminated. For example, one frequently used measure of the impact of a given disease is the cause-elimination life expectancy gain, the change in the life expectancy that would occur if all deaths due to that given cause were prevented. Because this is only a potential gain, the interpretation is that the mortality impact of a specific disease is measurable as the years of life lost due to the continued occurrence of deaths due to that disease. Numerically, this quantity is the cause-elimination life expectancy gain. For example, in Chapter 5 we present the life expectancies from the underlying-cause-elimination (Chiang, 1968) and pattern-of-failure-elimination (Manton *et al.*, 1976) life tables for the U.S. white male 1969 population for ischemic heart disease (IHD). In these data, the current life expectancy of 68.02 years increases to 73.74 years for the hypothetical elimination of IHD as an underlying cause of death. For the hypothetical elimination of all patterns of failure with IHD as a component, the resulting life expectancy was 75.13 years. Thus, the elimination of IHD could be expected to produce an increase in life expectancy of from 5.72 to 7.11 years.

One issue that is frequently mentioned in discussions of models with competing risks is the effect of risk dependency. In the usual formulation of the cause-elimination life table model, the risks are simply assumed to be independent. This could be problematic for analysis of underlying-cause mortality data because risks that are truly dependent may be mistakenly treated as independent. In this regard, the pattern-of-failure model is more flexible than the underlying-cause model in that the patterns are defined by combinations of one or more diseases. If a pair of diseases is suspected to be dependent, then the patterns with that disease pair can be used to define a death-state compartment that represents the mortality risk of the disease pair as an independent physiological process. For example, generalized arteriosclerosis (GA) is frequently reported as a causative factor in the development of IHD. This suggests the likelihood of a positive dependency for this pair of diseases. Yet, the 1969 U.S. white male multiple-cause life tables indicate that the average age at death for persons with both IHD and GA listed as causes of death is greater by about 5.1 years than for persons with IHD listed but not GA. Hence, it is also possible that there are two distinct underlying-disease processes with the IHD deaths in young adults that are related to such factors as hypertension, congenital anomaly, aneurism, thrombi, and emboli but not to arteriosclerosis. In contrast, IHD deaths with GA could represent an age-dependent disease process in which atherosclerotic deposits lead to acute circulatory failure.

The pattern-of-failure model, in effect, views the question of disease dependency as an issue of disease definition. Rather than dealing with mortality risks as separate diseases, this model deals with mortality risks as "lethal defects" defined by combinations of diseases. From this perspective, the analysis of single diseases involves a specialization of the lethal defects definition to patterns with the disease occurring only as the underlying cause. More generally, the lethal defects are identified with independent physiological processes so that the pattern-of-failure model is, by definition, a model of independent mortality risks. This point is central to the argument for applying the methods of independent competing risks to the pattern-of-failure analysis. In contrast, the argument for risk independence in the underlying-cause model is much weaker, with the absence of a computationally tractable alternative set of assumptions being the typically cited justification for assuming independence.

A second issue of concern in both the underlying-cause and pattern-of-failure forms of cause elimination relates to the substantive interpretation given to the term *elimination*. On one hand, the cause-elimination calculations might be regarded solely as a means to calibrate the impact of a mortality risk in terms of years of life lost. Alternatively, one might consider these calculations as estimates of the effects of eliminating deaths due to a given cause. In this latter case, several important substantive issues arise regarding the mechanism by which such elimination occurs, whether the elimination is complete or partial (Tsai *et al.*, 1978), whether other risks are also affected by the same mechanism (Schatzkin, 1980), whether the elimination requires a phase-in period, and whether the elimination of deaths also implies elimination of disease or disability or only the control of lethal sequelae of disease. These and other issues require representation in substantive analyses.

## *Multiple-Decrement Life Tables*

In Eq. (4.4.4) we find that the total force of mortality is the sum of two component forces defined for risk $\lambda$ and its complementary risk $\nu$. This suggests that we can rewrite (4.3.41) in the form

$$_n d_x = \int_x^{x+n} [\lambda(a) + \nu(a)] l_a \, da \qquad (4.4.5a)$$

$$= {}_n d_{x\lambda} + {}_n d_{x\nu}, \qquad (4.4.5b)$$

where

$$_n d_{x\lambda} = \int_x^{x+n} \lambda(a) l_a \, da \qquad (4.4.6)$$

and

$$_n d_{x\nu} = \int_x^{x+n} \nu(a) l_a \, da. \qquad (4.4.7)$$

The symbol $_n d_{x\lambda}$ represents the number of individuals just born who will die of cause $\lambda$ in the age interval $(x, x + n)$ and $_n d_{x\nu}$ represents the complementary number who will die in the age interval $(x, x + n)$ due to other causes than $\lambda$. The product $\lambda(a) l_a$ in (4.4.6) may be interpreted as an "instantaneous density" of deaths due to cause $\lambda$ in the cohort at age $a$. This is consistent with the interpretation given to the product $\mu(a) l_a$ in the comments following Eq. (4.3.41). Hence, the observable number of deaths due to cause $\lambda$ in the interval $(x, x + n)$ is obtained as the integral of the product $\lambda(a) l_a$ over this interval. Similar considerations apply to the interpretation of the product $\nu(a) l_a$.

The term *multiple decrement* arises from the representation of the $d_x$ column entries of the life table as the sum of several decrements of the form shown in (4.4.5b). Hence, $_nd_{x\lambda}$ is a decrement and denotes an entry at age $x$ in a multiple-decrement life table.

One can obtain an expression for the age-specific, cause-specific probability of death by rewriting (4.3.43) in the form

$$_nq_x = \int_x^{x+n} [\lambda(a) + \nu(a)] \exp\left[-\int_x^a \mu(w)\,dw\right] da \qquad (4.4.8a)$$

$$= {}_nq_{x\lambda} + {}_nq_{x\nu}, \qquad (4.4.8b)$$

where

$$_nq_{x\lambda} = \int_x^{x+n} \lambda(a) \exp\left[-\int_x^a \mu(w)\,dw\right] da \qquad (4.4.9)$$

and

$$_nq_{x\nu} = \int_x^{x+n} \nu(a) \exp\left[-\int_x^a \mu(w)\,dw\right] da. \qquad (4.4.10)$$

With these definitions, it is easy to show that

$$_nd_{x\lambda} = l_x\, {}_nq_{x\lambda} \qquad (4.4.11)$$

and

$$_nd_{x\nu} = l_x\, {}_nq_{x\nu}, \qquad (4.4.12)$$

so that the sum of these two equations yields

$$({}_nd_{x\lambda} + {}_nd_{x\nu}) = l_x({}_nq_{x\lambda} + {}_nq_{x\nu}), \qquad (4.4.13)$$

which is the multiple-decrement generalization of Eq. (4.3.6).

Equation (4.3.8) may also be generalized by defining cause-specific $l_{x\lambda}$ and $l_{x\nu}$ columns in the form

$$l_{x\lambda} = \sum_{i=x}^{\omega} d_{i\lambda} \qquad (4.4.14)$$

and

$$l_{x\nu} = \sum_{i=x}^{\omega} d_{i\nu}, \qquad (4.4.15)$$

so that the sum of these two equations yields

$$(l_{x\lambda} + l_{x\nu}) = \sum_{i=x}^{\omega} (d_{i\lambda} + d_{i\nu}), \qquad (4.4.16)$$

which is the multiple-decrement generalization of Eq. (4.3.8). The interpretation of $l_{x\lambda}$ is as the number of persons in a given cohort alive at age $x$ who will ultimately die from cause $\lambda$. Hence, $l_{0\lambda}$ represents the number of persons just born who will die as a result of cause $\lambda$. Also, because $l_0$ represents the total number of persons born in each cohort, the ratio $l_{0\lambda}/l_0$ represents the proportion of the cohort who will ultimately die of cause $\lambda$. In this case, the ratio $l_{0\lambda}/l_0$ can be interpreted as the probability that a randomly chosen person will ultimately die from cause $\lambda$. In the next chapter we shall see that this probability is near 0.165, or 16.5%, for cancer in the 1969 underlying-cause life tables for white males in the United States.

### *Cause-Elimination Life Tables*

A convenient starting point for discussion of competing risks involves the effect on total mortality that would occur if risk $\lambda$ or risk $\nu$ were the only component of the total force of mortality operating on the population. Consideration of risk $\nu$ alone leads to the cause-elimination life table model for the elimination of risk $\lambda$. Because we are concerned with total mortality, we consider replacing $\mu(x)$ in Fig. 1 with either $\mu_{\lambda \cdot \nu}(x)$ or $\mu_{\nu \cdot \lambda}(x)$, where

$$\mu_{\lambda \cdot \nu}(x) = \lim_{\Delta x \to 0} \frac{1}{\Delta x} \Pr[\text{dead due to cause } \lambda \text{ in age interval } (x, x + \Delta x), \text{ given survival to age } x; \text{ where } \lambda \text{ is the only risk}], \qquad (4.4.17)$$

$$\mu_{\nu \cdot \lambda}(x) = \lim_{\Delta x \to 0} \frac{1}{\Delta x} \Pr[\text{dead due to cause } \nu \text{ in age interval } (x, x + \Delta x), \text{ given survival to age } x; \text{ where } \nu \text{ is the only risk}]. \qquad (4.4.18)$$

If $\mu(x)$ in Fig. 1 is replaced with $\mu_{\nu \cdot \lambda}(x)$, then Eq. (4.3.17) needs to be replaced with

$$_{n}h_{x\nu \cdot \lambda} = \int_{x}^{x+n} \mu_{\nu \cdot \lambda}(a) \, da, \qquad (4.4.19)$$

from which we get the following generalizations of (4.3.23), (4.3.5), and (4.3.6):

$$_{n}q_{x\nu \cdot \lambda} = 1 - \exp(-_{n}h_{x\nu \cdot \lambda}), \qquad (4.4.20)$$

$$l_{xv\cdot\lambda} = l_0 \prod_{i=0}^{x-1} (1 - q_{iv\cdot\lambda}),$$ (4.4.21)

$$_n d_{xv\cdot\lambda} = l_{xv\cdot\lambda}\,_n q_{xv\cdot\lambda}.$$ (4.4.22)

The quantities $_n q_{xv\cdot\lambda}$, $l_{xv\cdot\lambda}$, and $_n d_{xv\cdot\lambda}$ are the parameters of the cause-elimination life table model for the elimination of deaths due to cause $\lambda$. By symmetry, an analogous set of parameters $_n q_{x\lambda\cdot v}$, $l_{x\lambda\cdot v}$, and $_n d_{x\lambda\cdot v}$ can be defined by using

$$_n h_{x\lambda\cdot v} = \int_x^{x+n} \mu_{\lambda\cdot v}(a)\,da.$$ (4.4.23)

The quantity $_n q_{x\lambda\cdot v}$ is sometimes called the *net* probability of death due to cause $\lambda$ in the age interval $(x, x + n)$ and can be distinguished from the $_n q_{x\lambda}$ quantity in (4.4.9), which is sometimes called the *crude* probability of death for cause $\lambda$ (Chiang, 1968).

In view of Eq. (4.4.5b), it is apparent that the crude probabilities in (4.4.8b) are computable from observed data through the multiple-decrement life table computations. In contrast, computation of the net probabilities $_n q_{x\lambda\cdot v}$ and $_n q_{xv\cdot\lambda}$ requires that certain additional assumptions be made. In particular, an assumption of *independent* competing risks is fundamental to the computation of cause-elimination life tables. This is the case for the cause-elimination calculations based on elimination of disease risk both as the underlying cause of death and as an element of a set of diseases under the pattern-of-failure representation of multiple-cause mortality.

The assumption of independent competing risks implies [but is not implied by; see Eqs. (4.4.47) and (4.4.48) for details] the condition that

$$\mu_{\lambda\cdot v}(x) = \lambda(x) \quad \text{and} \quad \mu_{v\cdot\lambda}(x) = v(x),$$ (4.4.24)

in which case (4.4.23) and (4.4.19) become

$$_n h_{x\lambda\cdot v} = \int_x^{x+n} \lambda(a)\,da$$ (4.4.25)

and

$$_n h_{xv\cdot\lambda} = \int_x^{x+n} v(a)\,da.$$ (4.4.26)

Hence, (4.4.24) is the necessary and sufficient condition under which the cause-elimination life table model becomes directly computable from the transition rates $\lambda(x)$ and $v(x)$, which describe the stochastic process that underlies the multiple-decrement life table model. This means that both types of life tables derive from consideration of the identical stochastic process model.

Other assumptions that are required for the computation of cause-elimination life tables are of a more trivial nature, primarily regarding the evaluation of the integrals (4.4.25) and (4.4.26). Chiang (1968) recommends use of

$$_nh_{x\lambda\cdot\nu} = {}_nh_x({}_nd_{x\lambda}/{}_nd_x)$$    (4.4.27)

and

$$_nh_{x\nu\cdot\lambda} = {}_nh_x({}_nd_{x\nu}/{}_nd_x),$$    (4.4.28)

which are maximum likelihood estimators if the ratio $\lambda(x)/\mu(x)$ is constant over the age interval $(x, x + n)$. For short age intervals, for example, $n < 5$ years, this assumption is likely to be satisfactory. Indeed, when $\lambda(x)$ and $\nu(x)$ are modeled from the same extreme value distribution, such as the exponential or Weibull distributions, then it can be shown that the constancy of the ratio $\lambda(x)/\mu(x)$ maintains not just for one age interval, but for the entire lifetime (David, 1970).

### The Concept of Independence of Risks

Up to this point, the discussion of the independence or dependence of mortality risks has been on an intuitive level. In part, this is because the connection between our concept of risk as a potential cause of death and our concept of a disease classification system for representing the medical facts surrounding death involves a certain amount of "slippage." This slippage occurs in three ways. First, a specific disease entity is isolated as a separate category of the ICD only when its frequency of occurrence or its importance as a morbid condition are judged to warrant it. Thus, the classification system may not permit each disease to be defined as a risk (e.g., mesothelioma is classified with cancer of trachea, bronchus, and lung, ICDA 162.1). Second, for reasons of diagnostic reliability, one may not wish to deal with detailed subcategories of diseases when defining the risks to be studied in a given analysis. That is, as a general rule, the less specific the disease definition, the more likely is the accuracy of the diagnosis. For example, Griffith (1976) noted that up to 15% of deaths certified as due to specific cancers were incorrect as to the site of the cancer or as to whether the death was due to cancer at all. This figure dropped to 4% when a more general disease definition encompassing all cancer sites was employed (Table 4, Chapter 2). Third, with the multiple-cause mortality data, it is possible to employ the pattern-of-failure definition of mortality risk in which several biomedically interrelated diseases are used to define a single risk or lethal defect. Thus, some aspects of disease dependence can be resolved through appropriate risk definitions.

In this section we shall focus on the concept of independence of mortality risks. By doing so we hope to clarify the relationship between risk independence and the more familiar concept of statistical independence. We also wish to clarify the relationship between statistical dependence and risk dependence and to indicate how these effects are represented in a stochastic compartment model. Once we have clarified these concepts, we shall be in a position to consider models of disease dependence in which additional health states are introduced and for which the various sets of exit transition rates are conditionally independent. Mathematically, the case of conditional independence in these more complex models turns out to be analogous to the case of complete risk independence in the model in Fig. 2. Thus, the stochastic compartment representation of morbidity and mortality provides an appropriate conceptual framework for discussion of issues of disease dependence.

If one compares the definition of $\mu_{\lambda\cdot\nu}(x)$ in (4.4.17) with the definition of $\lambda(x)$ in (4.4.1), then one can see that the difference is the qualification in (4.4.17): $\lambda$ is the only risk. This suggests that a viable definition of *independence* of risks $\lambda$ and $\nu$ is that the forces of mortality due to the risks $\lambda$ and $\nu$ are the same regardless of the presence or absence of the complementary risk $\nu$ or $\lambda$. This definition is given operational meaning in the conditions stated in (4.4.24). This definition applies to risks, not to diseases, although it suggests a definition of independence of diseases in which the development of each of two diseases proceeds at the same rate regardless of the presence or absence of the other disease of the pair. The analogy can be carried further. The absence of independence implies dependence, so that the dependence of two diseases might imply that the rate of development of either or both of two diseases changes when they occur simultaneously in an individual. This can be represented in the stochastic compartment model as a change in either of the conditions in (4.4.24) when one of the risks is removed as a force of mortality. We shall pursue discussion of models of this type in the next section.

We now show that statistical independence of the cause-specific ages at death is a sufficient condition for risk independence in (4.4.24). To this end, we consider the stochastic process that underlies the cause-elimination life table. In particular, we consider the distribution of age at death in the cause-elimination life table. We generalize the sampling scheme for the variate $X$ to the case in which at birth each individual is assigned a variate value for each risk so that the observed age at death $x$ is simply the smallest of these values. With only two risks to consider, we use $X_{\lambda\cdot\nu}$ and

$X_{\nu\cdot\lambda}$ to denote the variates, with $X_{\lambda\cdot\nu}$ representing the variate when risk $\nu$ is eliminated and $X_{\nu\cdot\lambda}$ representing it when $\lambda$ is eliminated. We also have generalizations of $F(x)$, $f(x)$, and $S(x)$:

$$F_{\lambda\cdot\nu}(x) = \Pr(X_{\lambda\cdot\nu} \leq x) = \int_0^x f_{\lambda\cdot\nu}(a)\, da, \tag{4.4.29}$$

$$S_{\lambda\cdot\nu}(x) = 1 - F_{\lambda\cdot\nu}(x) = \exp\left[-\int_0^x \mu_{\lambda\cdot\nu}(a)\, da\right], \tag{4.4.30}$$

$$f_{\lambda\cdot\nu}(x) = \mu_{\lambda\cdot\nu}(x) \exp\left[-\int_0^x \mu_{\lambda\cdot\nu}(a)\, da\right]. \tag{4.4.31}$$

An analogous set of equations may be written for the distribution of $X_{\nu\cdot\lambda}$. Also, from (4.4.30) it is apparent that Eq. (4.3.12) generalizes to

$$\mu_{\lambda\cdot\nu}(x) = -\frac{d}{dx}\ln S_{\lambda\cdot\nu}(x) \tag{4.4.32}$$

and by analogy that

$$\mu_{\nu\cdot\lambda}(x) = -\frac{d}{dx}\ln S_{\nu\cdot\lambda}(x). \tag{4.4.33}$$

A fundamental difference between the variate $X$ associated with the life table for total mortality and the variates $X_{\lambda\cdot\nu}$ and $X_{\nu\cdot\lambda}$ is that whereas $X$ is observable for each individual, $X_{\lambda\cdot\nu}$ and $X_{\nu\cdot\lambda}$ are not. In competing-risk theory this problem is dealt with by assuming that $X$ is the smaller of the two values $X_{\lambda\cdot\nu}$ and $X_{\nu\cdot\lambda}$. Hence,

$$X = \min(X_{\lambda\cdot\nu}, X_{\nu\cdot\lambda}). \tag{4.4.34}$$

In view of (4.4.34), Eq. (4.3.33) becomes,

$$S(x) = \Pr[\min(X_{\lambda\cdot\nu}, X_{\nu\cdot\lambda}) > x] \tag{4.4.35a}$$

$$= \int_x^\infty \int_x^\infty f(a_{\lambda\cdot\nu}, a_{\nu\cdot\lambda})\, da_{\nu\cdot\lambda}\, da_{\lambda\cdot\nu}, \tag{4.4.35b}$$

where $f(x_{\lambda\cdot\nu}, x_{\nu\cdot\lambda})$ is the bivariate probability density of $X_{\lambda\cdot\nu}$ and $X_{\nu\cdot\lambda}$. In dealing with bivariate distributions, one can define a joint probability distribution as

$$F(x_{\lambda\cdot\nu}, x_{\nu\cdot\lambda}) = \Pr(X_{\lambda\cdot\nu} \leq x_{\lambda\cdot\nu}, X_{\nu\cdot\lambda} \leq x_{\nu\cdot\lambda})$$

$$= \int_0^{x_{\lambda\cdot\nu}} \int_0^{x_{\nu\cdot\lambda}} f(a_{\lambda\cdot\nu}, a_{\nu\cdot\lambda})\, da_{\nu\cdot\lambda}\, da_{\lambda\cdot\nu} \tag{4.4.36}$$

and a joint survival function as

$$S(x_{\lambda\cdot\nu}, x_{\nu\cdot\lambda}) = \Pr(X_{\lambda\cdot\nu} > x_{\lambda\cdot\nu}, X_{\nu\cdot\lambda} > x_{\nu\cdot\lambda}) \tag{4.4.37a}$$

$$= \int_{x_{\lambda \cdot \nu}}^{\infty} \int_{x_{\nu \cdot \lambda}}^{\infty} f(a_{\lambda \cdot \nu}, a_{\nu \cdot \lambda}) \, da_{\nu \cdot \lambda} \, da_{\lambda \cdot \nu}. \qquad (4.4.37b)$$

In comparing (4.4.35b) with (4.4.37b), it is apparent that

$$S(x) = S(x, x) = \Pr(X_{\lambda \cdot \nu} > x, X_{\nu \cdot \lambda} > x), \qquad (4.4.38)$$

so that the order of the variables is relevant to the specification of the bivariate distribution if ambiguity is to be avoided in interpretation of symbols such as $S(x, x)$. An alternate notation that is frequently used is

$$S(x) = S(x_{\lambda \cdot \nu}, x_{\nu \cdot \lambda})\Big|_{x_{\lambda \cdot \nu} = x_{\nu \cdot \lambda} = x}, \qquad (4.4.39)$$

where the equalities following the vertical bar indicate constraints on $x_{\lambda \cdot \nu}$ and $x_{\nu \cdot \lambda}$ (both are set to the value $x$).

With this notation developed, we can revise definition (4.4.1) to express $\lambda(x)$ as a limiting form of the relative rate of decrease in $S(x, x)$ along the direction $x_{\lambda \cdot \nu}$. Hence, a generalization of (4.3.11) is obtained:

$$\lambda(x) = \lim_{\Delta x \to 0} \frac{1}{\Delta x} \left[ \frac{S(x, x) - S(x + \Delta x, x)}{S(x, x)} \right]$$

$$= -\frac{1}{S(x, x)} \lim_{\Delta x \to 0} \left[ \frac{S(x + \Delta x, x) - S(x, x)}{\Delta x} \right]. \qquad (4.4.40)$$

The limiting form of the final bracketed term is the time derivative of $S(x, x)$ with respect to $x_{\lambda \cdot \nu}$. Hence, we have

$$\lambda(x) = -\frac{1}{S(x_{\lambda \cdot \nu}, x_{\nu \cdot \lambda})} \frac{\partial}{\partial x_{\lambda \cdot \nu}} S(x_{\lambda \cdot \nu}, x_{\nu \cdot \lambda})\Big|_{x_{\lambda \cdot \nu} = x_{\nu \cdot \lambda} = x} \qquad (4.4.41a)$$

$$= -\frac{\partial}{\partial x_{\lambda \cdot \nu}} \ln S(x_{\lambda \cdot \nu}, x_{\nu \cdot \lambda})\Big|_{x_{\lambda \cdot \nu} = x_{\nu \cdot \lambda} = x}, \qquad (4.4.41b)$$

which is the bivariate analog to Eq. (4.3.12). A similar line of reasoning yields a corresponding expression for $\nu(x)$ as a partial derivative of the logarithm of $S(x)$:

$$\nu(x) = -\frac{\partial}{\partial x_{\nu \cdot \lambda}} \ln S(x_{\lambda \cdot \nu}, x_{\nu \cdot \lambda})\Big|_{x_{\lambda \cdot \nu} = x_{\nu \cdot \lambda} = x}. \qquad (4.4.42)$$

The two variates $X_{\lambda \cdot \nu}$ and $X_{\nu \cdot \lambda}$ are *statistically independent* if for all $x_{\lambda \cdot \nu}$ and $x_{\nu \cdot \lambda}$ the following condition holds:

$$\Pr(X_{\lambda \cdot \nu} > x_{\lambda \cdot \nu}, X_{\nu \cdot \lambda} > x_{\nu \cdot \lambda})$$

$$= \Pr(X_{\lambda \cdot \nu} > x_{\lambda \cdot \nu}) \Pr(X_{\nu \cdot \lambda} > x_{\nu \cdot \lambda}). \qquad (4.4.43)$$

Hence, the probability of the joint occurrence of the two events is equal to the product of the probabilities of the occurrence of each event separately. In terms of the survival functions, independence implies the condition

$$S(x_{\lambda \cdot \nu}, x_{\nu \cdot \lambda}) = S_{\lambda \cdot \nu}(x_{\lambda \cdot \nu})S_{\nu \cdot \lambda}(x_{\nu \cdot \lambda}). \tag{4.4.44}$$

Substituting (4.4.44) in (4.4.41b) yields

$$\lambda(x) = -\frac{\partial}{\partial x_{\lambda \cdot \nu}} \ln \left[ S_{\lambda \cdot \nu}(x_{\lambda \cdot \nu})S_{\nu \cdot \lambda}(x_{\nu \cdot \lambda}) \right] \Big|_{x_{\lambda \cdot \nu} = x_{\nu \cdot \lambda} = x} \tag{4.4.45a}$$

$$= -\frac{\partial}{\partial x_{\lambda \cdot \nu}} \ln S_{\lambda \cdot \nu}(x_{\lambda \cdot \nu})$$

$$\quad -\frac{\partial}{\partial x_{\lambda \cdot \nu}} \ln S_{\nu \cdot \lambda}(x_{\nu \cdot \lambda}) \Big|_{x_{\lambda \cdot \nu} = x_{\nu \cdot \lambda} = x} \tag{4.4.45b}$$

$$= -\frac{\partial}{\partial x} \ln S_{\lambda \cdot \nu}(x) - 0 \tag{4.4.45c}$$

$$= -\frac{d}{dx} \ln S_{\lambda \cdot \nu}(x) = \mu_{\lambda \cdot \nu}(x). \tag{4.4.45d}$$

Similarly, substituting (4.4.44) in (4.4.42) yields

$$\nu(x) = -\frac{d}{dx} \ln S_{\nu \cdot \lambda}(x) = \mu_{\nu \cdot \lambda}(x). \tag{4.4.46}$$

But Eq. (4.4.45d) and (4.4.46) are simply the two conditions given in (4.4.24) for the independence of competing risks $\lambda$ and $\nu$. Thus, we have shown that if the ages at death for risks $\lambda$ and $\nu$ are statistically independent, then the forces of mortality in the multiple-decrement and cause-elimination life table models will be pairwise equal as shown in (4.4.24).

Gail (1975) notes that the converse statement that (4.4.24) implies statistically independent ages at death does not hold. This means that the validity of the cause-elimination life table calculations based on (4.4.25) and (4.4.26) does not depend on an assumption of statistical independence but on the slightly weaker assumption defined by the conditions in (4.4.24). This becomes obvious when one realizes that (4.4.24) implies the following two equalities:

$$\frac{\partial}{\partial x_{\lambda \cdot \nu}} \ln S(x_{\lambda \cdot \nu}, x_{\nu \cdot \lambda}) \Big|_{x_{\lambda \cdot \nu} = x_{\nu \cdot \lambda} = x} = \frac{d}{dx} \ln S_{\lambda \cdot \nu}(x) \tag{4.4.47}$$

and

$$\frac{\partial}{\partial x_{\nu \cdot \lambda}} \ln S(x_{\lambda \cdot \nu}, x_{\nu \cdot \lambda}) \Big|_{x_{\lambda \cdot \nu} = x_{\nu \cdot \lambda} = x} = \frac{d}{dx} \ln S_{\nu \cdot \lambda}(x). \tag{4.4.48}$$

Condition (4.4.44) for statistical independence constrains $S(x_{\lambda \cdot \nu}, x_{\nu \cdot \lambda})$ at all points $(x_{\lambda \cdot \nu}, x_{\nu \cdot \lambda})$ in the plane defined by the variates $X_{\lambda \cdot \nu}$ and $X_{\nu \cdot \lambda}$. In contrast, condition (4.4.24) constrains $S(x_{\lambda \cdot \nu}, x_{\nu \cdot \lambda})$ only along the equi-angular line $x_{\lambda \cdot \nu} = x_{\nu \cdot \lambda}$ but imposes no constraints off this line. Hence, (4.4.24) cannot imply (4.4.44). In a later section of this chapter we shall show that (4.4.24) is satisfied if the risks are merely uncorrelated across heterogeneous individuals. In this case, however, a conditional form of (4.4.24) is also required that suggests the need for an assumption of conditional risk independence within each individual in which the presence or absence of one risk does not affect the development of any other risk.

A concept that is sometimes confused with risk independence is the notion of additivity of risks or, more precisely, of the forces of mortality or transition associated with a set of risks. With condition (4.4.24) one can revise (4.4.4) to express the total force of mortality as the sum of the forces of mortality in the disjoint cause-elimination life table models. Hence,

$$\mu(x) = \mu_{\lambda \cdot \nu}(x) + \mu_{\nu \cdot \lambda}(x), \qquad (4.4.49)$$

so that risk independence leads to additive forces of mortality as observed in the multiple-decrement life table model. As noted in (4.4.4), however, the property of additive forces of mortality in a multiple-decrement life table model is not an assumption at all but follows directly from the definitions (4.4.1) and (4.4.2). This implies that the computation of multiple-decrement life tables does not require any assumptions regarding the dependence or independence (or lack of correlation) of mortality risks.

In contrast, the cause-elimination life table model is based on the assumption of risk independence and with this assumption derives from the stochastic compartment model in Fig. 2 as the consistent discrete-time model. Thus, the assumption of risk independence is important because it permits assessment of the net or potential impact of a given risk, in which case one can then assess the effects of various efforts designed to modify that impact. In situations in which the assumption of risk independence is judged too unrealistic, progress can be made if one can specify conditions under which the competing risks are conditionally independent. This requires elaboration of the model in Fig. 2 to represent additional health states and/or correlated risks across heterogeneous individuals.

## 5   Models of Chronic Disease Morbidity and Mortality

### *A Stochastic Compartment Model with an Unobserved Morbid State*

In order to advance beyond the models specified in Figs. 1 and 2, we must introduce evidence from auxiliary sources. Specifically, if we assume that it is possible to know the rate of change with age of the force of

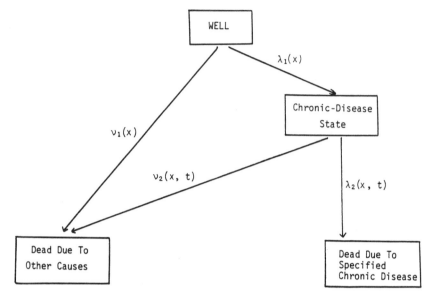

**Fig. 3.** States and transitions of a four-compartment system with two absorbing states and one unobserved intermediate morbid state.

transition from the well-state compartment to a chronic morbid-state compartment and to know the rate of change with the time spent in the morbid-state compartment of the force of transition to a given death-state compartment, then the distribution of persons in the chronic-disease state and the distribution of time spent within that state can be estimated as in Fig. 3.

Figure 3 displays a four-compartment stochastic process model of illness and death due to a specified chronic disease with competing risk adjustments for the censoring effects of other causes of death. In this model the transition rates are functions not only of the age $x$ of the individual, but also of the time $t$ spent in the chronic-disease-state compartment. Thus, this model could be used to generate two-dimensional life tables in which the $l_x$ column is decomposed as

$$l_x = l_{W,x} + \int_0^x l_{M,x,t}\, dt. \tag{4.5.1}$$

In Eq. (4.5.1), $l_{W,x}$ represents the number of persons alive at exact age $x$ who are free of the chronic disease and remain in the well-state compartment, and $l_{M,x,0}$ represents the density of persons who at exact age $x$

experience onset of the chronic disease; in general, $l_{M,x,t}$ represents the density of persons in the morbid state who at exact age $x$ have had the chronic disease for $t$ years. From (4.5.1) it is apparent that the total number of persons in the chronic-disease state at age $x$ can be defined as

$$l_{M,x} = \int_0^x l_{M,x,t} \, dt, \qquad (4.5.2)$$

so that $l_x$ can be expressed as the sum of the well and chronic-diseased population counts:

$$l_x = l_{W,x} + l_{M,x}. \qquad (4.5.3)$$

In Eq. (4.5.2) we have summed over the time in the chronic-disease-state compartment to generate age-specific morbidity estimates. For many chronic diseases, the duration of the disease will be correlated with the severity of the disease. This suggests the desirability of summing over age with $t$ held constant to generate duration-specific morbidity estimates for a population. For example, under stationary conditions, one can integrate $l_{M,x,t}$ over $x$ to obtain $l_{M,\cdot,t}$, which represents the instantaneous density of persons with chronic illness duration $t$. To obtain an interval estimate of the number of persons whose duration is $m$ to $m + 1$ years, we then integrate $l_{M,\cdot,t}$ from $t = m$ to $t = m + 1$ years, obtaining $L_{M,\cdot,m}$, where

$$L_{M,\cdot,m} = \int_m^{m+1} \int_t^\infty l_{M,a,t} \, da \, dt \qquad (4.5.4)$$

represents the number of persons alive in the population with chronic illness duration $t$, where $m \le t \le m + 1$. Morbidity estimates of this type can be useful in a number of applied problems. Additionally, by comparing the morbidity estimates derived under a given specialization of the model in Fig. 3 with independent estimates from epidemiologic sources, it is possible to evaluate the adequacy of parametric functions of disease onset and progression in describing the total disease process.

### Reduced Form Multiple-Decrement Computations

Application of the model to mortality data will normally require estimation of the multiple-decrement $d_x$ columns, $_nd_{x\lambda}$ and $_nd_{x\nu}$ [see Eqs. (4.4.6) and (4.4.7)]. In order to generate these estimates, it is necessary to "reduce" the model in Fig. 3 to the form in Fig. 2. In other words, we need to specify the transition rates in Fig. 2 as functions of the transition rates in Fig. 3. In this section we shall consider the general solution for these equations. In the next section we shall provide, by specification of certain independence assumptions, more tractable forms of solution. The nature of these assumptions should be consistent with the biomedical characteristics of the chronic disease process being analyzed.

To introduce a general methodology for simplifying the structure of a given compartmental system, we need to define a *transition density* for each of the transitions in Fig. 2. To this end we define

$$g_\lambda(x) = \lim_{\Delta x \to 0} \frac{1}{\Delta x} \text{ Pr[dead due to cause } \lambda$$
$$\text{in age interval } (x, x + \Delta x),$$
$$\text{given survival to age 0]}, \qquad (4.5.5)$$

$$g_\nu(x) = \lim_{\Delta x \to 0} \frac{1}{\Delta x} \text{ Pr[dead due to cause } \nu$$
$$\text{in age interval } (x, x + \Delta x),$$
$$\text{given survival to age 0]}, \qquad (4.5.6)$$

Interpretation of these transition densities can be made by reference to the distributions of age at death in the multiple-decrement life table. Let $X_\lambda$ denote the variate representing age at death due to cause $\lambda$ for the population subgroup $l_{0\lambda}$ whose ultimate cause of death will be $\lambda$. Then the probability density of $X_\lambda$ is proportional to $g_\lambda(x)$; that is,

$$f_\lambda(x) = g_\lambda(x)(l_0/l_{0\lambda}), \qquad (4.5.7)$$

where the ratio $l_0/l_{0\lambda}$ normalizes $f_\lambda(x)$ to unit probability mass. Similarly, it can be shown that

$$f_\nu(x) = g_\nu(x)(l_0/l_{0\nu}) \qquad (4.5.8)$$

is the density of the variate $X_\nu$, which represents age at death due to cause $\nu$ for the subgroup $l_{0\nu}$ that will ultimately die due to cause $\nu$.

Interpretation of these transition densities can also be made by reference to the transition rates $\lambda(x)$ and $\nu(x)$ in the compartmental system in Fig. 2. If one compares the definition of $g_\lambda(x)$ in (4.5.5) with the definition of $\lambda(x)$ in (4.4.1), then one can see that the difference is the qualification in (4.4.1): given survival to age $x$. The transition rate $\lambda(x)$ is defined as the limiting form of the conditional probability of death due to cause $\lambda$ at age $x$, given survival to that age. The transition density $g_\lambda(x)$ is the limiting form of the joint probability of death due to cause $\lambda$ at age $x$ and survival from birth (age 0) to that age. Because the joint probability of two events can always be obtained from the product of the marginal probability of one event times the conditional probability of the second event, given that the first event occurred, we can apply this principle to obtain the identity

$$g_\lambda(x) = \lambda(x) \exp\left\{-\int_0^x [\lambda(a) + v(a)]\, da\right\}, \tag{4.5.9}$$

where the exponential form of $S(x)$ derives from (4.3.14) with $\mu(a)$ replaced by the sum of $\lambda(a)$ and $v(a)$ as shown in (4.4.4). An analogous expression derives for $g_v(x)$:

$$g_v(x) = v(x) \exp\left\{-\int_0^x [\lambda(a) + v(a)]\, da\right\}. \tag{4.5.10}$$

In view of (4.5.9) and (4.5.10), it follows that interpretation of these transition densities can also be made by reference to the distribution of age at death $X$ in the life table for total mortality. Just as we saw in (4.4.4) that the transition rates governing the exit from a given compartment add to yield the overall transition rate of exit, it is also the case that the transition densities add to yield the overall probability density of the time to exit, which for the model in Fig. 2 is simply the age at death $X$. To see this, consider the sum of (4.5.9) and (4.5.10). This yields

$$g_\lambda(x) + g_v(x) = [\lambda(x) + v(x)] \exp\left\{-\int_0^x [\lambda(a) + v(a)]\, da\right\}$$

$$= \mu(x) \exp\left\{-\int_0^x \mu(a)\, da\right\} = f(x), \tag{4.5.11}$$

where the second line of this equation is simply the density $f(x)$ of $X$ given in (4.3.35). This additive property of the transition densities is reflected in the multiple-decrement life table in the additivity of $_n d_{x\lambda}$ and $_n d_{xv}$ seen in (4.4.5b). Indeed, because $l_a$ in (4.4.6) and (4.4.7) can be expressed as the product of $l_0$ and the exponential survival function appearing in (4.5.9) and (4.5.10), it follows that (4.4.6) and (4.4.7) are equivalent to

$$_n d_{x\lambda} = l_0 \int_x^{x+n} g_\lambda(a)\, da, \tag{4.5.12}$$

$$_n d_{xv} = l_0 \int_x^{x+n} g_v(a)\, da. \tag{4.5.13}$$

Hence, specification of the transition densities $g_\lambda(x)$ and $g_v(x)$ will be sufficient for multiple-decrement life table computations.

As noted in (4.5.9) and (4.5.10), it is always possible in compartment modeling to express a given transition density as the product of the corresponding transition rate times the survival probability, which can be expressed as an exponential function of the entire set of transition rates governing exit from the given compartment. Applying this fundamental principle to the model depicted in Fig. 3, we obtain the following expression for $g_\lambda(x)$:

$$g_\lambda(x) = \int_0^x \lambda_1(a_1) \exp\left\{- \int_0^{a_1} [\lambda_1(w) + \nu_1(w)]\, dw\right\}$$

$$\times \lambda_2(x, x - a_1)\ \exp\left\{- \int_{a_1}^x [\lambda_2(w, w - a_1)\right.$$

$$\left. + \nu_2(w, w - a_1)]\, dw\right\} da_1. \tag{4.5.14}$$

Equation (4.5.14) represents the condition that death due to the specified chronic disease at age $x$ requires (1) that the person first enters the chronic-disease-state compartment at age $a_1$ and (2) that the person is still alive at age $x$ so that he or she is available to die from the specified chronic disease at that time. The outer integral in (4.5.14) represents the summation over all possible $a_1$'s in the interval $(0, x)$, that is, the condition that $0 \le a_1 \le x$.

The expression for the transition density $g_\nu(x)$ in this model is slightly more complex due to there being two transitions to this death state. Nonetheless, the same principle of combining conditional probabilities applies. Hence,

$$g_\nu(x) = \nu_1(x) \exp\left\{- \int_0^x [\lambda_1(w) + \nu_1(w)]\, dw\right\}$$

$$+ \int_0^x \lambda_1(a_1) \exp\left\{- \int_0^{a_1} [\lambda_1(w) + \nu_1(w)]\, dw\right\}$$

$$\times \nu_2(x, x - a_1) \exp\left\{- \int_{a_1}^x [\lambda_2(w, w - a_1)\right.$$

$$\left. + \nu_2(w, w - a_1)]\, dw\right\} da_1. \tag{4.5.15}$$

In (4.5.15) the first term represents the transition from the well-state compartment to the death-due-to-other-causes compartment. As might be expected, this component is similar in form to Eq. (4.5.10), with the censoring effect modified to reflect the introduction of the chronic-disease-state compartment. The second component is similar to Eq. (4.5.14) except that $\lambda_2(x, x - a_1)$ is replaced with $\nu_2(x, x - a_1)$.

From (4.5.14) and (4.5.15), it is apparent that these expressions can be substituted in (4.5.12) or (4.5.13) to compute the multiple-decrement $d_x$ columns $_nd_{x\lambda}$ and $_nd_{x\nu}$. Because these columns also derive from the model in Fig. 2, it is instructive to examine the implications of the more detailed model in Fig. 3 for the transition rates in Fig. 2. Specifically, in view of (4.5.11), we have

$$S(x) = \int_x^\infty [g_\lambda(a) + g_\nu(a)]\, da, \tag{4.5.16}$$

so that by replacing the exponential terms in (4.5.9) and (4.5.10) with $S(x)$ as defined in (4.5.16), we obtain

$$\lambda(x) = g_\lambda(x) \Big/ \int_x^\infty [g_\lambda(a) + g_\nu(a)] \, da \qquad (4.5.17)$$

and

$$\nu(x) = g_\nu(x) \Big/ \int_x^\infty [g_\lambda(a) + g_\nu(a)] \, da, \qquad (4.5.18)$$

where $g_\lambda(x)$ is defined in (4.5.14) and $g_\nu(x)$ in (4.5.15). The important point derived from this demonstration is that if the model in Fig. 3 is correct, then the transition rates in Fig. 2 will generally be dependent since both $\lambda(x)$ and $\nu(x)$ are functions of all four of the transition rates specified in Fig. 3. In the next section we shall examine the conditions under which the model in Fig. 3 reduces to independent risks for the model in Fig. 2.

Before we consider risk independence, it will be useful to consider the relationship between the transition densities $g_\lambda(x)$ and $g_\nu(x)$ and the bivariate density $f(x_{\lambda \cdot \nu}, x_{\nu \cdot \lambda})$ defined in (4.4.35). We can revise (4.5.5) to express $g_\lambda(x)$ as a limiting form of the rate of decrease in $S(x, x)$ along the direction $x_{\lambda \cdot \nu}$. Hence,

$$g_\lambda(x) = \lim_{\Delta x \to 0} \frac{1}{\Delta x} [S(x, x) - S(x + \Delta x, x)]$$

$$= - \frac{\partial}{\partial x_{\lambda \cdot \nu}} S(x_{\lambda \cdot \nu}, x_{\nu \cdot \lambda}) \Big|_{x_{\lambda \cdot \nu} = x_{\nu \cdot \lambda} = x}, \qquad (4.5.19)$$

which is a generalization of (4.3.34). Also, in view of (4.4.41), it immediately follows that

$$\lambda(x) = g_\lambda(x)/S(x, x), \qquad (4.5.20)$$

which is simply an alternative form of (4.5.17). Again, we see that $\lambda(x)$ is a function of the bivariate survival function when the risks are dependent. The same argument also yields

$$\nu(x) = g_\nu(x)/S(x, x), \qquad (4.5.21)$$

where

$$g_\nu(x) = - \frac{\partial}{\partial x_{\nu \cdot \lambda}} S(x_{\lambda \cdot \nu}, x_{\nu \cdot \lambda}) \Big|_{x_{\lambda \cdot \nu} = x_{\nu \cdot \lambda} = x}. \qquad (4.5.22)$$

In view of (4.4.37b), it is apparent that we can replace the bivariate survival function in (4.5.19) with a double integral to obtain

$$g_\lambda(x) = -\left. \frac{\partial}{\partial x_{\lambda\cdot\nu}} \int_{x_{\lambda\cdot\nu}}^\infty \int_{x_{\nu\cdot\lambda}}^\infty f(a_{\lambda\cdot\nu}, a_{\nu\cdot\lambda})\, da_{\nu\cdot\lambda}\, da_{\lambda\cdot\nu} \right|_{x_{\lambda\cdot\nu} = x_{\nu\cdot\lambda} = x} \qquad (4.5.23a)$$

$$= \int_x^\infty f(x, a)\, da, \qquad (4.5.23b)$$

and in (4.5.22) to obtain

$$g_\nu(x) = \int_x^\infty f(a, x)\, da. \qquad (4.5.24)$$

To interpret these results, it is helpful to recall that $f_{\lambda\cdot\nu}(x)$ and $f_{\nu\cdot\lambda}(x)$ are the bivariate marginal densities and are obtainable from the joint density $f(x, x)$ by integration over the unwanted variable. Hence,

$$f_{\lambda\cdot\nu}(x) = \int_0^\infty f(x, a)\, da, \qquad (4.5.25)$$

$$f_{\nu\cdot\lambda}(x) = \int_0^\infty f(a, x)\, da, \qquad (4.5.26)$$

and it is seen that $g_\lambda(x)$ differs from $f_{\lambda\cdot\nu}(x)$ owing to the exclusion in the integral (4.5.23b) of all bivariate density values below $x_{\nu\cdot\lambda} = x$. Similarly, $g_\nu(x)$ excludes all values of $f(x_{\lambda\cdot\nu}, x_{\nu\cdot\lambda})$ below $x_{\lambda\cdot\nu} = x$.

### Independent Competing Risks

When condition (4.4.24) holds, the transition density $g_\lambda(x)$ in (4.5.9) can be written in the form

$$g_\lambda(x) = f_{\lambda\cdot\nu}(x) \exp\left[-\int_0^x \nu(a)\, da\right], \qquad (4.5.27)$$

where $f_{\lambda\cdot\nu}(x)$ is the probability density for the variate $X_{\lambda\cdot\nu}$ defined in (4.4.31). Hence, the transition density $g_\lambda(x)$ for the joint event of surviving to age $x$ and then dying of cause $\lambda$ is given by the product of the probability density of dying at age $x$ due to cause $\lambda$ times the probability of not dying due to cause $\nu$ before that age. Under the assumption of independent risks, these latter two factors are independent, so that their joint occurrence is governed by the product of their independent probabilities. This is different from the general form in (4.5.9), where the survival function employed was an exponential function of the entire set of transition rates governing exit from the given compartment.

Equation (4.5.27) can also be derived as a direct consequence of the assumed independence of the variates $X_{\lambda\cdot\nu}$ and $X_{\nu\cdot\lambda}$. It is instructive to see how this occurs because the derivation employs the relationship between $g_\lambda(x)$ and $f(x, x)$ developed in (4.5.23b). Recall that statistical independence implies the condition (4.4.43), which in terms of the marginal densities is

$$f(x_{\lambda \cdot \nu}, x_{\nu \cdot \lambda}) = f_{\lambda \cdot \nu}(x_{\lambda \cdot \nu}) f_{\nu \cdot \lambda}(x_{\nu \cdot \lambda}). \tag{4.5.28}$$

On substitution of (4.5.28) in (4.5.23b), one obtains

$$g_\lambda(x) = f_{\lambda \cdot \nu}(x) \int_x^\infty f_{\nu \cdot \lambda}(a) \, da \tag{4.5.29a}$$

$$= f_{\lambda \cdot \nu}(x) \exp\left[-\int_0^x \mu_{\nu \cdot \lambda}(a) \, da\right], \tag{4.5.29b}$$

where the relationship in (4.4.30) is used to introduce the exponential survival function in (4.5.29b). With (4.4.46), one then can replace $\mu_{\nu \cdot \lambda}(a)$ in (4.5.29b) with $\nu(a)$, thereby obtaining (4.5.27) from (4.5.23b) as a direct consequence of statistical independence. By following the same line of reasoning, it is easy to see that an analogous form to (4.5.27) also occurs for the transition density $g_\nu(x)$; that is,

$$g_\nu(x) = f_{\nu \cdot \lambda}(x) \exp\left[-\int_0^x \lambda(a) \, da\right]. \tag{4.5.30}$$

With (4.5.27) and (4.5.30) available, it is possible to establish the conditions that must be met for the model in Fig. 3 to reduce to an independent risk form of the model in Fig. 2. By comparing (4.5.27) and (4.5.14), we see that the sufficient conditions are (4.4.24) and (4.5.31), where

$$\nu_1(x) = \nu_2(x, t) = \nu(x). \tag{4.5.31}$$

With these conditions, (4.5.14) can be written in the form (4.5.27), with $f_{\lambda \cdot \nu}(x)$ defined as

$$f_{\lambda \cdot \nu}(x) = \int_0^x \lambda_1(a_1) \exp\left[-\int_0^{a_1} \lambda_1(w) \, dw\right]$$

$$\times \lambda_2(x, x - a_1) \exp\left[-\int_{a_1}^x \lambda_2(w, w - a_1) \, dw\right] da_1. \tag{4.5.32}$$

Similarly, (4.5.15) can be written in the form (4.5.30), with

$$\exp\left[-\int_0^x \lambda(a) \, da\right]$$

$$= S_{\lambda \cdot \nu}(x)$$

$$= \exp\left[-\int_0^x \lambda_1(a) \, da\right]$$

$$+ \int_0^x \lambda_1(a_1) \exp\left[-\int_0^{a_1} \lambda_1(w) \, dw\right]$$

$$\times \exp\left[-\int_{a_1}^x \lambda_2(w, w - a_1) \, dw\right] da_1. \tag{4.5.33}$$

Hence, in view of (4.4.31), $\lambda(a)$ is expressible as the ratio of (4.5.32) to (4.5.33) or

$$\lambda(x) = f_{\lambda \cdot \nu}(x)/S_{\lambda \cdot \nu}(x), \tag{4.5.34}$$

an expression which does *not* involve $\nu(x)$.

Equation (4.5.34) defines $\lambda(x)$ as a function only of $\lambda_1(x)$ and $\lambda_2(x, t)$, although due to the complexity of (4.5.32) and (4.5.33), some simplification of this relationship would appear to be desirable. Two types of simplification are likely to be of practical interest, both involving the $\lambda_2(x, t)$ transition rate.

First, we may wish to regard $\lambda_2(x, t)$ as a function only of age, denoted as $\lambda_2(x, \cdot)$, where the dot is used to nullify the argument $t$. In this case, we obtain

$$f_{\lambda \cdot \nu}(x) = \lambda_2(x, \cdot) \int_0^x \lambda_1(a_1) \exp\left[-\int_0^{a_1} \lambda_1(w) \, dw\right]$$
$$\times \exp\left[-\int_{a_1}^x \lambda_2(w, \cdot) \, dw\right] da_1, \tag{4.5.35}$$

which is the product of the force of mortality $\lambda_2(x, \cdot)$ times the probability that a person just born will be alive in the chronic-disease state at age $x$. This same probability occurs in $S_{\lambda \cdot \nu}(x)$ in the second term; that is,

$$S_{\lambda \cdot \nu}(x) = \exp\left[-\int_0^x \lambda_1(a) \, da\right] + \int_0^x \lambda_1(a_1)$$
$$\times \exp\left[-\int_0^{a_1} \lambda_1(w) \, dw\right] \exp\left[-\int_{a_1}^x \lambda_2(w, \cdot) \, dw\right] da_1. \tag{4.5.36}$$

The survival probability for cause $\lambda$ is the sum of the probability of avoiding onset of chronic disease plus the probability of avoiding death due to chronic disease given that onset has occurred. With (4.5.35) and (4.5.36), we can rewrite (4.5.34) in the form

$$\lambda(x) = \lambda_2(x, \cdot) \Big/ \left[ 1 + \frac{\exp\left[-\int_0^x \lambda_1(a) \, da\right]}{\int_0^x \lambda_1(a_1) \exp\left[-\int_0^{a_1} \lambda_1(w) \, dw\right] \times \exp\left[-\int_{a_1}^x \lambda_1(w, \cdot) \, dw\right] da_1} \right] \tag{4.5.37}$$

Here we see that $\lambda(x)$ is variably related to $\lambda_2(x, \cdot)$, with the divisor being a simple function of the ratio of the two probability terms in (4.5.36).

Second, we may wish to regard $\lambda_2(x, t)$ as a function only of time in the chronic-disease state, denoted as $\lambda_2(\cdot, t)$. In this case,

$$f_{\lambda \cdot \nu}(x) = \int_0^x \lambda_1(a_1) \exp\left[-\int_0^{a_1} \lambda_1(w)\, dw\right]$$
$$\times \lambda_2(\cdot, x - a_1) \exp\left[-\int_0^{x-a_1} \lambda_2(\cdot, w)dw\right] da_1, \quad (4.5.38)$$

and

$$S_{\lambda \cdot \nu}(x) = \exp\left[-\int_0^x \lambda_1(a)\, da\right] + \int_0^x \lambda_1(a_1) \exp\left[-\int_0^{a_1} \lambda_1(w)\, dw\right]$$
$$\times \exp\left[-\int_0^{x-a_1} \lambda_2(\cdot, w)\, dw\right] da_1. \quad (4.5.39)$$

Here we fail to obtain much simplification for the form of $\lambda(x)$ in (4.5.34). We do find, however, that $f_{\lambda \cdot \nu}(x)$ is now expressed in the form of the probability density of the sum of two independent random variables, for example, $A_{\lambda_1 \cdot \nu}$ and $T_{\lambda_2 \cdot \nu}$, where $A_{\lambda_1 \cdot \nu}$ denotes the age at onset of chronic disease and where $T_{\lambda_2 \cdot \nu}$ denotes the time to death measured from the onset of the disease and where both variates are independent of $X_{\nu \cdot \lambda}$. Hence, we can write (4.5.38) in the form

$$f_{\lambda \cdot \nu}(x) = \int_0^x f_{\lambda_1 \cdot \nu}(a) f_{\lambda_2 \cdot \nu}(x - a)\, da, \quad (4.5.40)$$

which is called the *convolution* of $f_{\lambda_1 \cdot \nu}(a)$ and $f_{\lambda_2 \cdot \nu}(t)$, where

$$f_{\lambda_1 \cdot \nu}(a) = \lambda_1(a) \exp\left[-\int_0^a \lambda_1(w)\, dw\right] \quad (4.5.41)$$

is the probability density function for the variate $A_{\lambda_1 \cdot \nu}$ and where

$$f_{\lambda_2 \cdot \nu}(t) = \lambda_2(\cdot, t) \exp\left[-\int_0^t \lambda_2(\cdot, w)\, dw\right] \quad (4.5.42)$$

is the probability density function for the variate $T_{\lambda_2 \cdot \nu}$. For any two random values $a_{\lambda_1 \cdot \nu}$ and $t_{\lambda_2 \cdot \nu}$, we then have

$$x_{\lambda \cdot \nu} = a_{\lambda_1 \cdot \nu} + t_{\lambda_2 \cdot \nu}, \quad (4.5.43)$$

which has the density given in (4.5.40) and which expresses the age at death $X_{\lambda \cdot \nu}$ due to cause $\lambda$ as the sum of the age at onset of chronic disease and the duration of that disease.

The choice between either of the above two simplifications of $\lambda_2(x, t)$ should be based on available biomedical data and insight into the nature of the mortality risk of the specific disease. Except for this choice, the assumptions leading from (4.5.31) to (4.5.34) are simply the two conditions of independence in (4.4.24). Hence, the independence assumptions in this form of the compartment model in Fig. 3 are no different from the independence assumptions underlying the standard cause-elimination life table calculations for the same chronic disease. This, however, does not mean that the models are substantively equivalent. For the model in Fig. 2, cause elimination means that the transition rate $\lambda(x)$ is nullified and the risk $\lambda$ is made inactive. For the model in Fig. 3, cause elimination is not uniquely defined because $\lambda(x)$ is nullified if either the risk $\lambda_1$ or $\lambda_2$ is made inactive. From the structure of that model, however, it is obvious that the method of cause elimination will have important substantive implications because if $\lambda_2$ is deactivated, then there may be substantial health care and treatment costs that would not occur if $\lambda_1$ were deactivated.

### Extensions to Dependent Chronic Disease Processes

For the model in Fig. 3, the assumption (4.5.31) that the presence of the chronic disease does not affect the force of mortality due to other causes of death appears reasonable. That is, if it is suspected that such a dependency exists, then it is likely that the chronic disease affects only the risk of other diseases that are physiologically related. For example, IHD and stroke are both related to an underlying process of atherogenesis. As a consequence, it may be most appropriate to employ multiple-cause data in the analysis of this pair of diseases. As noted previously, the pattern-of-failure model provides a relatively simple method of dealing with dependency by associating the physiological dependency with an independent lethal defect mechanism. An alternative strategy would require specification of a model such as in Fig. 4.

Figure 4 displays a 12-compartment stochastic process model of dependency between a pair of chronic diseases, labeled A and B. Note that the five transitions to the death-from-other-causes state are specified with the same $\nu$-transition rate to reflect a simple generalization of the independence assumption in (4.5.31). The remaining six death-state compartments specify which disease causes death (A or B), although the transition rates are permitted to differ according to the chronic-disease compartment from which the transition occurs and as a function of the ages of entry $a_1$ and $a_2$ into both prior and current compartments. For example, chronic disease A can cause death by itself from chronic-disease state A and in combination with chronic disease B from chronic-disease state BA (with A occurring first) or from chronic-disease state AB (with B occurring first). By permitting these states to have different transition rates, it is possible to specify different assumptions about the nature of the disease dependency. Note that the model can also be used to specify not only that the forces of mortality are dependent, but also that the onset

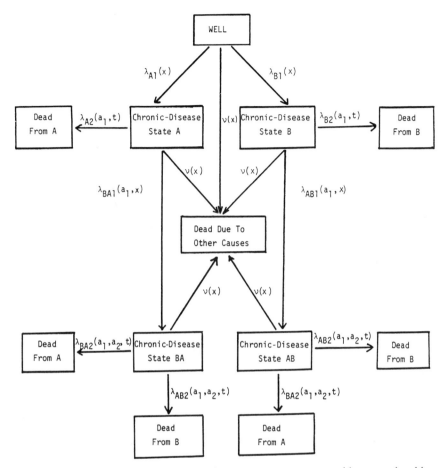

**Fig. 4.** States and transitions of a twelve-compartment system with seven absorbing states and four unobserved intermediate morbid states.

of the chronic diseases are dependent. For example, if the onset of B is more likely given the onset of A, then the transition rate $\lambda_{B1}(x)$ would be smaller than the transition rate $\lambda_{BA1}(a_1, x)$, although both transition rates govern the onset of B. The general solution for the model in Fig. 4 is derived by application of similar conditional probability calculations as employed for the model in Fig. 3. These equations are presented in Manton and Stallard (1980). However, because application of this model requires substantial specialization, we shall not reproduce these equations here. Instead, we shall in a later chapter deal with the equations appropriate to the specialized applications of the model.

When we refer to a model such as that in Fig. 4 as a model of disease dependency, we also need to stress that it is a model that explains disease dependency rather than one in which the exit risks from any given compartment are dependent. The primary method of representing risk dependency in compartmental modeling is through the introduction of additional compartments for which the exit risks are conditionally independent given the set of time variables at entry to those compartments. The goals of bioactuarial modeling require that the level of detail in the compartment model be such that the assumption of conditional independence of all sets of exit risks is biomedically plausible. Otherwise, if we allow conditional dependence, the effects of intervention cannot be assessed because the intervention would affect transition rates for risks other than the target risk in an unspecified way.

Thus, in discussing the effects of risk dependency it is important to keep in mind the goals of the modeling effort. For example, we have seen in earlier sections of this chapter that the multiple-decrement life table model could be developed from a stochastic compartment model where conditional (on birth) independence was assumed, such as in Fig. 2, with condition (4.4.24). Alternatively, the multiple-decrement life table model can be developed from the stochastic compartment model in Fig. 3 where an explicit dependence between $\lambda(x)$ and $\nu(x)$ is identified in (4.5.17) and (4.5.18). This dependence occurs even if the exit transition rates from each compartment in Fig. 3 are conditionally independent. Here, conditional independence refers to the independence of risk $\nu_1$ and $\lambda_1$ given $x$ and of $\nu_2$ and $\lambda_2$ given $x$ and $t$. As noted, if these risks are conditionally independent, then the model in Fig. 3 will represent a satisfactory bioactuarial model. Otherwise, we may need to use an even more complex model such as in Fig. 4 to achieve conditional independence.

Conditional independence of the exit risks of a given compartment model is not a sufficient condition to guarantee that the model is appropriate to a given analytic situation. For example, the cause-elimination life table model derives from the stochastic compartment model in Fig. 2 under the assumption of independent competing risks, as stated in condition (4.4.24). However, the cause-elimination life table model can also be derived from the stochastic compartment model in Fig. 3 if, in addition to (4.4.24), condition (4.5.31) is imposed. With condition (4.5.31), it becomes possible for both compartment models to satisfy the assumption of conditional independence of their respective exit risks when describing the same mortality data, although they clearly have very different implications for the results of biomedical intervention in the disease process. For the model in Fig. 2, the disease is represented as a single risk $\lambda$, whereas in Fig. 3 the disease is represented by the two risks $\lambda_1$ and $\lambda_2$. The model in Fig. 3 may be more appropriate for representing a chronic disease because it can represent the elimination of the lethal sequelae of chronic disease through nullification of the risk $\lambda_2$ whereas the model in Fig. 2 cannot. Substantively, such an effect might correspond to the introduction of new treatment protocols for patients, such as insulin therapy for diabetes or renal dialysis for kidney failure.

# 6  Population Heterogeneity

## *Basic Concepts*

To achieve the goals of bioactuarial modeling, we must employ models that are consistent with a continuous-state–continuous-time stochastic process model of human morbidity and mortality. In previous sections of this chapter we have dealt with the issue of generating discrete-time life table models from an underlying discrete-state–continuous-time stochastic process model. In this section we shall show how these discrete-state models can be related to continuous-state models so that parameter estimates derived from the discrete-state models will be consistent with a continuous-state process.

A fundamental assumption in continuous-state models is that the probability of occurrence of specific types of morbidity or mortality is functionally related to values of the set of physiological variables that are relevant to the specific health event. Thus, the continuous-state models are explicitly formulated at the level of the individual person, and they employ physiological data collected at that level. In contrast, the discrete-state models are formulated at the level of groups of individuals and are generally restricted to information on the numbers of persons dying by age, race, sex, and cause of death. We attempt to extend this information by using stochastic compartment methods to infer the prior distribution of these persons by compartment and by various inferred times of compartmental entry and exit. Thus, the main consideration in such a system is the temporal change in the conditional density of persons, by race and sex, in each specified compartment given the set of time variables at entry to that compartment. In the life table for total mortality, the initial values of these conditional densities are simply the radix value $l_0$ (because all persons enter the alive state at birth) and the age at death density $f(x)$ (representing the continuous-time analog to the life table $d_x$ column). In the life table model for chronic-disease mortality derived from Fig. 3, the initial values of these conditional densities are the radix values $l_{W,0}$, a set of continuous-time densities defined by the parameters $l_{M,x,0}$ (representing the number of persons who at exact age $x$ initiate the chronic disease), and a set of continuous-time densities recording entry into the two death states. The densities associated with the death states are not of interest to this discussion because death is an absorbing state. Instead, the densities of interest are the ones corresponding to living populations whose initial values are the radix values $l_0$, $l_{W,0}$, and $l_{M,x,0}$ or similarly defined continuous-time functions.

To facilitate our discussion, we shall define a *risk set* as a group of individuals who enter a given compartment at the same time (and at the same age—we are dealing only with cohort models in this chapter) and whose times of entry into all prior compartments are identical. Hence, with only the information recorded under this model, the individual members of the risk set are indistinguishable, so that there is no basis on which to account for individual differences in various exit transition rates. Nonetheless, the continuous-state model implies that such differences do exist, so that the fundamental problem is to account for the effects of these differences in models of population mortality. This problem is frequently referred to as the issue of *population heterogeneity*. In using this terminology, however, one needs to keep in mind that this is a form of residual variation because the individual differences occur among members of a risk set who represent not only a demographically homogeneous population subgroup, but also one that has a common health history inferred from the model.

The definition of risk sets given in the preceding discussion is consistent with the terminology used in discussing independence of risks in the preceding sections of this chapter. Indeed, the concept of conditional independence of risks, introduced in the preceding section as a condition to be satisfied in bioactuarial modeling, is equivalent to the condition of independent exit risks for each risk set of the model. This is because the defining conditions of a risk set are a common set of times of entry into all prior compartments of the model, conditions that are the same as in the discussion of conditional independence of the preceding section. Furthermore, we saw previously that one means of modeling dependence involved adding compartments to the model with dependent risks. Because the use of additional compartments also implies the presence of population heterogeneity, it is clear that steps taken to remedy one problem also can remedy the other. This suggests that an understanding of the issue of risk independence also requires an understanding of the issue of population heterogeneity.

## *Mortality Selection*

The essential issue of population heterogeneity is the operation of differential forces of mortality on the members of a risk set that differentially remove or select out certain individuals with unfavorable values of physiological variables. We can begin our study of the effects of mortality selection by considering a single risk set formed at age $x_0$ with individual forces of mortality defined for each age $x_0 + t$ as

$$\mu(t|z) = \lim_{\Delta t \to 0} \frac{1}{\Delta t} \text{ Pr[dead in time interval } (t, t + \Delta t),$$
$$\text{given survival to time } t$$
$$\text{and risk factor level } z]. \tag{4.6.1}$$

In formulating this definition, we have chosen to deal with time in such a way that the special case $x_0 = 0$ implies that the risk set is a birth cohort and that the time $t$ is a measure of age. This is done so that the results of this section can be applied to the life table models presented earlier while still maintaining sufficient generality to be applied to risk sets defined for the more complex compartmental systems. The risk factor $Z$ is a fixed (over time) latent variable introduced to give explicit representation to the concept of population heterogeneity. For the variate $Z$, we define an associated probability density function $f_{Z|(t)}(z|(t))$ to represent the density of $Z$ among the risk set members who are still alive at time $t$. Because the risk set is assumed to be initially formed at time $t = 0$, the initial density of $Z$ at this time will be denoted by $f_{Z|(0)}(z|(0))$, which is the density of $Z$ prior to the operation of mortality selection. Because the value $Z$ is fixed for each individual over time, any changes that occur in the density $f_{Z|(t)}(z|(t))$ over time must occur as the result of the selective removal by mortality of those individuals with unfavorable values of $\mu(t|z)$. Hence, the assumption of fixed $Z$ values permits us to study the dynamics of a pure mortality selection process. Later, we shall consider the more general case of time varying $Z$ values.

Just as age at death was treated as a random variable $X$ in an earlier section, we shall define a variate $T$ to denote the time to death $t$ measured from the time of formation of the risk set. The following conditional functions are defined:

$$F_{T|Z}(t|z) = \text{Pr}(T \leq t|Z = z), \tag{4.6.2}$$

$$S_{T|Z}(t|z) = \text{Pr}(T > t|Z = z) = 1 - F_{T|Z}(t|z), \tag{4.6.3}$$

$$f_{T|Z}(t|z) = -\frac{\partial}{\partial t} S_{T|Z}(t|z), \tag{4.6.4}$$

and

$$\mu(t|z) = -\frac{\partial}{\partial t} \ln S_{T|Z}(t|z). \tag{4.6.5}$$

Note that $\mu(t|z)$ might have been denoted by $\mu_{T|Z}(t|z)$. We have used the simpler notation because we use the hazard function of a distribution only when it is a waiting-time distribution such as age at death $X$ or time to death $T$. Given the initial condition

$$S_{T|Z}(0|z) = 1, \tag{4.6.6}$$

it may be shown by a similar argument to that leading to (4.3.14) that $S_{T|Z}(t|z)$ can be expressed as an exponential survival function of $\mu(t|z)$:

$$S_{T|Z}(t|z) = \exp\left[-\int_0^t \mu(a|z)\, da\right]. \tag{4.6.7}$$

In order to make the connection between these results and those of the preceding sections of this chapter, we need to define the marginal force of mortality at age $x_0 + t$ for the risk set formed at age $x_0$ as

$$\mu(t) = \lim_{\Delta t \to 0} \frac{1}{\Delta t} \Pr[\text{dead in time interval } (t, t + \Delta t),$$
$$\text{given survival to time } t]. \tag{4.6.8}$$

Except for the use of $t$ in place of $x$, definition (4.6.8) is identical to definition (4.3.10). Hence, the following functions define the marginal distribution of $T$:

$$F_T(t) = \Pr(T \le t), \tag{4.6.9}$$

$$S_T(t) = \Pr(T > t) = 1 - F_T(t), \tag{4.6.10}$$

$$f_T(t) = -\frac{d}{dt} S_T(t), \tag{4.6.11}$$

and

$$\mu(t) = -\frac{d}{dt} \ln S_T(t). \tag{4.6.12}$$

As in (4.3.14), the initial condition

$$S_T(0) = 1, \tag{4.6.13}$$

yields the solution

$$S_T(t) = \exp\left[-\int_0^t \mu(a)\, da\right]. \tag{4.6.14}$$

Again, we note that $\mu(t)$ might have been denoted $\mu_T(t)$ but was not, so that we could simplify our hazard function notation.

The use of the term *marginal* in describing (4.6.8)–(4.6.14) needs some explanation because it makes sense only when contrasted with the term *conditional* in describing (4.6.1)–(4.6.7). In fact, $S_T(t)$ is the survival function for the risk set in the same sense as $S(x)$ is the survival function for the life table birth cohort. For example, from Eq. (4.3.19) one can see that $l_x$ is given by the product $l_0 S(x)$, so that $S(x)$ is the survival probability that describes the observed survivorship proportion at each age $x$ in a cohort. Likewise, $S_T(t)$ is the survival probability that describes the observed survivorship proportion at each time $t$ in the risk set. Hence, when discussing marginal probabilities, we are discussing probabilities that describe observed or observable data. This can be a significant point if our theoretical perspective leads to specification of functional forms, not in terms of the marginal distributions, but in terms of the conditional distributions of the model. For example, functional forms derived from biomedical or clinical studies of temporal changes in individual risks lead to specification of the conditional force of mortality $\mu(t|z)$, not the marginal force of mortality $\mu(t)$. Conversely, we need to stress that inferences concerning temporal changes in individual risks may be in error if they are based on $\mu(t)$ rather than on $\mu(t|z)$.

The effects of mortality selection on a heterogeneous population can be completely described through examination of the change over time of the density of $Z$ among survivors to each time. It is significant that $f_{Z|(t)}(z|(t))$ is defined conditionally on survival to time $t$ because Bayes's formula then permits us to define it in terms of the initial density $f_{Z|(0)}(z|(0))$ and the conditional survival probability $S_{T|Z}(t|z)$ given that the individual with risk factor level $z$ is alive at time $t = 0$. Hence,

$$f_{Z|(t)}(z|(t)) = S_{T|Z}(t|z)f_{Z|(0)}(z|(0))/S_T(t), \qquad (4.6.15)$$

where $S_T(t)$ is the marginal survival probability defined in (4.6.10).

By integrating $f_{Z|(t)}(z|(t))$ over the entire range $R_Z$ of $z$, we obtain by definition

$$\int_{R_Z} f_{Z|(t)}(z|(t)) \, dz = 1. \qquad (4.6.16)$$

In view of (4.6.15), this yields the identity

$$S_T(t) = \int_{R_Z} S_{T|Z}(t|z)f_{Z|(0)}(z|(0)) \, dz \qquad (4.6.17a)$$

$$= \mathscr{E}_{Z|(0)}\{S_{T|Z}(t|z)\}, \qquad (4.6.17b)$$

where the symbol $\mathscr{E}_{Z|(t)}\{\cdot\}$ denotes the mathematical expectation of the function in braces based on $f_{Z|(t)}(z|(t))$. Hence, the marginal survival function $S_T(t)$ is simply the average of the conditional survival functions $S_{T|Z}(t|z)$ among the risk set members alive at time $t = 0$.

In view of (4.6.7) and (4.6.14), it is apparent that (4.6.15) can be rewritten in terms of the exponential form

$$f_{Z|(t)}(z|(t)) = \exp\left\{\int_0^t [\mu(a) - \mu(a|z)]\, da\right\} f_{Z|(0)}(z|(0)). \quad (4.6.18)$$

This is important to facilitating our study of the change over time in the density of $Z$. In particular, differentiation of (4.6.18) with respect to time $t$ simply multiplies the expression on the right by the quantity $[\mu(t) - \mu(t|z)]$, in which case we obtain

$$\frac{\partial}{\partial t} f_{Z|(t)}(z|(t)) = [\mu(t) - \mu(t|z)]f_{Z|(t)}(z|(t)). \quad (4.6.19)$$

From (4.6.19) we see that if the conditional force of mortality $\mu(t|z)$ is larger than the marginal force of mortality $\mu(t)$, then the sign of the bracketed term will be negative and the density of survivors at that point $z$ will decrease over time. Conversely, if $\mu(t|z)$ is less than $\mu(t)$, the sign of the bracketed term will be positive and the density of survivors at that point $z$ will increase over time. Thus, individuals with relatively low values of $\mu(t|z)$ will have relatively higher survival chances.

The marginal force of mortality $\mu(t)$ can be further characterized by using the integral of (4.6.19). Specifically, by taking the time derivative of (4.6.16), we obtain

$$0 = \frac{d}{dt} \int_{R_z} f_{Z|(t)}(z|(t))\, dz \quad (4.6.20a)$$

$$= \int_{R_z} \frac{\partial}{\partial t} f_{Z|(t)}(z|(t))\, dz, \quad (4.6.20b)$$

where we assume the order of integration and differentiation in (4.6.20a) are interchangeable as shown in (4.6.20b). Then replacing the differential expression in (4.6.20b) with the expression on the right of (4.6.19) and separating the terms, we obtain

$$\int_{R_z} \mu(t)f_{Z|(t)}(z|(t))\, dz = \int_{R_z} \mu(t|z)f_{Z|(t)}(z|(t))\, dz. \quad (4.6.21)$$

Factoring $\mu(t)$ outside the integral on the left and using (4.6.16) to dispose of the remaining expression, we obtain

$$\mu(t) = \int_{R_z} \mu(t|z) f_{Z|(t)}(z|(t)) \, dz \qquad (4.6.22a)$$

$$= \mathscr{E}_{Z|(t)}\{\mu(t|z)\}. \qquad (4.6.22b)$$

Hence, the marginal force of mortality $\mu(t)$ is simply the average of the conditional force of mortality $\mu(t|z)$ among the risk set members who are still alive at time $t$. However, it is *not* the average among the risk set members who are alive at time 0. One needs to be careful to specify properly the time frame when dealing with average values in a selected population. For example, using (4.6.11) and (4.6.4) to obtain $f_T(t)$ from the time derivative of (4.6.17a), we find that

$$f_T(t) = \int_{R_z} f_{T|Z}(t|z) f_{Z|(0)}(z|(0)) \, dz \qquad (4.6.23a)$$

$$= \mathscr{E}_{Z|(0)}\{f_{T|Z}(t|z)\}, \qquad (4.6.23b)$$

which shows that the marginal density $f_T(t)$ is an average of the conditional density $f_{T|Z}(t|z)$ among the initial risk set members alive at time 0, not at time $t$.

### Frailty

In order to be more specific about the effects of mortality selection on the density of $Z$, we need to be more specific about our assumptions concerning the conditional force of mortality $\mu(t|z)$. We might assume that $Z$ is a measure of frailty that operates to increase the force of mortality in a multiplicative manner. In this case, it is reasonable to define a standard force of mortality $\mu(t|1)$ against which the conditional force of mortality for any individual may be compared. Specifically, we have by assumption

$$\mu(t|z) = z\mu(t|1), \qquad (4.6.24)$$

from which it trivially follows that

$$z = \mu(t|z)/\mu(t|1), \qquad (4.6.25)$$

so that $z$ is seen to be a measure of relative risk or of relative susceptibility. Such measures are frequently assessed for specific population subgroups in epidemiologic studies, so that it is natural to consider them in our treatment of population heterogeneity. Indeed, with the assumption that $Z$ is fixed over time for each individual, Eq. (4.6.24) defines a *proportional hazards model* (Menken *et al.*, 1981; Trussell and Hammerslough, 1983), a model form widely used by demographers when $Z$ is an observed covariate.

In view of (4.6.24), it is apparent that $f_{Z|(t)}(z|(t))$ is defined only for nonnegative values of $z$ so that the range $R_Z$ is the interval $(0, \infty)$. Furthermore, in view of (4.6.22b), it follows that

$$\mu(t) = \mathscr{E}_{Z|(t)}(z)\mu(t|1), \tag{4.6.26}$$

so that the mean of $Z$ can be set to any arbitrary value because (4.6.26) shows that it can be absorbed into the standard force of mortality as a proportionality constant. Given this behavior, a reasonable choice is to set the initial mean to unity, that is,

$$\mathscr{E}_{Z|(0)}(z) = 1, \tag{4.6.27}$$

in which case (4.6.26) yields

$$\mu(0) = \mu(0|1), \tag{4.6.28}$$

so that the cohort force of mortality $\mu(t)$ and the standard force of mortality $\mu(t|1)$ coincide at the time origin of the risk set.

Because (4.6.27) gives only the initial mean value of $Z$, it is important to establish how this value changes over time as mortality selectively removes individuals with high $Z$ values. We can do this by considering the basic definition of the mean value of $Z$. We have

$$\mathscr{E}_{Z|(t)}(z) = \int_0^\infty z f_{Z|(t)}(z|(t))\,dz, \tag{4.6.29}$$

where the range $R_Z$ is now explicitly represented due to our frailty assumption (4.6.24). The change in the mean of $Z$ is described by the time derivative of (4.6.29). Hence,

$$\frac{d}{dt}\mathscr{E}_{Z|(t)}(z) = \frac{d}{dt}\int_0^\infty z f_{Z|(t)}(z|(t))\,dz \tag{4.6.30a}$$

$$= \int_0^\infty z \frac{\partial}{\partial t} f_{Z|(t)}(z|(t))\,dz \tag{4.6.30b}$$

$$= \int_0^\infty z[\mu(t) - \mu(t|z)]f_{Z|(t)}(z|(t))\,dz, \tag{4.6.30c}$$

where the modifications are based on (4.6.20b) and (4.6.19). Using (4.6.26) to eliminate $\mu(t)$ and (4.6.24) to eliminate $\mu(t|z)$, we can rewrite (4.6.30c) as

$$\frac{d}{dt}\mathscr{E}_{Z|(t)}(z) = \int_0^\infty z[\mathscr{E}_{Z|(t)}(z) - z]\mu(t|1)f_{Z|(t)}(z|(t))\,dz \tag{4.6.31a}$$

$$= \{[\mathscr{E}_{Z|(t)}(z)]^2 - \mathscr{E}_{Z|(t)}(z^2)\}\mu(t|1) \tag{4.6.31b}$$

$$= -\operatorname{var}_{Z|(t)}(z)\mu(t|1), \tag{4.6.31c}$$

where $\text{var}_{Z|(t)}(z)$ denotes the variance of $z$ among members of the risk set who survive to age $t$. Because both the variance of $z$ and the standard force of mortality $\mu(t|1)$ are assumed to be positive, the negative sign in (4.6.31c) implies that $\mathscr{E}_{Z|(t)}(z)$ will be a strictly decreasing function of time. In other words, the average frailty in a cohort will decline as those members with higher values of $Z$ are selectively removed. From (4.6.27) and (4.6.31c), it is apparent that (4.6.26) implies the inequality for $t > 0$ of

$$\mu(t) < \mu(t|1). \qquad (4.6.32)$$

The substantive implication of (4.6.32) is that the marginal force of mortality $\mu(t)$ in a heterogeneous risk set will tend to diverge away from the standard force of mortality $\mu(t|1)$ in the risk set. For example, in the simple case in which the standard force of mortality is constant, such as in a select clinical population, the conditional force of mortality for each individual will also be constant, but the observed force of mortality will decline over time. That is, given the condition

$$\mu(t|1) = \mu(0|1), \qquad (4.6.33)$$

it will be the case that for $0 < t < t'$,

$$\mu(0) > \mu(t) > \mu(t'), \qquad (4.6.34)$$

so that $\mu(t)$ will be a monotonic decreasing function of time. Because the mortality data for such persons provide direct estimates of $\mu(t)$ but not of $\mu(t|1)$, it is apparent that such data will not distinguish between the following two situations: (1) heterogeneous forces of mortality constant for each individual and (2) decreasing forces of mortality for a homogeneous group of individuals. Essentially, this same point was also noted by Sheps and Menken (1973, p. 69) in their analysis of fertility risks.

A central issue in mortality selection involves the functional relationship between the marginal force of mortality $\mu(t)$ at time $t$ and the standard force of mortality $\mu(t|1)$ at the same time. This relationship is given explicitly in (4.6.22a) in terms of the density $f_{Z|(t)}(z|(t))$ but not in terms of the initial density $f_{Z|(0)}(z|(0))$. With $Z$ assumed fixed over time, this latter specification requires that we assume the functional form of the conditional force of mortality $\mu(t|z)$ for individual members of the risk set. Indeed, limiting this choice to just one or a few plausible alternatives is one possible way in which the biomedical sciences and clinical studies of survival can provide input into a bioactuarial model.

We can establish the required relationship by using (4.6.17a) to replace $S_T(t)$ in (4.6.12) so that we have

$$\mu(t) = -\frac{d}{dt} \ln \int_{R_Z} S_{T|Z}(t|z) f_{Z|(0)}(z|(0)) \, dz. \qquad (4.6.35)$$

Then we replace $S_{T|Z}(t|z)$ with the exponential survival function defined in (4.6.7) but only after using (4.6.24) to factor $z$ outside the integral in (4.6.7). This permits (4.6.35) to be revised to

$$\mu(t) = -\frac{d}{dt} \ln \int_0^\infty \exp\left[-z \int_0^t \mu(a|1)\, da\right] f_{Z|(0)}(z|(0))\, dz \quad (4.6.36a)$$

$$= -\frac{d}{dt} \ln \mathscr{L}_{Z|(0)}\left\{\int_0^t \mu(a|1)\, da\right\}, \quad (4.6.36b)$$

where $\mathscr{L}_{Z|(0)}\{\cdot\}$ denotes the Laplace transform of the probability density $f_{Z|(0)}(z|(0))$. Because the Laplace transform is routinely provided, when it exists, for standard statistical distributions, the relationship (4.6.36b) provides a convenient method of representing selection effects due to population heterogeneity in bioactuarial models with fixed frailty.

### Competing Risks

The assumption that the risk set is heterogeneous with respect to un-measured risk variables has important implications for our treatment of competing risks and, specifically, for the conditions under which the cause-elimination life table calculations are valid. In an earlier section we saw that condition (4.4.24) was necessary and sufficient to generate an independent competing risk model. With heterogeneity this is still the case, the difference being that we no longer can assume (4.4.24) because it refers to marginal forces of mortality whereas our model is specified in terms of conditional forces of mortality, as in (4.6.36b). Instead, we are required to make the appropriate assumptions concerning the conditional forces of mortality that lead to condition (4.4.24) as a consequence. It turns out that these assumptions will include an analogous condition to (4.4.24) for the conditional forces of mortality.

Consider the compartmental system in Fig. 5 with transition rates $\lambda(t|z_\lambda)$ and $\nu(t|z_\nu)$, where $Z_\lambda$ and $Z_\nu$ are the risk factors associated with the risks $\lambda$ and $\nu$, respectively. This compartmental system is analogous to the system studied in Fig. 2 except that this new system is conditional on the pair of risk factors $Z_\lambda$ and $Z_\nu$. As in the models discussed earlier, we assume that $Z_\lambda$ and $Z_\nu$ are fixed over time for each individual. We define

$$\lambda(t|z_\lambda) = \lim_{\Delta t \to 0} \frac{1}{\Delta t} \text{Pr[dead due to cause } \lambda$$
$$\text{in time interval } (t,\, t + \Delta t),$$
$$\text{given survival to time } t$$
$$\text{and risk factor level } Z_\lambda = z_\lambda], \quad (4.6.37)$$

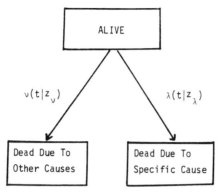

**Fig. 5.** States and transitions of a three-compartment system with two absorbing states in which transition rates are conditional on frailty variates.

$$\nu(t|z_\nu) = \lim_{\Delta t \to 0} \frac{1}{\Delta t} \text{Pr[dead due to cause } \nu$$
$$\text{in time interval } (t,\, t + \Delta t),$$
$$\text{given survival to time } t$$
$$\text{and risk factor level } Z_\nu = z_\nu]. \quad (4.6.38)$$

Using similar reasoning as that leading to (4.4.4), we obtain

$$\mu(t|z_\lambda,\, z_\nu) = \lambda(t|z_\lambda) + \nu(t|z_\nu), \quad (4.6.39)$$

where $\mu(t|z_\lambda,\, z_\nu)$ is the conditional total force of mortality, that is,

$$\mu(t|z_\lambda,\, z_\nu) = \lim_{\Delta t \to 0} \frac{1}{\Delta t} \text{Pr[dead in time interval } (t,\, t + \Delta t),$$
$$\text{given survival to time } t$$
$$\text{and risk factor levels } Z_\lambda = z_\lambda$$
$$\text{and } Z_\nu = z_\nu]. \quad (4.6.40)$$

We also need the hazard rates for each risk acting alone:

$$\mu_{\lambda \cdot \nu}(t|z_\lambda) = \lim_{\Delta t \to 0} \frac{1}{\Delta t} \text{Pr[dead due to cause } \lambda$$
$$\text{in time interval } (t,\, t + \Delta t),$$
$$\text{given survival to time } t$$
$$\text{and risk factor level } Z_\lambda = z_\lambda,$$
$$\text{where } \lambda \text{ is the only risk]}, \quad (4.6.41)$$

$$\mu_{\nu \cdot \lambda}(t|z_\nu) = \lim_{\Delta t \to 0} \frac{1}{\Delta t} \text{Pr[dead due to cause } \nu$$
$$\text{in time interval } (t,\, t + \Delta t),$$
$$\text{given survival to time } t$$
$$\text{and risk factor level } Z_\nu = z_\nu,$$
$$\text{where } \nu \text{ is the only risk]}. \quad (4.6.42)$$

The assumption of conditionally independent competing risks implies but is not implied by the condition that

$$\mu_{\lambda \cdot \nu}(t|z_\lambda) = \lambda(t|z_\lambda) \qquad \text{and} \qquad \mu_{\nu \cdot \lambda}(t|z_\nu) = \nu(t|z_\nu), \qquad (4.6.43)$$

which is the same as (4.4.24) if the risk set is homogeneous. Just as (4.4.24) derives when the condition of statistical independence in (4.4.44) is true at least along the line $x_{\lambda \cdot \nu} = x_{\nu \cdot \lambda} = x$, (4.6.43) likewise derives from the analogous relationship for the conditional survival functions

$$S_{T_{\lambda \cdot \nu}, T_{\nu \cdot \lambda}|Z_\lambda, Z_\nu}(t, t|z_\lambda, z_\nu) = S_{T_{\lambda \cdot \nu}|Z_\lambda}(t|z_\lambda) S_{T_{\nu \cdot \lambda}|Z_\nu}(t|z_\nu), \qquad (4.6.44)$$

where the survival probabilities have the following interpretations:

$$S_{T_{\lambda \cdot \nu}, T_{\nu \cdot \lambda}|Z_\lambda, Z_\nu}(t_{\lambda \cdot \nu}, t_{\nu \cdot \lambda}|z_\lambda, z_\nu) = \Pr[T_{\lambda \cdot \nu} > t_{\lambda \cdot \nu}, T_{\nu \cdot \lambda} > t_{\nu \cdot \lambda}|Z_\lambda = z_\lambda, Z_\nu = z_\nu],$$

$$(4.6.45)$$

$$S_{T_{\lambda \cdot \nu}|Z_\lambda}(t_{\lambda \cdot \nu}|z_\lambda) = \Pr[T_{\lambda \cdot \nu} > t_{\lambda \cdot \nu}|Z_\lambda = z_\lambda]$$

$$= \exp\left[-\int_0^{t_{\lambda \cdot \nu}} \mu_{\lambda \cdot \nu}(t|z_\lambda)\, dt\right], \qquad (4.6.46)$$

$$S_{T_{\nu \cdot \lambda}|Z_\nu}(t_{\nu \cdot \lambda}|z_\nu) = \Pr[T_{\nu \cdot \lambda} > t_{\nu \cdot \lambda}|Z_\nu = z_\nu]$$

$$= \exp\left[-\int_0^{t_{\nu \cdot \lambda}} \mu_{\nu \cdot \lambda}(t|z_\nu)\, dt\right]. \qquad (4.6.47)$$

The conditions under which (4.4.24) holds are the same conditions under which (4.4.44) holds on the line $x_{\lambda \cdot \nu} = x_{\nu \cdot \lambda} = x$. Hence, in our current generalized notation, we require that

$$S_{T_{\lambda \cdot \nu}, T_{\nu \cdot \lambda}}(t, t) = S_{T_{\lambda \cdot \nu}}(t) S_{T_{\nu \cdot \lambda}}(t), \qquad (4.6.48)$$

which is the marginal distribution form of the condition (4.6.44), where the survival probabilities have the following interpretations:

$$S_{T_{\lambda \cdot \nu}, T_{\nu \cdot \lambda}}(t_{\lambda \cdot \nu}, t_{\nu \cdot \lambda}) = \Pr[T_{\lambda \cdot \nu} > t_{\lambda \cdot \nu}, T_{\nu \cdot \lambda} > t_{\nu \cdot \lambda}], \qquad (4.6.49)$$

$$S_{T_{\lambda \cdot \nu}}(t_{\lambda \cdot \nu}) = \Pr[T_{\lambda \cdot \nu} > t_{\lambda \cdot \nu}]$$

$$= \exp\left[-\int_0^{t_{\lambda \cdot \nu}} \mu_{\lambda \cdot \nu}(t)\, dt\right], \qquad (4.6.50)$$

$$S_{T_{\nu \cdot \lambda}}(t_{\nu \cdot \lambda}) = \Pr[T_{\nu \cdot \lambda} > t_{\nu \cdot \lambda}]$$

$$= \exp\left[-\int_0^{t_{\nu \cdot \lambda}} \mu_{\nu \cdot \lambda}(t)\, dt\right]. \qquad (4.6.51)$$

Because (4.6.48) refers to a joint marginal survival function with respect to the variates $Z_\lambda$ and $Z_\nu$, it is natural to examine the expectation integral that defines this marginal survival function:

$$S_{T_{\lambda\cdot\nu}, T_{\nu\cdot\lambda}}(t, t) = \mathscr{E}_{Z_\lambda, Z_\nu|(0)}\{S_{T_{\lambda\cdot\nu}, T_{\nu\cdot\lambda}|Z_\lambda, Z_\nu}(t, t|z_\lambda, z_\nu)\} \qquad (4.6.52a)$$

$$= \int_{R_{Z_\lambda}} \int_{R_{Z_\nu}} S_{T_{\lambda\cdot\nu}, T_{\nu\cdot\lambda}|Z_\lambda, Z_\nu}(t, t|z_\lambda, z_\nu)$$

$$\times f_{Z_\lambda, Z_\nu|(0)}(z_\lambda, z_\nu|(0))\, dz_\nu\, dz_\lambda, \qquad (4.6.52b)$$

where $f_{Z_\lambda, Z_\nu|(0)}(z_\lambda, z_\nu|(0))$ is the joint probability density of $Z_\lambda$ and $Z_\nu$ among the initial risk set members.

In view of (4.6.17b) and (4.6.52a), we also see that (4.6.48) is equivalent to the condition that the joint marginal survival function is the product of the expectations of the individual marginal survival functions; that is,

$$\mathscr{E}_{Z_\lambda, Z_\nu|(0)}\{S_{T_{\lambda\cdot\nu}, T_{\nu\cdot\lambda}|Z_\lambda, Z_\nu}(t, t|z_\lambda, z_\nu)\}$$

$$= \mathscr{E}_{Z_\lambda|(0)}\{S_{T_{\lambda\cdot\nu}|Z_\lambda}(t|z_\lambda)\}\mathscr{E}_{Z_\nu|(0)}\{S_{T_{\nu\cdot\lambda}|Z_\nu}(t|z_\nu)\}, \qquad (4.6.53)$$

where

$$\mathscr{E}_{Z_\lambda|(0)}\{S_{T_{\lambda\cdot\nu}|Z_\lambda}(t|z_\lambda)\} = \int_{R_{Z_\lambda}} S_{T_{\lambda\cdot\nu}|Z_\lambda}(t|z_\lambda) f_{Z_\lambda|(0)}(z_\lambda|(0))\, dz_\lambda, \qquad (4.6.54)$$

$$\mathscr{E}_{Z_\nu|(0)}\{S_{T_{\nu\cdot\lambda}|Z_\nu}(t|z_\nu)\} = \int_{R_{Z_\nu}} S_{T_{\nu\cdot\lambda}|Z_\nu}(t|z_\nu) f_{Z_\nu|(0)}(z_\nu|(0))\, dz_\nu. \qquad (4.6.55)$$

Because the left side of (4.6.53) is the expression in (4.6.52b) whereas the right side is the product of (4.6.54) and (4.6.55), it is apparent that equality will be obtained in (4.6.53), and hence in (4.6.48) and (4.4.24), if conditions (4.6.44) and (4.6.56) both hold, where (4.6.56) is

$$f_{Z_\lambda, Z_\nu|(0)}(z_\lambda, z_\nu|(0)) = f_{Z_\lambda|(0)}(z_\lambda|(0)) f_{Z_\nu|(0)}(z_\nu|(0)). \qquad (4.6.56)$$

Whereas conditional risk independence at the individual level implies condition (4.6.44), which, in turn, implies condition (4.6.43), condition (4.6.56) is a condition of statistical independence of the risk factors $Z_\lambda$ and $Z_\nu$, which is a condition of marginal independence.

Actually, condition (4.6.56) is slightly stronger than necessary. If (4.6.44) holds, then (4.6.52b) becomes

$$S_{T_{\lambda\cdot\nu}, T_{\nu\cdot\lambda}}(t, t) = \int_{R_{Z_\lambda}} \int_{R_{Z_\nu}} S_{T_{\lambda\cdot\nu}|Z_\lambda}(t|z_\lambda) S_{T_{\nu\cdot\lambda}|Z_\nu}(t|z_\nu)$$

$$\times f_{Z_\lambda, Z_\nu|(0)}(z_\lambda, z_\nu|(0))\, dz_\nu\, dz_\lambda \qquad (4.6.57a)$$

$$= \mathscr{E}_{Z_\lambda, Z_\nu|(0)}\{S_{T_{\lambda\cdot\nu}|Z_\lambda}(t|z_\lambda) S_{T_{\nu\cdot\lambda}|Z_\nu}(t|z_\nu)\}. \qquad (4.6.57b)$$

Hence, (4.6.53) and (4.6.48) are replaced with

$$\mathscr{E}_{Z_\lambda, Z_\nu|(0)}\{S_{T_{\lambda\cdot\nu}|Z_\lambda}(t|z_\lambda) S_{T_{\nu\cdot\lambda}|Z_\nu}(t|z_\nu)\}$$

$$= \mathscr{E}_{Z_\lambda|(0)}\{S_{T_{\lambda\cdot\nu}|Z_\lambda}(t|z_\lambda)\}\mathscr{E}_{Z_\nu|(0)}\{S_{T_{\nu\cdot\lambda}|Z_\nu}(t|z_\nu)\}, \qquad (4.6.58)$$

an expression that is obviously true if (4.6.56) is true but one that is also true if, instead of (4.6.56), the risk factors $Z_\lambda$ and $Z_\nu$ are merely *uncorrelated* [see Kendall and Stuart (1969, Vol. 1, p. 52)].

Even if condition (4.6.43) holds for individuals so that the risks are "biomedically independent," it follows that if the risk factors $Z_\lambda$ and $Z_\nu$ are correlated, then condition (4.6.58) will not hold and (4.4.24) will be invalid. This means that certain types of risk dependence can be represented as effects of correlated risk factors operating on heterogeneous risk sets. For example, cigarette smoking is cited as a risk factor for several diseases so that it might be reasonable to represent its health impact in a heterogeneous population model with correlated risk factors. Naturally, given these effects, the standard cause-elimination life table calculations will no longer be an accurate model of the effect of eliminating a given risk.

For practical purposes, we regard (4.6.43) as a fundamental assumption of bioactuarial modeling. Without this condition, there is an unspecified dependence between pairs of risks that implies the existence of additional unmeasured risk factors. In this case, by increasing the number of compartments in the model and by specifying the presence of additional heterogeneous risk sets, one can specify the sources of this dependence. With this additional specification, condition (4.6.43) can then be satisfied for each risk set. This suggests that a properly specified bioactuarial model may be defined as one in which condition (4.6.43) is satisfied for each risk set. In this case, all sources of risk dependence are represented through correlated risk factors or through the specification of additional compartments.

## 7   Risk-Factor Dynamics

### Basic Concepts

The assumption that the individual frailty variate $Z$ is fixed over the life of an individual in the model of total mortality is a simplification. For example, from various epidemiologic studies the effects of cigarette smoking, exercise, weight control, nutrition, and other factors on mortality risks have been confirmed, so that change in any of these factors violates the assumption of fixed frailty. The same problem also arises in modeling cause-specific mortality by using $Z_\lambda$ to represent fixed susceptibility, because risk factors for cause-specific mortality are also subject to change. In this section we shall generalize our model of population heterogeneity to represent the effects of change in risk factor levels. As in the previous section we shall focus on a model of total mortality in a single risk set formed at age $x_0$ with the forces of mortality indicated for each age $x_0 + t$. Although we focus on a model of total mortality, the results also apply directly to cause-specific mortality under the assumption (4.6.56) of independent risk factors and the assumption (4.6.43) of conditionally independent competing risks. The assumption (4.6.56) of independent risk factors may be inappropriate, however, as in the case of heart disease and lung cancer where cigarette consumption is a risk factor for both.

We begin by defining the individual force of mortality at age $x_0 + t$ as

$$\mu(t|y(t)) = \lim_{\Delta t \to 0} \frac{1}{\Delta t} \text{Pr[dead in time interval } (t, t + \Delta t),$$
$$\text{given survival to time } t$$
$$\text{and risk factor level } y(t)]. \qquad (4.7.1)$$

One can see that this definition differs from $\mu(t|z)$ in (4.6.1) in that the risk factor $y(t)$ is an explicit function of $t$. For the variate $Y(t)$, we define an associated probability density function $f_{Y(t)|(t)}(y(t)|(t))$ to represent the density of $Y(t)$ among the risk set members who are still alive at time $t$. One can see that the notation required to deal with time-varying risk factor values in a risk set subject to differential mortality is somewhat cumbersome. We shall avoid the temptation to simplify this notation, however, in the interest of maintaining precision. Hence, we use $f_{Y(t_1)|(t_0)}(y(t_1)|(t_0))$ to represent the density of $Y(t)$ at time $t_1$ among the risk-set members who are alive at time $t_0$. If $t_0 > t_1$, then these values are distributed as a subset of the values for members alive at time $t_1$. If $t_1 > t_0$, then some of these values are hypothetical extrapolations because some members of $(t_0)$ will not be alive at $t_1$ and hence will not be members of $(t_1)$.

It is important to emphasize that $\mu(t|y(t))$ is to be regarded primarily as a function of $y(t)$. In the random walk model (Woodbury and Manton, 1977), $Y(t)$ is a vector and the function is a quadratic risk function. With $y(t)$ as a scalar quantity, this suggests

$$\mu(t|y(t)) = y^2(t)\mu(t|1), \qquad (4.7.2)$$

where $\mu(t|1)$ is the standard force of mortality at the risk factor level $y(t) = 1$ or at $y(t) = -1$ because (4.7.2) implies $\mu(t|-1) = \mu(t|1)$. If $Y(t)$ is constant, then (4.7.2) simplifies to (4.6.24) with $z = y^2(\cdot)$, so that the quadratic risk function is not inconsistent with the proportional hazard assumption made in the frailty model. Alternatively, one could simplify (4.7.2) by replacing $y^2(t)$ with $y(t)$ as

$$\mu(t|y(t)) = y(t)\mu(t|1) \qquad (4.7.3)$$

and by making the appropriate change to the density $f_{Y(t)|(t)}(y(t)|(t))$ to restrict its range to the interval $(0, \infty)$.

Because we assume that we have no direct measurement of $Y(t)$, the choice between the functional forms (4.7.2), (4.7.3), or any other form is arbitrary, so that we choose to deal with (4.7.3) for its simplicity.

Some further assumptions will be useful for expository purposes. We define

$$\mathscr{E}_{Y(t_1)|(t_0)}(y(t_1)) = \int_0^\infty y(t_1)f_{Y(t_1)|(t_0)}(y(t_1)|(t_0))\, dy(t_1), \qquad (4.7.4)$$

which is the expectation of $y(t_1)$ among the risk-set members alive at $t_0$. Without loss of generality, we assume that

$$\mathscr{E}_{Y(t)|(0)}(y(t)) = \mathscr{E}_{Y(0)|(0)}(y(0)), \qquad (4.7.5)$$

which states that the average value of $Y(t)$ is constant over time in the risk set where the averaging is taken over the members alive at time 0. As noted, some of these values are hypothetical because the group alive at time $t$ is a biased subset of the original group. If (4.7.5) is not initially true, then one can replace $y(t)$ in (4.7.3) with

$$y(t) \leftarrow y(t)\mathscr{E}_{Y(0)|(0)}(y(0))/\mathscr{E}_{Y(t)|(0)}(y(t)), \qquad (4.7.6)$$

in which case the ratio of the expectations in (4.7.6) is absorbed into $\mu(t|1)$. This adjustment is consistent with the interpretation of $Y(t)$ as a measure of relative risk that is free of the effects of mortality selection.

Assumption (4.7.5) specifies a model in which there is no *drift*. This differs from the random walk model discussed in Section 2, although it is not a critical difference. The random walk model employs a quadratic force of mortality but does not employ a concept of a standard force of mortality. In terms of Eq. (4.7.2), this is equivalent to assuming that $\mu(t|1) = 1$ for all values of $t$. In contrast, the model being developed here does employ a standard force of mortality so that any change in the mean values of $y(t)$ due to drift can be absorbed into the standard force of mortality. Hence, drift is implicitly represented in this model.

With implicit representation of the effects of drift, the remaining two risk factor dynamics we need to consider are the effects of diffusion and regression. These are the risk factor dynamics represented in the random walk model so that their representation in our model of mortality selection will recast that model to an equivalent level of generality. Unfortunately, assumption (4.7.5) is not sufficient by itself to specify the effects of diffusion and regression on individual risk variable values. Basically, we can identify three plausible scenarios.

First, it is possible that the only changes in $Y(t)$ are random changes so that risk variable dynamics can be adequately represented as a diffusion process without regression effects. In this case, the conditional expectation of $Y(t_1)$ given $y(t_0)$ is simply $y(t_0)$ or, more formally,

$$\mathscr{E}_{Y(t_1)|Y(t_0),(t_0)}(y(t_1)|y(t_0)) = y(t_0). \qquad (4.7.7)$$

Hence, if $y(t_0)$ denotes the present value of $Y(t)$, then the expected future values of $Y(t)$ are the same value $y(t_0)$. However, if $y(t_0)$ is changed in some manner, then the expected future values of $Y(t)$ are also changed. In this sense, the effects of a given change can be regarded as permanent. This type of diffusion process might well represent such changes as initiation or cessation of cigarette smoking, weight gain or weight loss, initiation of treatment for hypertension, and other effects that tend to be relatively permanent.

Second, it is possible that a diffusion process is accompanied by one of two types of regression processes—a homeostatic process that returns each individual to his or her own unique frailty value $z$ or a homeostatic process that tends to move an individual toward the population mean value $\mathscr{E}_{Z|(0)}(z)$. In the first case, the conditional expectation of $Y(t_1)$ given $y(t_0)$ and homeostatic frailty value of $Z$ depends on the time path of the return to homeostasis. To illustrate, suppose that the rate of return is proportional to the difference of $y(t_0)$ and $z$; that is,

$$\frac{d}{dt}\,\mathscr{E}_{Y(t)|Y(t_0),Z,(t_0)}(y(t)|y(t_0),z)\Big|_{t=t_0} = -k(y(t_0) - z), \qquad (4.7.8)$$

where $k$ is the homeostatic constant. Hence,

$$\mathscr{E}_{Y(t_1)|Y(t_0),Z,(t_0)}(y(t_1)|y(t_0),z) = (y(t_0) - z)\exp[-k(t_1 - t_0)] + z. \qquad (4.7.9)$$

For $k = 0$ this reduces to (4.7.7), so that the model is a special case of (4.7.9). Alternatively, for $k = \infty$ the equation reduces to

$$\mathscr{E}_{Y(t_1)|Y(t_0),Z,(t_0)}(y(t_1)|y(t_0),z) = z, \qquad (4.7.10)$$

which is the fixed frailty model, where the effects of diffusion are instantaneously reversed, so that $Y(t)$ is constant over time and is well represented by the variate $Z$.

To represent a homeostatic process in which an individual moves toward the population mean value, we can revise (4.7.8) by replacing $Z$ with $\mathscr{E}_{Z|(0)}(z)$:

$$\frac{d}{dt}\,\mathscr{E}_{Y(t)|Y(t_0),\mathscr{E}_{Z|(0)}(z),(t_0)}(y(t)|y(t_0),\mathscr{E}_{Z|(0)}(z))\Big|_{t=t_0}$$

$$= -k(y(t_0) - \mathscr{E}_{Z|(0)}(z)), \qquad (4.7.11)$$

where $k$ is again interpreted as a homeostatic constant. Hence,

$$\mathscr{E}_{Y(t_1)|Y(t_0),\mathscr{E}_{Z|(0)}(z),(t_0)}(y(t_1)|y(t_0),\mathscr{E}_{Z|(0)}(z))$$

$$= [y(t_0) - \mathscr{E}_{Z|(0)}(z)]\exp[-k(t_1 - t_0)] + \mathscr{E}_{Z|(0)}(z). \qquad (4.7.12)$$

For $k = 0$ this also reduces to (4.7.7), so that that model is a special case of (4.7.12). For $k = \infty$ the equation reduces to

$$\mathscr{E}_{Y(t_1)|Y(t_0),\mathscr{E}_{Z|(0)}(z),(t_0)}(y(t_1)|y(t_0), \mathscr{E}_{Z|(0)}(z)) = \mathscr{E}_{Z|(0)}(z), \qquad (4.7.13)$$

which is the homogeneous population model where the effects of diffusion are instantaneously reversed so that all individuals in the population have the same value of $Y(t)$; that is, $Y(t) = \mathscr{E}_{Z|(0)}(z) = 1$.

Given the results of numerous epidemiologic studies that the development of "excess risk" due to various environmental and occupational exposures occurs over many years and is frequently of a permanent nature, it is unlikely that either of the homeostatic constants just discussed is very different from zero. Hence, the main potential difficulty with application of the fixed frailty model is the biases that may result from failure to represent the effects of diffusion on $Y(t)$. Naturally, if the duration of the study is short and the rate of diffusion is small, then those biases will tend to be minimized.

### Diffusion

In order to be more precise about the effects of diffusion, we need a model of diffusion. To develop such a model, we need some preliminary results. To this end, we define the positive valued integrable random function $R(t)$ with $r(0) = 1$ such that for any $t \geq 0$

$$\mathscr{E}_{R(t)|(0)}(r(t)) = 1 \qquad (4.7.14)$$

and the nonnegative valued random function $H(t)$ such that for any $t \geq 0$

$$h(t) = \int_0^t r(a)\mu(a|1)\,da. \qquad (4.7.15)$$

We assume that $Y(0)$ and $R(t)$ are independently distributed among the risk-set members alive at time 0 and that $Y(t)$ is obtained from the product of $Y(0)$ and $R(t)$. Hence,

$$y(t) = y(0)r(t), \qquad (4.7.16)$$

and

$$\mathscr{E}_{Y(t)|(0)}(y(t)) = \mathscr{E}_{Y(0)|(0)}(y(0))\mathscr{E}_{R(t)|(0)}(r(t)). \qquad (4.7.17)$$

Furthermore, in view of (4.7.14), it is apparent that

$$\mathscr{E}_{Y(t)|Y(0),(0)}(y(t)|y(0)) = y(0)\mathscr{E}_{R(t)|(0)}(r(t)) = y(0) \qquad (4.7.18)$$

as described in (4.7.7).

With the random functions $H(t)$ and $R(t)$, we can generalize the expression for the marginal survival function $S_T(t)$ in (4.6.17a) to account for the effects of diffusion.

In view of (4.7.3) and (4.7.16), we have

$$\mu(t|y(0), \ r(t)) = y(0)r(t)\mu(t|1), \qquad (4.7.19)$$

in which case the conditional probability of surviving to time $t$ is

$$S_{T|Y(0),H(t)}(t|y(0), \ h(t)) = \exp\left[-\int_0^t \mu(a|y(0), \ r(a)) \ da\right] \quad (4.7.20a)$$

$$= \exp[-y(0)h(t)], \qquad (4.7.20b)$$

where $h(t)$ is introduced as a result of (4.7.15). The survival probability therefore depends on $H(t)$, not on $R(t)$, although one would expect that these two random functions are highly correlated. The marginal survival probability is obtainable, as before, by using Bayes's formula for the joint density of $Y(0)$ and $H(t)$:

$$f_{Y(0),H(t)|(t)}(y(0), \ h(t)|(t)) = S_{T|Y(0),H(t)}(t|y(0), \ h(t))$$

$$\times f_{Y(0),H(t)|(0)}(y(0), \ h(t)|(0))/S_T(t). \qquad (4.7.21)$$

As in (4.6.16), we have

$$\int_0^\infty \int_0^\infty f_{Y(0),H(t)|(t)}(y(0), \ h(t)|(t)) \ dh(t) \ dy(0) = 1, \qquad (4.7.22)$$

in which case (4.7.21) and (4.7.22) imply

$$S_T(t) = \int_0^\infty \int_0^\infty S_{T|Y(0),H(t)}(t|y(0), \ h(t))$$

$$\times f_{Y(0),H(t)|(0)}(y(0), \ h(t)|(0)) \ dh(t) \ dy(0) \qquad (4.7.23a)$$

$$= \mathscr{E}_{Y(0),H(t)|(0)}\{S_{T|Y(0),H(t)}(t|y(0), \ h(t))\}. \qquad (4.7.23b)$$

As before, the marginal survival probability $S_T(t)$ is the expected value of the conditional survival probability that, with diffusion being represented, is conditional on both $Y(0)$ and $H(t)$. It is significant that $Y(0)$ and $H(t)$ are initially independent, because $H(t)$ is functionally related to the sequence of $R(t)$ values as seen in (4.7.15) and $R(t)$ is independent of $Y(0)$. Hence the following factorization holds:

$$f_{Y(0),H(t)|(0)}(y(0), \ h(t)|(0)) = f_{Y(0)|(0)}(y(0)|(0))f_{H(t)|(0)}(h(t)|(0)), \quad (4.7.24)$$

where the terms on the right are the marginal densities of $Y(0)$ and $H(t)$. With (4.7.20b) used to replace the conditional survival function in (4.7.21), one obtains

$$f_{Y(0),H(t)|(t)}(y(0), h(t)|(t)) = \exp[- y(0)h(t)]f_{Y(0)|(0)}(y(0)|(0))$$

$$\times f_{H(t)|(0)}(h(t)|(0))/S_T(t). \qquad (4.7.25)$$

Because the exponential term in (4.7.25) does not factor into a product of terms involving $y(0)$ and $h(t)$ separately, it is apparent that the distributions of $Y(0)$ and $H(t)$ among the survivors to time $t$ are dependent distributions. In other words. the effects of diffusion operate selectively on the distribution of $Y(0)$. To see this, integrate $h(t)$ out of (4.7.25):

$$f_{Y(0)|(t)}(y(0)|(t)) = \int_0^\infty f_{Y(0),H(t)|(t)}(y(0), h(t)|(t)) \, dh(t) \qquad (4.7.26a)$$

$$= f_{Y(0)|(0)}S_T^{-1}(t) \int_0^\infty \exp[- y(0)h(t)]$$

$$\times f_{H(t)|(0)}(h(t)|(0)) \, dh(t) \qquad (4.7.26b)$$

$$= f_{Y(0)|(0)}S_T^{-1}(t)\mathscr{L}_{H(t)|(0)}[y(0)], \qquad (4.7.26c)$$

where $\mathscr{L}_{H(t)|(0)}[\cdot]$ denotes the Laplace transform of the probability density $f_{H(t)|(0)}(h(t)|(0))$.

Division by $S_T(t)$ on the right side of Bayes's formula in (4.7.21) serves the purpose of normalizing the joint probability mass to unity in (4.7.22). One can gain insight into the effects of diffusion by removing this normalization from the calculations. Let $g_{Y(0),H(t)|(t)}(y(0), h(t)|(t))$ be the unnormalized joint density of $Y(0)$ and $H(t)$ among survivors at time $t$, and let $g_{Y(0)|(t)}(y(0)|(t))$ and $g_{H(t)|(t)}(h(t)|(t))$ be the corresponding unnormalized marginal density functions. Then

$$g_{Y(0),H(t)|(t)}(y(0), h(t)|(t)) = \exp[- y(0)h(t)]$$

$$\times f_{Y(0),H(t)|(0)}(y(0), h(t)|(0)), \qquad (4.7.27)$$

and in view of (4.7.26c),

$$g_{Y(0)|(t)}(y(0)|(t)) = f_{Y(0)|(0)}(y(0)|(0))\mathscr{L}_{H(t)|(0)}[y(0)]. \qquad (4.7.28)$$

The Laplace transform in (4.7.28) is the expectation of $\exp[-y(0)h(t)]$; that is,

$$\mathscr{L}_{H(t)|(0)}[y(0)] = \mathscr{E}_{H(t)|(0)}\{\exp[-y(0)h(t)]\}. \qquad (4.7.29)$$

This can lead to a useful inequality if we can define the expectation of $h(t)$ as

$$\mathscr{E}_{H(t)|(0)}(h(t)) = \int_0^t \mathscr{E}_{R(a)|(0)}(r(a))\mu(a|1) \, da \qquad (4.7.30a)$$

$$= \int_0^t \mu(a|1) \, da, \qquad (4.7.30b)$$

which is simply the cumulative standard force of mortality. Equation (4.7.30a) follows directly from the Fubini theorem [see Liptser and Shiryayev (1977, Vol. 1, p. 21)]. Here we have used the fact that the expectation of $R(t)$ is 1 as assumed in (4.7.14) and the property that the integral in (4.7.15) can be represented as the limiting form of a sum of an ever-increasing number of random variables. We assume that this limit exists as it would if $R(t)$ were governed by a Brownian motion process. With these restrictions on $R(t)$, we observe that the exponential function is a convex function of $h(t)$ so that the conditions of Jensen's inequality imply

$$\mathscr{E}_{H(t)|(0)}\{\exp[-y(0)h(t)]\} > \exp\left[-y(0)\int_0^t \mu(a|1)\,da\right], \quad (4.7.31)$$

where the integral on the right is due to (4.7.30b). In view of (4.7.28) and (4.7.29), we obtain the inequality

$$g_{Y(0)|(t)}(y(0)|(t)) > f_{Y(0)|(0)}(y(0)|(0)) \exp\left[-y(0)\int_0^t \mu(a|1)\,da\right]. \quad (4.7.32)$$

To interpret this fundamental inequality in terms of the fixed frailty model, we define a corresponding unnormalized density of $Z$ among survivors at time $t$. This is done by multiplying (4.6.15) by $S_T(t)$ and using (4.6.7) to replace $S_{T|Z}(t|z)$ with the exponential survival form

$$g_{Z|(t)}(z|(t)) = f_{Z|(0)}(z|(0)) \exp\left[-z\int_0^t \mu(a|1)\,da\right]. \quad (4.7.33)$$

Hence, setting $Z = Y(0)$ in (4.7.33), one obtains from (4.7.32) the following equivalent form of inequality:

$$g_{Y(0)|(t)}(y(0)|(t)) > g_{Z|(t)}(z|(t))|_{z=y(0)}. \quad (4.7.34)$$

Hence, the probability of surviving to time $t$ is greater for any value of $z$ under the diffusion model than under the fixed frailty model. Hence, on integration of (4.7.34), one obtains

$$\mathscr{E}_{Y(0)|(0)}\{S_{T|Y(0)}(t|y(0))\} > \mathscr{E}_{Z|(0)}\{S_{T|Z}(t|z)\}|_{z=y(0)}, \quad (4.7.35)$$

which simply states that the overall surviving proportion is greater under the diffusion model than under the fixed frailty model.

The preceding inequalities arise under the assumption of a common age trajectory of the standard force of mortality $\mu(t|1)$ in the two types of models. In actual application, one frequently observes the marginal survival function $S_T(t)$ so that equality in (4.7.35) is forced to occur, in which case the standard forces of mortality in the two types of models cannot be equal. By using $\mu^*(t|1)$ to represent the estimate of the standard force of mortality in the fixed frailty model and $\mu^{**}(t|1)$ to represent the estimate in the diffusion model, it is apparent that for equality to be attained in (4.7.35) the following condition must hold for all $t > 0$:

$$\mu^{**}(t|1) > \mu^*(t|1) > \mu(t),$$ (4.7.36)

where the second inequality is a restatement of (4.6.32). The substantive implication of (4.7.36) is that the effects of diffusion and population heterogeneity are incremental so that the marginal force of mortality in the risk set diverges away from the standard force of mortality when fixed heterogeneity is initially present but that the divergence is more rapid when both dynamics are simultaneously occurring. Diffusion does *not* cancel out the bias of population heterogeneity.

One can gain further insight into the effects of a diffusion process by considering how other results obtained for the fixed frailty model are modified. The conditional density of death at time $t$ can be written as

$$f_{T|Y(0),H(t),R(t)}(t|y(0), h(t), r(t))$$

$$= y(0)r(t)\mu(t|1) \exp[-y(0)h(t)].$$ (4.7.37)

The marginal density $f_T(t)$ is then obtained as in (4.6.23b) as the average of the conditional densities in (4.7.37) among the risk set members alive at time 0, or

$$f_T(t) = \mathscr{E}_{Y(0),H(t),R(t)|(0)}\{f_{T|Y(0),H(t),R(t)}(t|y(0), h(t), r(t))\}$$ (4.7.38a)

$$= \mu(t|1) \int_0^\infty \int_0^\infty \int_0^\infty y(0)r(t) \exp[-y(0)h(t)]$$

$$\times f_{H(t),R(t)|(0)}(h(t), r(t)|(0))$$

$$\times f_{Y(0)|(0)}(y(0)|(0)) \, dh(t) \, dr(t) \, dy(0).$$ (4.7.38b)

Equation (4.7.38b) can be simplified by replacing $y(0)$ with its value in (4.7.16), namely,

$$y(0) = y(t)/r(t),$$ (4.7.39)

and observing that the density of $Y(t)$ is of the form

$$f_{Y(t)|(t)}(y(t)|(t)) = \frac{1}{S_T(t)} \int_0^\infty f_{Y(0)|(0)}(y(t)/r(t)|(0))$$

$$\times f_{R(t)|(0)}(r(t)|(0))(1/r(t))$$

$$\times \left[ \int_0^\infty \exp[-y(t)h(t)/r(t)] \right.$$

$$\left. \times f_{H(t)|R(t),(0)}(h(t)|r(t), (0)) \, dh(t) \right] dr(t).$$ (4.7.40)

Thus, (4.7.38b) can be written as

$$f_T(t) = \mu(t|1) \left\{ \int_0^\infty y(t) f_{Y(t)|(t)}(y(t)|(t)) \, dy(t) \right\} S_T(t) \qquad (4.7.41a)$$

$$= \mu(t|1) \mathscr{E}_{Y(t)|(t)}(y(t)) S_T(t), \qquad (4.7.41b)$$

where $\mathscr{E}_{Y(t)|(t)}(y(t))$ is the average of $Y(t)$ among survivors to time $t$. By dividing both sides of (4.7.41b) by $S_T(t)$ and noting that the left side yields $\mu(t)$, we obtain

$$\mu(t) = \mathscr{E}_{Y(t)|(t)}(y(t)) \mu(t|1), \qquad (4.7.42)$$

which is an important generalization of (4.6.26) because it shows that the marginal force of mortality is the average of the individual forces of mortality even in the case where the risk variate $Y(t)$ is changing over time.

As the final task of this section we shall comment on the implications of the assumption that $R(t)$ is governed by a Brownian motion process. As seen in (4.7.14), we require that

$$\mathscr{E}_{R(t)|(0)}(r(t)) = 1, \qquad (4.7.43)$$

which simply states that we expect $Y(t)$ to have the same value as $Y(0)$, because (4.7.16) implies

$$\mathscr{E}_{Y(t)|Y(0),(0)}(y(t)|y(0)) = y(0) \mathscr{E}_{R(t)|(0)}(r(t)). \qquad (4.7.44)$$

If $B(t)$ is a Brownian motion process, then $b(t)$ is normally distributed with zero mean and variance given by

$$\text{var}_{B(t)}[b(t)] = t \, \text{var}_{B(t)}[b(1)] \qquad (4.7.45a)$$

$$= t\sigma_B^2, \qquad (4.7.45b)$$

where $\sigma_B^2$ denotes the variance of $B(t)$ in the unit time interval. Note that the variance in (4.7.45b) is proportional to $t$, not to $t^2$, so that the Brownian motion process involves the sum of independent increments over each subinterval in the range $(0, t)$. Condition (4.7.14) will be satisfied if

$$r(t) = \exp[b(t) - \tfrac{1}{2}t\sigma_B^2]. \qquad (4.7.46)$$

Because the Brownian motion process is additive, we also have the general form for any time interval $\Delta t = t_1 - t_0$:

$$r(\Delta t) = \exp[b(\Delta t) - \tfrac{1}{2} \Delta t \, \sigma_B^2], \qquad (4.7.47)$$

where $r(\Delta t)$ is a function only of the length of the interval, not the time coordinates $t_0$ or $t_1$. This means that we can shift the origin of the time interval to the point $t_0 = 0$ and use $t$ in place of $t_1$ without loss of generality.

Our main concern is with the change over time in $f_{Y(t)|(t)}(y(t)|(t))$ as diffusion and selective mortality simultaneously operate on this density. Hence, we are interested in the differential equation that generalizes (4.6.19) to the case of a diffusion process. Using (4.7.39) to define $y(0)$, we obtain the change in $Y(\cdot)$ as

$$\Delta y(t) = y(t) - y(0) \tag{4.7.48a}$$

$$= y(t)(1 - 1/r(t)). \tag{4.7.48b}$$

The following results are needed:

$$\mathscr{E}_{R(t)|(0)}(1/r(t)) = \exp(t\sigma_B^2), \tag{4.7.49}$$

$$\mathscr{E}_{R(t)|(0)}[(1 - 1/r(t))/r(t)] = \exp(t\sigma_B^2) - \exp(3t\sigma_B^2), \tag{4.7.50}$$

$$\mathscr{E}_{R(t)|(0)}[(1 - 1/r(t))^2/r(t)] = \exp(t\sigma_B^2) - 2\exp(3t\sigma_B^2) + \exp(6t\sigma_B^2). \tag{4.7.51}$$

We rewrite (4.7.40) in the form

$$f_{Y(t)|(t)}(y(t)|(t)) \doteq \int_0^\infty f_{Y(0)|(0)}(y(t)/r(t)|(0))$$

$$\times f_{R(t)|(0)}(r(t)|(0))(1/r(t))\, dr(t)$$

$$- \int_0^\infty f_{Y(0)|(0)}(y(t)/r(t)|(0))$$

$$\times f_{R(t)|(0)}(r(t)|(0))(1/r(t))$$

$$\times \int_0^\infty [y(t)h(t)/r(t) - \int_0^t \mu(a)\, da]$$

$$\times f_{H(t)|R(t),(0)}(h(t)|r(t),(0))\, dh(t)\, dr(t), \tag{4.7.52}$$

where the exponential term in (4.7.40) is expanded in a Taylor series with only the first two terms retained. Higher-order terms will be of order $o(t)$, which means that they converge to zero faster than $t$ and hence that the ratio $o(t)/t$ converges to zero as $t$ approaches zero.

To simplify (4.7.52), we replace $f_{Y(0)|(0)}(\cdot)$ in the first term with the three-term Taylor expansion

$$f_{Y(0)|(0)}(y(t)/r(t)|(0)) \doteq f_{Y(0)|(0)}(y(t)|(0))$$

$$- f'_{Y(0)|(0)}(y(t)|(0))y(t)$$

$$\times [1 - 1/r(t)] + \tfrac{1}{2}f''_{Y(0)|(0)}(y(t)|(0))$$

$$\times y^2(t)[1 - 1/r(t)]^2, \tag{4.7.53}$$

where prime denotes differentiation with respect to $y(t)$. We retain only the first terms of the Taylor expansions of $f_{Y(0)|(0)}(\cdot)$ and $1/r(t)$ in the second term of (4.7.52): this yields

$$f_{Y(t)|(t)}(y(t)|(t)) = f_{Y(0)|(0)}(y(t)|(0)) \exp(t\sigma_B^2) - f'_{Y(0)|(0)}(y(t)|(0))y(t)$$

$$\times \left[\exp(t\sigma_B^2) + \exp(3t\sigma_B^2)\right] + \frac{1}{2} f''_{Y(0)|(0)}(y(t)|(0))y^2(t)$$

$$\times \{\exp(t\sigma_B^2) - 2 \exp(3t\sigma_B^2) + \exp(6t\sigma_B^2)\}$$

$$+ \int_0^t [\mu(a) - \mu(a|y(t))] \, da \times f_{Y(0)|(0)}(y(t)|(0)) + o(t).$$

$$(4.7.54)$$

By letting $t$ approach 0, the following differential equation is obtained:

$$\frac{\partial}{\partial t} f_{Y(t)|(t)}(y(t)|(t)) = \sigma_B^2 f_{Y(t)|(t)}(y(t)|(t)) + 2y(t)\sigma_B^2 f'_{Y(t)|(t)}(y(t)|(t))$$

$$+ \frac{1}{2} y^2(t)\sigma_B^2 f''_{Y(t)|(t)}(y(t)|(t)) + [\mu(t) - \mu(t|y(t))]$$

$$\times f_{Y(t)|(t)}(y(t)|(t)). \qquad (4.7.55)$$

This equation can be used in projections of the density $f_{Y(t)|(t)}(y(t)|(t))$ forward in time in a manner analogous to the methods of Manton and Woodbury (1983). Naturally, this requires that the functional form of $f_{Y(t)|(t)}(y(t)|(t))$ be specified for some point in time $t = t_0$. Yashin *et al.* (1985) consider very general stochastic process models, of which (4.7.55) is a special case.

In examining (4.7.55), one can see that if the diffusion variance $\sigma_B^2$ becomes 0, then the form reduces to that of (4.6.19). Alternatively, if $\sigma_B^2$ is "small," then the first three terms of (4.7.55) may be small enough that $Y(t)$ may be treated as fixed for short time intervals.

One can also generalize (4.6.30b) to obtain the time derivative of the mean of $Y(t)$:

$$\frac{d}{dt} \mathcal{E}_{Y(t)|(t)}(y(t)) = \int_0^\infty y(t) \frac{\partial}{\partial t} f_{Y(t)|(t)}(y(t)|(t)) \, dy(t) \qquad (4.7.56a)$$

$$= \int_0^\infty y(t)[\mu(t) - \mu(t|y(t))]$$

$$\times f_{Y(t)|(t)}(y(t)|(t)) \, dy(t) \qquad (4.7.56b)$$

$$= -\mathrm{var}_{Y(t)|(t)}(y(t))\mu(t|1), \qquad (4.7.56c)$$

which is analogous to (4.6.31c). To obtain (4.7.56b), one need only consider that the first three terms of (4.7.55) describe a pure diffusion process with no change in the mean value. Hence, on integration only the final term is nonzero and that is the term shown in (4.7.56b). The expression in (4.5.56c) then is obtained by using the same steps as used in obtaining (4.6.31c) from (4.6.30c). The difference, however, is that the variance of $Y(t)$ in (4.7.56c) is subject to the effects of diffusion whereas the variance of $Z$ in (4.6.31c) is not.

## 8   Summary

In this chapter we have developed a conceptual framework for mortality analysis that is consistent with the most general process theories of morbidity and mortality. The mathematical apparatus for dealing with these concepts derives from the theory of stochastic processes. In the most general model, the mortality process is represented as a continuous-time–continuous-state stochastic process, with individuals exhibiting random trajectories through the state space and with death represented as the probabilistic removal of the individual from that space. By imposing a range of constraints or assumptions on this general model, one can develop specialized models appropriate for the analysis of specific types of mortality data. We have indicated the nature of these assumptions in the preceding sections of this chapter for analysis of total and cause-specific mortality and for analysis of the effects of cause elimination. Special attention was given to the role of the independence assumption in competing risk calculations. When independence cannot be assumed, the strategy proposed was to develop models in which the transition rates were conditionally independent. This strategy will likely involve elaboration of the model structure to include health states for which the entrance and exit transitions are not directly observable. Alternatively, the model structure may be elaborated to represent individual differences in health-state transition rates by using either a fixed frailty model or one in which frailty changes over time.

## References

Chiang, C. L. 1968. *Introduction to stochastic processes in biostatistics*. New York: Wiley.
David, H. A. 1970. On Chiang's proportionality assumptions in the theory of competing risks. *Biometrics* **26**:336–339.
Economos, A. C. 1982. Rate of aging, rate of dying and the mechanism of mortality. *Archives of Gerontology and Geriatrics* **1**:3–27.
Gail, M. 1975. A review and critique of some models used in competing risk analysis. *Biometrics* **31**:209–222.

Griffith, G. 1976. Cancer surveillance with particular reference to the uses of mortality data. *International Journal of Epidemiology* **5**:69–76.

Jacquez, J. A. 1972. *Compartment analysis in biology and medicine*. Amsterdam: Elsevier.

Jordan, C. W. 1975. *The Society of Actuaries textbook on life contingencies*. Chicago: Society of Actuaries.

Kendall, M. G., and Stuart, A. 1969. *The advanced theory of statistics*. New York: Hafner.

Liptser, R. S., and Shiryayev, A. N. 1977. *Statistics of random processes*. New York: Springer-Verlag.

Manton, K. G., and Stallard, E. 1980. A stochastic compartment model representation of chronic disease dependence: Techniques for evaluating parameters of partially unobserved age inhomogeneous stochastic processes. *Theoretical Population Biology* **18**:57–75.

Manton, K. G., Tolley, H. D., and Poss, S. S. 1976. Life table techniques for multiple-cause mortality. *Demography* **13**:541–564.

Manton, K. G., and Woodbury, M. A. 1983. Models of the process of risk factor change and risk selection for multiple disease endpoints in the Kaunas study population. Report for development of Integrated Programme for Noncommunicable Disease Prevention and Control, World Health Organization, Geneva.

Manton, K. G., Woodbury, M. A., and Stallard, E. 1979. Analysis of the components of CHD risk in the Framingham study: New multivariate procedures for the analysis of chronic disease development. *Computers and Biomedical Research* **12**:109–123.

Menken, J., Trussell, J., Stempel, D., and Babakol, O. 1981. Proportional hazards life table models: An illustrative analysis of socio-demographic influences on marriage dissolution in the United States. *Demography* **18**: 181–200.

Preston, S. H., Keyfitz, N., and Schoen, R. 1972. *Causes of death: Life tables for national populations*. New York and London: Seminar Press.

Sacher, G. A., and Trucco, E. 1962. The stochastic theory of mortality. *Annals of the New York Academy of Sciences* **96**:985–1007.

Schatzkin, A. 1980. How long can we live? A more optimistic view of potential gains in life expectancy. *American Journal of Public Health* **70**:1199–1200.

Sheps, M., and Menken, J. 1973. *Mathematical models of conception and birth*. Chicago: University of Chicago Press.

Trussell, J., and Hammerslough, C. 1983. A hazards model analysis of the covariates of infant and child mortality in Sri Lanka. *Demography* **20**:1–26.

Tsai, S. P., Lee, E. S., and Hardy, R. J. 1978. The effect of a reduction in leading causes of death: Potential gains in life expectancy. *American Journal of Public Health* **68**:966–971.

Woodbury, M. A., and Manton, K. G. 1977. A random walk model of human mortality and aging. *Theoretical Population Biology* **11**:37–48.

Woodbury, M. A., and Manton, K. G. 1982. Stochastic compartment models. In *Encyclopedia of statistical sciences* (S. Kotz, N. L. Johnson, and C. B. Read, eds.), Vol. 2, pp. 71–75. New York: Wiley.

Woodbury, M. A., Manton, K. G., and Stallard, E. 1979. Longitudinal analysis of the dynamics and risks of coronary heart disease in the Framingham study. *Biometrics* **35**:575–585.

Yashin, A. I., Manton, K. G., and Vaupel, J. W. 1985. Mortality and aging in a heterogeneous population: A stochastic process model with observed and unobserved variables. *Theoretical Population Biology* [in press (February 1985)].

# Chapter 5 | Life Table Methods for the Analysis of Underlying- and Multiple-Cause Mortality Data

## 1 Introduction

In this chapter we shall study a variety of life table methods for the analysis of cause-specific mortality data. These methods are based on multiple-decrement and cause-elimination life table models that should be familiar to demographers and actuaries who have studied underlying-cause mortality data. Application of these methods to multiple-cause mortality data, however, is novel and requires that modification and elaboration be given to the interpretation of the results derived from these models. In particular, it is necessary with multiple-cause data to pay special attention to definitions of risks as disease or disease combinations, to assumptions concerning independence of risks, and to the substantive interpretation of cause-elimination calculations.

A useful working hypothesis is that cause-specific mortality is best described as the end result of a discrete-state–continuous-time stochastic process for which end-result data are collected at regular age and time intervals. The properties of such processes have been described in the prior chapter, in which it was shown that the multiple-decrement life table derives from a variety of processes that can be characterized according to the following: (1) number and definitions of several unobserved health states, (2) assumptions concerning independence or dependence of various health-state transitions or changes, and (3) assumptions concerning the heterogeneity of individuals with regard to unobserved risk factors. Hence, the working hypothesis implies that interpretation of cause-specific life table analyses can be meaningfully made only when it is linked to the characteristics of the process that gives rise to the specific results. We

138

illustrate these ideas through analyses of life table parameters for five specific chronic diseases based on 1969 U.S. mortality and population data. These five diseases are cancer (ICDA-8, 140-209), diabetes mellitus (ICDA-8, 250), ischemic heart disease (ICDA-8, 410-414), stroke (ICDA-8, 430-438), and generalized arteriosclerosis (ICDA-8, 440).

As discussed in Chapters 2 and 3, the choice of the calendar year 1969 as the basis of these life tables results from the fact that the NCHS provided an early release of multiple-cause mortality data for 1969 for this study. With these data we have the requisite information to examine the role of chronic diseases both as underlying causes of death and as contributory causes of death. The selection of these particular five chronic diseases for analysis is based on their major role in mortality: numerically, these are among the most frequently reported chronic diseases in both underlying-cause and multiple-cause mortality tabulations (see Table 2, Chapter 3). Additionally, high frequencies of these diseases are observed in both race- and sex-specific tabulations, so that an important issue that can be addressed with numerical examples is the development of life table methods for assessing differentials in the age dependence of the force of mortality of such chronic diseases across the four race–sex-groups. Although the study of such demographic variation in cause-specific mortality is an important topic in its own right and provides a rationalization of the differential changes in total mortality over recent years, we also wish to emphasize that the developers of bioactuarial models of the population health state must be sensitive to these differentials and must include some mechanism for their representation in the models. Obviously, without an awareness of the precise nature of these demographic differentials, it would be difficult to select an appropriate mechanism for their bioactuarial representation.

This chapter is organized into seven sections. First, we shall present life tables for total mortality for the 1969 U.S. population stratified by race (white and black) and sex (male and female). These life tables provide a "baseline" for comparison with the cause-specific life tables. Second, we shall present the multiple-decrement life tables for the five specified chronic diseases. These tables include both underlying- and multiple-cause decrements. Third, we shall present the cause-elimination life tables for the independent competing risk model for both underlying- and multiple-cause definitions of mortality risks. Fourth, we shall present life table extensions that evaluate the effects of cause elimination on the specific subset of the population affected by such elimination rather than the total population effect. These methods are designed to assess the gains in life expectancy for the portion of the population that would be "saved" from death if the hypothetical elimination actually occurred.

Fifth, we shall present life table methods that generalize the concept of cause elimination to represent the effects of delaying the age at death due to a specific cause. These methods provide a strategy for evaluating the population health impact of specific biomedical innovations, which includes as a special case the standard impact assessment of the hypothetical but unlikely biomedical innovation that completely eliminates the disease as a mortality risk. Sixth, we shall present life table methods for extending the calculations on saved persons to represent the effects on persons with specific "background" chronic disabilities. These methods employ a conceptual approach explicitly based on the representation of disease dependency in a stochastic compartment model. Finally, the summary section will review the possible roles and dependencies between the four noncancer chronic diseases in causing death. Extensions of these methods to the analysis of other chronic degenerative diseases are also discussed.

## 2  Total Mortality

Table 1 is the complete current life table for the 1969 white male population. The most prominent feature of this table is its length. The descriptor *complete* refers not to the number of life table columns presented, but to the presentation of life table parameters by single years of age over the age range 0, 1, 2, ..., 98, 99+. The descriptor *current* means that the life table parameters refer to a given calendar year (1969) or period. Thus, the 100 age categories represent a cross section of the 1969 mortality experience of 100 cohorts (i.e., persons born in the same calendar year) born in 1870 or earlier and in 1871, 1872, ..., 1969. The use of such a cross section means that the life table is interpreted as applying not to any given cohort, but to a "synthetic cohort" derived from the cross section of the 100 cohorts employed in its construction. In Chapter 6 we shall examine the effects of population heterogeneity and differential rates of mortality selection across successive cohorts on the interpretation of the period life table as representing the mortality experience of a synthetic cohort. Although it will be seen that the period life table is somewhat biased if the cohorts are heterogeneous and mortality rates are declining over successive cohorts, we shall deal with the period life table in this chapter for four reasons. First, considerable effort is involved in producing disease-specific models to generate precise numerical estimates of the unbiased period life table for the five chronic diseases. Second, the most appropriate use for the adjusted period life table, which requires the evaluation of a number of substantive factors in making the adjustments, is to analyze the

**Table 1**

White Male Complete 1969 Current Life Table

| Age at start of interval $(x, x + 1)$, $x$ | Probability of dying in interval $(x, x + 1)$, $_1q_x$ | Number living at age $x$, $l_x$ | Number dying in interval $(x, x + 1)$, $_1d_x$ | Observed life expectancy at age $x$, $\overset{\circ}{e}_x$ | Cumulative force of mortality over interval $(x, x + 1)$, $_1h_x$ |
|---|---|---|---|---|---|
| 0 | 0.0209523 | 100,000 | 2,095 | 68.02 | 0.0211749 |
| 1 | 0.0011673 | 97,905 | 114 | 68.48 | 0.0011680 |
| 2 | 0.0008271 | 97,790 | 81 | 67.56 | 0.0008274 |
| 3 | 0.0007079 | 97,710 | 69 | 66.61 | 0.0007082 |
| 4 | 0.0005871 | 97,640 | 57 | 65.66 | 0.0005872 |
| 5 | 0.0005371 | 97,583 | 52 | 64.70 | 0.0005372 |
| 6 | 0.0005167 | 97,531 | 50 | 63.73 | 0.0005168 |
| 7 | 0.0004692 | 97,480 | 46 | 62.76 | 0.0004693 |
| 8 | 0.0004261 | 97,435 | 42 | 61.79 | 0.0004262 |
| 9 | 0.0004259 | 97,393 | 41 | 60.82 | 0.0004260 |
| 10 | 0.0003710 | 97,352 | 36 | 59.85 | 0.0003711 |
| 11 | 0.0003680 | 97,315 | 36 | 58.87 | 0.0003680 |
| 12 | 0.0004476 | 97,280 | 44 | 57.89 | 0.0004477 |
| 13 | 0.0005087 | 97,236 | 49 | 56.91 | 0.0005088 |
| 14 | 0.0006592 | 97,187 | 64 | 55.94 | 0.0006595 |
| 15 | 0.0008491 | 97,123 | 82 | 54.98 | 0.0008495 |
| 16 | 0.0012715 | 97,040 | 123 | 54.03 | 0.0012723 |
| 17 | 0.0015462 | 96,917 | 150 | 53.09 | 0.0015474 |
| 18 | 0.0019837 | 96,767 | 192 | 52.18 | 0.0019856 |
| 19 | 0.0020432 | 96,575 | 197 | 51.28 | 0.0020452 |
| 20 | 0.0019703 | 96,378 | 190 | 50.38 | 0.0019723 |
| 21 | 0.0019816 | 96,188 | 191 | 49.48 | 0.0019835 |
| 22 | 0.0020610 | 95,997 | 198 | 48.58 | 0.0020632 |
| 23 | 0.0018256 | 95,799 | 175 | 47.68 | 0.0018273 |
| 24 | 0.0017905 | 95,624 | 171 | 46.76 | 0.0017921 |
| 25 | 0.0017127 | 95,453 | 163 | 45.85 | 0.0017142 |
| 26 | 0.0016017 | 95,290 | 153 | 44.92 | 0.0016030 |
| 27 | 0.0015398 | 95,137 | 146 | 44.00 | 0.0015410 |
| 28 | 0.0017081 | 94,991 | 162 | 43.06 | 0.0017095 |
| 29 | 0.0016162 | 94,828 | 153 | 42.14 | 0.0016175 |
| 30 | 0.0016411 | 94,675 | 155 | 41.20 | 0.0016424 |
| 31 | 0.0017108 | 94,520 | 162 | 40.27 | 0.0017123 |
| 32 | 0.0016907 | 94,358 | 160 | 39.34 | 0.0016922 |
| 33 | 0.0018245 | 94,198 | 172 | 38.40 | 0.0018261 |
| 34 | 0.0019679 | 94,027 | 185 | 37.47 | 0.0019698 |
| 35 | 0.0020899 | 93,842 | 196 | 36.55 | 0.0020921 |
| 36 | 0.0022428 | 93,645 | 210 | 35.62 | 0.0022453 |
| 37 | 0.0025025 | 93,435 | 234 | 34.70 | 0.0025057 |

(*continued*)

**Table 1** (*Continued*)

| Age at start of interval $(x, x + 1)$, $x$ | Probability of dying in interval $(x, x + 1)$, $_1q_x$ | Number living at age $x$, $l_x$ | Number dying in interval $(x, x + 1)$, $_1d_x$ | Observed life expectancy at age $x$, $\overset{\circ}{e}_x$ | Cumulative force of mortality over interval $(x, x + 1)$, $_1h_x$ |
|---|---|---|---|---|---|
| 38 | 0.0027341 | 93,202 | 255 | 33.79 | 0.0027379 |
| 39 | 0.0029960 | 92,947 | 278 | 32.88 | 0.0030005 |
| 40 | 0.0033321 | 92,668 | 309 | 31.98 | 0.0033377 |
| 41 | 0.0035778 | 92,359 | 330 | 31.08 | 0.0035842 |
| 42 | 0.0041779 | 92,029 | 384 | 30.19 | 0.0041866 |
| 43 | 0.0045306 | 91,645 | 415 | 29.31 | 0.0045409 |
| 44 | 0.0049351 | 91,229 | 450 | 28.45 | 0.0049474 |
| 45 | 0.0055873 | 90,779 | 507 | 27.58 | 0.0056030 |
| 46 | 0.0059167 | 90,272 | 534 | 26.74 | 0.0059343 |
| 47 | 0.0066297 | 89,738 | 595 | 25.89 | 0.0066518 |
| 48 | 0.0071074 | 89,143 | 634 | 25.06 | 0.0071328 |
| 49 | 0.0079639 | 88,509 | 705 | 24.24 | 0.0079958 |
| 50 | 0.0087899 | 87,804 | 772 | 23.43 | 0.0088287 |
| 51 | 0.0098201 | 87,033 | 855 | 22.63 | 0.0098686 |
| 52 | 0.0106644 | 86,178 | 919 | 21.85 | 0.0107217 |
| 53 | 0.0119829 | 85,259 | 1,022 | 21.08 | 0.0120553 |
| 54 | 0.0130437 | 84,237 | 1,099 | 20.33 | 0.0131295 |
| 55 | 0.0142587 | 83,139 | 1,185 | 19.59 | 0.0143614 |
| 56 | 0.0159340 | 81,953 | 1,306 | 18.87 | 0.0160623 |
| 57 | 0.0171666 | 80,647 | 1,384 | 18.17 | 0.0173157 |
| 58 | 0.0189298 | 79,263 | 1,500 | 17.48 | 0.0191112 |
| 59 | 0.0203835 | 77,762 | 1,585 | 16.80 | 0.0205941 |
| 60 | 0.0219090 | 76,177 | 1,669 | 16.14 | 0.0221525 |
| 61 | 0.0245462 | 74,508 | 1,829 | 15.49 | 0.0248525 |
| 62 | 0.0269731 | 72,679 | 1,960 | 14.87 | 0.0273436 |
| 63 | 0.0281952 | 70,719 | 1,994 | 14.27 | 0.0286003 |
| 64 | 0.0311815 | 68,725 | 2,143 | 13.67 | 0.0316780 |
| 65 | 0.0349063 | 66,582 | 2,324 | 13.09 | 0.0355301 |
| 66 | 0.0359949 | 64,258 | 2,313 | 12.55 | 0.0366587 |
| 67 | 0.0400404 | 61,945 | 2,480 | 12.00 | 0.0408641 |
| 68 | 0.0437909 | 59,465 | 2,604 | 11.48 | 0.0447787 |
| 69 | 0.0462107 | 56,861 | 2,628 | 10.98 | 0.0473125 |
| 70 | 0.0498726 | 54,233 | 2,705 | 10.49 | 0.0511592 |
| 71 | 0.0540907 | 51,528 | 2,787 | 10.01 | 0.0556085 |
| 72 | 0.0578441 | 48,741 | 2,819 | 9.55 | 0.0595845 |
| 73 | 0.0607843 | 45,922 | 2,791 | 9.11 | 0.0627101 |
| 74 | 0.0645451 | 43,130 | 2,784 | 8.67 | 0.0667224 |
| 75 | 0.0723173 | 40,347 | 2,918 | 8.23 | 0.0750655 |
| 76 | 0.0757248 | 37,429 | 2,834 | 7.83 | 0.0787454 |

**Table 1** (*Continued*)

| Age at start of interval $(x, x + 1)$, $x$ | Probability of dying in interval $(x, x + 1)$, $_1q_x$ | Number living at age $x$, $l_x$ | Number dying in interval $(x, x + 1)$, $_1d_x$ | Observed life expectancy at age $x$, $\overset{\circ}{e}_x$ | Cumulative force of mortality over interval $(x, x + 1)$, $_1h_x$ |
|---|---|---|---|---|---|
| 77 | 0.0833550 | 34,595 | 2,884 | 7.44 | 0.0870350 |
| 78 | 0.0880640 | 31,711 | 2,793 | 7.07 | 0.0921855 |
| 79 | 0.0926741 | 28,918 | 2,680 | 6.70 | 0.0972536 |
| 80 | 0.1043485 | 26,238 | 2,738 | 6.33 | 0.1102039 |
| 81 | 0.1083951 | 23,500 | 2,547 | 6.01 | 0.1147322 |
| 82 | 0.1180333 | 20,953 | 2,473 | 5.68 | 0.1256010 |
| 83 | 0.1290414 | 18,480 | 2,385 | 5.38 | 0.1381608 |
| 84 | 0.1423236 | 16,095 | 2,291 | 5.10 | 0.1535284 |
| 85 | 0.1510931 | 13,805 | 2,086 | 4.86 | 0.1638058 |
| 86 | 0.1644481 | 11,719 | 1,927 | 4.64 | 0.1796628 |
| 87 | 0.1645237 | 9,792 | 1,611 | 4.45 | 0.1797533 |
| 88 | 0.1626120 | 8,181 | 1,330 | 4.23 | 0.1774678 |
| 89 | 0.1831088 | 6,850 | 1,254 | 3.96 | 0.2022494 |
| 90 | 0.2063161 | 5,596 | 1,155 | 3.73 | 0.2310700 |
| 91 | 0.2184424 | 4,441 | 970 | 3.57 | 0.2464665 |
| 92 | 0.2346818 | 3,471 | 815 | 3.43 | 0.2674636 |
| 93 | 0.2611492 | 2,657 | 694 | 3.33 | 0.3026593 |
| 94 | 0.2344391 | 1,963 | 460 | 3.33 | 0.2671465 |
| 95 | 0.2308577 | 1,503 | 347 | 3.20 | 0.2624793 |
| 96 | 0.2584335 | 1,156 | 299 | 3.00 | 0.2989904 |
| 97 | 0.2619608 | 857 | 225 | 2.88 | 0.3037583 |
| 98 | 0.2716418 | 633 | 172 | 2.72 | 0.3169623 |
| 99 | 1.0000000 | 461 | 461 | 2.55 | |

morbidity–mortality process of each disease independently. Third, in using the period life table as a baseline for comparison with cause-specific life tables, we shall be concerned primarily with *differences* in life table parameters. This suggests that if two life table parameters are equally biased, their difference will be unbiased and hence will provide a valid indication of the population mortality effect of the given mortality risk. Finally, many of our mortality comparisons will be made at middle age and early old age during which any effects of heterogeneity will still be small.

The 1969 white male life table consists of six columns, five of which are presented in most published life tables and a sixth column that is directly related to the stochastic compartment model representation of total mortality (Chapter 4, Fig. 1). The five standard columns are the age category and the $q_x$, $l_x$, $d_x$, and $\overset{\circ}{e}_x$ columns; the new column is the $h_x$ column. Note that with the exception of the $\overset{\circ}{e}_x$ column, these parameters have been described in Chapter 4 in the context of cohort life table interpretations. However, because of the "synthetic cohort" interpretation of the period life table, it will be useful to reconsider the meaning of these quantities. We also need to consider the data and methods of constructing these life tables from available mortality and population data.

## Data

Total and cause-specific life tables for a given period (e.g., calendar year or set of calendar years) can be constructed with two types of data. The first is the mortality data, which needs to be tabulated by age, race, sex, and cause. This topic was discussed in Chapter 3, in which it was indicated that questions of disease definition can be resolved by consideration of both underlying-cause and pattern-of-failure tabulation methods. We shall employ the symbol $_nD_x^{1969}$ with the year as a superscript to denote the total number of deaths in the age interval $x$ to $x + n$ in the year 1969 for an arbitrary race–sex-group. For cause-specific mortality counts we shall employ the symbol $_nD_{x\lambda}^{1969}$ to denote the mortality counts for the given cause and $_nD_{x\nu}^{1969}$ to denote the mortality counts for all remaining causes. In dealing with single year of age mortality data (i.e., $n = 1$) for a given calendar year, we shall simplify the symbols to $D_x$, $D_{x\lambda}$, and $D_{x\nu}$. Given these definitions, it follows that $D_x$ is simply the sum of deaths due to the cause of interest and deaths due to all other causes:

$$D_x = D_{x\lambda} + D_{x\nu}. \tag{5.2.1}$$

Note also that the subscripts $\lambda$ and $\nu$ were chosen to be consistent with the description of the stochastic compartment model in Chapter 4, Fig. 2.

The second type of data required for life table construction is the set of age-specific population counts to represent the number of persons at risk to mortality. While it can be anticipated that the mortality data provide virtually 100% coverage of the deaths in the population, the available counts of the population are known to have serious errors in terms of underenumeration, age misreporting, and race misclassification. Siegel (1974) provides a "preferred" set ("set D, adjusted") of age-, race-, and sex-specific adjustment factors, which we employed in adjusting the April 1, 1970, published population counts for these errors. The Siegel adjustments were for 5-year age-groups up to age 74 with an aggregate adjustment for ages 75+, so that it may be anticipated that some residual age misreporting errors remained in these data. The overall adjustment was 2.5% for white males and 1.4% for white females; substantially larger adjustments of 9.9 and 5.5% were indicated for black males and black females, respectively.

In attempting to obtain reliable population counts by each year of age up to age 109, we encountered two additional difficulties. First, for ages 85 to 99, the published census counts were by 5-year age-groups. Second, for ages 100 and over, the published census counts were the totals for this age category and were grossly exaggerated due to a misunderstanding on the part of a substantial number of respondents (about 100,000 persons) on the procedure for indicating age. To deal with the first difficulty, we employed the public use sample (PUS) 1-in-100 computer tapes to estimate the single-year age distributions within each of the three 5-year age categories: 85–89, 90–94, and 95–99. These tapes are made available for statistical analysis by the U.S. Bureau of the Census and contain a 1% sample of the complete decennial census data files for individual residents of the United States. A pro rata adjustment was employed to match the single and 5-year age totals. With the Siegel (1974) adjustment for ages 75+ applied to the 85–99-year age-groups, this yielded our working estimates of population counts by single years of age in the age range 0–99.

With chronic disease mortality primarily affecting the elderly population, we wished to extend the working age range out to 109 years of age. Given the unreliable nature of the census counts for ages 100 and over, we decided not to employ the PUS counts but instead to employ the 1969 mortality counts at and beyond age 100 to estimate this missing data. The basic idea employed was very simple and is known as an *extinct cohort* method (Rosenwaike, 1979, 1981). The population at age 109, $P_{109}$, was assumed to be equal to the number of deaths at age 109 or older:

$$P_{109} = D_{109+} . \tag{5.2.2}$$

Then, under the assumption of a stable population above age 100 (an assumption that also justifies use of 1969 mortality counts), the following recursive estimates were obtained:

$$P_{108} = P_{109} + D_{108} ,$$
$$P_{107} = P_{108} + D_{107} , \tag{5.2.3}$$
$$\vdots$$
$$P_{100} = P_{101} + D_{100} .$$

A strict interpretation of stable population dynamics would require that each estimated $P_x$ in (5.2.3) be deflated by an amount approximately one-half the number of deaths at that age, i.e., by $\frac{1}{2}D_x$. We did not make this adjustment because the actual population is not stable but is increasing in size. With this procedure it was possible to extend the working age range up to age 109+, although because of the greater uncertainty surrounding these data, we terminated our life tables at age 99 and used these additional data only to compute the final life expectancy at age 99.

With the adjusted single-year age population estimates corresponding to April 1, 1970, a backward projection method was employed to generate population estimates corresponding to July 1, 1969. For this purpose, we employed the formula

$$P_x^{1969} = 0.75P_{x+1}^{1970} + 0.25P_x^{1970} + 0.75D_x^{1969}. \tag{5.2.4}$$

Note that $P_x^{1970}$ refers to the adjusted census counts for the age interval $x$ to $x + 1$ on April 1, 1970, but that $P_x^{1969}$ refers to the midyear estimate for July 1, 1969. With these estimates, it was possible to estimate denominators $N_x^{1969}$ for mortality rates by using the simple formula

$$N_x^{1969} = P_x^{1969} + 0.5D_x^{1969}, \tag{5.2.5}$$

so that $N_x$ represents the January 1 estimate of the population who, if they survived to the following July 1, would, on average, report their age as the value $x$, that is, in the interval $(x, x + 1)$. A more refined treatment would attempt to improve on the approximations (5.2.4) and (5.2.5). However, given the major adjustments already employed for census underenumeration, race misclassification, and age misreporting, it would be difficult to justify such refinements as substantive improvements.

### Life Table Construction

The current life tables for total mortality are constructed from the entries in the $q_x$ column. These $q_x$'s are derived from the mortality and population data via the equation

$$q_x = D_x/N_x. \tag{5.2.6}$$

Thus, $q_x$ represents the observed probability of death in the age interval $x$ to $x + 1$. The $h_x$ column is derived from the $q_x$ column by a logarithmic transformation

$$h_x = -\ln(1 - q_x). \tag{5.2.7}$$

As discussed in Chapter 4, $h_x$ represents the observed cumulative force of mortality over the age interval $(x, x + 1)$, that is,

$$h_x = \int_x^{x+1} \mu(a)\, da. \tag{5.2.8}$$

In Table 1, it can be seen that $q_x$ and $h_x$ are virtually identical when $q_x$ is less than 0.05. Note, however, that at the older ages the values of $h_x$ are substantially higher than the corresponding $q_x$'s. These differences reflect the fact that $q_x$ is a probability measure that must be contained in the range 0 to 1 while $h_x$ is unbounded above.

The $l_x$ and $d_x$ columns are derived from the $q_x$ column via the recursive formulas

$$d_x = l_x q_x,$$ (5.2.9)

and

$$l_{x+1} = l_x - d_x,$$ (5.2.10)

where the initial birth cohort size or *radix* value $l_0$ is arbitrarily set to the value 100,000 persons and each entry in the $l_x$ and $d_x$ columns is then rounded to the nearest integer value. Thus, the interpretation of these two columns is based on the application of the mortality schedule implied by the $q_x$ column to a synthetic cohort of 100,000 persons.

The $\overset{\circ}{e}_x$ column represents the age-specific life expectancy in this synthetic cohort. For example, Table 1 shows that at birth $\overset{\circ}{e}_0$ is 68.02 years. This figure represents the average number of years to be lived by white males born in 1969 if the age-specific mortality probabilities faced by these persons remain at the values reported in the $q_x$ column. Alternatively, this figure represents the average age at death $X$ for the members of the synthetic cohort. In terms of the age at death probability density $f(x)$ discussed in Chapter 4, we have the interpretation

$$\overset{\circ}{e}_0 = \mathscr{E}(x)$$ (5.2.11a)

$$= \int_0^\infty x f(x) \, dx.$$ (5.2.11b)

The life expectancy at other ages represents the number of years yet to be lived by persons alive at the specified age. For example, at age 65, $\overset{\circ}{e}_{65}$ is 13.09 years. This figure indicates that white males who are exactly age 65 in 1969 will, on average, live to age 78.09 if the age-specific mortality probabilities in the $q_x$ column apply. Alternatively, this figure may be interpreted as representing the difference between the average age at death for persons who die past age 65 and the current age of these persons (i.e., 65).

In general, for any age we can interpret $\overset{\circ}{e}_x$ as

$$\overset{\circ}{e}_x = \left[ \int_x^\infty (a - x) f(a) \, da \right] \Big/ \left[ \int_x^\infty f(a) \, da \right].$$ (5.2.12)

The normalizing constant formed by the denominator of (5.2.12) is the probability $_x p_0$ that an individual just born will die after age $x$. Evaluation of (5.2.12) requires a discrete-time approximation to the integral in the numerator. To generate such an approximation, observe that Eq. (4.3.37b) implies

$$d_x = l_0 \int_x^{x+1} f(a) \, da. \tag{5.2.13}$$

With (5.2.13) we can approximate (5.2.12) by introducing an age-specific constant $b_x$ to represent the fraction of each age interval lived by the $d_x$ persons who die in that age interval. Hence,

$$\overset{\circ}{e}_x = \frac{1}{l_x} \sum_{i=x}^{\omega} (i + b_i - x) \, d_i. \tag{5.2.14}$$

In general, we set $b_x = 0.5$ to represent a midpoint approximation. However, Chiang (1968) suggests that below age 5 the approximation is improved by setting $b_0 = 0.10$, $b_1 = 0.43$, $b_2 = 0.45$, $b_3 = 0.47$, and $b_4 = 0.49$. The final age category $\omega$ (age 109 or more) is open ended. To deal with this, we assume that the hazard rate $\mu(a)$, $a > \omega - 1$ is constant and can be approximated by $h_{\omega-1}$, which represents the last computed hazard rate. This assumption yields

$$b_\omega = 1/h_{\omega-1}. \tag{5.2.15}$$

This approximation has the advantage of permitting both total and cause-elimination life tables to be *closed out* in an identical manner. In addition, this assumption appears to be consistent with empirical data (Wilkin, 1981). The final reported $q_x$ is set to 1.0, by convention.

Although we closed out these life tables at age 109, we report life-table parameters only up to age 99. Only the parameter $\overset{\circ}{e}_{99}$ is affected by this because (5.2.15) would yield an estimate of 3.15 years whereas (5.2.14) produced the 2.55-year estimate actually obtained. This shows that the final life expectancies are sensitive to the age at which the life table is closed out. Furthermore, in interpreting these life table parameters, it is necessary to distinguish between numerical and statistical precision. For example, both the $q_x$ and $h_x$ columns are printed with seven significant digits. This is because we will use these tables in comparisons with cause-specific life tables and hence will be concerned with differences in the various life table parameters. The underlying computations were carried out with 14-decimal-digit floating point precision, which implies that the printed 7 decimal digits are numerically precise. In contrast, the statistical precision of these data is influenced to an unknown degree by the effects of age misreporting in both mortality and population data as well as by the effects of census underenumeration (Siegel, 1974). Thus, whereas the life expectancy at birth is shown to be 68.02 years, these enumeration and age misreporting effects suggest that we interpret this numerically precise quantity as representing a life expectancy of *about* 68 years.

## Abbreviated Life Tables

Because of its length, a complete life table such as the one presented in Table 1 is often difficult to work with. Table 2 contains a more manageable, abbreviated version of the complete current life table for the 1969 U.S. white male population. This life table presents the life table parameters by 5-year age categories in the range 0–4, 5–9, 10–14, ..., 90–94, and 95+. Here we need to distinguish between the terms *abbreviated* and *abridged*. The latter term is often used to describe life tables with 5-year age categories. However, the computations of the $q_x$ column in these

**Table 2**

White Male Abbreviated 1969 Current Life Table

| Age at start of interval $(x, x + 5)$, $x$ | Probability of dying in interval $(x, x + 5)$, $_5q_x$ | Number living at age $x$, $l_x$ | Number dying in interval $(x, x + 5)$, $_5d_x$ | Observed life expectancy at age $x$, $\overset{\circ}{e}_x$ | Cumulative force of mortality over interval $(x, x + 5)$, $_5h_x$ |
|---|---|---|---|---|---|
| 0 | 0.0241688 | 100,000 | 2,417 | 68.02 | 0.0244657 |
| 5 | 0.0023727 | 97,583 | 232 | 64.70 | 0.0023755 |
| 10 | 0.0023522 | 97,352 | 229 | 59.85 | 0.0023550 |
| 15 | 0.0076705 | 97,123 | 745 | 54.98 | 0.0077000 |
| 20 | 0.0095920 | 96,378 | 924 | 50.38 | 0.0096383 |
| 25 | 0.0081519 | 95,453 | 778 | 45.85 | 0.0081853 |
| 30 | 0.0088038 | 94,675 | 833 | 41.20 | 0.0088428 |
| 35 | 0.0125026 | 93,842 | 1,173 | 36.55 | 0.0125814 |
| 40 | 0.0203861 | 92,668 | 1,889 | 31.98 | 0.0205968 |
| 45 | 0.0327687 | 90,779 | 2,975 | 27.58 | 0.0333177 |
| 50 | 0.0531398 | 87,804 | 4,666 | 23.43 | 0.0546038 |
| 55 | 0.0837304 | 83,139 | 6,961 | 19.59 | 0.0874447 |
| 60 | 0.1259581 | 76,177 | 9,595 | 16.14 | 0.1346269 |
| 65 | 0.1854700 | 66,582 | 12,349 | 13.09 | 0.2051440 |
| 70 | 0.2560524 | 54,233 | 13,887 | 10.49 | 0.2957847 |
| 75 | 0.3496762 | 40,347 | 14,108 | 8.23 | 0.4302849 |
| 80 | 0.4738802 | 26,238 | 12,434 | 6.33 | 0.6422263 |
| 85 | 0.5946235 | 13,805 | 8,208 | 4.86 | 0.9029390 |
| 90 | 0.7314736 | 5,596 | 4,093 | 3.73 | 1.3148059 |
| 95 | 1.0000000 | 1,503 | 1,503 | 3.20 | |

abridged life tables are based on mortality and population counts that are tabulated by 5-year age intervals.

In contrast, our abbreviated life tables are based on the complete life table $q_x$ columns already described. The $l_x$ and $\overset{\circ}{e}_x$ columns are identical to the complete life tables. The $q_x$, $d_x$, and $h_x$ columns are computed from the complete life table as follows:

$$_5q_x = 1 - \prod_{i=x}^{x+4} (1 - q_i), \tag{5.2.16}$$

$$_5d_x = \sum_{i=x}^{x+4} d_i, \tag{5.2.17}$$

$$_5h_x = \sum_{i=x}^{x+4} h_i. \tag{5.2.18}$$

**Table 3**

White Female Abbreviated 1969 Current Life Table

| Age at start of interval $(x, x + 5)$, $x$ | Probability of dying in interval $(x, x + 5)$, $_5q_x$ | Number living at age $x$, $l_x$ | Number dying in interval $(x, x + 5)$, $_5d_x$ | Observed life expectancy at age $x$, $\overset{\circ}{e}_x$ | Cumulative force of mortality over interval $(x, x + 5)$, $_5h_x$ |
|---|---|---|---|---|---|
| 0 | 0.0186882 | 100,000 | 1,869 | 75.60 | 0.0188650 |
| 5 | 0.0016456 | 98,131 | 161 | 72.03 | 0.0016469 |
| 10 | 0.0014477 | 97,970 | 142 | 67.14 | 0.0014487 |
| 15 | 0.0028786 | 97,828 | 282 | 62.24 | 0.0028828 |
| 20 | 0.0032555 | 97,546 | 318 | 57.41 | 0.0032608 |
| 25 | 0.0034620 | 97,229 | 337 | 52.59 | 0.0034680 |
| 30 | 0.0048499 | 96,892 | 470 | 47.76 | 0.0048617 |
| 35 | 0.0074379 | 96,422 | 717 | 42.98 | 0.0074657 |
| 40 | 0.0119021 | 95,705 | 1,139 | 38.28 | 0.0119735 |
| 45 | 0.0181598 | 94,566 | 1,717 | 33.71 | 0.0183267 |
| 50 | 0.0272998 | 92,849 | 2,535 | 29.29 | 0.0276794 |
| 55 | 0.0394963 | 90,314 | 3,567 | 25.04 | 0.0402975 |
| 60 | 0.0582065 | 86,747 | 5,049 | 20.96 | 0.0599693 |
| 65 | 0.0934684 | 81,698 | 7,636 | 17.09 | 0.0981294 |
| 70 | 0.1470946 | 74,061 | 10,894 | 13.58 | 0.1591067 |
| 75 | 0.2292921 | 63,167 | 14,484 | 10.46 | 0.2604458 |
| 80 | 0.3578315 | 48,684 | 17,421 | 7.80 | 0.4429045 |
| 85 | 0.5174306 | 31,263 | 16,176 | 5.73 | 0.7286305 |
| 90 | 0.6751875 | 15,087 | 10,186 | 4.29 | 1.1245071 |
| 95 | 1.0000000 | 4,900 | 4,900 | 3.64 | |

In particular, it should be noted that (5.2.16) and (5.2.18) maintain the relationship (5.2.7) in these abbreviated life tables:

$$_5h_x = -\ln(1 - {_5q_x}).$$  (5.2.19)

Tables 3, 4, and 5 contain the corresponding abbreviated life tables for white females, black males, and black females in the 1969 U.S. population. These life tables were computed by the same methods as employed in computing the abbreviated life tables for white males.

Examination of these tables shows that although there is a substantial race difference in life expectancy, there are also substantial sex differences within each race group. For example, Table 2 shows a white male life expectancy $\overset{\circ}{e}_0$ of 68.02 years. For white females, Table 3 shows a life expectancy of 75.60 years (7.58 years more). Black males have the lowest

**Table 4**

Black Male Abbreviated 1969 Current Life Table

| Age at start of interval $(x, x + 5)$, $x$ | Probability of dying in interval $(x, x + 5)$, $_5q_x$ | Number living at age $x$, $l_x$ | Number dying in interval $(x, x + 5)$, $_5d_x$ | Observed life expectancy at age $x$, $\overset{\circ}{e}_x$ | Cumulative force of mortality over interval $(x, x + 5)$, $_5h_x$ |
|---|---|---|---|---|---|
| 0 | 0.0440850 | 100,000 | 4,408 | 61.20 | 0.0450863 |
| 5 | 0.0032606 | 95,592 | 312 | 59.00 | 0.0032659 |
| 10 | 0.0035107 | 95,280 | 335 | 54.18 | 0.0035169 |
| 15 | 0.0116957 | 94,945 | 1,110 | 49.37 | 0.0117647 |
| 20 | 0.0186138 | 93,835 | 1,747 | 44.92 | 0.0187892 |
| 25 | 0.0192873 | 92,088 | 1,776 | 40.72 | 0.0194757 |
| 30 | 0.0245602 | 90,312 | 2,218 | 36.47 | 0.0248668 |
| 35 | 0.0327825 | 88,094 | 2,888 | 32.32 | 0.0333319 |
| 40 | 0.0463570 | 85,206 | 3,950 | 28.33 | 0.0474659 |
| 45 | 0.0619329 | 81,256 | 5,032 | 24.58 | 0.0639338 |
| 50 | 0.0919093 | 76,224 | 7,006 | 21.04 | 0.0964110 |
| 55 | 0.1200187 | 69,218 | 8,307 | 17.90 | 0.1278547 |
| 60 | 0.1638779 | 60,911 | 9,982 | 15.00 | 0.1789806 |
| 65 | 0.2450537 | 50,929 | 12,480 | 12.44 | 0.2811086 |
| 70 | 0.3020202 | 38,448 | 11,612 | 10.67 | 0.3595652 |
| 75 | 0.3386832 | 26,836 | 9,089 | 9.22 | 0.4135222 |
| 80 | 0.4364471 | 17,747 | 7,746 | 7.76 | 0.5734941 |
| 85 | 0.4803913 | 10,002 | 4,805 | 6.91 | 0.6546793 |
| 90 | 0.5113686 | 5,197 | 2,658 | 6.33 | 0.7161468 |
| 95 | 1.0000000 | 2,539 | 2,539 | 5.57 | |

**Table 5**

Black Female Abbreviated 1969 Current Life Table

| Age at start of interval $(x, x + 5)$, $x$ | Probability of dying in interval $(x, x + 5)$, $_5q_x$ | Number living at age $x$, $l_x$ | Number dying in interval $(x, x + 5)$, $_5d_x$ | Observed life expectancy at age $x$, $\overset{\circ}{e}_x$ | Cumulative force of mortality over interval $(x, x + 5)$, $_5h_x$ |
|---|---|---|---|---|---|
| 0 | 0.0358844 | 100,000 | 3,588 | 69.06 | 0.0365440 |
| 5 | 0.0022567 | 96,412 | 218 | 66.61 | 0.0022593 |
| 10 | 0.0020091 | 96,194 | 193 | 61.76 | 0.0020111 |
| 15 | 0.0046776 | 96,001 | 449 | 56.88 | 0.0046885 |
| 20 | 0.0066383 | 95,552 | 634 | 52.13 | 0.0066604 |
| 25 | 0.0087377 | 94,917 | 829 | 47.46 | 0.0087761 |
| 30 | 0.0138393 | 94,088 | 1,302 | 42.86 | 0.0139360 |
| 35 | 0.0209767 | 92,786 | 1,946 | 38.42 | 0.0211999 |
| 40 | 0.0309826 | 90,840 | 2,814 | 34.19 | 0.0314727 |
| 45 | 0.0410455 | 88,025 | 3,613 | 30.20 | 0.0419116 |
| 50 | 0.0580883 | 84,412 | 4,903 | 26.38 | 0.0598438 |
| 55 | 0.0759988 | 79,509 | 6,043 | 22.84 | 0.0790419 |
| 60 | 0.1097722 | 73,466 | 8,065 | 19.51 | 0.1162779 |
| 65 | 0.1742782 | 65,402 | 11,398 | 16.60 | 0.1914974 |
| 70 | 0.1981905 | 54,004 | 10,703 | 14.58 | 0.2208842 |
| 75 | 0.2171336 | 43,301 | 9,402 | 12.56 | 0.2447932 |
| 80 | 0.2973035 | 33,899 | 10,078 | 10.37 | 0.3528302 |
| 85 | 0.3523964 | 23,820 | 8,394 | 8.71 | 0.4344765 |
| 90 | 0.4421612 | 15,426 | 6,821 | 7.12 | 0.5836853 |
| 95 | 1.0000000 | 8,605 | 8,605 | 5.87 | |

life expectancy, 61.20 years (Table 4), whereas black females have a 69.06-year life expectancy (7.86 years more than the black males).

If instead of examining life expectancy at birth we examine the life expectancies at older ages, then the sex differentials tend to be the dominant demographic differential. For example, at age 65, $\overset{\circ}{e}_{65}$ is 13.09 for white males and 12.44 for black males; $\overset{\circ}{e}_{65}$ is 17.09 for white females and 16.60 for black females.

A more complete picture of these race–sex differentials can be obtained by examining Fig. 1, which contains plots of the distributions of ages at death for the four race–sex groups. Before examining these plots, however, it will be useful to contrast our life tables with official life tables produced by the NCHS. This will be of aid in developing a feel for the actual level of precision to be attributed to these life table parameters. The most closely matched life tables produced by the NCHS are the official

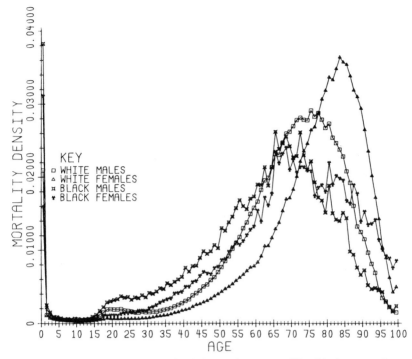

**Fig. 1.** Distributions of age at death in 1969 complete current life table, by sex and race.

U.S. decennial life tables for 1969 to 1971 (NCHS, 1975). These life tables are based on the average of 3 years of mortality data, centered on 1970, which is 1 year later than for our life tables. Two other important differences in methods need to be noted. First, whereas our population data were adjusted by using the Siegel (1974) adjustments for undercount, the NCHS data were not. Second, at ages 95 and over (and in some cases at ages 85–94), the NCHS life tables were based on death rates derived from the Medicare program, not from the ratio of mortality and census counts. Despite these methodological differences, the life tables for the white population exhibit a remarkable degree of similarity. For white males, the NCHS reported a 67.94-year life expectancy; we estimated 68.02 years. At age 65, the NCHS reported a 13.02-year life expectancy; we estimated 13.09 years. For white females, the correspondence was also good: at birth, 75.49 years (NCHS) versus 75.60 years; at age 65, 16.93 years (NCHS) versus 17.09 years. For the black population, some sizable differences were noted that appear primarily to be a result of the large undercount adjustments [i.e., 9.9% for males or 5.5% for females (Siegel,

1974)], which we made to the population counts for blacks but which were not made by NCHS. For black males, the life expectancy comparisons are: at birth, 60.00 years (NCHS data) versus 61.20 years; at 65, 12.53 years (NCHS) versus 12.44 years. For black females, the life expectancy comparisons are: at birth, 68.32 years (NCHS) versus 69.06 years; at 65, 15.67 years (NCHS) versus 16.60 years. Hence, these differences in the life expectancy estimates for blacks suggest that a reasonable confidence interval should have a range of up to 1 year or more. With these caveats in mind, we can now turn our attention to Fig. 1.

The four plots in Fig. 1 are derived from the complete life table by using the following approximation based on Eq. (4.3.37b):

$$f(x + \tfrac{1}{2}) = d_x/l_0. \tag{5.2.20}$$

Here it is seen that white females have the greatest ages at death as well as the most peaked distribution. The distributions for white males and females are, relatively, much smoother than for black males and females. This reflects the greater stability in the $d_x$'s induced by the larger white population counts. For example, for white females, $d_{65}$ is based on a population count of 747,685; for black females, $d_{65}$ is based on a population count of 61,926.

The average age at death for each race–sex-group is the $\overset{\circ}{e}_0$ value reported in Tables 2–5. However, as shown in Fig. 1, there is a large component of infant and childhood mortality. Hence, comparisons of adult mortality might be better summarized by considering the life expectancy at some other age. For example, at age 10, the life expectancies in Tables 2–5 are 59.85, 67.14, 54.18, and 61.76, respectively, which implies an average age at death of 69.85, 77.14, 64.18, and 71.76. Here we see that black females have an average age at death 1.91 years greater than white males, that is, $71.76 - 69.85 = 1.91$. However, Fig. 1 also shows that the distribution for U.S. black females is much flatter than for U.S. white males, which explains the 3.51-year life expectancy differential at age 65 for these two groups, that is, $16.60 - 13.09 = 3.51$.

As discussed, representation of mortality risks in terms of the distribution of ages at death is mathematically equivalent to representation of the stochastic compartment model in terms of the transition rate $\mu(x)$. Nonetheless, because we deal with a stochastic process, we need to think of the transition rates as the fundamental quantities of interest. To see this, consider Fig. 2, which contains plots of the hazard rates for the four race–sex-groups based on the approximation

$$\mu(x + \tfrac{1}{2}) = h_x, \tag{5.2.21}$$

where $h_x$ is obtained from the complete life table for each race–sex-group.

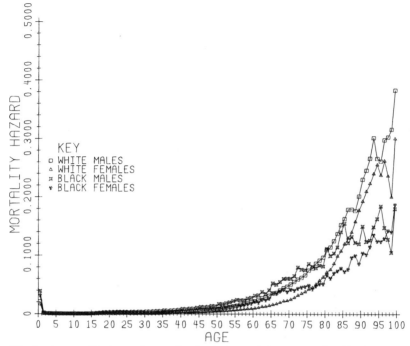

**Fig. 2.** Age-specific force of mortality in 1969 complete current life table, by sex and race.

Three comments need to be made. First, it is seen that all four race–sex-groups exhibit a substantial increase in the force of mortality with increasing age. Second, within race, males have higher hazard rates than females at almost every age. Third, within sex, blacks have substantially higher mortality hazards than whites at early ages. However, beyond about age 75, blacks have lower mortality hazards than whites. This latter observation has been termed the "black–white crossover" phenomenon and has been the subject of much recent debate over whether it is in fact "real" and, if so, how one explains the phenomenon in the face of the known socioeconomic and biomedical disadvantages of blacks at all ages in the U.S. population. The next chapter will review evidence of the validity of the crossover and review a range of biological mechanisms that could contribute to its occurrence. Specific numerical calculations will be developed under the assumptions of a fixed frailty model of the type considered in Section 6 of Chapter 4. Some substantive implications of the alternative explanations of the crossover will be identified.

## 3   Multiple-Decrement Life Tables

As discussed in Chapter 4, the transformation of stochastic compartment models from continuous to discrete time leads to the multiple-decrement decomposition of the complete life table for total mortality.

### *Methods*

With cause-specific mortality counts denoted by $D_{x\lambda}$ (cause of interest) and $D_{x\nu}$ (all other causes), the corresponding life table quantities $d_{x\lambda}$ and $d_{x\nu}$ are computed as follows:

$$d_{x\lambda} = d_x(D_{x\lambda}/D_x),  \tag{5.3.1}$$

and

$$d_{x\nu} = d_x(D_{x\nu}/D_x).  \tag{5.3.2}$$

The multiple-decrement survivorship columns are computed by using Eqs. (4.4.14) and (4.4.15), that is,

$$l_{x\lambda} = \sum_{i=x}^{\omega} d_{i\lambda} ,  \tag{5.3.3}$$

and

$$l_{x\nu} = \sum_{i=x}^{\omega} d_{i\nu} .  \tag{5.3.4}$$

The multiple-decrement mortality rate columns are computed by using

$$q_{x\lambda} = d_{x\lambda}/l_x ,  \tag{5.3.5}$$

and

$$q_{x\nu} = d_{x\nu}/l_x .  \tag{5.3.6}$$

The multiple-decrement hazard rate columns are computed by using

$$h_{x\lambda} = h_x(D_{x\lambda}/D_x) = h_x(d_{x\lambda}/d_x),  \tag{5.3.7}$$

and

$$h_{x\nu} = h_x(D_{x\nu}/D_x) = h_x(d_{x\nu}/d_x),  \tag{5.3.8}$$

which are sometimes termed the *proportional hazard formulas.*

Chiang (1968) shows that (5.3.7) and (5.3.8) are maximum likelihood estimators of these hazards if the ratio $\lambda(x)/\mu(x)$ is constant over the age interval $(x, x + n)$, where

$$_nh_{x\lambda} = \int_x^{x+n} \lambda(a)\ da \qquad (5.3.9)$$

and

$$_nh_{xv} = \int_x^{x+n} v(a)\ da \qquad (5.3.10)$$

and where the total force of mortality $\mu(x)$ is the sum

$$\mu(x) = \lambda(x) + v(x). \qquad (5.3.11)$$

Formulas (5.3.7) and (5.3.8) contain the same expressions as seen on the right side of formulas (4.4.27) and (4.4.28). This means that under the assumption of independence of the risks $\lambda$ and $v$, the following identity holds:

$$_nh_{x\lambda\cdot v} = {}_nh_{x\lambda} \quad \text{and} \quad _nh_{xv\cdot\lambda} = {}_nh_v, \qquad (5.3.12)$$

so that the hazard rates in the multiple-decrement life table and in the cause-elimination life table are the same. In fact, to avoid redundancy, we present $_nh_{x\lambda}$(or $_nh_{x\lambda\cdot v}$) in the multiple-decrement life tables and $_nh_{xv}$ (or $_nh_{xv\cdot\lambda}$) in the cause-elimination life tables.

The following additive properties apply to the multiple-decrement life table parameters:

$$d_x = d_{x\lambda} + d_{xv}, \qquad (5.3.13)$$

$$l_x = l_{x\lambda} + l_{xv}, \qquad (5.3.14)$$

$$q_x = q_{x\lambda} + q_{xv}, \qquad (5.3.15)$$

$$h_x = h_{x\lambda} + h_{xv}. \qquad (5.3.16)$$

Hence, the multiple-decrement life tables for any number of disjoint causes of death may be computed independently by appropriate redefinition of cause $\lambda$ as each table is developed.

The property of addivity in (5.3.13)–(5.3.16) does not hold for the multiple-decrement life expectancy columns. Instead the multiple-decrement life table $\mathring{e}_{x\lambda}$ and $\mathring{e}_{xv}$ columns represent the weighted decomposition of the $\mathring{e}_x$ column in the life table for total mortality, that is,

$$\mathring{e}_x = (l_{x\lambda}\mathring{e}_{x\lambda} + l_{xv}\mathring{e}_{xv})/l_x. \qquad (5.3.17)$$

Thus, $\mathring{e}_{x\lambda}$ represents the expected number of years to be lived by the $l_{x\lambda}$ persons alive at age $x$ who will eventually succumb to the specified mortality risk. Similar interpretations apply to $\mathring{e}_{xv}$ as the expected number of years yet to be lived by the $l_{xv}$ persons alive at age $x$ who will eventually die of a cause other than the specified mortality risk. In terms of the probability densities of the observed age at death $X_\lambda$ due to cause $\lambda$ or age at death $X_\nu$ due to cause $\nu$, we have by analogy to (5.2.11a) and (5.2.11b):

$$\overset{\circ}{e}_{0\lambda} = \mathscr{E}_\lambda(x) \tag{5.3.18a}$$

$$= \int_0^\infty x f_\lambda(x) \, dx \tag{5.3.18b}$$

and

$$\overset{\circ}{e}_{0\nu} = \mathscr{E}_\nu(x) \tag{5.3.19a}$$

$$= \int_0^\infty x f_\nu(x) \, dx, \tag{5.3.19b}$$

where $f_\lambda(x)$ and $f_\nu(x)$ are defined in Eqs. (4.5.7) and (4.5.8) and represent the densities of the variates $X_\lambda$ and $X_\nu$, respectively.

In general, for any age $x$, we can interpret $\overset{\circ}{e}_{x\lambda}$ or $\overset{\circ}{e}_{x\nu}$ analogously to (5.2.12), that is,

$$\overset{\circ}{e}_{x\lambda} = \left[ \int_x^\infty (a - x) f_\lambda(a) \, da \right] \bigg/ \left[ \int_x^\infty f_\lambda(a) \, da \right] \tag{5.3.20a}$$

$$= \left[ \int_x^\infty (a - x) g_\lambda(a) \, da \right] \bigg/ \left[ \int_x^\infty g_\lambda(a) \, da \right], \tag{5.3.20b}$$

and

$$\overset{\circ}{e}_{x\nu} = \left[ \int_x^\infty (a - x) f_\nu(a) \, da \right] \bigg/ \left[ \int_x^\infty f_\nu(a) \, da \right] \tag{5.3.21a}$$

$$= \left[ \int_x^\infty (a - x) g_\nu(a) \, da \right] \bigg/ \left[ \int_x^\infty g_\nu(a) \, da \right], \tag{5.3.21b}$$

where $g_\lambda(x)$ and $g_\nu(x)$ are the transition densities defined in Eqs. (4.5.5) and (4.5.6). These equations are evaluated via a discrete-time approximation similar to that in (5.2.14):

$$\overset{\circ}{e}_{x\lambda} = \frac{1}{l_{x\lambda}} \sum_{i=x}^{\omega} (i + b_i - x) \, d_{i\lambda}, \tag{5.3.22}$$

and

$$\overset{\circ}{e}_{x\nu} = \frac{1}{l_{x\nu}} \sum_{i=x}^{\omega} (i + b_i - x) \, d_{i\nu}, \tag{5.3.23}$$

where the $b_x$'s are the same as in (5.2.14). Note that by substituting (5.3.22) and (5.3.23) in (5.3.17) and manipulating the result via (5.3.13), one can obtain (5.2.14), thereby demonstrating that the approximations (5.3.22) and (5.3.23) are consistent with (5.2.14).

As with life tables for total mortality, the abbreviated versions of the multiple-decrement life tables differ from the complete versions in the $q_x$, $d_x$, and $h_x$ columns but not in the $l_x$ and $\mathring{e}_x$ columns. The abbreviated life tables are computed as follows:

$$_5q_{x\lambda} = {}_5d_{x\lambda}/l_x, \tag{5.3.24}$$

$$_5d_{x\lambda} = \sum_{i=x}^{x+4} d_{i\lambda}, \tag{5.3.25}$$

$$_5h_{x\lambda} = \sum_{i=x}^{x+4} h_{i\lambda}. \tag{5.3.26}$$

A similar set of equations may be written for the computation of $_5q_{x\nu}$, $_5d_{x\nu}$, and $_5h_{x\nu}$.

## Results

Tables 6–10 contain the 1969 white male abbreviated multiple-decrement life table columns described above for five chronic diseases under

**Table 6**

White Male Multiple-Decrement 1969 Life Tables for Cancer

| Age at start of interval $(x, x + 5)$, $x$ | Probability of dying in interval $(x, x + 5)$, $_5q_{x\lambda}$ | Number living at age $x$, $l_{x\lambda}$ | Number dying in interval $(x, x + 5)$, $_5d_{x\lambda}$ | Observed life expectancy at age $x$, $\mathring{e}_{x\lambda}$ | Cumulative force of mortality over interval $(x, x + 5)$, $_5h_{x\lambda}$ |
|---|---|---|---|---|---|
| | | Underlying-cause definition | | | |
| 0 | 0.0003725 | 16,486 | 37 | 68.08 | 0.0003806 |
| 5 | 0.0004120 | 16,448 | 40 | 63.23 | 0.0004125 |
| 10 | 0.0003009 | 16,408 | 29 | 58.38 | 0.0003013 |
| 15 | 0.0004630 | 16,379 | 45 | 53.48 | 0.0004645 |
| 20 | 0.0005478 | 16,334 | 53 | 48.62 | 0.0005505 |
| 25 | 0.0006989 | 16,281 | 67 | 43.77 | 0.0007018 |
| 30 | 0.0009195 | 16,214 | 87 | 38.94 | 0.0009236 |
| 35 | 0.0016609 | 16,127 | 156 | 34.13 | 0.0016716 |
| 40 | 0.0031687 | 15,971 | 294 | 29.44 | 0.0032023 |
| 45 | 0.0057174 | 15,678 | 519 | 24.94 | 0.0058145 |
| 50 | 0.0107131 | 15,159 | 941 | 20.70 | 0.0110098 |
| 55 | 0.0182690 | 14,218 | 1,519 | 16.89 | 0.0190869 |

*(continued)*

**Table 6** (*Continued*)

| Age at start of interval $(x, x + 5)$, $x$ | Probability of dying in interval $(x, x + 5)$, $_5q_{x\lambda}$ | Number living at age $x$, $l_{x\lambda}$ | Number dying in interval $(x, x + 5)$, $_5d_{x\lambda}$ | Observed life expectancy at age $x$, $\overset{\circ}{e}_{x\lambda}$ | Cumulative force of mortality over interval $(x, x + 5)$, $_5h_{x\lambda}$ |
|---|---|---|---|---|---|
| | | Underlying-cause definition | | | |
| 60 | 0.0278170 | 12,699 | 2,119 | 13.60 | 0.0297335 |
| 65 | 0.0396282 | 10,580 | 2,639 | 10.79 | 0.0437590 |
| 70 | 0.0494881 | 7,942 | 2,684 | 8.54 | 0.0569903 |
| 75 | 0.0589260 | 5,258 | 2,377 | 6.64 | 0.0719352 |
| 80 | 0.0628261 | 2,880 | 1,648 | 5.17 | 0.0840218 |
| 85 | 0.0612317 | 1,232 | 845 | 3.99 | 0.0912363 |
| 90 | 0.0560312 | 387 | 314 | 3.07 | 0.0979330 |
| 95 | 0.0485695 | 73 | 73 | 2.72 | |
| | | Pattern-of-failure definition | | | |
| 0 | 0.0003936 | 19,303 | 39 | 69.15 | 0.0004021 |
| 5 | 0.0004236 | 19,264 | 41 | 64.29 | 0.0004241 |
| 10 | 0.0003108 | 19,223 | 30 | 59.42 | 0.0003111 |
| 15 | 0.0004754 | 19,192 | 46 | 54.51 | 0.0004770 |
| 20 | 0.0005652 | 19,146 | 54 | 49.63 | 0.0005680 |
| 25 | 0.0007263 | 19,092 | 69 | 44.77 | 0.0007294 |
| 30 | 0.0009539 | 19,022 | 90 | 39.92 | 0.0009581 |
| 35 | 0.0017351 | 18,932 | 163 | 35.10 | 0.0017463 |
| 40 | 0.0033191 | 18,769 | 308 | 30.38 | 0.0033542 |
| 45 | 0.0060307 | 18,462 | 547 | 25.84 | 0.0061332 |
| 50 | 0.0113678 | 17,914 | 998 | 21.55 | 0.0116831 |
| 55 | 0.0196194 | 16,916 | 1,631 | 17.66 | 0.0204990 |
| 60 | 0.0304565 | 15,285 | 2,320 | 14.26 | 0.0325635 |
| 65 | 0.0447956 | 12,965 | 2,983 | 11.34 | 0.0494992 |
| 70 | 0.0583424 | 9,982 | 3,164 | 8.97 | 0.0672726 |
| 75 | 0.0721190 | 6,818 | 2,910 | 6.98 | 0.0881933 |
| 80 | 0.0822093 | 3,908 | 2,157 | 5.39 | 0.1102114 |
| 85 | 0.0842767 | 1,751 | 1,163 | 4.16 | 0.1262429 |
| 90 | 0.0841056 | 588 | 471 | 3.15 | 0.1473072 |
| 95 | 0.0778443 | 117 | 117 | 2.76 | |

**Table 7**

White Male Multiple-Decrement 1969 Life Tables for DM

| Age at start of interval $(x, x + 5)$, $x$ | Probability of dying in interval $(x, x + 5)$, $_5q_{x\lambda}$ | Number living at age $x$, $l_{x\lambda}$ | Number dying in interval $(x, x + 5)$, $_5d_{x\lambda}$ | Observed life expectancy at age $x$, $\overset{\circ}{e}_{x\lambda}$ | Cumulative force of mortality over interval $(x, x + 5)$, $_5h_{x\lambda}$ |
|---|---|---|---|---|---|
| | | Underlying-cause definition | | | |
| 0 | 0.0000084 | 1,470 | 1 | 70.32 | 0.0000085 |
| 5 | 0.0000088 | 1,469 | 1 | 65.36 | 0.0000088 |
| 10 | 0.0000082 | 1,468 | 1 | 60.39 | 0.0000082 |
| 15 | 0.0000146 | 1,467 | 1 | 55.42 | 0.0000147 |
| 20 | 0.0000374 | 1,466 | 4 | 50.48 | 0.0000376 |
| 25 | 0.0000883 | 1,462 | 8 | 45.59 | 0.0000887 |
| 30 | 0.0001530 | 1,454 | 14 | 40.84 | 0.0001537 |
| 35 | 0.0002101 | 1,440 | 20 | 36.23 | 0.0002114 |
| 40 | 0.0002617 | 1,420 | 24 | 31.69 | 0.0002643 |
| 45 | 0.0004605 | 1,396 | 42 | 27.20 | 0.0004681 |
| 50 | 0.0006944 | 1,354 | 61 | 22.96 | 0.0007142 |
| 55 | 0.0011710 | 1,293 | 97 | 18.91 | 0.0012240 |
| 60 | 0.0018652 | 1,195 | 142 | 15.23 | 0.0019973 |
| 65 | 0.0032091 | 1,053 | 214 | 11.92 | 0.0035482 |
| 70 | 0.0042763 | 840 | 232 | 9.30 | 0.0049422 |
| 75 | 0.0063072 | 608 | 254 | 6.89 | 0.0077364 |
| 80 | 0.0076786 | 353 | 201 | 5.10 | 0.0103125 |
| 85 | 0.0078896 | 152 | 109 | 3.76 | 0.0118713 |
| 90 | 0.0064510 | 43 | 36 | 2.78 | 0.0110484 |
| 95 | 0.0457516 | 7 | 7 | 2.34 | |
| | | Pattern-of-failure definition | | | |
| 0 | 0.0000149 | 5,740 | 1 | 71.67 | 0.0000151 |
| 5 | 0.0000126 | 5,739 | 1 | 66.69 | 0.0000127 |
| 10 | 0.0000115 | 5,738 | 1 | 61.70 | 0.0000115 |
| 15 | 0.0000242 | 5,737 | 2 | 56.72 | 0.0000243 |
| 20 | 0.0000562 | 5,734 | 5 | 51.74 | 0.0000565 |
| 25 | 0.0001232 | 5,729 | 12 | 46.78 | 0.0001238 |
| 30 | 0.0002259 | 5,717 | 21 | 41.87 | 0.0002269 |
| 35 | 0.0003564 | 5,696 | 33 | 37.02 | 0.0003586 |
| 40 | 0.0006010 | 5,662 | 56 | 32.22 | 0.0006073 |
| 45 | 0.0012661 | 5,607 | 115 | 27.52 | 0.0012878 |
| 50 | 0.0024447 | 5,492 | 215 | 23.04 | 0.0025154 |
| 55 | 0.0044514 | 5,277 | 370 | 18.86 | 0.0046548 |
| 60 | 0.0077183 | 4,907 | 588 | 15.08 | 0.0082566 |

(*continued*)

**Table 7** (*Continued*)

| Age at start of interval $(x, x + 5)$, $x$ | Probability of dying in interval $(x, x + 5)$, $_5q_{x\lambda}$ | Number living at age $x$, $l_{x\lambda}$ | Number dying in interval $(x, x + 5)$, $_5d_{x\lambda}$ | Observed life expectancy at age $x$, $\overset{\circ}{e}_{x\lambda}$ | Cumulative force of mortality over interval $(x, x + 5)$, $_5h_{x\lambda}$ |
|---|---|---|---|---|---|
| | | Pattern-of-failure definition | | | |
| 65 | 0.0132049 | 4,319 | 879 | 11.77 | 0.0146250 |
| 70 | 0.0187587 | 3,440 | 1,017 | 9.11 | 0.0216715 |
| 75 | 0.0253723 | 2,422 | 1,024 | 6.88 | 0.0310847 |
| 80 | 0.0303599 | 1,399 | 797 | 5.15 | 0.0407415 |
| 85 | 0.0303242 | 602 | 419 | 3.87 | 0.0451965 |
| 90 | 0.0273138 | 183 | 153 | 2.86 | 0.0466029 |
| 95 | 0.0206254 | 31 | 31 | 2.63 | |

**Table 8**

White Male Multiple-Decrement 1969 Life Tables for IHD

| Age at start of interval $(x, x + 5)$, $x$ | Probability of dying in interval $(x, x + 5)$, $_5q_{x\lambda}$ | Number living at age $x$, $l_{x\lambda}$ | Number dying in interval $(x, x + 5)$, $_5d_{x\lambda}$ | Observed life expectancy at age $x$, $\overset{\circ}{e}_{x\lambda}$ | Cumulative force of mortality over interval $(x, x + 5)$, $_5h_{x\lambda}$ |
|---|---|---|---|---|---|
| | | Underlying-cause definition | | | |
| 0 | 0.0000084 | 39,251 | 1 | 72.23 | 0.0000085 |
| 5 | 0.0000034 | 39,250 | 0 | 67.24 | 0.0000034 |
| 10 | 0.0000033 | 39,250 | 0 | 62.24 | 0.0000033 |
| 15 | 0.0000170 | 39,250 | 2 | 57.24 | 0.0000171 |
| 20 | 0.0000511 | 39,248 | 5 | 52.24 | 0.0000514 |
| 25 | 0.0001592 | 39,243 | 15 | 47.25 | 0.0001600 |
| 30 | 0.0006393 | 39,228 | 61 | 42.26 | 0.0006426 |
| 35 | 0.0022709 | 39,168 | 213 | 37.32 | 0.0022865 |
| 40 | 0.0057311 | 38,954 | 531 | 32.51 | 0.0057931 |
| 45 | 0.0117864 | 38,423 | 1,070 | 27.92 | 0.0119891 |
| 50 | 0.0211793 | 37,353 | 1,860 | 23.64 | 0.0217687 |
| 55 | 0.0345847 | 35,494 | 2,875 | 19.74 | 0.0361246 |
| 60 | 0.0529544 | 32,618 | 4,034 | 16.25 | 0.0565932 |

**Table 8** (*Continued*)

| Age at start of interval $(x, x+5)$, $x$ | Probability of dying in interval $(x, x+5)$, $_5q_{x\lambda}$ | Number living at age $x$, $l_{x\lambda}$ | Number dying in interval $(x, x+5)$, $_5d_{x\lambda}$ | Observed life expectancy at age $x$, $\overset{\circ}{e}_{x\lambda}$ | Cumulative force of mortality over interval $(x, x+5)$, $_5h_{x\lambda}$ |
|---|---|---|---|---|---|
| | | Underlying-cause definition | | | |
| 65 | 0.0785615 | 28,585 | 5,231 | 13.17 | 0.0869168 |
| 70 | 0.1095304 | 23,354 | 5,940 | 10.54 | 0.1264910 |
| 75 | 0.1491205 | 17,414 | 6,017 | 8.29 | 0.1834422 |
| 80 | 0.2043454 | 11,397 | 5,362 | 6.36 | 0.2770848 |
| 85 | 0.2594506 | 6,035 | 3,582 | 4.86 | 0.3940549 |
| 90 | 0.3224716 | 2,454 | 1,805 | 3.71 | 0.5825067 |
| 95 | 0.4318031 | 649 | 649 | 3.15 | |
| | | Pattern-of-failure definition | | | |
| 0 | 0.0000266 | 45,712 | 3 | 72.56 | 0.0000270 |
| 5 | 0.0000094 | 45,709 | 1 | 67.57 | 0.0000094 |
| 10 | 0.0000093 | 45,708 | 1 | 62.57 | 0.0000093 |
| 15 | 0.0000275 | 45,707 | 3 | 57.57 | 0.0000276 |
| 20 | 0.0000804 | 45,705 | 8 | 52.57 | 0.0000808 |
| 25 | 0.0002193 | 45,697 | 21 | 47.58 | 0.0002204 |
| 30 | 0.0007248 | 45,676 | 69 | 42.60 | 0.0007285 |
| 35 | 0.0024870 | 45,607 | 233 | 37.66 | 0.0025039 |
| 40 | 0.0061742 | 45,374 | 572 | 32.84 | 0.0062411 |
| 45 | 0.0127008 | 44,802 | 1,153 | 28.22 | 0.0129191 |
| 50 | 0.0230118 | 43,649 | 2,021 | 23.90 | 0.0236529 |
| 55 | 0.0382664 | 41,628 | 3,181 | 19.93 | 0.0399776 |
| 60 | 0.0598575 | 38,447 | 4,560 | 16.35 | 0.0639922 |
| 65 | 0.0912400 | 33,887 | 6,075 | 13.20 | 0.1009855 |
| 70 | 0.1295865 | 27,812 | 7,028 | 10.52 | 0.1497409 |
| 75 | 0.1792295 | 20,784 | 7,231 | 8.23 | 0.2205033 |
| 80 | 0.2451247 | 13,553 | 6,432 | 6.30 | 0.3321828 |
| 85 | 0.3093137 | 7,121 | 4,270 | 4.81 | 0.4694446 |
| 90 | 0.3761485 | 2,851 | 2,105 | 3.69 | 0.6776768 |
| 95 | 0.4963407 | 746 | 746 | 3.16 | |

## Table 9

White Male Multiple-Decrement 1969 Life Tables for Cerebrovascular Accidents

| Age at start of interval $(x, x + 5)$, $x$ | Probability of dying in interval $(x, x + 5)$, $_5q_{x\lambda}$ | Number living at age $x$, $l_{x\lambda}$ | Number dying in interval $(x, x + 5)$, $_5d_{x\lambda}$ | Observed life expectancy at age $x$, $\overset{\circ}{e}_{x\lambda}$ | Cumulative force of mortality over interval $(x, x + 5)$, $_5h_{x\lambda}$ |
|---|---|---|---|---|---|
| | | Underlying-cause definition | | | |
| 0 | 0.0000842 | 9,543 | 8 | 76.50 | 0.0000856 |
| 5 | 0.0000261 | 9,535 | 3 | 71.56 | 0.0000262 |
| 10 | 0.0000356 | 9,532 | 3 | 66.58 | 0.0000357 |
| 15 | 0.0000644 | 9,529 | 6 | 61.61 | 0.0000646 |
| 20 | 0.0000692 | 9,523 | 7 | 56.64 | 0.0000696 |
| 25 | 0.0001404 | 9,516 | 13 | 51.68 | 0.0001410 |
| 30 | 0.0001982 | 9,503 | 19 | 46.75 | 0.0001992 |
| 35 | 0.0003948 | 9,484 | 37 | 41.84 | 0.0003973 |
| 40 | 0.0006736 | 9,447 | 62 | 36.99 | 0.0006806 |
| 45 | 0.0012219 | 9,384 | 111 | 32.22 | 0.0012427 |
| 50 | 0.0022235 | 9,273 | 195 | 27.57 | 0.0022866 |
| 55 | 0.0039574 | 9,078 | 329 | 23.11 | 0.0041365 |
| 60 | 0.0075240 | 8,749 | 573 | 18.87 | 0.0080570 |
| 65 | 0.0142325 | 8,176 | 948 | 15.01 | 0.0158276 |
| 70 | 0.0257928 | 7,228 | 1,399 | 11.62 | 0.0299586 |
| 75 | 0.0433429 | 5,830 | 1,749 | 8.79 | 0.0537634 |
| 80 | 0.0705792 | 4,081 | 1,852 | 6.46 | 0.0963683 |
| 85 | 0.0971167 | 2,229 | 1,341 | 4.76 | 0.1479011 |
| 90 | 0.1179476 | 888 | 660 | 3.58 | 0.2103419 |
| 95 | 0.1516966 | 228 | 228 | 2.94 | |
| | | Pattern-of-failure definition | | | |
| 0 | 0.0002964 | 15,115 | 30 | 75.82 | 0.0003015 |
| 5 | 0.0001418 | 15,085 | 14 | 70.96 | 0.0001420 |
| 10 | 0.0001231 | 15,071 | 12 | 66.03 | 0.0001233 |
| 15 | 0.0002480 | 15,059 | 24 | 61.08 | 0.0002489 |
| 20 | 0.0002536 | 15,035 | 24 | 56.17 | 0.0002549 |
| 25 | 0.0002890 | 15,011 | 28 | 51.26 | 0.0002903 |
| 30 | 0.0003690 | 14,983 | 35 | 46.35 | 0.0003706 |
| 35 | 0.0006461 | 14,948 | 61 | 41.45 | 0.0006501 |
| 40 | 0.0010877 | 14,887 | 101 | 36.61 | 0.0010991 |
| 45 | 0.0019765 | 14,787 | 179 | 31.84 | 0.0020107 |
| 50 | 0.0035667 | 14,607 | 313 | 27.20 | 0.0036683 |
| 55 | 0.0065589 | 14,294 | 545 | 22.73 | 0.0068560 |
| 60 | 0.0123630 | 13,749 | 942 | 18.53 | 0.0132444 |

**Table 9** (*Continued*)

| Age at start of interval $(x, x + 5)$, $x$ | Probability of dying in interval $(x, x + 5)$, $_5q_{x\lambda}$ | Number living at age $x$, $l_{x\lambda}$ | Number dying in interval $(x, x + 5)$, $_5d_{x\lambda}$ | Observed life expectancy at age $x$, $\overset{\circ}{e}_{x\lambda}$ | Cumulative force of mortality over interval $(x, x + 5)$, $_5h_{x\lambda}$ |
|---|---|---|---|---|---|
| | | Pattern-of-failure definition | | | |
| 65 | 0.0233121 | 12,807 | 1,552 | 14.69 | 0.0259115 |
| 70 | 0.0419973 | 11,255 | 2,278 | 11.35 | 0.0487670 |
| 75 | 0.0694394 | 8,977 | 2,802 | 8.56 | 0.0859870 |
| 80 | 0.1102527 | 6,176 | 2,893 | 6.30 | 0.1502999 |
| 85 | 0.1455450 | 3,283 | 2,009 | 4.68 | 0.2214458 |
| 90 | 0.1708852 | 1,273 | 956 | 3.54 | 0.3049713 |
| 95 | 0.2109115 | 317 | 317 | 2.97 | |

**Table 10**

White Male Multiple-Decrement 1969 Life Tables for GA

| Age at start of interval $(x, x + 5)$, $x$ | Probability of dying in interval $(x, x + 5)$, $_5q_{x\lambda}$ | Number living at age $x$, $l_{x\lambda}$ | Number dying in interval $(x, x + 5)$, $_5d_{x\lambda}$ | Observed life expectancy at age $x$, $\overset{\circ}{e}_{x\lambda}$ | Cumulative force of mortality over interval $(x, x + 5)$, $_5h_{x\lambda}$ |
|---|---|---|---|---|---|
| | | Underlying-cause definition | | | |
| 0 | 0.0 | 1,725 | 0 | 82.79 | 0.0 |
| 5 | 0.0 | 1,725 | 0 | 77.79 | 0.0 |
| 10 | 0.0 | 1,725 | 0 | 72.79 | 0.0 |
| 15 | 0.0000006 | 1,725 | 0 | 67.79 | 0.0000006 |
| 20 | 0.0 | 1,725 | 0 | 62.79 | 0.0 |
| 25 | 0.0000009 | 1,725 | 0 | 57.79 | 0.0000009 |
| 30 | 0.0000030 | 1,725 | 0 | 52.79 | 0.0000030 |
| 35 | 0.0000040 | 1,725 | 0 | 47.80 | 0.0000040 |
| 40 | 0.0000146 | 1,724 | 1 | 42.81 | 0.0000147 |
| 45 | 0.0000307 | 1,723 | 3 | 37.84 | 0.0000314 |
| 50 | 0.0000831 | 1,720 | 7 | 32.90 | 0.0000858 |
| 55 | 0.0002306 | 1,713 | 19 | 28.02 | 0.0002412 |
| 60 | 0.0005628 | 1,694 | 43 | 23.31 | 0.0006025 |

(*continued*)

**Table 10** (*Continued*)

| Age at start of interval $(x, x + 5)$, $x$ | Probability of dying in interval $(x, x + 5)$, ${}_5q_{x\lambda}$ | Number living at age $x$, $l_{x\lambda}$ | Number dying in interval $(x, x + 5)$, ${}_5d_{x\lambda}$ | Observed life expectancy at age $x$, $\overset{\circ}{e}_{x\lambda}$ | Cumulative force of mortality over interval $(x, x + 5)$, ${}_5h_{x\lambda}$ |
|---|---|---|---|---|---|
| | | Underlying-cause definition | | | |
| 65 | 0.0013451 | 1,651 | 90 | 18.85 | 0.0015006 |
| 70 | 0.0029968 | 1,561 | 163 | 14.77 | 0.0034836 |
| 75 | 0.0064571 | 1,399 | 261 | 11.18 | 0.0080806 |
| 80 | 0.0146405 | 1,138 | 384 | 8.13 | 0.0201446 |
| 85 | 0.0263056 | 754 | 363 | 5.98 | 0.0408255 |
| 90 | 0.0464428 | 391 | 260 | 4.35 | 0.0872672 |
| 95 | 0.0871590 | 131 | 131 | 3.52 | |
| | | Pattern-of-failure definition | | | |
| 0 | 0.0000026 | 15,394 | 0 | 78.39 | 0.0000026 |
| 5 | 0.0000017 | 15,393 | 0 | 73.39 | 0.0000017 |
| 10 | 0.0000011 | 15,393 | 0 | 68.39 | 0.0000011 |
| 15 | 0.0000017 | 15,393 | 0 | 63.39 | 0.0000017 |
| 20 | 0.0000057 | 15,393 | 1 | 58.39 | 0.0000057 |
| 25 | 0.0000174 | 15,392 | 2 | 53.40 | 0.0000175 |
| 30 | 0.0000571 | 15,391 | 5 | 48.40 | 0.0000574 |
| 35 | 0.0001677 | 15,385 | 16 | 43.42 | 0.0001689 |
| 40 | 0.0004720 | 15,370 | 44 | 38.46 | 0.0004771 |
| 45 | 0.0010946 | 15,326 | 99 | 33.56 | 0.0011139 |
| 50 | 0.0025144 | 15,227 | 221 | 28.76 | 0.0025874 |
| 55 | 0.0052401 | 15,006 | 436 | 24.14 | 0.0054829 |
| 60 | 0.0108717 | 14,570 | 828 | 19.78 | 0.0116500 |
| 65 | 0.0218100 | 13,742 | 1,452 | 15.81 | 0.0242575 |
| 70 | 0.0394334 | 12,290 | 2,139 | 12.36 | 0.0457675 |
| 75 | 0.0683194 | 10,151 | 2,756 | 9.42 | 0.0848353 |
| 80 | 0.1180198 | 7,395 | 3,097 | 6.97 | 0.1614364 |
| 85 | 0.1733789 | 4,298 | 2,393 | 5.20 | 0.2658513 |
| 90 | 0.2440279 | 1,905 | 1,366 | 3.87 | 0.4446314 |
| 95 | 0.3586161 | 539 | 539 | 3.23 | |

both underlying-cause and pattern-of-failure definitions of mortality risk. The five chronic diseases are cancer (CA), diabetes mellitus (DM), ischemic heart disease (IHD), cerebrovascular accidents (stroke), and generalized arteriosclerosis (GA). For the underlying-cause definition of the mortality risks, the multiple-decrement life tables are mutually exclusive and additive. That is, each death is represented in only one $d_{x\lambda}$ column, so that the sum of all the $d_{x\lambda}$ entries reproduces the life table number of deaths attributed to these five chronic diseases. In contrast, the pattern-of-failure definition of the mortality risks represents, for each chronic disease, the life table number of deaths for persons with that chronic disease mentioned anywhere on the death certificate. As a consequence, the pattern-of-failure life table will represent each death in as many $d_{x\lambda}$ columns as there are mentions of the five chronic diseases on the reported death certificate. Note, however, that within the $d_{x\lambda}$ column for a specific chronic disease, each death is counted only one time.

These five tables display, for the white male population in 1969, the most salient aspects of cause-specific mortality due to these major chronic degenerative diseases. For example, the $q_{x\lambda}$'s, which are often termed the cause-specific *crude probabilities* of death, represent the probabilities that must be reproduced by any bioactuarial model that fits the data. Comparison of the $q_{x\lambda}$'s with the corresponding $h_{x\lambda}$'s reveals that there are substantial differences due to the effects of competing risks, especially at the older ages. Given the independence assumption in (5.3.12), an exponential transformation analogous to Eq. (4.4.20),

$$_{n}q_{x\lambda \cdot v} = 1 - \exp(-_{n}h_{x\lambda}),$$
(5.3.27)

can be employed to generate what is often termed the *net probability* of death, or the mortality probability for the cause $\lambda$ under the assumption that it is the only cause of death operating on the population. For example, for cancer, using the underlying-cause definition we have $_{5}h_{x\lambda} = 0.0912363$ for white males at age 85. Applying the above transformation, we find the net probability to be 0.0871980. This can be compared with the corresponding $_{5}q_{x\lambda} = 0.0612317$, where it is seen that about 30% [i.e., $(1 - 0.0612317/0.0871980) \times 100$] of the persons who would have died of cancer are censored by other causes of death in the age interval 85–89.

The $l_{x\lambda}$'s represent the numbers of persons in an initial birth cohort of 100,000 persons who will ultimately die of the given disease (underlying-cause definition) or with the given disease mentioned somewhere on the death certificate (pattern-of-failure definition). For example, at birth, the $l_{0\lambda}$'s in Table 6 show that 16.486% of white males (that is, 16,486 of 100,000 persons) will die with cancer as the underlying cause but that 19.303% will die with cancer mentioned. This implies that 2.817%, that is, 19.303 − 16.486, will die with cancer as an associated, nonunderlying cause. For IHD, Table 8 shows that 39.251% will die with IHD as the underlying cause but that 45.712% will die with IHD as a pattern of failure. For stroke, Table 9 shows that 9.543% will die with stroke as the underlying cause but that 15.115% will die with stroke as a pattern of failure. For DM, Table 7 shows that only 1.470% will die with DM as an underlying cause but that 5.740% will die with DM as a pattern of failure. For GA, Table 10 shows that only 1.725% will die with GA as an underlying cause but that 15.394% will die with GA as a pattern of failure.

Corresponding multiple-decrement life table columns for the five chronic diseases under the two definitions of mortality risk were similarly computed for the 1969 white female, black male, and black female populations. To facilitate comparisons of these tables, we shall employ graphs based on the complete multiple-decrement life tables, of which the results for $l_{0\lambda}$ and $\mathring{e}_{0\lambda}$ are presented in Tables 11 and 12. We shall consider two types of graphs. The first is the distribution of age at death for a specific chronic disease. These are computed by using the multiple-decrement analog to (5.2.20):

$$f_\lambda(x + \tfrac{1}{2}) = d_{x\lambda}/l_{0\lambda}, \qquad (5.3.28)$$

where $l_{0\lambda}$ is displayed in Table 11.

In Fig. 3 we present the race- and sex-specific distributions of age at death for deaths to each of the five chronic diseases under the underlying-cause definition of mortality risk. This graph permits comparison of the distributions of age at death across the five chronic diseases.

In Fig. 4 we present the race–sex-specific distribution of age at death for deaths to each of the five chronic diseases under the pattern-of-failure definition of mortality risk. Differences between Figs. 3 and 4 reflect the

**Table 11**

Multiple-Decrement 1969 Life Table Cause-Specific $l_{0\lambda}$ Entries[a]

| Race–sex category | Cancer | | DM | | IHD | | Cerebro-vascular accidents | | GA | |
|---|---|---|---|---|---|---|---|---|---|---|
| | UCD | TM | UCD | TM | UCD | TM | UCD | TM | UCD | TM |
| White males | 16,486 | 19,303 | 1,470 | 5,740 | 39,251 | 45,712 | 9,543 | 15,115 | 1,725 | 15,394 |
| White females | 15,470 | 17,696 | 2,442 | 8,644 | 38,059 | 45,331 | 15,011 | 22,884 | 3,252 | 22,579 |
| Black males | 15,073 | 16,926 | 1,593 | 4,171 | 27,416 | 31,804 | 11,094 | 16,798 | 1,307 | 10,229 |
| Black females | 12,722 | 14,217 | 3,593 | 9,114 | 31,731 | 37,296 | 16,151 | 24,431 | 2,300 | 15,929 |

[a] Underlying cause definition of mortality risk (UCD); pattern-of-failure (total mention) definition of mortality risk (TM).

**Table 12**

Multiple-Decrement 1969 Life Table Life Expectancies $\mathring{e}_{0\lambda}$ (in Years)[a]

| Race–sex category | Cancer | | DM | | IHD | | Cerebro-vascular accidents | | GA | |
|---|---|---|---|---|---|---|---|---|---|---|
| | UCD | TM | UCD | TM | UCD | TM | UCD | TM | UCD | TM |
| White males | 68.08 | 69.15 | 70.32 | 71.67 | 72.23 | 72.56 | 76.50 | 75.82 | 82.79 | 78.39 |
| White females | 69.30 | 70.44 | 74.60 | 75.73 | 80.48 | 80.38 | 81.10 | 80.62 | 87.10 | 83.88 |
| Black males | 65.76 | 66.44 | 64.70 | 66.59 | 69.80 | 69.97 | 70.53 | 70.03 | 80.67 | 76.72 |
| Black females | 65.36 | 66.19 | 68.61 | 69.76 | 76.56 | 76.32 | 75.76 | 75.34 | 87.39 | 82.09 |

[a] Underlying cause definition of mortality risk (UCD); pattern-of-failure (total mention) definition of mortality risk (TM).

effects of the additional mentions of chronic disease in the multiple-cause data, that is, because each distribution is normalized to a probability mass of unity. The mean values of each distribution may be obtained from the corresponding $\mathring{e}_{0\lambda}$ entries in Table 12. For example, the mean age of death $\mathring{e}_{0\lambda}$ due to cancer is obtained from Table 12 for white males as either 68.08 years in the underlying-cause category (Fig. 3) or as 69.15 years in the pattern-of-failure category (Fig. 4). The conclusion to be drawn from examination of Figs. 3 and 4 is that the shapes of the cause-specific distributions of age at death are quite distinct but have a general tendency to be more peaked for higher mean values.

In Fig. 5 we present comparisons of the race- and sex-specific distributions of age at death for each of the five chronic diseases under the underlying-cause definition of mortality risk. The corresponding plots for each of the five chronic diseases under the pattern-of-failure definition of mortality risk are presented in Fig. 6. These plots illustrate the tremendous advantage experienced by white females with respect to IHD, stroke, and GA mortality.

The second type of graph represents the comparisons in terms of the age-specific force of mortality $\lambda(a)$. For each chronic disease we approximate the force of mortality in an analogous manner to (5.2.21):

$$\lambda(x + \tfrac{1}{2}) = h_{x\lambda}. \qquad (5.3.29)$$

In Fig. 7 we present the race- and sex-specific graphs comparing the force of mortality due to cancer under the underlying-cause definition of

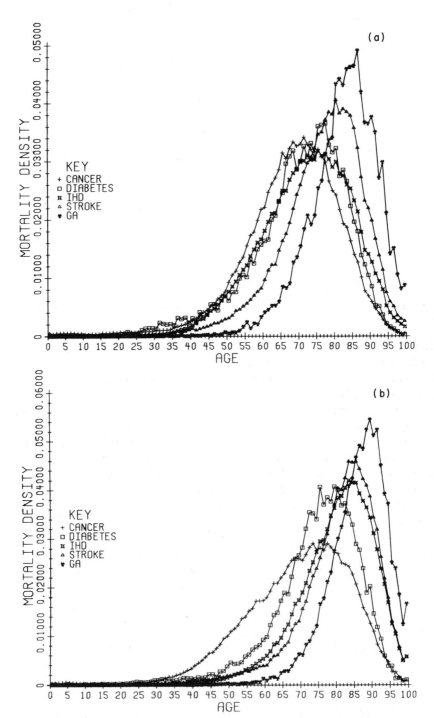

**Fig. 3.** Distributions of age at death in 1969 multiple-decrement life tables for five chronic diseases, under the underlying-cause definition of mortality risk, by sex and race. (a) White males, (b) white females.

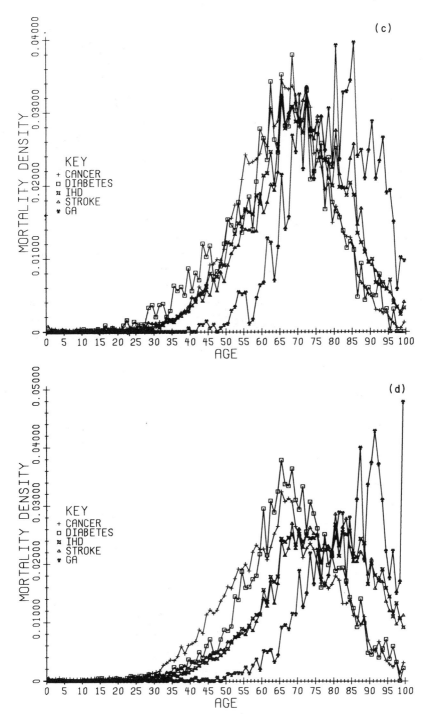

**Fig. 3** (*continued*). (c) Black males, (d) black females.

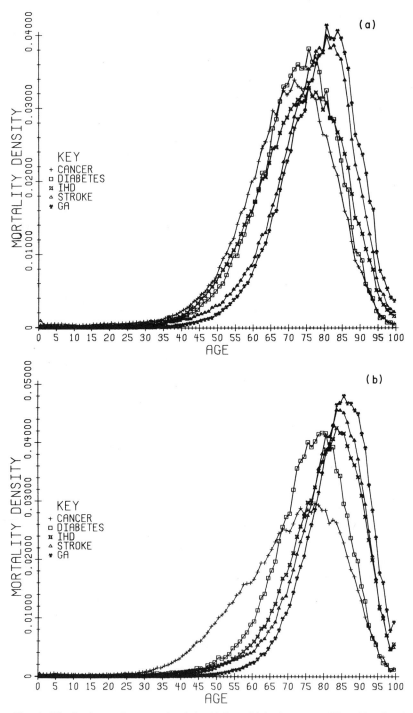

**Fig. 4.** Distributions of age at death in 1969 multiple-decrement life tables for five chronic diseases, under the pattern-of-failure definition of mortality risk, by sex and race. (a) White males, (b) white females.

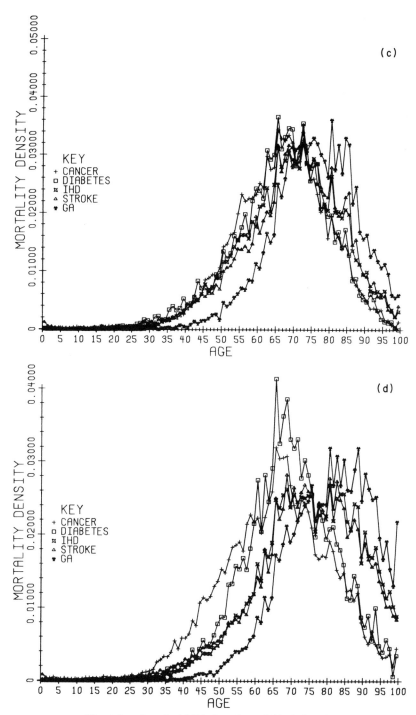

**Fig. 4** (*continued*). (c) Black males, (d) black females.

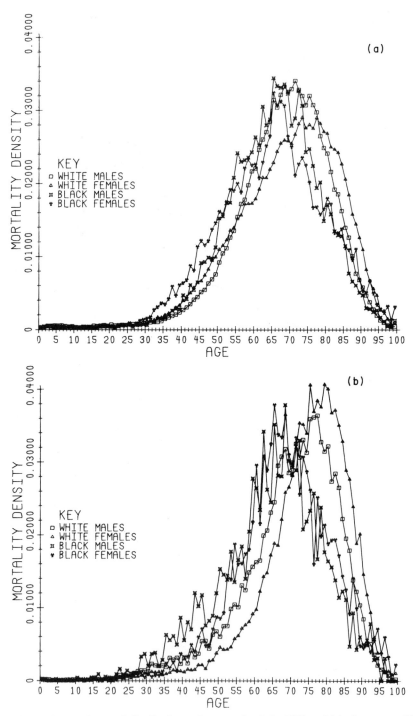

**Fig. 5.** Comparisons of distributions of age at death in 1969 multiple-decrement life tables across four race–sex-groups for five chronic diseases, under the underlying-cause definition of mortality risk. (a) Cancer, (b) diabetes mellitus.

174

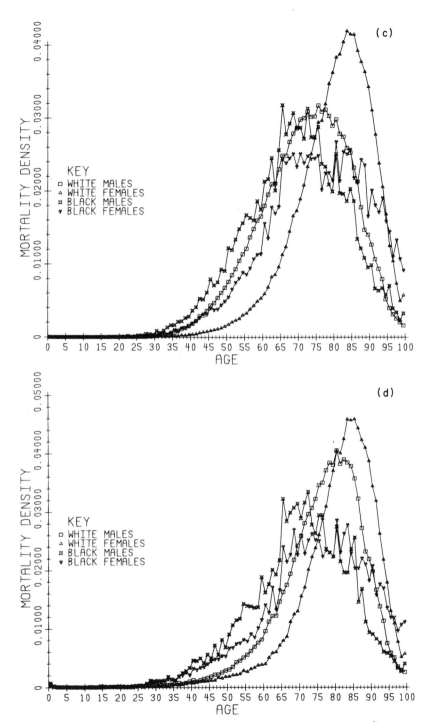

**Fig. 5** (*continued*). (c) Ischemic heart disease, (d) stroke (*continued*).

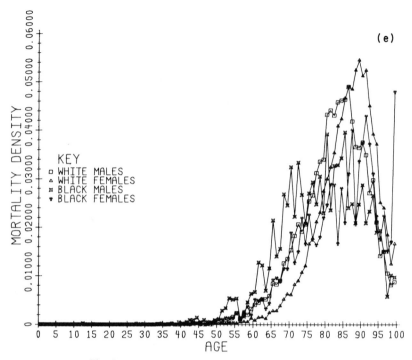

**Fig. 5** (*continued*). (e) Generalized arteriosclerosis.

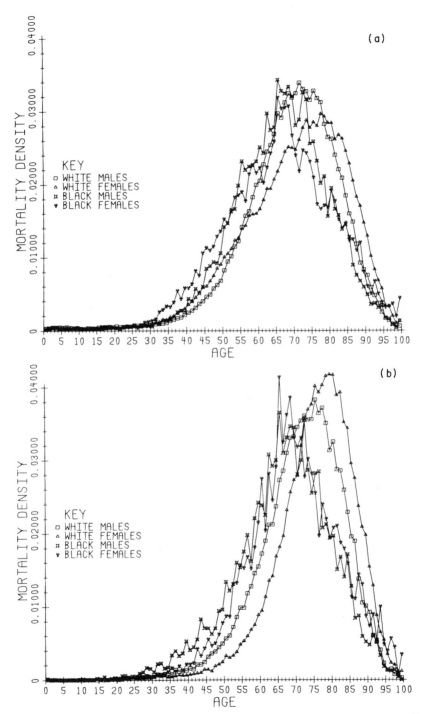

**Fig. 6.** Comparisons of distributions of age at death in 1969 multiple-decrement life tables across four race–sex-groups for five chronic diseases, under the pattern-of-failure definition of mortality risk. (a) Cancer, (b) diabetes mellitus (*continued*).

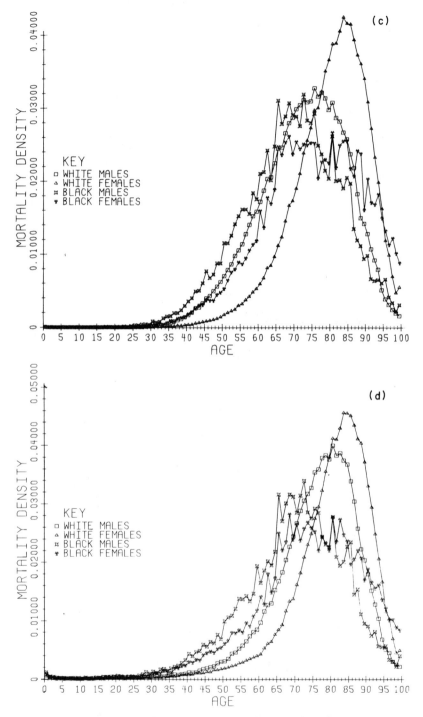

**Fig. 6** (*continued*). (c) Ischemic heart disease, (d) stroke.

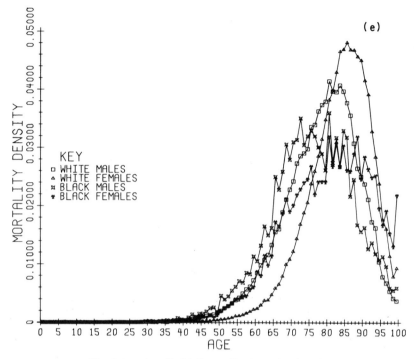

**Fig. 6** (*continued*). (e) Generalized arteriosclerosis.

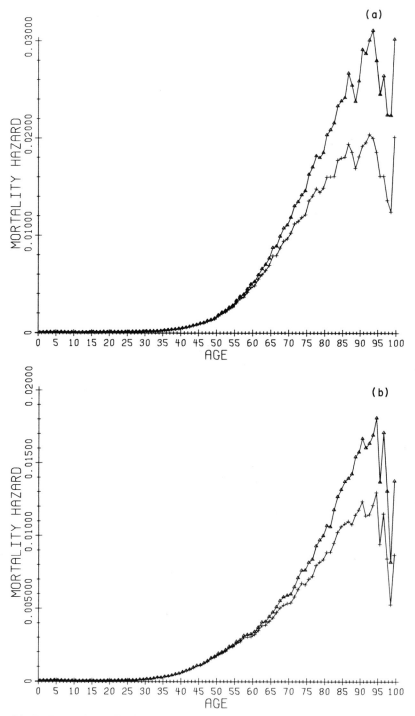

**Fig. 7.** Force of mortality in 1969 multiple-decrement life tables for cancer, under underlying-cause (+) and pattern-of-failure (Δ) definitions of mortality risk, by sex and race. (a) White males, (b) white females.

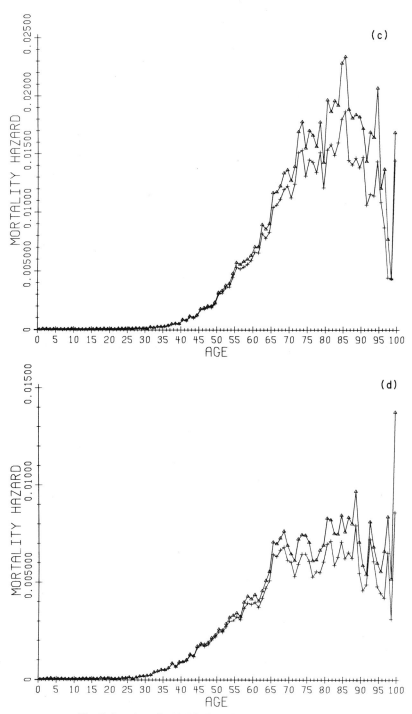

**Fig. 7** (*continued*). (c) Black males, (d) black females.

mortality risk with the force of mortality due to cancer under the pattern-of-failure definition of mortality risk. The corresponding plots for DM, IHD, stroke, and GA are presented in Figs. 8–11. In each graph it can be seen that when a divergence occurs, the difference between the two types of hazard rates becomes progressively larger over age, indicating the greater impact of multiple-cause data at advanced ages.

In Fig. 12 we present comparisons of the race- and sex-specific force of mortality for each of the five chronic diseases under the underlying-cause definition of mortality risk. The corresponding plots for each of the five chronic diseases under the pattern-of-failure definition of mortality risk are presented in Fig. 13. There are major differences between the race–sex-groups in these plots that suggest that blacks have higher average hazard rates at younger ages but not necessarily at older ages.

## 4   Cause-Elimination Life Tables

While we have seen in the preceding section that the multiple-decrement life tables provide basic descriptions of the impact of a given chronic disease, both in terms of the distribution of ages at death due to the chronic disease and in terms of the age dependence of the chronic disease force of mortality, it is desirable also to have a one-parameter measure of the health impact of the chronic disease. A frequently employed summary measure of this kind is the cause-elimination life table life expectancy gain, denoted $\Delta \overset{\circ}{e}_{0 \cdot \lambda}$. This parameter represents the change in life expectancy that would be obtained under the hypothetical elimination of the specified chronic disease, given that the mortality risk represented by the chronic disease is independent of all other mortality risks. Hence, in cases in which gross violations of the independence assumption are known to occur, this summary measure will be inappropriate.

### *Methods*

The cause-elimination life table life expectancy gain can be computed for any age $x$ as the difference in the $\overset{\circ}{e}_x$ columns of two life tables:

$$\Delta \overset{\circ}{e}_{x \cdot \lambda} = \overset{\circ}{e}_{xv \cdot \lambda} - \overset{\circ}{e}_x. \tag{5.4.1}$$

The first life table is an observed life table for total mortality, such as Tables 1–5. This life table provides the age-specific life expectancy $\overset{\circ}{e}_x$ in Eq. (5.4.1). The second life table is a hypothetical life table for total mortality in which the component force of mortality $\lambda(x)$ due to the mortality risk being "eliminated" is set to zero. In this case, we assume condition (5.3.12) so that the new total force of mortality is given, not by $_n h_x$, but by $_n h_{xv}$ as defined in (5.3.10) or (5.3.8). Hence, we have

$$h_{xv \cdot \lambda} = h_{xv} = h_x - h_{x\lambda}, \tag{5.4.2}$$

$$q_{xv \cdot \lambda} = 1 - \exp(-h_{xv \cdot \lambda}), \tag{5.4.3}$$

$$d_{xv \cdot \lambda} = l_{xv \cdot \lambda} \, q_{xv \cdot \lambda}, \tag{5.4.4}$$

$$l_{(x+1)v \cdot \lambda} = l_{xv \cdot \lambda} - d_{xv \cdot \lambda}, \tag{5.4.5}$$

and

$$\mathring{e}_{xv \cdot \lambda} = \frac{1}{l_{xv \cdot \lambda}} \sum_{i=x}^{\omega} (i + b_i - x) \, d_{iv \cdot \lambda}, \tag{5.4.6}$$

where $b_x$ is the same as in (5.2.14), except for $b_\omega$, which is computed as

$$b_\omega = 1/h_{(\omega-1)v \cdot \lambda} \tag{5.4.7}$$

instead of as in (5.2.15).

As in (5.2.16)–(5.2.18), abbreviated life table parameters can be obtained by using

$$_5 q_{xv \cdot \lambda} = 1 - \prod_{i=x}^{x+4} (1 - q_{iv \cdot \lambda}), \tag{5.4.8}$$

$$_5 d_{xv \cdot \lambda} = \sum_{i=x}^{x+4} d_{xv \cdot \lambda}, \tag{5.4.9}$$

$$_5 h_{xv \cdot \lambda} = \sum_{i=x}^{x+4} h_{xv \cdot \lambda}. \tag{5.4.10}$$

In view of (5.4.2) it is apparent that the cause-elimination life table for cause $\lambda$ can be easily constructed if the life table hazard columns for total mortality and multiple-decrement mortality are available. In this case, $_5 h_{xv \cdot \lambda}$ in (5.4.10) can be directly obtained as

$$_5 h_{xv \cdot \lambda} = {}_5 h_x - {}_5 h_{x\lambda}. \tag{5.4.11}$$

### Results

In Table 13 we present the cause-elimination life table life expectancy gains for the white male, white female, black male, and black female 1969 current life tables under the hypothetical elimination of each of the five chronic diseases both under the underlying-cause definition of mortality risk and under the pattern-of-failure definition of mortality risk.

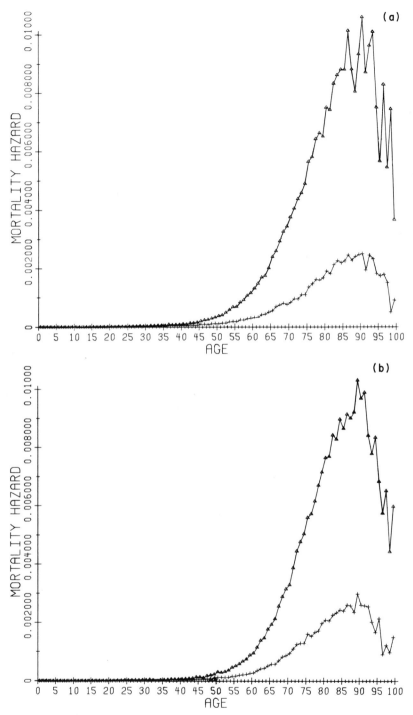

**Fig. 8.** Force of mortality in 1969 multiple-decrement life tables for diabetes mellitus, under underlying-cause (+) and pattern-of-failure (Δ) definitions of mortality risk, by sex and race. (a) White males, (b) white females.

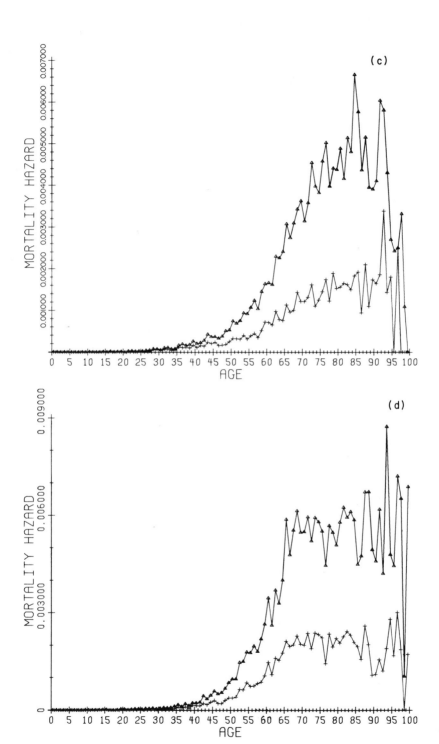

**Fig. 8** (*continued*). (c) Black males, (d) black females.

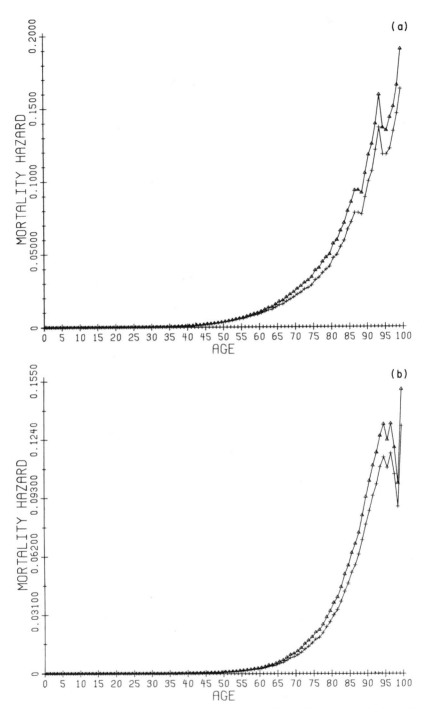

**Fig. 9.** Force of mortality in 1969 multiple-decrement life tables for ischemic heart disease, under underlying-cause (+) and pattern-of-failure (Δ) definitions of mortality risk, by sex and race. (a) White males, (b) white females.

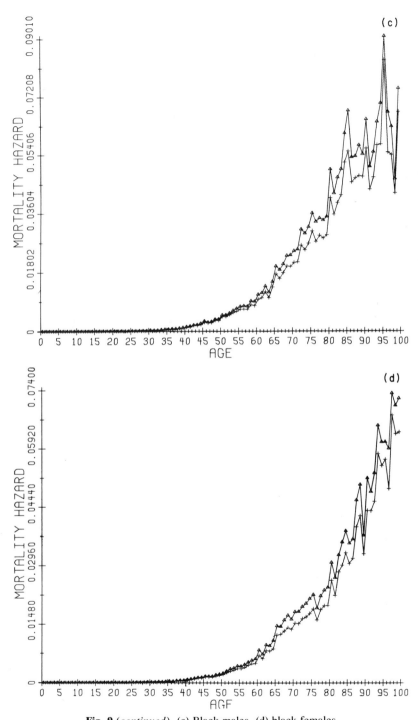

**Fig. 9** (*continued*). (c) Black males, (d) black females.

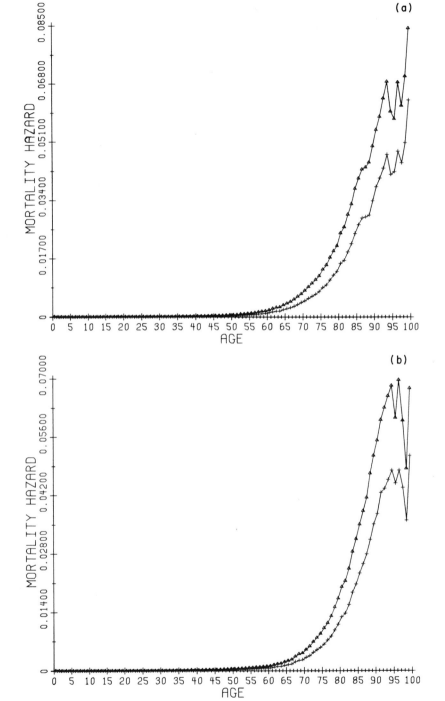

**Fig. 10.** Force of mortality in 1969 multiple-decrement life tables for stroke, under underlying-cause (+) and pattern-of-failure (Δ) definitions of mortality risk, by sex and race. (a) White males, (b) white females.

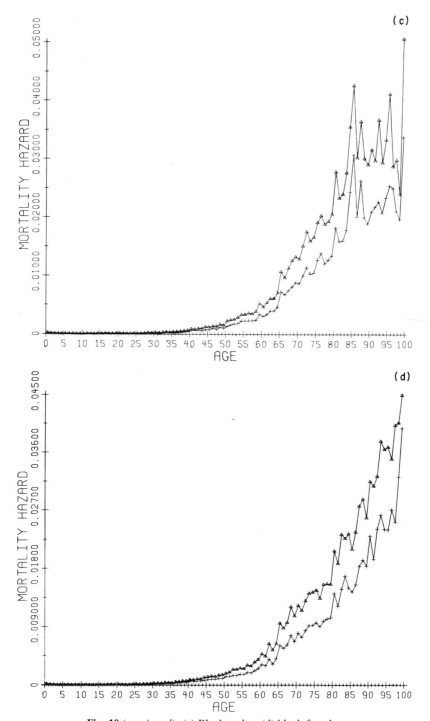

**Fig. 10** (*continued*). (c) Black males, (d) black females.

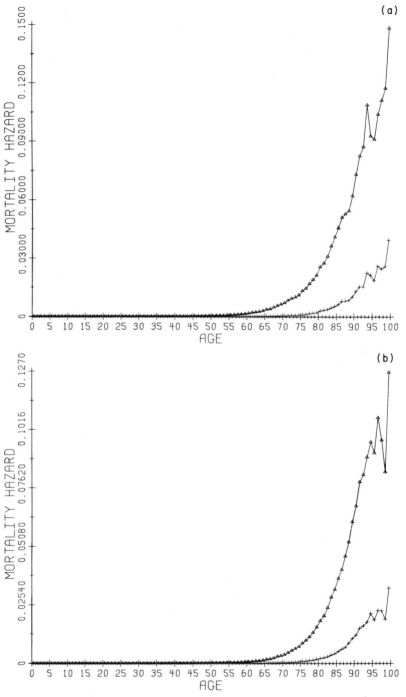

**Fig. 11.** Force of mortality in 1969 multiple-decrement life tables for generalized arteriosclerosis, under underlying-cause (+) and pattern-of-failure (Δ) definitions of mortality risk, by sex and race. (a) White males, (b) white females.

190

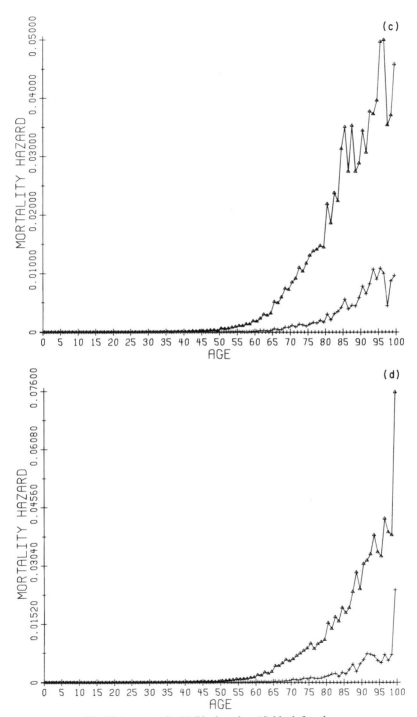

**Fig. 11** (*continued*). (c) Black males, (d) black females.

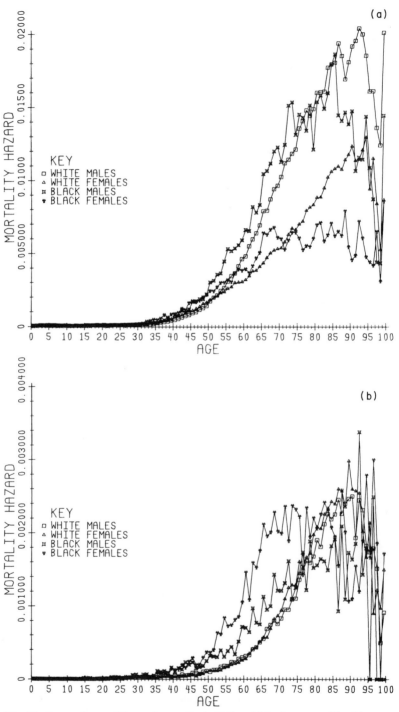

**Fig. 12.** Comparisons of force of mortality in 1969 multiple-decrement life tables across four race–sex-groups for five chronic diseases, under the underlying-cause definition of mortality risk. (a) Cancer, (b) diabetes mellitus.

192

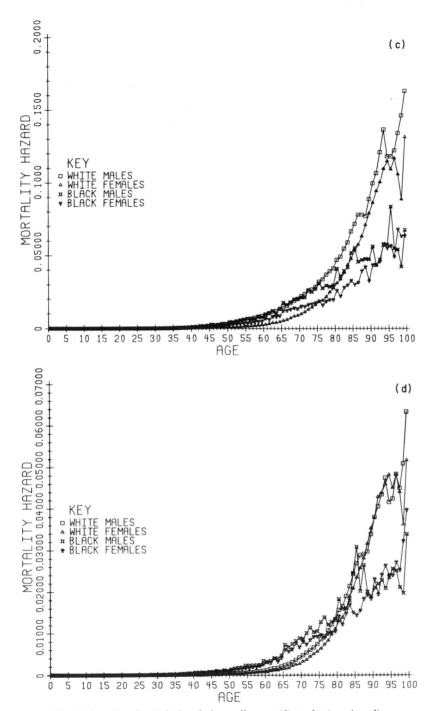

**Fig. 12** (*continued*). (c) Ischemic heart disease, (d) stroke (*continued*).

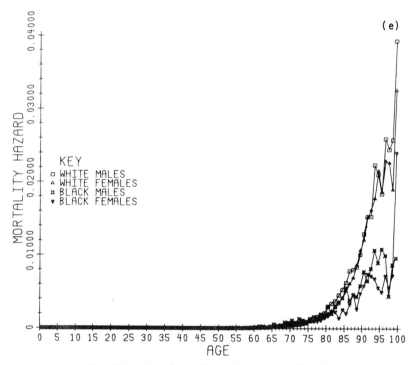

**Fig. 12** (*continued*). (e) Generalized arteriosclerosis.

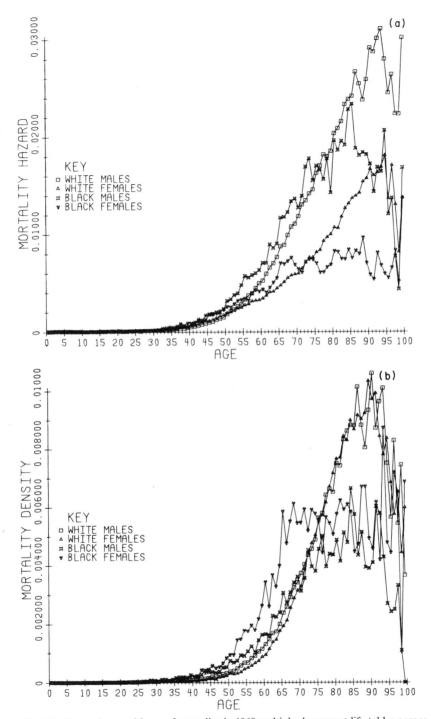

**Fig. 13.** Comparisons of force of mortality in 1969 multiple-decrement life tables across four race–sex-groups for five chronic diseases, under the pattern-of-failure definition of mortality risk. (a) Cancer, (b) diabetes mellitus (*continued*).

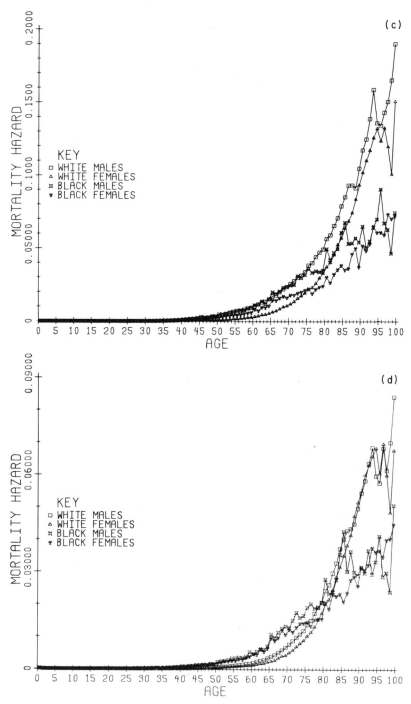

**Fig. 13** (*continued*). (c) Ischemic heart disease, (d) stroke.

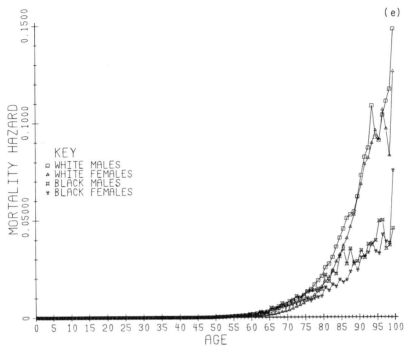

**Fig. 13** (*continued*). (e) Generalized arteriosclerosis.

**Table 13**

Cause-Elimination 1969 Life Table Life Expectancy Gains (in Years) for the Elimination of Five Chronic Diseases[a]

| Race–sex category | Cancer | | DM | | IHD | | Cerebro-vascular accidents | | GA | |
|---|---|---|---|---|---|---|---|---|---|---|
| | UCD | TM | UCD | TM | UCD | TM | UCD | TM | UCD | TM |
| White males | 2.30 | 2.64 | 0.17 | 0.64 | 5.72 | 7.11 | 0.91 | 1.57 | 0.11 | 1.46 |
| White females | 2.57 | 2.83 | 0.29 | 1.00 | 4.65 | 6.02 | 1.44 | 2.39 | 0.20 | 2.12 |
| Black males | 2.31 | 2.59 | 0.23 | 0.57 | 4.43 | 5.42 | 1.48 | 2.42 | 0.11 | 1.16 |
| Black females | 2.47 | 2.73 | 0.59 | 1.50 | 5.73 | 7.42 | 2.44 | 4.02 | 0.20 | 2.03 |

[a] Underlying cause definition of mortality risk (UCD); pattern-of-failure (total mentions) definition of mortality risk (TM).

Because these are only *potential* gains, it is natural to reverse the interpretation and treat these figures as the average years of life lost due to each specific cause. For example, the table suggests that white males lose 2.30 years of life due to cancer in its underlying-cause role or 2.64 years due to cancer in all roles. In each case, the pattern-of-failure figure is larger than the corresponding underlying-cause figure with the difference reflecting the associated-cause impact of the disease.

In the preceding section we saw that there were important differentials in the distributions of ages at death among the four race–sex-groups. Further insight into these differentials can be obtained by comparing the cause-elimination life table life expectancy gains at ages past birth, that is, $\Delta \mathring{e}_{x \cdot \lambda}$. In Fig. 14 we present comparisons of the race- and sex-specific $\Delta \mathring{e}_{x \cdot \lambda}$'s for each of the five chronic diseases under the underlying-cause definition of mortality risk. The corresponding plots for each of the five chronic diseases under the pattern-of-failure definition of mortality risk are presented in Fig. 15.

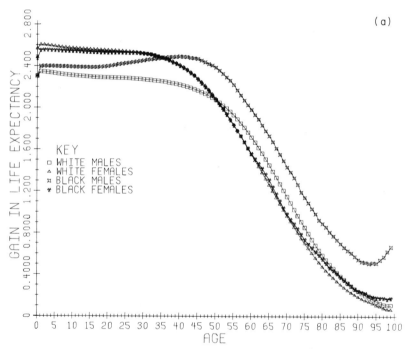

**Fig. 14.** Comparisons of years gain in life expectancy in 1969 cause-elimination life tables across four race–sex-groups for five chronic diseases, under the underlying-cause definition of mortality risk. (a) Cancer.

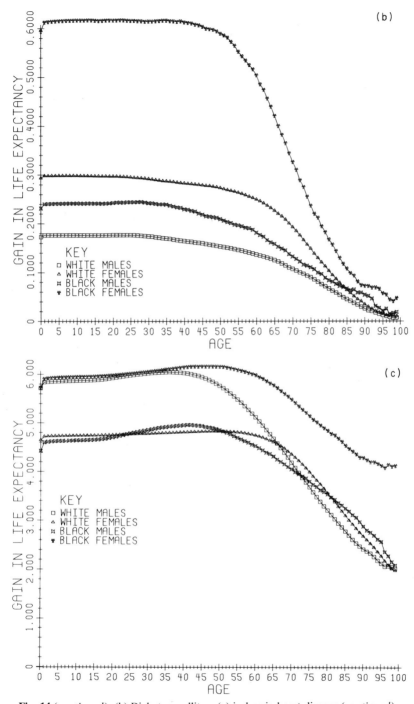

**Fig. 14** (*continued*). (b) Diabetes mellitus, (c) ischemic heart disease (*continued*).

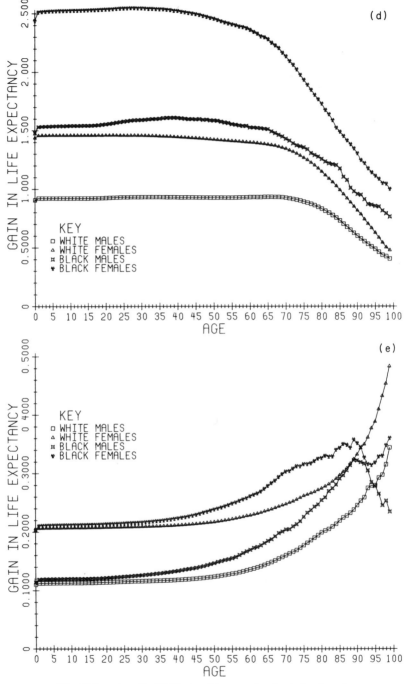

**Fig. 14** (*continued*). (d) Stroke, (e) generalized arteriosclerosis.

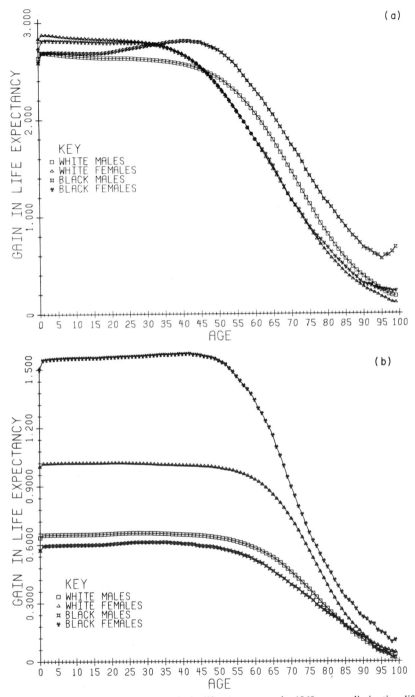

**Fig. 15.** Comparisons of years gain in life expectancy in 1969 cause-elimination life tables across four race–sex-groups for five chronic diseases, under the pattern-of-failure definition of mortality risk. (a) Cancer, (b) diabetes mellitus (*continued*).

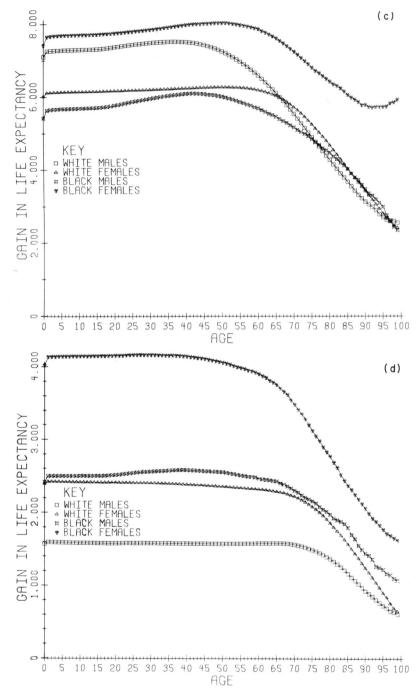

**Fig. 15** (*continued*). (c) Ischemic heart disease, (d) stroke.

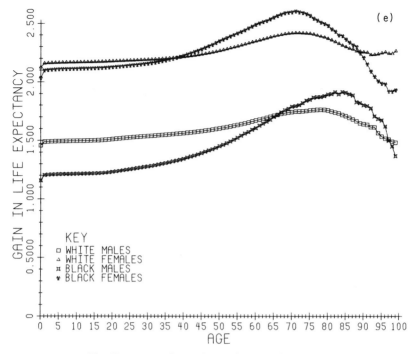

**Fig. 15** (*continued*). (e) Generalized arteriosclerosis.

In these two figures one can see that the mortality impact of each chronic disease risk remains relatively constant up to about 50 years of age, at which point, except for GA, it begins a rapid decline. Interestingly, the shapes of the cause-specific plots are similar between the underlying-cause and the pattern-of-failure definitions of risk despite the overall differences in level of effect between the two definitions. This suggests that the age-specific plots corresponding to the two types of cause elimination summarized in Table 13 are approximately related by a simple multiplicative constant.

## 5  Cause-Elimination Effects on Saved Population

In the preceding section we saw that the health impact of a given chronic disease could be summarized by a single measure $\Delta \overset{\circ}{e}_{0\cdot\lambda}$, the cause-elimination life table life expectancy gain. The difficulty with this measure is that it is not possible to say whether a given $\Delta \overset{\circ}{e}_{0\cdot\lambda}$ represents a large gain in life expectancy for a small portion of the population or whether it represents a small gain in life expectancy for a large portion of the population. To resolve this difficulty, we can define a second summary measure $\Delta \mathring{e}_{0\lambda\cdot\lambda}$, which explicitly represents the gain in life expectancy for the specific subset of the population affected by the hypothetical elimination of the mortality risk, again under the assumption of independence.

In generating such a measure by using only cause-of-death mortality data, one is restricted to defining population components solely on the basis of the prevalence of disease at the time of death. Such a component is defined by the $l_{0\lambda}$ parameter in the multiple-decrement life table as the number of persons who will eventually succumb to the specified mortality risk. The key word here is *eventually*, because at any time prior to death, an individual member of $l_{0\lambda}$ may or may not exhibit symptoms of the disease risk $\lambda$. Hence, the definition of $l_{0\lambda}$ or, more generally, of $l_{x\lambda}$ is not equivalent to a concept of prevalence of disease in a living population. For a living population, one needs to identify individual cases of disease in order to define a population component for subsequent follow-up, as in the various cancer patient survival studies such as in the Third National Cancer Survey (TNCS) and Surveillance, Epidemiology, and End Results (SEER) programs sponsored by the National Cancer Institute (NCI) (Axtell *et al.*, 1976).

### Methods

In defining such a measure, we consider the population at a given age to be comprised of two subsets of size $l_{x\lambda}$ and $l_{x\nu}$, where $l_{x\lambda}$ can be obtained from the multiple-decrement life tables, which were summarized in Tables 11 and 12, and where $l_{x\nu}$ can be obtained from $l_x$ (Tables 2–5) by subtraction. Clearly, if it is assumed that risks $\lambda$ and $\nu$ are independent, then the $l_{x\nu}$ persons who will die of other causes will not benefit at all from the elimination of the risk $\lambda$: the $l_{x\lambda}$ persons constituting the saved population will achieve *all* the benefit. Thus, the life expectancy gain in the total population $\Delta \mathring{e}_{0\cdot\lambda}$ will represent the weighted average of the gain in the unaffected group (no gain) and in the saved population group $\Delta \mathring{e}_{0\lambda\cdot\lambda}$. To see this, let us express the cause-elimination life table life expectancy in the form

$$\mathring{e}_{x\nu\cdot\lambda} = [l_{x\lambda}\mathring{e}_{x\lambda\cdot\lambda} + l_{x\nu}\mathring{e}_{x\nu}]/l_x, \qquad (5.5.1)$$

where $\mathring{e}_{x\lambda\cdot\lambda}$ represents the unknown life expectancy for the $l_{x\lambda}$ persons affected by cause elimination. Subtracting (5.3.17) from (5.5.1) yields $\Delta \mathring{e}_{x\cdot\lambda}$ as defined in (5.4.1):

$$\Delta \mathring{e}_{x\cdot\lambda} = \Delta \mathring{e}_{x\lambda\cdot\lambda}(l_{x\lambda}/l_x), \qquad (5.5.2)$$

where by definition

$$\Delta \mathring{e}_{x\lambda\cdot\lambda} = \mathring{e}_{x\lambda\cdot\lambda} - \mathring{e}_{x\lambda}. \tag{5.5.3}$$

From (5.5.2) we solve for $\Delta \mathring{e}_{x\lambda\cdot\lambda}$:

$$\Delta \mathring{e}_{x\lambda\cdot\lambda} = \Delta \mathring{e}_{x\cdot\lambda}(l_x/l_{x\lambda}). \tag{5.5.4}$$

Equation (5.5.2) shows that the cause-elimination life table life expectancy gain $\Delta \mathring{e}_{x\cdot\lambda}$ is an age-specific function of the life expectancy gain in the saved population $\Delta \mathring{e}_{x\lambda\cdot\lambda}$, with the adjustment multiplier being the age-specific relative frequency of death due to the eliminated cause $l_{x\lambda}/l_x$. Hence, the prevalence of the disease at the time of death has explicit representation in these equations. Substantively, the equation shows that a cause elimination that has a substantial impact on a given subset of the population as measured by their changed life expectancy $\Delta \mathring{e}_{x\lambda\cdot\lambda}$ will show up as a relatively trivial impact unless the proportion of the population receiving the impact is large. Equation (5.5.4) shows how $\Delta \mathring{e}_{x\lambda\cdot\lambda}$ can be computed from the three types of life tables presented in the previous sections: total-mortality life tables $(l_x)$, multiple-decrement life tables $(l_{x\lambda})$, and cause-elimination life tables $(\Delta \mathring{e}_{x\cdot\lambda})$.

## Results

Table 14 presents the saved persons' life expectancy gains for the 1969 current life tables for white males, white females, black males, and black

**Table 14**

Cause-Elimination Life Table Life Expectancy Gains (in Years) for the Saved Population $l_{0\lambda}$ for the Elimination of Five Chronic Diseases[a]

| Race–sex category | Cancer | | DM | | IHD | | Cerebrovascular accidents | | GA | |
|---|---|---|---|---|---|---|---|---|---|---|
| | UCD | TM | UCD | TM | UCD | TM | UCD | TM | UCD | TM |
| White males | 13.97 | 13.65 | 11.75 | 11.10 | 14.57 | 15.55 | 9.49 | 10.39 | 6.38 | 9.47 |
| White females | 16.59 | 16.01 | 12.02 | 11.58 | 12.21 | 13.27 | 9.57 | 10.45 | 6.24 | 9.41 |
| Black males | 15.31 | 15.29 | 14.52 | 13.72 | 16.14 | 17.05 | 13.33 | 14.39 | 8.75 | 11.32 |
| Black females | 19.45 | 19.17 | 16.35 | 16.46 | 18.04 | 19.88 | 15.11 | 16.46 | 8.88 | 12.76 |

[a] Underlying-cause definition of mortality risk (UCD); pattern-of-failure (total mentions) definition of mortality risk (TM).

females. Table 14 eliminates each of the five chronic diseases both under the underlying-cause and pattern-of-failure definitions of mortality risk.

Three general comments can be made concerning Table 14. First, whereas Table 13 indicates relatively small life expectancy gains for the less frequent diseases (e.g., DM or GA), Table 14 shows large gains in life expectancy for the saved population component. Second, the gains in Table 14 are negatively correlated with the average age at death due to the disease as can be seen by comparison with the $\mathring{e}_{0\lambda}$ values in Table 12. Third, whereas the pattern-of-failure gains in Table 13 are always larger than the corresponding underlying-cause gains, in Table 14 the pattern-of-failure gains may be larger or smaller than the corresponding underlying-cause gains because each measure in Table 14 is adjusted for the effects of differences in the prevalence of the disease risk at the time of death.

As was done with the cause-elimination life table life expectancy gains at ages past birth, we can gain further insight into these race–sex differentials by comparing the plots of $\Delta\mathring{e}_{x\lambda\cdot\lambda}$ over age. Figure 16 presents compari-

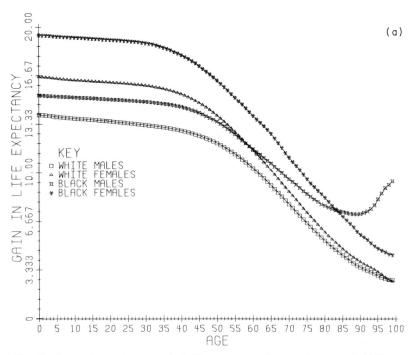

**Fig. 16.** Comparisons of years gain in life expectancy for saved persons in 1969 cause-elimination life tables across four race–sex-groups for five chronic diseases, under the underlying-cause definition of mortality risk. (a) Cancer.

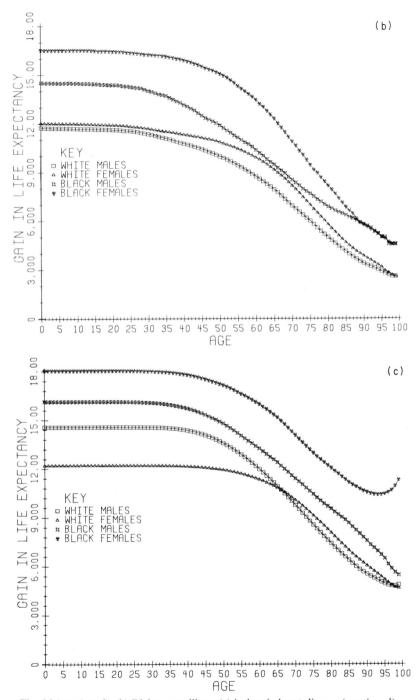

**Fig. 16** (*continued*). (b) Diabetes mellitus, (c) ischemic heart disease (*continued*).

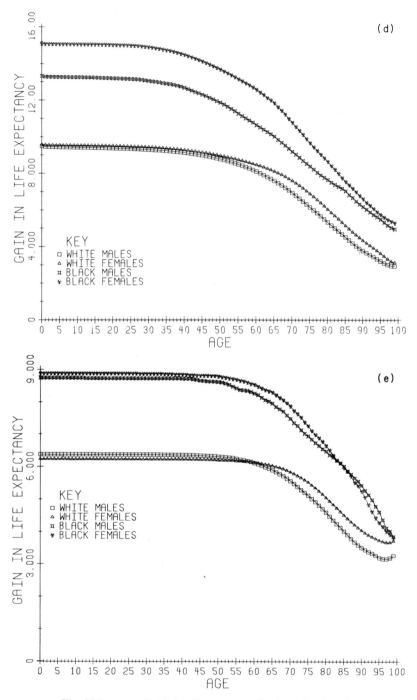

**Fig. 16** (*continued*). (d) Stroke, (e) generalized arteriosclerosis.

sons of the race- and sex-specific $\Delta\mathring{e}_{x\lambda\cdot\lambda}$'s for each of the five chronic diseases under the underlying-cause definition of mortality risk. The corresponding plots for each of the five chronic diseases under the pattern-of-failure definition of mortality risk are presented in Fig. 17.

As in Figures 14 and 15 one can see that the mortality impact of each chronic risk remains relatively constant up to about 50 years of age, when it begins a rapid decline, even in the graphs for GA that increased previously. It is significant to note that even at age 85 the life expectancy gains are still in the 3–9-year range, indicating the large potential benefits in life that would accrue as a result of successful "elimination" activities. However, it needs to be stressed that the validity of these calculations is premised on the assumption of risk independence, an assumption that is frequently made in conducting cause-elimination life table calculations.

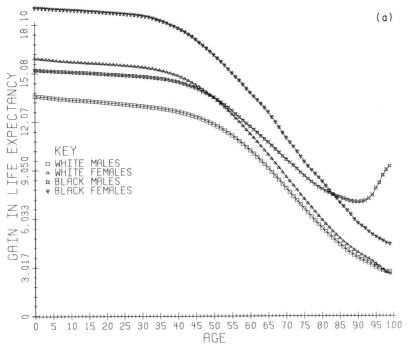

**Fig. 17.** Comparisons of years gain in life expectancy for saved persons in 1969 cause-elimination life tables across four race–sex-groups for five chronic diseases, under the pattern-of-failure definition of mortality risk. (a) Cancer (*continued*).

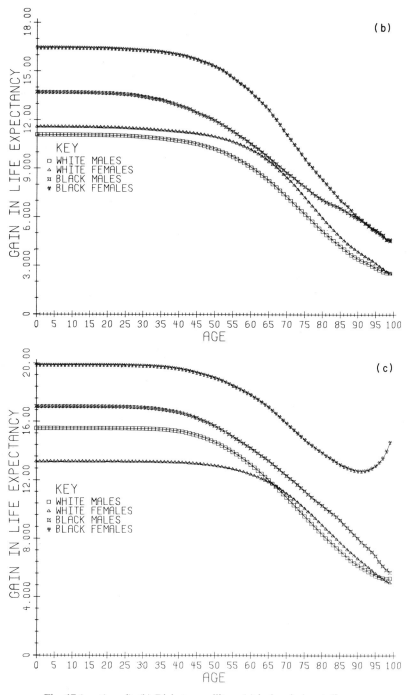

**Fig. 17** (*continued*). (b) Diabetes mellitus, (c) ischemic heart disease.

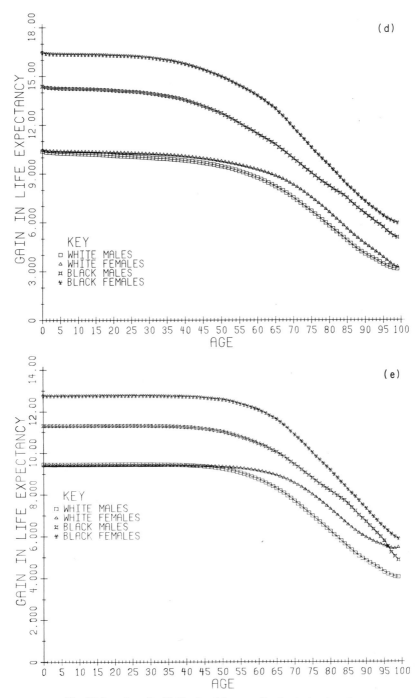

**Fig. 17** (*continued*). (d) Stroke, (e) generalized arteriosclerosis.

211

## 6    Cause-Delay Life Tables

The cause-elimination life table calculations presented in the preceding two sections are designed to provide measures of the total population impact and saved population impact of a given mortality risk defined by the disease of interest. In our case, the mortality risk was defined to be any one of five chronic diseases operating as either an underlying cause or in the pattern-of-failure mode. However, it is important to emphasize that the same calculations would apply in the analysis of acute diseases from which full "recovery" is possible, for example, infectious or parasitic diseases. This means that the independent competing-risk cause-elimination life table model provides a flexible and generally applicable methodology for assessing the population impact of any mortality risk that can be operationally defined in the vital statistics data on mortality. However, it also means that the independent competing-risk cause-elimination life table model fails to distinguish the biomedical processes characteristic of acute causes of mortality from the long-term, age-dependent processes characteristic of the chronic degenerative diseases that we are focusing on. Indeed, this model does not recognize any process characteristics of disease; instead, it views each death as operating in an instantaneous "shock" mode and does not consider any biological processes leading to the death. Thus, the model, by viewing death as a shock, makes no distinction between a death due to IHD and a death due to a gunshot wound. However, in attempting to develop bioactuarial models of the health state of a population, it is clear that a model that fails to make such a basic distinction will be of limited utility.

In this section we shall address this issue of cause elimination of chronic degenerative diseases by considering an independent competing-risk model that was specifically formulated to recognize the development of, and subsequent mortality due to, a given chronic disease as a process that unfolds over time. This model to which we refer is the stochastic compartment model presented in Fig. 3 of Chapter 4 with the specialization to independent waiting-time distributions. In Fig. 18 we display the specialized form of the model.

In Chapter 4 it was shown that the general form of this model could be "reduced" to a model in which the transition to the chronic-disease-state compartment was not displayed [see Fig. 2, and Eqs. (4.5.31) and (4.5.34) in Chapter 4]. This simplified model is the model presumed to underlie the independent competing-risk cause-elimination life table calculations. However, in dealing with chronic disease processes, the simplified or reduced model is inappropriate for consideration of anything other than the complete elimination of the mortality risk.

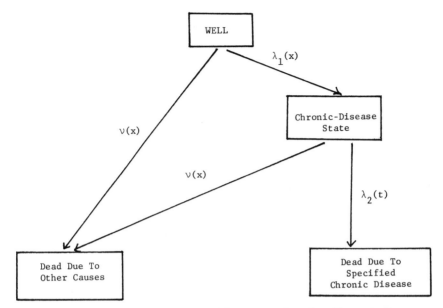

**Fig. 18.** A stochastic compartment model representation of an illness–death process with independent waiting-time distributions.

From Fig. 18, however, we can identify two approaches to the partial reduction of the force of mortality for a given chronic disease. The first is by prevention of the occurrence of the disease. This involves a modification of the transition rate $\lambda_1(x)$ that governs the onset of the chronic disease. Such a modification can be achieved through a variety of policy initiatives. For example, cigarette smoking behavior has been linked to the onset of a number of specific cancers (e.g., lung cancer) as well as to the development of both IHD and stroke. Presumably, efforts to reduce cigarette consumption effect a reduction in the transition rate $\lambda_1(x)$ for these diseases. In this regard, the reduction of $\lambda_1(x)$ to zero, equivalent to complete prevention, is one form of cause elimination.

The second approach to the partial reduction of the force of mortality for a given chronic disease involves the medical management of the disease within the affected population. This involves a modification of the transition rate $\lambda_2(t)$, which governs the transition from the chronic-disease-state compartment to the chronic-disease–death-state compartment. For example, subsequent to the introduction of insulin treatment, the mortality rates for DM were greatly reduced. In the past decade, the coronary bypass procedure has been argued to reduce the mortality risk associated with occlusion of the coronary arteries. Elsewhere, new chemotherapeutic techniques are being tested for cancer treatment. Such activities clearly reduce the force of mortality in a chronically disabled subgroup of the population, that is, the transition rate $\lambda_2(t)$ for these diseases. In this regard, the reduction of $\lambda_2(t)$ to zero, equivalent to completely effective treatment, would be a second form of cause elimination. Note that in this second form of cause elimination, there is no necessity to assume that the prevalence of the disease is abated. Indeed, with transition rate $\lambda_2(t)$ reduced, these chronically disabled persons will survive longer, which implies that the prevalence of the disease may actually increase in living populations, as suggested by Kramer (1980).

Often, innovative biomedical treatment protocols for specific chronic diseases are evaluated for effectiveness in clinical follow-up studies that produce measures of the increased survival due to the specific treatment. Additionally, the relative effectiveness of different treatment protocols is often determined by comparison of the increased survival time associated with each treatment. Presumably, the treatment protocol that results in the greatest increase in survival time will be the one selected for general dissemination unless it is prohibitively expensive.

Another important component in this assessment involves measures of the population level effect of the general dissemination of such innovative biomedical treatment protocols. The cause-delay life table model is designed to translate the clinically observed increase in survival time into the population gain in life expectancy that would occur if the treatment protocol were made available to the general population.

## Methods

Let $\bar{t}_0$ denote the average time between the onset of a chronic disease and the time of death due to the chronic disease. Let $\bar{t}_j$ denote the average time between the onset of the chronic disease and the time of death due to the chronic disease, given that a specific treatment of interest is being employed. Let $\Delta \bar{t}_j$ represent the increase in survival time under the specified treatment, that is,

$$\Delta \bar{t}_j = \bar{t}_j - \bar{t}_0. \qquad (5.6.1)$$

We call $\Delta \bar{t}_j$ the delay time for the $j$th treatment.

Because we are dealing with an age-dependent chronic disease whose onset occurs primarily in middle and older ages (e.g., any of the five chronic diseases that we are focusing on), we can approximate $\lambda(x)$ in Eq. (4.5.34) with the simple origin shift on the $\lambda_1(x)$ transition rate:

$$\lambda(x) \doteq \lambda_1(x - \bar{t}_0). \qquad (5.6.2)$$

Under the specified treatment, $\bar{t}_0$ is then replaced by $\bar{t}_j$ to yield

$$\lambda(x) \doteq \lambda_1(x - \bar{t}_j) \qquad (5.6.3a)$$

$$\doteq \lambda(x - \Delta\bar{t}_j). \qquad (5.6.3b)$$

Equation (5.6.3b) shows that the delay of $\Delta\bar{t}_j$ years will have the effect of shifting the age at which a given force of mortality is operating by $\Delta\bar{t}_j$ years. The adequacy of this last approximation depends only on the size of $\Delta\bar{t}_j$, not $\bar{t}_j$, so that (5.6.3b) will be "better than (5.6.3a) in general.

It is now necessary to transform this effect from continuous time to discrete time. To do this, we shall represent the delay time by $\Delta x_j$, where $\Delta x_j$ represents $\Delta t_j$ in the discrete age units of the life table. The corresponding equation to (5.6.3b) is then expressed in terms of the cumulative hazard:

$$h_{x\lambda j} = h_{(x - \Delta x_j)\lambda}, \qquad (5.6.4)$$

where

$$h_{x\lambda j} = 0, \quad \text{if} \quad \Delta x_j > x. \qquad (5.6.5)$$

From (5.3.16) the total force of mortality is the sum of the two component forces of mortality:

$$h_x = h_{x\nu} + h_{x\lambda}. \qquad (5.6.6)$$

From (5.4.2) the effect of elimination of risk $\lambda$ is to nullify $h_{x\lambda}$ in (5.6.6) so that the total force of mortality becomes

$$h_{x\nu\cdot\lambda} = h_{x\nu}. \qquad (5.6.7)$$

The cause-delay model does not nullify $h_{x\lambda}$ in (5.6.6) but instead replaces it by $h_{x\lambda j}$, so that the total force of mortality, denoted by $h_{x\nu\cdot\lambda j}$, becomes

$$h_{x\nu\cdot\lambda j} = h_{x\nu} + h_{x\lambda j}. \qquad (5.6.8)$$

For no delay, $\Delta x_j = 0$ and $h_{x\lambda 0} = h_{x\lambda}$, so that

$$h_{x\nu\cdot\lambda j}\Big|_{\Delta x_j = 0} = h_x. \qquad (5.6.9)$$

Alternatively, for $\Delta x_j > x$, $h_{x\lambda j} = 0$, so that

$$h_{x\nu\cdot\lambda j}\Big|_{\Delta x_j > x} = h_{x\nu\cdot\lambda}. \qquad (5.6.10)$$

From (5.6.10) it can be seen that the cause-elimination life table model is a special case of the cause-delay model in which the delay time $\Delta x_j$ is longer than the age of the oldest survivor at his time of death.

The cause-delay calculations are simple generalizations of (5.4.3)–(5.4.10), with $h_{xv \cdot \lambda j}$ given by (5.6.8):

$$q_{xv \cdot \lambda j} = 1 - \exp(-h_{xv \cdot \lambda j}), \tag{5.6.11}$$

$$d_{xv \cdot \lambda j} = l_{xv \cdot \lambda j} \, q_{xv \cdot \lambda j}, \tag{5.6.12}$$

$$l_{(x+1)v \cdot \lambda j} = l_{xv \cdot \lambda j} - d_{xv \cdot \lambda j}, \tag{5.6.13}$$

and

$$\overset{\circ}{e}_{xv \cdot \lambda j} = \frac{1}{l_{xv \cdot \lambda j}} \sum_{i=x}^{\omega} (i + b_i - x) \, d_{iv \cdot \lambda j}, \tag{5.6.14}$$

where $b_x$ is the same as in (5.2.14) and (5.4.6), except for $b_\omega$, which is computed as

$$b_\omega = 1/h_{(\omega-1)v \cdot \lambda j}, \tag{5.6.15}$$

instead of as in (5.2.15) or (5.4.7).

Finally, the population gain in life expectancy that would occur if the $j$th treatment protocol were made available to the general population is computed as the difference in the $\overset{\circ}{e}_x$ columns in the cause-delay life table and the observed life table for total mortality:

$$\Delta \overset{\circ}{e}_{x \cdot \lambda j} = \overset{\circ}{e}_{xv \cdot \lambda j} - \overset{\circ}{e}_x. \tag{5.6.16}$$

### Results

In Table 15 we present the cause-delay life table life expectancy gains for the 1969 current life tables for white males, white females, black males, and black females under the hypothetical delay of 1, 2, 3, 5, 10, and 15 years' time for each of the five chronic diseases both under the underlying-cause and pattern-of-failure definitions of mortality risk.

Examination of Table 15 shows that there is a substantial difference between the impact of a given treatment in a clinical population and in the general population, with the life expectancy gain in the general population being much smaller than the clinical delay time. However, in evaluating these gains it is important to recognize that the effect of a given delay cannot be greater than the effect of the total elimination of the disease. This suggests that we can evaluate the effects of the various delays in Table 15 by comparing them with the effects of the total elimination of the disease presented in Table 13. In Table 16 each effect in Table 15 is represented as a percentage of the cause-elimination life table life expectancy gain in Table 13, that is, as $(\Delta \overset{\circ}{e}_{x \cdot \lambda j} / \Delta \overset{\circ}{e}_{x \cdot \lambda}) \cdot 100$.

**Table 15**

Cause-Delay 1969 Life Table Life Expectancy Gains (in Years) for Six Hypothetical Delay Times[a]

| Delay time | Cancer | | DM | | IHD | | Cerebro-vascular accidents | | GA | |
|---|---|---|---|---|---|---|---|---|---|---|
| | UCD | TM | UCD | TM | UCD | TM | UCD | TM | UCD | TM |
| White males | | | | | | | | | | |
| 1.00 | 0.16 | 0.19 | 0.01 | 0.06 | 0.38 | 0.45 | 0.09 | 0.15 | 0.02 | 0.15 |
| 2.00 | 0.31 | 0.37 | 0.03 | 0.11 | 0.75 | 0.88 | 0.17 | 0.28 | 0.03 | 0.28 |
| 3.00 | 0.46 | 0.53 | 0.04 | 0.15 | 1.09 | 1.29 | 0.25 | 0.40 | 0.04 | 0.41 |
| 5.00 | 0.72 | 0.84 | 0.06 | 0.24 | 1.74 | 2.05 | 0.38 | 0.62 | 0.06 | 0.62 |
| 10.00 | 1.25 | 1.45 | 0.10 | 0.40 | 3.05 | 3.64 | 0.61 | 1.00 | 0.09 | 1.00 |
| 15.00 | 1.62 | 1.87 | 0.13 | 0.50 | 4.00 | 4.83 | 0.74 | 1.24 | 0.10 | 1.22 |
| White females | | | | | | | | | | |
| 1.00 | 0.15 | 0.17 | 0.02 | 0.08 | 0.37 | 0.44 | 0.14 | 0.22 | 0.03 | 0.22 |
| 2.00 | 0.30 | 0.34 | 0.05 | 0.16 | 0.72 | 0.86 | 0.27 | 0.42 | 0.06 | 0.41 |
| 3.00 | 0.43 | 0.49 | 0.07 | 0.24 | 1.04 | 1.26 | 0.39 | 0.61 | 0.08 | 0.60 |
| 5.00 | 0.69 | 0.78 | 0.10 | 0.37 | 1.64 | 1.99 | 0.60 | 0.94 | 0.11 | 0.91 |
| 10.00 | 1.23 | 1.39 | 0.17 | 0.62 | 2.79 | 3.46 | 0.96 | 1.54 | 0.17 | 1.47 |
| 15.00 | 1.64 | 1.83 | 0.22 | 0.78 | 3.55 | 4.46 | 1.17 | 1.90 | 0.19 | 1.78 |
| Black males | | | | | | | | | | |
| 1.00 | 0.15 | 0.17 | 0.02 | 0.04 | 0.27 | 0.31 | 0.10 | 0.16 | 0.01 | 0.10 |
| 2.00 | 0.29 | 0.33 | 0.03 | 0.08 | 0.52 | 0.61 | 0.21 | 0.32 | 0.02 | 0.19 |
| 3.00 | 0.42 | 0.47 | 0.04 | 0.11 | 0.76 | 0.89 | 0.30 | 0.46 | 0.03 | 0.27 |
| 5.00 | 0.67 | 0.75 | 0.07 | 0.18 | 1.22 | 1.43 | 0.47 | 0.73 | 0.05 | 0.42 |
| 10.00 | 1.18 | 1.33 | 0.12 | 0.31 | 2.17 | 2.56 | 0.82 | 1.27 | 0.08 | 0.71 |
| 15.00 | 1.56 | 1.75 | 0.16 | 0.41 | 2.88 | 3.43 | 1.05 | 1.65 | 0.10 | 0.89 |
| Black females | | | | | | | | | | |
| 1.00 | 0.12 | 0.14 | 0.04 | 0.09 | 0.33 | 0.39 | 0.16 | 0.24 | 0.02 | 0.15 |
| 2.00 | 0.24 | 0.27 | 0.07 | 0.17 | 0.61 | 0.73 | 0.31 | 0.47 | 0.03 | 0.29 |
| 3.00 | 0.36 | 0.40 | 0.10 | 0.26 | 0.92 | 1.09 | 0.45 | 0.68 | 0.06 | 0.44 |
| 5.00 | 0.58 | 0.65 | 0.16 | 0.41 | 1.44 | 1.71 | 0.71 | 1.08 | 0.09 | 0.67 |
| 10.00 | 1.06 | 1.18 | 0.29 | 0.74 | 2.60 | 3.13 | 1.24 | 1.93 | 0.14 | 1.17 |
| 15.00 | 1.45 | 1.61 | 0.39 | 0.98 | 3.49 | 4.24 | 1.63 | 2.57 | 0.17 | 1.49 |

[a] Underlying-cause definition of mortality risk (UCD); pattern-of-failure (total mentions) definition of mortality risk (TM).

**Table 16**

Representation of Cause-Delay 1969 Life Table Life Expectancy Gain as a Percentage of Corresponding Cause-Elimination Life Table Life Expectancy Gain for Six Hypothetical Delay Times[a]

| Delay time | Cancer | | DM | | IHD | | Cerebro-vascular accidents | | GA | |
|---|---|---|---|---|---|---|---|---|---|---|
| | UCD | TM | UCD | TM | UCD | TM | UCD | TM | UCD | TM |
| | | | | | White males | | | | | |
| 1.00 | 6.97 | 7.13 | 8.21 | 8.70 | 6.70 | 6.30 | 10.07 | 9.25 | 14.70 | 10.01 |
| 2.00 | 13.58 | 13.86 | 15.84 | 16.78 | 13.08 | 12.33 | 19.22 | 17.75 | 27.27 | 19.36 |
| 3.00 | 19.82 | 20.21 | 22.91 | 24.27 | 19.15 | 18.10 | 27.56 | 25.56 | 37.97 | 27.80 |
| 5.00 | 31.26 | 31.81 | 35.51 | 37.62 | 30.35 | 28.84 | 41.94 | 39.24 | 55.41 | 42.47 |
| 10.00 | 54.26 | 54.98 | 59.27 | 62.65 | 53.29 | 51.28 | 67.15 | 64.02 | 80.83 | 68.47 |
| 15.00 | 70.45 | 71.12 | 74.63 | 78.44 | 69.89 | 67.94 | 81.64 | 78.90 | 91.98 | 83.46 |
| | | | | | White females | | | | | |
| 1.00 | 5.90 | 6.10 | 8.06 | 8.37 | 7.95 | 7.34 | 10.00 | 9.21 | 15.14 | 10.21 |
| 2.00 | 11.54 | 11.91 | 15.60 | 16.21 | 15.44 | 14.33 | 19.12 | 17.71 | 27.72 | 19.50 |
| 3.00 | 16.92 | 17.44 | 22.63 | 23.54 | 22.47 | 20.94 | 27.43 | 25.54 | 39.06 | 28.06 |
| 5.00 | 26.93 | 27.68 | 35.32 | 36.74 | 35.22 | 33.08 | 41.81 | 39.34 | 56.50 | 42.87 |
| 10.00 | 47.94 | 48.91 | 59.55 | 61.96 | 60.08 | 57.44 | 67.05 | 64.43 | 82.17 | 69.15 |
| 15.00 | 63.86 | 64.77 | 75.26 | 78.11 | 76.45 | 74.16 | 81.42 | 79.39 | 92.79 | 83.89 |
| | | | | | Black males | | | | | |
| 1.00 | 6.46 | 6.46 | 6.70 | 7.09 | 6.00 | 5.70 | 7.05 | 6.62 | 8.91 | 8.24 |
| 2.00 | 12.66 | 12.65 | 13.05 | 13.78 | 11.77 | 11.19 | 14.03 | 13.07 | 20.82 | 16.24 |
| 3.00 | 18.31 | 18.32 | 19.04 | 20.10 | 17.25 | 16.43 | 20.60 | 19.23 | 29.50 | 23.60 |
| 5.00 | 29.08 | 29.09 | 30.04 | 31.63 | 27.53 | 26.32 | 32.12 | 30.20 | 43.65 | 36.59 |
| 10.00 | 51.30 | 51.29 | 52.29 | 54.69 | 49.01 | 47.26 | 55.20 | 52.55 | 70.07 | 61.36 |
| 15.00 | 67.55 | 67.51 | 68.22 | 70.85 | 65.11 | 63.28 | 71.15 | 68.46 | 84.43 | 77.25 |
| | | | | | Black females | | | | | |
| 1.00 | 5.05 | 5.12 | 5.93 | 5.95 | 5.75 | 5.30 | 6.58 | 6.04 | 9.45 | 7.53 |
| 2.00 | 9.84 | 9.98 | 11.41 | 11.58 | 10.73 | 9.80 | 12.69 | 11.72 | 16.91 | 14.34 |
| 3.00 | 14.66 | 14.81 | 17.09 | 17.15 | 16.03 | 14.68 | 18.30 | 16.95 | 28.00 | 21.58 |
| 5.00 | 23.57 | 23.85 | 27.30 | 27.41 | 25.18 | 23.12 | 28.94 | 26.97 | 42.45 | 33.16 |
| 10.00 | 43.03 | 43.43 | 48.74 | 49.04 | 45.41 | 42.24 | 50.75 | 48.10 | 68.73 | 57.35 |
| 15.00 | 58.67 | 59.09 | 65.12 | 65.52 | 60.89 | 57.21 | 66.65 | 63.92 | 83.10 | 73.40 |

[a] Underlying-cause definition of mortality risk (UCD); pattern-of-failure (total mentions) definition of mortality risk (TM).

In Table 16 we see that the effects of even modest delays of the time of death due to a given chronic disease can yield a sizable proportion of the cause-elimination life table life expectancy gains. Therefore, for white males, a 3-year delay in the cancer patient survival time would yield about 20% (19.82% by the underlying-cause definition; 20.21% by the pattern-of-failure definition) of the gain in life expectancy obtainable from the complete elimination of cancer as a mortality risk. This would be roughly equivalent to a 20% reduction in the rate of cancer incidence, although the policy implications of the two approaches could be vastly different.

As seen in Table 15, the population impact of a given delay is greatly influenced by the relative frequency of death to the specified chronic disease. A similar effect was noted earlier with the cause-elimination life table life expectancy gain. Previously, we saw that this effect could be removed by computing a life expectancy gain $\Delta \mathring{e}_{x\lambda\cdot\lambda}$ specifically designed to represent the effect of cause elimination in the saved population. With the cause-delay life table model, we can compute an analogous measure to (5.5.4):

$$\Delta \mathring{e}_{x\lambda\cdot\lambda j} = \Delta \mathring{e}_{x\cdot\lambda j}(l_x/l_{x\lambda}). \qquad (5.6.17)$$

The difference between (5.5.4) and (5.6.17) is that whereas the former measure $\Delta \mathring{e}_{x\lambda\cdot\lambda}$ represents the life expectancy gain in a population subgroup saved from the eliminated cause, the latter measure $\Delta \mathring{e}_{x\lambda\cdot\lambda j}$ represents the life expectancy gain in the same population subgroup when only a portion of the subgroup is saved. The delay of the time of death to the specified chronic disease permits some portion of this group to succumb to other causes of death during the delay interval $\Delta x_j$. In Table 17 we present the effects of the various delays when the transformation (5.6.17) is applied to Table 15 to represent the effects on this potentially saved population.

Examination of Table 17 shows that by expressing the delay in terms of its effect on the specific population subgroup that will benefit from the delay, the realized gain in life expectancy will be much closer to the delay time, although there still appear to be diminishing returns for the larger delays. This is due to the fact that with increasing delays, the censoring effects of other causes of death will have more time to operate, thereby reducing the likelihood that any given individual will live to experience the full benefit of the delay. This effect is well known in clinical follow-up studies in which the survival probabilities are frequently divided by the expected survival probabilities in the general population to obtain the *relative survival rate,* a measure that better represents the mortality risks associated with the target disease.

**Table 17**

Cause-Delay 1969 Life Table Life Expectancy Gain (in Years) for the Saved Population $l_{0\lambda}$ for Six Hypothetical Delay Times[a]

| Delay time | Cancer | | DM | | IHD | | Cerebro-vascular accidents | | GA | |
|---|---|---|---|---|---|---|---|---|---|---|
| | UCD | TM | UCD | TM | UCD | TM | UCD | TM | UCD | TM |
| | | | | | White males | | | | | |
| 1.00 | 0.97 | 0.97 | 0.96 | 0.97 | 0.98 | 0.98 | 0.96 | 0.96 | 0.94 | 0.96 |
| 2.00 | 1.90 | 1.89 | 1.86 | 1.86 | 1.91 | 1.92 | 1.82 | 1.84 | 1.74 | 1.83 |
| 3.00 | 2.77 | 2.76 | 2.69 | 2.69 | 2.79 | 2.81 | 2.61 | 2.65 | 2.42 | 2.63 |
| 5.00 | 4.37 | 4.34 | 4.17 | 4.17 | 4.42 | 4.48 | 3.98 | 4.08 | 3.54 | 4.02 |
| 10.00 | 7.58 | 7.51 | 6.96 | 6.95 | 7.76 | 7.97 | 6.37 | 6.65 | 5.16 | 6.48 |
| 15.00 | 9.84 | 9.71 | 8.77 | 8.71 | 10.18 | 10.56 | 7.75 | 8.19 | 5.87 | 7.90 |
| | | | | | White females | | | | | |
| 1.00 | 0.98 | 0.98 | 0.97 | 0.97 | 0.97 | 0.97 | 0.96 | 0.96 | 0.94 | 0.96 |
| 2.00 | 1.91 | 1.91 | 1.88 | 1.88 | 1.89 | 1.90 | 1.83 | 1.85 | 1.73 | 1.83 |
| 3.00 | 2.81 | 2.79 | 2.72 | 2.73 | 2.74 | 2.78 | 2.62 | 2.67 | 2.44 | 2.64 |
| 5.00 | 4.47 | 4.43 | 4.25 | 4.26 | 4.30 | 4.39 | 4.00 | 4.11 | 3.53 | 4.03 |
| 10.00 | 7.95 | 7.83 | 7.16 | 7.18 | 7.34 | 7.62 | 6.42 | 6.74 | 5.13 | 6.51 |
| 15.00 | 10.59 | 10.37 | 9.05 | 9.05 | 9.34 | 9.84 | 7.79 | 8.30 | 5.79 | 7.89 |
| | | | | | Black males | | | | | |
| 1.00 | 0.99 | 0.99 | 0.97 | 0.97 | 0.97 | 0.97 | 0.94 | 0.95 | 0.78 | 0.93 |
| 2.00 | 1.94 | 1.94 | 1.89 | 1.89 | 1.90 | 1.91 | 1.87 | 1.88 | 1.82 | 1.84 |
| 3.00 | 2.80 | 2.80 | 2.77 | 2.76 | 2.78 | 2.80 | 2.74 | 2.77 | 2.58 | 2.67 |
| 5.00 | 4.45 | 4.45 | 4.36 | 4.34 | 4.44 | 4.49 | 4.28 | 4.34 | 3.82 | 4.14 |
| 10.00 | 7.86 | 7.84 | 7.59 | 7.50 | 7.91 | 8.06 | 7.36 | 7.56 | 6.13 | 6.95 |
| 15.00 | 10.34 | 10.32 | 9.91 | 9.72 | 10.51 | 10.79 | 9.48 | 9.85 | 7.38 | 8.74 |
| | | | | | Black females | | | | | |
| 1.00 | 0.98 | 0.98 | 0.98 | 0.98 | 1.00 | 1.00 | 0.99 | 0.99 | 0.84 | 0.96 |
| 2.00 | 1.91 | 1.91 | 1.89 | 1.91 | 1.94 | 1.95 | 1.92 | 1.93 | 1.50 | 1.83 |
| 3.00 | 2.85 | 2.84 | 2.82 | 2.82 | 2.89 | 2.92 | 2.76 | 2.79 | 2.49 | 2.75 |
| 5.00 | 4.58 | 4.57 | 4.51 | 4.51 | 4.54 | 4.60 | 4.37 | 4.44 | 3.77 | 4.23 |
| 10.00 | 8.37 | 8.33 | 8.06 | 8.07 | 8.19 | 8.40 | 7.67 | 7.92 | 6.10 | 7.32 |
| 15.00 | 11.41 | 11.33 | 10.76 | 10.78 | 10.99 | 11.37 | 10.07 | 10.52 | 7.38 | 9.37 |

[a] Underlying-cause definition of mortality risk (UCD); pattern-of-failure (total mentions) definition of mortality risk (TM).

In interpreting the preceding results for the saved population subgroup $l_{x\lambda}$, one needs to be mindful of the definition of $l_{x\lambda}$ in (5.3.3) as the number of persons alive at age $x$ whose ultimate cause of death will be cause $\lambda$. This is *not* the same as the population subgroup $l_{M,x}$ defined in Eq. (4.5.2) as the number of persons alive at age $x$ who are currently in the chronic-disease state represented by the risk $\lambda_1$ in Fig. 18. Although there is likely to be some overlap between the two sets of persons denoted by $l_{x\lambda}$ and $l_{M,x}$, it is also the case (1) that some of the $l_{x\lambda}$ persons will develop the disease beyond age $x$ and hence will not be contained in $l_{M,x}$ and (2) that some of the $l_{M,x}$ persons will die from other causes $v$ and hence will not be contained in $l_{x\lambda}$. That is, membership in the group of saved persons $l_{x\lambda}$ is determined at the time of death by the cause of death and represents persons who succumb to risk $\lambda$. In contrast, membership in the group $l_{M,x}$ is determined at the time of onset of the chronic disease and represents persons who succumb to risk $\lambda_1$. Life-table methods for analysis of the group $l_{M,x}$ were briefly introduced in Chapter 4 and will be discussed in more detail in Chapter 8. An awareness of the character of chronic-disease mortality as the end point of a biomedical process with one or more intermediate morbid states can enhance one's appreciation of the types of activities implied and possibilities of effects involved in discussions of cause elimination or cause delay. In particular, if the model in Fig. 18 is at all plausible, then the $l_x$ persons alive at age $x$ are not all equally likely to die from cause $\lambda$ because only the subgroup $l_{M,x}$ is exposed directly to the mortality risk $\lambda_2$. Thus, although our model cannot identify the individual members of the subgroup $l_{x\lambda}$, it is sensible to suppose that such a group does exist and that with successful delay of death to cause $\lambda$ by $\Delta x_j$ years, their life expectancy could increase in the manner exhibited in Table 17 if the independence assumptions (4.5.31) and (4.5.34) are approximately true.

Our treatment of the cause-delay model has focused on delay of the mortality risk $\lambda_2(t)$. The method can also be interpreted as applying to the risk $\lambda_1(x)$ so that delay is a form of partial prevention. In both cases, the model approximations lead to a delay in the cause-specific force of mortality $\lambda(x)$ as shown in (5.6.4). Other authors have presented models for describing medical and public health progress in terms of a proportional reduction in $\lambda(x)$. For example, Tsai *et al.* (1978) derived a net probability of death formula that in our notation is of the form

$$q_{xv\cdot\lambda\pi} = 1 - \exp[-h_{xv\cdot\lambda\pi}], \tag{5.6.18}$$

where

$$h_{xv\cdot\lambda\pi} = h_{xv} + (1 - \pi)h_{x\lambda} \tag{5.6.19}$$

and where $\pi$ is the proportional reduction in $h_{x\lambda}$. For no reduction, $\pi = 0$, so that

$$h_{xv\cdot\lambda 0} = h_x, \tag{5.6.20}$$

while for complete elimination, $\pi = 1$, so that

$$h_{xv\cdot\lambda 1} = h_{xv\cdot\lambda}. \tag{5.6.21}$$

Equations (5.6.20) and (5.6.21) are thus analogous to (5.6.9) and (5.6.10). Keyfitz (1977) carried this one step further by developing an approximation that predicts the change in life expectancy when the value of $\pi$ is small, for example, on the order of 0.01. This level of reduction results in life expectancy gains that are roughly additive so that the relative impact of various causes can be evaluated with a linear measure.

## 7  Life Table Methods for Dependent Disease Processes

The necessary assumption for the independent competing-risk cause-elimination life table calculations, which we have employed in previous sections to compute various measures of life expectancy gains, is that the force of mortality from the risk $\lambda$ being delayed or eliminated is independent of the force of mortality from the risk $v$, defined as all other causes of death. This condition was formally stated as Eq. (4.4.24) in the form

$$\mu_{\lambda\cdot v}(x) = \lambda(x) \qquad \text{and} \qquad \mu_{v\cdot\lambda}(x) = v(x). \tag{5.7.1}$$

One can see that (5.7.1) ensures the validity of the computational formula (5.4.2) used in the calculation of the cause-elimination life table for risk $\lambda$.

When dealing with dependent disease processes, several complications arise. The condition of independence (5.7.1) applies to risks, not to diseases, so that there are issues of definition to be resolved. In particular, (5.7.1) suggests a definition of independence of diseases in which the rates of development of each of several diseases proceed at the same pace regardless of the presence or absence of any or all of the other diseases. This definition suggests that one approach to dependent diseases treats them as dependent risks that can be represented in a compartment model with unobserved morbidity states that explain the dependence. A second approach is the pattern-of-failure definition of risk in which combinations of diseases are employed in defining independent risks. This approach recognizes that the categories of disease obtained from aggregation of a broad range of ICDA codes are frequently quite heterogeneous, so that the level of dependence of a disease pair is highly variable over specific code combinations.

Operationally, the two approaches to disease dependence are distinguished as follows. In the first case, the number of risks in the model is held constant but the number of unobserved health-state compartments is increased so that the change in the transition rates implied by failure of (5.7.1) is explained by varying forces of mortality over the unobserved compartments. In the second case, the number of risks in the model is increased, implying that the number of observed death-state compartments is also increased in direct proportion. Naturally, a third approach for disease dependence could be developed by combining these two approaches, for example, if neither alone was viewed as satisfactory.

Our ability to implement practical computational methods that incorporate these various representations of dependent disease processes is primarily restricted by the limited information content of the available vital statistics mortality data. For this reason, in the absence of strong evidence supporting the necessity for explicitly modeling a given mode of dependence, the assumption of independence is usually made. Practically, if underlying-cause mortality data are the only data available, then the assumption of independence can be avoided only in cases in which additional information on the form of dependence is obtainable from auxiliary data or theory. If multiple-cause mortality data are available, one can deal with dependence in the ways described.

### Methods

The first approach employs the combination of diseases to structure the outcomes of a stochastic compartment model of disease dependency. Such a model was presented in Fig. 4, Chapter 4. However, we shall illustrate the approach by considering a simplified version of this model, which is displayed in Fig. 19.

In Fig. 19 the transition rate $\lambda_B(x)$, which governs the mortality risk associated with disease B, is assumed to be unchanged by the onset of chronic disease A. This is the necessary condition for biomedical independence of the pair of diseases A and B. Additionally, the transition rate $\nu(x)$, which governs the mortality risk associated with other causes of death, is assumed to be unchanged by the onset of chronic disease A. Thus, chronic disease A is assumed to be a nonlethal "background" chronic disability with no effect on mortality. This lack of a mortality risk for disease A, which is assumed for purposes of simplicity, could be substantively meaningful if it were a result of an effective biomedical management of the disease such as discussed in the cause-delay model. Obviously, condition (5.7.1) is satisfied so that the mortality risk for disease B is independent of the mortality risk for other causes of death.

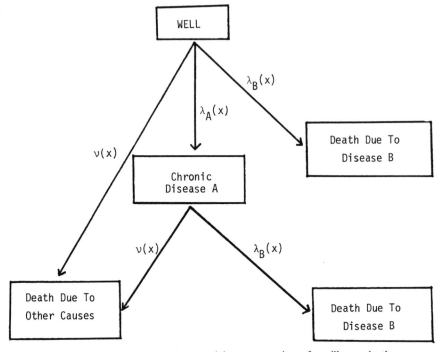

**Fig. 19.** A stochastic compartment model representation of an illness–death process with independent multiple causes of death.

With multiple-cause mortality data, only the death states in Fig. 19 are observable. Hence, the observable transition rates are those indicated in Fig. 20, in which the death states are seen to be pattern-of-failure death states, although in view of Fig. 19 our risks are not the pattern-of-failure risks.

Note that the transition rates $\nu(x)$ and $\lambda_B(x)$ in Fig. 20 are the same as in Fig. 19. Also, whereas the multiple-decrement methods discussed earlier required us to deal with only two decrements, that is, as in Eq. (5.3.11),

$$\mu(x) = \nu(x) + \lambda(x), \qquad (5.7.2)$$

the model in Fig. 20 requires that we deal with a further decomposition of $\lambda(x)$ into two components, $\lambda_{BA}(x)$ and $\lambda_B(x)$. Thus Eq. (5.3.11) is replaced by

$$\mu(x) = \nu(x) + \lambda_B(x) + \lambda_{BA}(x). \qquad (5.7.3)$$

Following the methods of reduced form multiple-decrement calculations introduced in Section 5 of Chapter 4, we define two new transi-

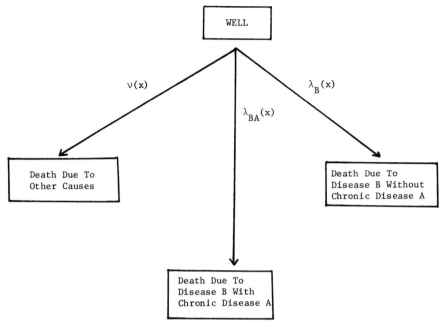

**Fig. 20.** Reduced form of the stochastic compartment model of the illness–death process depicted in Fig. 19.

tion densities

$$g_{\lambda_B}(x) = \lim_{\Delta x \to 0} \frac{1}{\Delta x} \Pr[\text{dead due to cause } \lambda_B \\ \text{in age interval } (x, x + \Delta x), \\ \text{given survival to age } 0], \qquad (5.7.4)$$

$$g_{\lambda_{BA}}(x) = \lim_{\Delta x \to 0} \frac{1}{\Delta x} \Pr[\text{dead due to cause } \lambda_{BA} \\ \text{in age interval } (x, x + \Delta x), \\ \text{given survival to age } 0]. \qquad (5.7.5)$$

In view of the independence of the risk $\lambda_B$ in Fig. 19, it follows that these transition densities are related to the transition density $g_\lambda(x)$ defined in (4.5.5) by

$$g_{\lambda_B}(x) = g_\lambda(x) \exp\left\{ -\int_0^x \lambda_A(a)\, da \right\}, \qquad (5.7.6)$$

$$g_{\lambda_{BA}}(x) = g_\lambda(x) \left\{ 1 - \exp\left[ -\int_0^x \lambda_A(a)\, da \right] \right\}, \qquad (5.7.7)$$

in which case it obviously follows that

$$g_\lambda(x) = g_{\lambda_B}(x) + g_{\lambda_{BA}}(x). \tag{5.7.8}$$

With the transition densities in hand, the multiple-decrement life table column $d_{x\lambda}$ is decomposed into $d_{x\lambda_B}$ and $d_{x\lambda_{BA}}$, where

$$d_{x\lambda_B} = l_0 \int_x^{x+1} g_{\lambda_B}(a) \, da, \tag{5.7.9}$$

$$d_{x\lambda_{BA}} = l_0 \int_x^{x+1} g_{\lambda_{BA}}(a) \, da, \tag{5.7.10}$$

where (5.7.8) implies additivity of these decrements:

$$d_{x\lambda} = d_{x\lambda_B} + d_{x\lambda_{BA}}. \tag{5.7.11}$$

With multiple-cause mortality counts for disease B recorded without or with disease A as $D_{x\lambda_B}$ and $D_{x\lambda_{BA}}$, we have

$$D_{x\lambda} = D_{x\lambda_B} + D_{x\lambda_{BA}}, \tag{5.7.12}$$

so that empirical estimates of $d_{x\lambda_B}$ and $d_{x\lambda_{BA}}$ are obtained, by analogy to (5.3.1) or (5.3.2) as

$$d_{x\lambda_B} = d_x(D_{x\lambda_B}/D_x), \tag{5.7.13}$$

and

$$d_{x\lambda_{BA}} = d_x(D_{x\lambda_{BA}}/D_x), \tag{5.7.14}$$

Other mutiple-decrement life table columns can be computed by using equations analogous to (5.3.3), (5.3.5), (5.3.7), and (5.3.22):

$$l_{x\lambda_B} = \sum_{i=x}^{\omega} d_{i\lambda_B}, \tag{5.7.15}$$

$$q_{x\lambda_B} = d_{x\lambda_B}/l_x, \tag{5.7.16}$$

$$h_{x\lambda_B} = h_x(D_{x\lambda_B}/D_x) = h_x(d_{x\lambda_B}/d_x), \tag{5.7.17}$$

and

$$\mathring{e}_{x\lambda_B} = \left(\frac{1}{l_{x\lambda_B}}\right) \sum_{i=x}^{\omega} (i + b_i - x) \, d_{i\lambda_B}, \tag{5.7.18}$$

where the $b_x$'s are the same as in (5.2.14). A similar set of equations applies to the computations for the risk $\lambda_{BA}$.

As in (5.3.17), we can also represent the multiple-decrement life expectancy $\mathring{e}_{x\lambda}$ as the weighted average of the life expectancies $\mathring{e}_{x\lambda_B}$ and $\mathring{e}_{x\lambda_{BA}}$:

$$\mathring{e}_{x\lambda} = (l_{x\lambda_B}\mathring{e}_{x\lambda_B} + l_{x\lambda_{BA}}\mathring{e}_{x\lambda_{BA}})/l_{x\lambda}, \tag{5.7.19}$$

where (5.7.9) and (5.7.15) jointly imply

$$l_{x\lambda_B} = l_0 \int_x^\infty g_{\lambda_B}(a) \, da \tag{5.7.20}$$

and

$$l_{x\lambda_{BA}} = l_0 \int_x^\infty g_{\lambda_{BA}}(a) \, da, \tag{5.7.21}$$

which in view of (5.7.8) obviously satisfy the simple additive condition

$$l_{x\lambda} = l_0 \int_x^\infty g_\lambda(a) \, da = l_{x\lambda_B} + l_{x\lambda_{BA}}. \tag{5.7.22}$$

Recall from (5.3.18b) that $\mathring{e}_{0\lambda}$ is defined as

$$\mathring{e}_{0\lambda} = \int_0^\infty x f_\lambda(x) \, dx, \tag{5.7.23}$$

where $f_\lambda(x)$ is given by

$$f_\lambda(x) = (l_0/l_{0\lambda})g_\lambda(x), \tag{5.7.24}$$

as shown in Eq. (4.5.7). Similarly, we have

$$\mathring{e}_{0\lambda_B} = \int_0^\infty x f_{\lambda_B}(x) \, dx \tag{5.7.25}$$

and

$$\mathring{e}_{0\lambda_{BA}} = \int_0^\infty x f_{\lambda_{BA}}(x) \, dx, \tag{5.7.26}$$

where by analogy to (5.7.24)

$$f_{\lambda_B}(x) = \frac{l_0}{l_{0\lambda_B}} g_{\lambda_B}(x) \tag{5.7.27a}$$

$$= \frac{l_0}{l_{0\lambda_B}} g_\lambda(x) \exp\left\{ - \int_0^x \lambda_A(a) \, da \right\} \tag{5.7.27b}$$

and

$$f_{\lambda_{BA}}(x) = \frac{l_0}{l_{0\lambda_{BA}}} g_{\lambda_{BA}}(x) \tag{5.7.28a}$$

$$= \frac{l_0}{l_{0\lambda_{BA}}} g_\lambda(x) \left\{ 1 - \exp\left[ - \int_0^x \lambda_A(a) \, da \right] \right\}. \tag{5.7.28b}$$

From (5.7.27b) and (5.7.28b) it is apparent that the probability densities $f_{\lambda_B}(x)$ and $f_{\lambda_{BA}}(x)$ are directly proportional to the transition densities

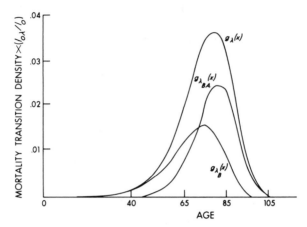

**Fig. 21.** Hypothetical decomposition of mortality transition density $g_\lambda(x)$ into a component due to cause $\lambda_B$, which represents disease B without mention of disease A, and a component due to cause $\lambda_{BA}$, which represents the joint occurrence of diseases A and B. The decomposition assumes an illness–death process with independent multiple causes of death such as depicted in Fig. 19.

$g_{\lambda_B}(x)$ and $g_{\lambda_{BA}}(x)$, respectively. In Fig. 21 we present a plot of the "typical" relationship of $g_{\lambda_B}(x)$ and $g_{\lambda_{BA}}(x)$ to $g_\lambda(x)$ under the reasonable assumption that the cumulative transition intensity represented by the integral $\int_0^x \lambda_A(a)\,da$ is a continuous increasing function of age $x$ with an initial value 0. This simply means that the ratio $g_{\lambda_B}(x)/g_\lambda(x)$ is a decreasing function of $x$, in which case the ratio $f_{\lambda_B}(x)/f_\lambda(x)$ is also a decreasing function of $x$. Conversely, the ratio $f_{\lambda_{BA}}(x)/f_\lambda(x)$ must be an increasing function of $x$, so that (5.7.23), (5.7.25), and (5.7.26) jointly imply the following inequality:

$$\overset{\circ}{e}_{0\lambda_B} < \overset{\circ}{e}_{0\lambda} < \overset{\circ}{e}_{0\lambda_{BA}}. \tag{5.7.29}$$

In words, the average age at death from cause $\lambda_B$ obtained from the transition density $g_{\lambda_B}(x)$ is less than the average age at death from cause $\lambda_{BA}$ obtained from the transition density $g_{\lambda_{BA}}(x)$. The location of $\overset{\circ}{e}_{0\lambda}$ in this inequality is due to (5.7.19), where $\overset{\circ}{e}_{0\lambda}$ is a weighted average of $\overset{\circ}{e}_{0\lambda_B}$ and $\overset{\circ}{e}_{0\lambda_{BA}}$. Furthermore, if $\lambda_A(x)$ is a positive for all $x$, then (5.7.29) generalizes to

$$\overset{\circ}{e}_{x\lambda_B} < \overset{\circ}{e}_{x\lambda} < \overset{\circ}{e}_{x\lambda_{BA}}. \tag{5.7.30}$$

The significance of (5.7.30) is that it specifies a set of conditions on the multiple-decrement life expectancies, which if not satisfied implies that the assumption of disease independence is empirically contradicted. The alternative, that disease dependence is operating, must then be accepted.

If disease dependence is operating, then one needs to revise the model in Fig. 19 so that one or both of the exit transition rates from the compartment labeled chronic disease A are permitted to vary from the corresponding exit transition rates from the well-state compartment. An alternative approach is to discard the model in Fig. 19 entirely and deal directly with the model in Fig. 20 by using the pattern-of-failure definition of mortality risk. In this case, the multiple-decrement life-table computations developed in the preceding continue to be applicable. The difference is that the risk $\lambda_A$ is removed from the model thereby nullifying equations (5.7.6), (5.7.7), (5.7.27b), (5.7.28b), (5.7.29), and (5.7.30), so that there is no longer any restriction on the relative size of $\mathring{e}_{0\lambda_B}$ and $\mathring{e}_{0\lambda_{BA}}$. Obviously, the conditions of Fig. 21 also are nullified. In this case, the disease B is a component of two independent risks $\lambda_B$ and $\lambda_{BA}$, which differ according to whether disease A is present. Hence, the diseases A and B function only as *indicators* of the cause of death but are not themselves the cause.

### Results

We shall illustrate the above models by considering the possibility of a dependence between DM and IHD, between DM and stroke, between GA and IHD, and between GA and stroke. In doing so, we shall treat either DM or GA as the background chronic disease A and assume that no deaths are directly attributable to these diseases. This, of course, is only a rough approximation that is not fully supported by the data. We shall treat either IHD or stroke as the disease B. The deaths due to IHD, that is, deaths with IHD listed anywhere on the death certificate, are subclassified into those that mention DM versus those that do not mention DM. This is required by the structure of the model in Fig. 20. Similarly, to test the DM-stroke dependency, the deaths with stroke listed anywhere on the death certificate are subclassified into those which do or do not mention DM. To test the GA–IHD dependency, the deaths due to IHD are subclassified into those that do or do not mention GA, whereas the test of GA–stroke dependency is conducted by subclassifying the deaths due to stroke into those that do or do not mention GA.

In Table 18 we present the multiple-decrement life expectancies $\mathring{e}_{0\lambda}$ for IHD as a pattern of failure, for IHD occurring without mention of DM $\mathring{e}_{0\lambda_B}$ and for IHD occurring with mention of DM $\mathring{e}_{0\lambda_{BA}}$, based on the 1969 current-life tables for white males, white females, black males, and black females.

In Table 18 we see that for all four race–sex-groups, the average age at death for IHD with DM is less than the average age at death for IHD

**Table 18**

Multiple-Decrement 1969 Life Table Life Expectancies (in Years)
for All Deaths with IHD Mentioned and for the Component
Deaths That Do and Do Not Have DM Mentioned

| Race–sex category | IHD | IHD without DM | IHD with DM | DM (as UCD)[a] |
|---|---|---|---|---|
| White males | 72.56 | 72.63 | 71.80 | 70.32 |
| White females | 80.38 | 80.93 | 76.06 | 74.60 |
| Black males | 69.97 | 70.08 | 68.14 | 64.70 |
| Black females | 76.32 | 77.01 | 70.95 | 68.61 |

[a] Underlying-cause definition of mortality risk (UCD).

without DM—an observation that clearly contradicts the inequality
(5.7.29). Thus, under the assumptions of the model, we can conclude that
dependence between IHD and DM is operating. The column labeled IHD
in Table 18 presents the pattern-of-failure life expectancies for IHD that
were previously presented in Table 12. These are the weighted averages
of the life expectancies in the second and third columns of the table as
shown in Eq. (5.7.19).

Of course, the assumption that no deaths are directly attributable to
DM complicates the interpretation of these results. The fourth column in
Table 18 presents the life expectancies for deaths due to DM as the
underlying cause that were previously presented in Table 12. This is a
group of persons for which IHD is mentioned 30–50% of the time (see
Table 8, Chapter 3), so that the DM-without-IHD deaths constitute just
over one-half of these deaths or about 10–15% of the total mentions of
DM. However, the fact that for all four race–sex-groups the life expectancies for IHD with DM are larger than for DM as an underlying cause, as
would be expected because the acquisition of IHD among diabetics would
not be concurrent with the onset of DM, suggests that the dependency
noted in the preceding discussion is reasonable.

In Table 19 we present the corresponding multiple-decrement life expectancies for testing the DM–stroke dependency. In this table we see
that for all four race–sex-groups the average age at death for stroke with
DM is less than the average age at death for a stroke without DM. As in
Table 18, these results contradict the inequality (5.7.29); this implies dependence between stroke and DM. Also note that the life expectancies for
stroke with DM are larger than for DM as an underlying cause, which

**Table 19**

Multiple-Decrement 1969 Life Table Life Expectancies (in Years) for
All Deaths with Cerebrovascular Accidents Mentioned and for the
Component Deaths That Do and Do Not Have DM Mentioned

| Race–sex category | Stroke | Stroke without DM | Stroke with DM | DM (as UCD)[a] |
|---|---|---|---|---|
| White males | 75.82 | 75.94 | 74.48 | 70.32 |
| White females | 80.62 | 80.94 | 77.66 | 74.60 |
| Black males | 70.03 | 70.08 | 69.38 | 64.70 |
| Black females | 75.34 | 75.81 | 71.64 | 68.61 |

[a] Underlying-cause definition of mortality risk (UCD).

again suggests that the role of DM as an associated cause of death involves a mechanism by which DM accelerates the biological processes for
other chronic degenerative diseases such as IHD or stroke.

In Table 20 we present the multiple-decrement life expectancies for
testing the GA–IHD dependency. In this table we see that for all four
race–sex-groups the inequality (5.7.29) is satisfied, which suggests that
independence of IHD and GA cannot be rejected. In Table 21 we present
the corresponding multiple-decrement life expectancies for testing the
GA–stroke dependency. Again, we see that for all four race–sex-groups
the inequality (5.7.29) is satisfied.

**Table 20**

Multiple-Decrement 1969 Life Table Life Expectancies (in Years)
for All Deaths with IHD Mentioned and for the Component
Deaths That Do and Do Not Have GA Mentioned

| Race–sex category | IHD | IHD without GA | IHD with GA | GA (as UCD)[a] |
|---|---|---|---|---|
| White males | 72.56 | 71.71 | 76.82 | 82.79 |
| White females | 80.38 | 79.57 | 83.26 | 87.10 |
| Black males | 69.97 | 69.08 | 75.92 | 80.67 |
| Black females | 76.32 | 75.17 | 81.94 | 87.39 |

[a] Underlying-cause definition of mortality risk (UCD).

**Table 21**

Multiple-Decrement 1969 Life Table Life Expectancies (in Years) for
All Deaths with Cerebrovascular Accidents Mentioned and for the
Component Deaths That Do and Do Not Have GA Mentioned

| Race–sex category | Stroke | Stroke without GA | Stroke with GA | GA (as UCD)[a] |
|---|---|---|---|---|
| White males | 75.82 | 74.24 | 79.16 | 82.79 |
| White females | 80.62 | 79.10 | 83.32 | 87.10 |
| Black males | 70.03 | 68.15 | 75.95 | 80.67 |
| Black females | 75.34 | 73.46 | 80.50 | 87.39 |

[a] Underlying-cause definition of mortality risk (UCD).

Examination of the fourth column of Table 20 (or Table 21) shows that the age at death due to GA as an underlying cause is much larger than for either IHD or stroke deaths that mention GA as an associated cause. Thus, the fact that GA is a disease of the very old (>80) is the likely explanation of our inability to confirm the presence of dependence between either IHD or stroke and GA. This, of course, raises the issue of how one deals with the generally accepted role of GA in circulatory disease mortality. One possibility is to employ the lethal defect pattern-of-failure model to deal with IHD without GA and IHD with GA as two distinct and independent mortality risks. For example, the mortality risk of IHD without GA could be related to factors such as hypertension, congenital anomaly, aneurism, thrombi, and emboli. This would be consistent with the observation of a substantial number of IHD deaths in the 30–50-year age range when GA is not yet operating (see Fig. 4, IHD versus GA). In contrast, the mortality risk of IHD with GA could represent an age-dependent disease process in which atherosclerotic deposits that accumulate over time lead to acute circulatory failure manifest as either IHD or stroke death. In this way, the dependence is explicitly recognized in defining the mortality risks, but the life table calculations can be conducted in the same manner as for any other independent mortality risks for the mortality risks defined in Fig. 20.

A second possibility is to employ the stochastic compartment model techniques to specify explicitly the transition rates in Fig. 19 as functions of age or time in the chronic disability compartment. Obviously, this second approach would be much more difficult, involving estimation of unobservable parameters. As a consequence, the pattern-of-failure approach would appear to be the method of choice.

# 8 Summary

In this chapter we have employed the stochastic compartment model concepts to motivate a variety of life table strategies for the analysis of cause-specific mortality. These life table methods were illustrated by application to a set of five chronic diseases: cancer, diabetes mellitus, ischemic heart disease, cerebrovascular accidents, and generalized arteriosclerosis. The five chronic diseases were employed to represent both underlying-cause and pattern-of-failure definitions of mortality risk. The population impacts of these diseases were studied from the perspective of the distribution of ages at death, a perspective that leads to the commonly employed measure of life expectancy at birth. The multiple-decrement life expectancies were employed to uncover the major race–sex differentials in the cause-specific analyses. The effects of the additional information in multiple-cause mortality data were assessed via the pattern-of-failure definition of mortality risk. For DM and GA, it was found that the pattern-of-failure definition of mortality risk implied a greatly increased population impact of these diseases vis-à-vis the underlying-cause definition. For the three other diseases, there was a more modest, although still substantial, difference in the perceived mortality impact between the pattern-of-failure and the underlying-cause definition of mortality risks.

Cause-elimination calculations were approached from three different perspectives. First, to summarize the population impact of the five chronic diseases, the independent competing-risk cause-elimination life table life expectancy gains were computed. These summary measures seem to carry much of the information on cause-specific differentials across race–sex observed in the multiple-decrement life table comparisons for the total age span. Second, to control for the effects of the relative frequency of disease, a second cause-elimination life-table life expectancy gain targeted to the specific population that would benefit from the disease elimination (the saved population) was examined. Third, two methods of cause elimination were discussed in the context of the stochastic compartment model of an illness–death process. The first of these methods involves the prevention of the onset of chronic disease; the second involves biomedical innovations that result in a delay of the time to death, given that the person has the chronic disease. Methods of evaluating the total population impact and the saved population impact of clinical or experimental treatment protocols were presented and evaluated against the baseline standard defined by the cause-elimination methods previously employed.

Disease dependency in multiple-cause data was approached from two perspectives, each of which seems to have validity in certain appropriate circumstances. The pattern-of-failure approach was used to deal with dependency by exhausting all information on disease combinations in multiple-cause mortality data. A second approach involved specialization of the stochastic compartment disease-dependency model to establish the conditions for biomedical independence. The four noncancer chronic diseases were selectively tested pairwise for disease dependence in a manner consistent with current epidemiological thinking. The role of DM appeared to accelerate both IHD and stroke; GA showed no indication of such an effect.

These various analyses indicated that the richness of the multiple-cause information can be fully exploited by developing flexible strategies for representing the various roles that chronic diseases may exhibit in the processes leading to mortality. An important aspect of these methods is that the calculations can be performed in a direct manner and do not require the estimation of unobservable parameters. As a consequence, it is possible to conduct similar analyses of other chronic diseases in a straightforward and inexpensive manner.

Although we have focused on chronic degenerative disease processes, one should be aware that many of these methods can be applied directly to acute disease processes. Indeed, the occurrence of acute diseases is often the result of the impaired body defense mechanisms associated with chronic disease. This would suggest the applicability of even the cause-delay and disease-dependency models discussed in the last two sections to the analysis of acute diseases in multiple-cause mortality data.

# References

Axtell, L. M., Asire, A. J., and Myers, M. H. 1976. Cancer patient survival. Report No. 5, U.S. Department of Health, Education and Welfare Pub. No. (NIH) 77-992, Bethesda, Maryland.

Chiang, C. L. 1968. *Introduction to stochastic processes in biostatistics*. New York: Wiley.

Keyfitz, N. 1977. What difference would it make if cancer were eradicated? An examination of the Taeuber paradox. *Demography* **14**:411–418.

Kramer, M. 1980. The rising pandemic of mental disorders and associated chronic diseases and disabilities. In *Epidemiologic research as basis for the organization of extramural psychiatry. Acta Psychiatrica Scandinavia,* Suppl. 285, Vol. 62.

NCHS (National Center for Health Statistics). 1975. United States life tables: 1969–71. U.S. Department of Health, Education and Welfare Pub. No. (HRA) 75-1150, U.S. *Decennial life tables for 1969–71,* Vol. 1, No. 1. Rockville, Maryland: Public Health Service.

Rosenwaike, I. 1979. A new evaluation of United States census data on the extreme aged. *Demography* **16**:279–288.

Rosenwaike, I. 1981. A note on new estimates of the mortality of the extreme aged. *Demography* **18**:257–266.

Siegel, J. S. 1974. Estimates of coverage of the population by sex, race and age in the 1970 census. *Demography* **11**:1–23.

Tsai, S. P., Lee, E. S., and Hardy, R. J. 1978. The effect of a reduction in leading causes of death: Potential gains in life expectancy. *American Journal of Public Health* **68**:966–971.

Wilkin, J. C. 1981. Recent trends in the mortality of the aged. *Transactions of the Society of Actuaries* **33**:11–44.

# Chapter 6

## Life Tables for Heterogeneous Populations: Cohort versus Period Life Table Computations, an Examination of the Black–White Mortality Crossover

## 1 Introduction

It is well known that the construction of a cohort or generation life table differs from the construction of a current or period life table. Strictly speaking, a cohort life table should be constructed by using the recorded age at death of each member of the cohort to develop direct counts of the quantities in the $d_x$ column of the life table. In this case, the $l_x$ column can be developed from Eq. (4.3.8) and the $q_x$ column from Eq. (4.3.9a). Furthermore, because the life table radix $l_0$ is simply the total number of deaths at all ages in the cohort, this value is the initial birth size of the cohort and is not arbitrarily determined as in the period life table. Construction of the period life table is based on making estimates of $q_x$ from annual age-specific death rates or mortality counts for the given period or calendar year. An example of this was seen in Chapter 5, where $q_x$ was estimated by

$$q_x^y = D_x^y/(P_x^y + 0.5D_x^y). \qquad (6.1.1)$$

where $D_x^y$ denotes the number of deaths in the age interval $(x, x + 1)$ in calendar year $y$ and $P_x^y$ denotes the number of persons alive on July 1 of the year $y$ and whose age is in the interval $(x, x + 1)$.

Unfortunately, the data required for construction of true cohort life tables for total mortality in human populations do not often exist. Consequently, it is customary to develop approximate life tables for cohorts by using estimates of $q_x$ derived from an appropriate sequence of period life tables. Consider a cohort born in the 1-year interval $(y - \frac{1}{2}, y + \frac{1}{2})$, which is centered on the date January 1 of the year $y$. The $q_x$ column for the life

236

table, which approximately describes their total mortality, is based on the sequence $q_0^y, q_1^{y+1}, ..., q_\omega^{y+\omega}$, which in general involves terms of the form

$$q_x^{y+x} = D_x^{y+x}/(P_x^{y+x} + 0.5D_x^{y+x}). \tag{6.1.2}$$

In an array of $q_x^y$'s by age and calendar year, the terms in (6.1.2) would appear along one of the diagonals beginning at year $y$.

Given the use of an approximation such as (6.1.2) in the construction of cohort life tables, it appears that for practical considerations the construction of cohort life tables and period life tables is essentially identical except for the choice of obtaining the $q_x$'s from the diagonals, as opposed to the columns, of the array of $q_x^y$'s by age and calendar year. Hence, the period life table represents a synthetic cohort life table that comprises the mortality experience of each of the cohorts alive in the given year.

Unfortunately, if the population is heterogeneous and if mortality rates are declining over successive birth cohorts, then the period life tables constructed by using (6.1.1) will no longer represent a consistent merger of the mortality experiences of each of the component cohorts because the entries in the $q_x$ column will be inconsistent with average age-specific mortality levels in any real cohort. That is, in a heterogeneous cohort, the mortality rate $q_x^y$ at age $x$ in year $y$ represents the average mortality rate among survivors alive at age $x$. But the number of survivors alive at age $x$ and their distribution of longevity characteristics depend on the set of prior mortality rates to which they were exposed, that is, the set $q_0^{y-x}$, $q_1^{y-x+1}, ..., q_{x-1}^{y-1}$. In a period life table based on (6.1.1), the mortality rate $q_x^y$ represents the average mortality rate among a group of individuals whose prior mortality rates is the set $q_0^y, q_1^y, ..., q_{x-1}^y$. Because the two sequences of prior rates will generally be different and because the set in the cohort life table is consistent with a process of mortality selection, it must be the case that the set in the period life table is inconsistent with such a process. In other words, changing the extent of mortality selection at younger ages also changes the characteristics of the group of survivors alive at age $x$, so that the mortality rate $q_x^y$ must also change. The extent to which $q_x^y$ must change in the period life table, for example, to the new value $\tilde{q}_x^y$, in order to be consistent with a selection process on a synthetic cohort represents the extent of bias present in period life tables calculated by using formulas such as (6.1.1).

As might be anticipated, the extent of heterogeneity bias in a period life table is largely determined by the extent of heterogeneity in each cohort that contributes a mortality rate to its construction. Unfortunately, other than classification by age, race, sex, and geographic region of residence, direct data on cohort heterogeneity are not available in standard demographic data, and we must rely on models that incorporate the best available sets of assumptions and auxiliary evidence to investigate the likely extent of such bias. In this chapter we shall first present a very elementary model of heterogeneity that can be used to develop estimates of the adjusted mortality rates $\bar{q}_x^y$. We shall then approach the issue of estimating the parameters of this model by evaluating the role of heterogeneity as one possible factor in the black–white crossover in total mortality rates. This phenomenon was observed in Chapter 5 but was not discussed in detail. Here we shall review a wide array of evidence and the various arguments made concerning the reality of this phenomenon so that the implications for the magnitude of heterogeneity bias can be adequately evaluated.

By focusing on the black–white mortality crossover in this chapter, we hope to sensitize the reader to the range of implications associated with attempts to use vital statistics data to draw conclusions about the patterns of mortality and of mortality changes in a national population. Past efforts at explaining the crossover have tended to stress (1) the effects of mortality selection on a heterogeneous population, (2) the implications of different age trajectories of individual mortality risks, or (3) the effects of differential data quality between whites and blacks at the advanced ages.

We do not argue that an accounting for the effects of data error and population heterogeneity can provide a complete explanation of the crossover or even that focusing narrowly on just the crossover without also accounting for the long period of convergence of mortality rates at younger ages is desirable. An entirely satisfactory explanation of the crossover requires consideration of the mortality differentials across the entire age span and surely must include consideration of the role of basic aging processes and of the external environment in morbidity and mortality. For example, we saw in Chapter 5 that there were notable differences in the cause of death structure between the races—differences that are frequently ignored in analyses of total mortality but that contribute to the crossover.

The presentation of concrete numerical results frequently aids in the understanding of complex issues, even if the results are only illustrative. Other authors (e.g., Kitagawa and Hauser, 1973; Bayo, 1972) have presented such results to illustrate the "narrowing" of the crossover that could occur when the numerator and denominator data for mortality rates were obtained from the same source. Rather than repeat such calculations here, we shall instead illustrate the narrowing or reversal of the crossover that could occur when one controls for the effects of mortality selection. In doing so, however, we shall use the life table data developed by Coale and Zelnick (1963) and by Coale and Rives (1973) because these data incorporate the best available adjustments for census enumeration error.

The high quality of these adjustments is attested to by the fact that the U.S. Bureau of the Census adopted the same methodology to develop estimates of enumeration error in the 1960 and 1970 censuses (Siegel, 1974) and in the 1980 census (Passel *et al.*, 1982).

## 2  Gamma-Distributed Frailty

### Basic Concepts

An elementary model of population heterogeneity that leads to relatively simple adjustments of the mortality rates in period life tables derives from the assumption of gamma-distributed frailty in each successive cohort. In this section we shall combine the results obtained in Section 6, Chapter 4, with the assumption that the frailty variate $Z$ is gamma distributed. Notationally, we use $X$ and $x$ in place of $T$ and $t$ because our risk set is a cohort and time $t$ is age $x$. Also, to emphasize that the cohort is heterogeneous, we denote the marginal survival function as $S_X(x)$ instead of as $S(x)$ and the marginal density as $f_X(x)$ instead of as $f(x)$.

Development of a life-table model with fixed frailty by using the gamma distribution represents perhaps the simplest parametric model that is capable of representing the effects of mortality selection. Other authors (e.g., Keyfitz and Littman, 1979; Heckman and Singer, 1982) have presented nonparametric models, although the use of such models in the present analysis would entail substantial analytic difficulties. Hougaard (1982) has suggested that the inverse Gaussian distribution be considered as an alternative to the gamma distribution, but this is still a parametric approach.

Probably the major criticism of our model, and of the other alternatives just noted, is their assumption that the frailty variate is fixed for life. There is ample evidence from various longitudinal studies (e.g., the studies conducted in Framingham, or in Evans County) that key physiological risk variables do change over the life span and that the effects of fat in diet, nutrition, cigarette smoking, hypertension, exercise, radiation, toxic chemicals, and other factors can modify one's mortality risks. Although the assumption of fixed frailty is probably acceptable when the analysis is for short periods of follow-up (e.g., <10 years), its use in models of the total life span may lead to biased results. Whereas the fixed frailty model cannot represent the various risk-factor changes cited, a dynamic frailty model based on a diffusion process such as studied in Section 7 of Chapter 4 can represent these effects. Under a diffusion process with dynamic frailty, one obtains a larger estimate of the standard force of mortality

$\mu(x|1)$ than under the fixed frailty model if one assumes the same initial distribution. The difference between the two estimates depends on the size of the diffusion variance relative to the initial frailty variance, a ratio that depends on the length of time over which the diffusion process operates. Thus, failure to account for diffusion in a life table model may result in bias in both the standard force of mortality $\mu(x|1)$ and in the assumed initial distribution of frailty because some of the diffusion variance may be assumed erroneously to be part of the initial frailty variance. In this latter case, however, some compensation may occur because the increase in the variance of the initial distribution implies a compensatory increase in the estimated standard force of mortality—thereby moving it closer to the true value so that its bias is reduced. A formal treatment of dynamic frailty, however, is beyond the scope of this analytic effort.

With fixed frailty, the basic relationship we deal with is (4.6.26):

$$\mu(x) = \mathscr{E}_{Z|(x)}(z)\mu(x|1), \tag{6.2.1}$$

which states that the marginal force of mortality in a heterogeneous cohort is the product of the average value of $Z$ among survivors alive at age $x$, denoted as $(x)$, times a standard force of mortality $\mu(x|1)$, which is the average force of mortality that would be observed if no prior selection had occurred. Frailty operates multiplicatively, so that for any level of $Z$ we have

$$\mu(x|z) = z\mu(x|1). \tag{6.2.2}$$

The conditional expectation in (6.2.1) can be defined as

$$\mathscr{E}_{Z|(x)}(z) = \int_0^\infty z f_{Z|(x)}(z|(x)) \, dz, \tag{6.2.3}$$

where $f_{Z|(x)}(z|(x))$ is the probability density of $Z$ among the survivors alive at age $x$. The initial density of $Z$ at birth in the cohort is assumed to be a gamma density, which can be written in the form

$$f_{Z|(0)}(z|(0)) = \left(\frac{zs}{\zeta}\right)^s \frac{\exp(-zs/\zeta)}{z\Gamma(s)} , \tag{6.2.4}$$

with mean parameter $\zeta$ and shape parameter $s$, both of which are positive in value. In view of (4.6.27), we can set the mean $\zeta$ to unity, in which case the cohort force of mortality and the standard force of mortality will be initially equal, that is, $\mu(0) = \mu(0|1)$. This leaves only the parameter $s$ as an unknown parameter.

The Laplace transform of (6.2.4) has the general form

$$\mathscr{L}_{Z|(0)}(u) = 1/[1 + u\zeta/s]^s , \tag{6.2.5}$$

so that, with $\zeta = 1$, Eq. (4.6.36b) yields the following analytic expression for the marginal force of mortality $\mu(x)$:

$$\mu(x) = \mu(x|1)/[1 + (1/s) \int_0^x \mu(a|1) \, da].$$ (6.2.6)

In view of (6.2.1) and (6.2.6) we have the general solution to (6.2.3)

$$\mathscr{E}_{Z|(x)}(z) = 1/[1 + (1/s) \int_0^x \mu(a|1) \, da],$$ (6.2.7)

which is a strictly decreasing function of time as required by condition (4.6.31c). In view of (4.6.18), we have, using (6.2.6) and (6.2.2) to evaluate the exponential term,

$$f_{Z|(x)}(z|(x)) = \left\{ z[s + \int_0^x \mu(a|1) \, da] \right\}^s \frac{\exp\left\{ -z[s + \int_0^x \mu(a|1) \, da] \right\}}{z\Gamma(s)},$$

(6.2.8)

which shows that the density of frailty among survivors alive at age $x$ is a gamma density with mean $\mathscr{E}_{Z|(x)}(z)$ and shape $s$.

Equation (6.2.8) exhibits two useful properties of the gamma distribution as the initial distribution in a fixed frailty model. First, if the initial distribution of frailty in a cohort is a gamma distribution, then, under a multiplicative model of mortality selection as in (6.2.2), the distribution will remain a distribution of the gamma form with the same shape parameter $s$. This means that a parsimonious description of a mortality selection process can be generated by using the gamma distribution because only one new parameter must be introduced. Furthermore, because the gamma form is a general form that includes as special cases several standard distributions including the exponential and chi-squared distributions, the choice of the gamma form is not particularly restrictive in terms of the range of possible shapes to which it can conform. Second, the constancy of the shape parameter implies constancy over age of the coefficient of variation of $Z$, that is, because

$$s = [CV_{Z|(x)}]^{-2}.$$ (6.2.9)

Hence, the relative degree of heterogeneity among the survivors alive at any age in the cohort is unaffected by mortality selection. If it is desired to modify (6.2.9) so that the distribution of frailty becomes relatively more homogeneous with time, then one might follow Hougaard's (1982) suggestion of replacing the gamma density with an inverse Gaussian density, which is also a member of the class of nonnegative exponential families. Unfortunately, this alternative seems to run counter to our results concerning the effects of diffusion in a dynamic frailty model so that the gamma distribution remains the distribution of choice. Indeed, even if one accepts Hougaard's (1982) argument that mortality selection might reduce the coefficient of variation of the frailty variate, this effect could be opposed by the effects of diffusion that tend to increase it, so that, on balance, it could remain fairly constant as predicted by use of the gamma distribution in (6.2.8). Thus, use of the gamma distribution can be rationalized in several ways.

### Standard Individual Life Tables

As discussed, the cohort life table mortality rates reflect not only the forces of mortality operating at each given age but also the degree of mortality selection occurring at all prior ages. We can remove the effects of prior mortality selection by constructing life tables based on the standard force of mortality $\mu(x|1)$ rather than on the cohort force of mortality. Because such life tables reflect the hypothetical mortality experience of an individual at the average or standard level of frailty in the model with gamma-distributed frailty, we shall refer to them as standard individual life tables (Vaupel et al., 1979). These are distinguished from cohort life tables in that they reflect the mortality experience faced by individuals at the initial average frailty level $Z = 1$. These life tables are not restricted to the standard frailty level since (6.2.2) implies that their hazard column $h_{x|1}$ [see (6.2.12a) below] may be multiplied by any desired value of $z$ to obtain the hazard column and associated life table for that level of frailty. Hence, these life tables for various levels of $Z$ are closely related to the concepts of the "life table with covariates" models recently appearing in the demographic literature (e.g., Trussell and Hammerslough, 1983) and in the biostatistical literature (e.g., Cox, 1972, 1975; Kalbfleisch and Prentice, 1980), the main difference being that our frailty covariate $Z$ is not observed.

To develop such life tables, we first observe that the marginal survival function $S_X(x)$ may be written, as implied in (4.6.35) and (4.6.36), in the form

$$S_X(x) = \mathscr{L}_{Z|(0)} \left\{ \int_0^x \mu(a|1) \, da \right\} \tag{6.2.10a}$$

$$= 1 \bigg/ \left[ 1 + (1/s) \int_0^x \mu(a|1) \, da \right]^s, \tag{6.2.10b}$$

where (6.2.10b) is a direct consequence of (6.2.5) and (6.2.10a). In view of (6.2.10b), it is obvious that (6.2.6) may be solved to yield

$$\mu(x|1) = \mu(x)/[S_X(x)]^{1/s}, \tag{6.2.11}$$

which expresses the standard force of mortality $\mu(x|1)$ as a simple function of the cohort force of mortality $\mu(x)$ and the cohort survivorship function $S_X(x)$.

Because $S_X(x)$ is equivalent to the life table parameter $_xp_0$, we have from (6.2.11) the following useful definition:

$$h_{x|1} = \int_x^{x+1} \mu(a|1) \, da \tag{6.2.12a}$$

$$= s\left[\left(\frac{1}{_{x+1}p_0}\right)^{1/s} - \left(\frac{1}{_xp_0}\right)^{1/s}\right], \tag{6.2.12b}$$

where $h_{x|1}$ is a cumulative standard force of mortality for the age interval $(x, x + 1)$. Using $h_{x|1}$ in analogous relationships to the cohort life table functions in Chapter 5, one can easily define the corresponding functions $q_{x|1}$, $l_{x|1}$, $d_{x|1}$, and $\overset{\circ}{e}_{x|1}$, which form the columns of the standard individual life table.

### Adjusted Period Life Tables

Consider an array of $h_{x|1}^y$'s by age and year. If we construct a life table by using the sequence of cumulative hazards obtained from a diagonal of this table beginning, for example, with $h_{0|1}^y$, then we obtain the life table for the standard individual from the cohort born in year $y$. Alternatively, if we obtain the hazards from a column of this table, for example, $h_{x|1}^y$, then we obtain the life table for the standard individual from a synthetic cohort corresponding to the period life table population in year $y$. This life table can then be modified by using the relationship in (6.2.6) to produce an adjusted period life table that is consistent with the standard individual life table and hence with the implied mortality selection on the synthetic cohort (Vaupel *et al.*, 1979).

The age-specific force of mortality in the cohort life table is obtained from (6.2.6) as

$$h_x = \int_x^{x+1} \mu(a) \, da \tag{6.2.13a}$$

$$= s \ln\left(\frac{1 + \int_0^{x+1} \mu(a|1) \, da/s}{1 + \int_0^x \mu(a|1) \, da/s}\right) \tag{6.2.13b}$$

$$= s \ln\left(1 + \frac{h_{x|1}}{s + _xh_{0|1}}\right), \tag{6.2.13c}$$

where $h_{x|1}$ is defined in (6.2.12b) and where

$$_xh_{0|1} = \int_0^x \mu(a|1) \, da \qquad (6.2.14a)$$

$$= \sum_{i=0}^{x-1} h_{i|1} . \qquad (6.2.14b)$$

We can rewrite (6.2.14b) to be explicit about the use of cohort data, in which case,

$$_xh_{0|1}^{y-x} = \sum_{i=0}^{x-1} h_{i|1}^{y-x+i}, \qquad (6.2.15)$$

so that (6.2.13c) becomes

$$h_x^y = s \ln \left(1 + \frac{h_{x|1}^y}{s + {_xh_{0|1}^{y-x}}}\right). \qquad (6.2.16)$$

For a synthetic cohort, the cumulative standard force of mortality prior to age $x$ is obtained as

$$_x\tilde{h}_{0|1}^y = \sum_{i=0}^{x-1} h_{i|1}^y \qquad (6.2.17)$$

and the age-specific synthetic cohort force of mortality as in (6.2.16) with $_x\tilde{h}_{0|1}^y$ replacing $_xh_{0|1}^{y-x}$:

$$\tilde{h}_x^y = s \ln \left(1 + \frac{h_{x|1}^y}{s + {_x\tilde{h}_{0|1}^y}}\right). \qquad (6.2.18)$$

Again, using $\tilde{h}_x^y$ in analogous relationships to the cohort life table functions in Chapter 5, we can define the corresponding functions $\tilde{q}_x^y$, $\tilde{l}_x^y$, $\tilde{d}_x^y$, and $\tilde{e}_x^y$, which form the columns of the adjusted period life table for the year $y$.

It is instructive to express the adjusted mortality rate $\tilde{q}_x^y$ as a function of the set of unadjusted mortality rates $q_x^y$ in (6.1.1). To this end, we start with the analogous relationship to (4.3.23), that is,

$$\tilde{q}_x^y = 1 - \exp[-\tilde{h}_x^y] \qquad (6.2.19a)$$

$$= 1 - \left(1 + \frac{h_{x|1}^y}{s + {_x\tilde{h}_{0|1}^y}}\right)^{-s}. \qquad (6.2.19b)$$

Using (6.2.12b) to replace $h_{x|1}^y$, we obtain

$$\tilde{q}_x^y = 1 - \left\{1 + \left[\left(\frac{1}{{_{x+1}p_0^{y-x}}}\right)^{1/s} - \left(\frac{1}{{_xp_0^{y-x}}}\right)^{1/s}\right]\left[\frac{1}{1 + {_x\tilde{h}_{0|1}^y}/s}\right]\right\}^{-s}, \qquad (6.2.20)$$

where

$$_xp_0^{y-x} = l_x^y/l_0^{y-x}. \qquad (6.2.21)$$

Define the probability of surviving to age $x$ in the adjusted life table as

$$_x\bar{p}_0^y = \bar{l}_x^y/\bar{l}_0^y, \qquad (6.2.22)$$

so that by analogy to (6.2.10b) we have

$$_x\bar{p}_0^y = 1/[1 + {}_x\bar{h}_{0/1}^y s]^s. \qquad (6.2.23)$$

Also note that

$$_{x+1}p_0^{y-x} = {}_xp_0^{y-x}(1 - q_x^y). \qquad (6.2.24)$$

Using (6.2.23) and (6.2.24), we can rewrite (6.2.20) in the form

$$\bar{q}_x^y = 1 - \left[1 + \left(\frac{_x\bar{p}_0^y}{_xp_0^{y-x}}\right)^{1/s}\left(\frac{1}{(1 - q_x^y)^{1/s}} - 1\right)\right]^{-s}. \qquad (6.2.25)$$

Hence, the adjusted period life table mortality probability $\bar{q}_x^y$ is a function of three factors: (1) the cohort mortality probability $q_x^y$; (2) the ratio of the survivorship proportions at age $x$ in the two types of life tables $_x\bar{p}_0^y/_xp_0^{y-x}$ or, alternatively, just $\bar{l}_x^y/l_x^y$; and (3) the shape parameter $s$ of the frailty distribution.

From (6.2.25) it can be seen that there are two possible ways in which $\bar{q}_x^y$ and $q_x^y$ would be equal. The first possibility is that the population is, in fact, homogeneous. In this case, the parameter $s$ has an infinitely large value, so that the limiting form of (6.2.25) as $s$ approaches infinity yields the equality between $\bar{q}_x^y$ and $q_x^y$. The second possibility is that the mortality experiences of all successive cohorts involved in the period cross section, as measured by $l_x^y$, are identical to the mortality experience of the synthetic cohort, as measured by $\bar{l}_x^y$. In this case, the ratio $\bar{l}_x^y/l_x^y$ will always be unity, so that (6.2.25) again simplifies to yield the equality between $\bar{q}_x^y$ and $q_x^y$.

The historical reality is that the mortality experience of successive cohorts in most societies has been characterized by substantial declines in the age-specific mortality probabilities $q_x^y$ and corresponding increases in the probabilities of survival to each given age $_xp_0^{y-x}$ or $l_x^y/l_0^{y-x}$. This eliminates the second possibility above, so that $\bar{q}_x^y$ and $q_x^y$ will be different if the population is heterogeneous. Indeed, the fact that $l_x^y$ is an increasing function of time $y$ suggests that the direction of bias in unadjusted period life table parameters can be established. Specifically, $q_x$ and $d_x$ will be smaller than the corresponding $\bar{q}_x$ and $\bar{d}_x$, while $l_x$ and $\mathring{e}_x$ will be larger than the corresponding $\tilde{l}_x$ and $\tilde{\mathring{e}}_x$. Having established the direction of bias in the unadjusted period life tables, the critical question then concerns the magnitude of this bias. This is an empirical issue that we shall investigate in the remaining sections of this chapter.

## 3  The Black–White Mortality Crossover

A major substantive implication of population heterogeneity is that comparison of unadjusted mortality rates may be misleading if two populations have faced very different prior sets of mortality rates at younger ages. One such comparison that has been the subject of longstanding controversy involves the interpretation to be given to the black–white crossover in mortality rates. In this section we shall define mortality *crossover* and *convergence,* array and discuss the extant evidence of a black–white mortality crossover in the U.S. population, and provide a list of possible causes of a black–white mortality crossover–convergence in the U.S. population. In the next section we shall apply the adjustments developed in Section 2 to study the implications of such adjustments for explanations of the crossover phenomenon.

### *Definitions of Mortality Crossover and Convergence*

A mortality crossover (or convergence) is an attribute of the relative rate of change and level of age-specific mortality rates in two population groups. Actually, there are several conditions that must exist before a mortality crossover is said to exist between two populations. First, it must be possible to identify one of the populations as disadvantaged on a variety of social, economic, and public health variables. Second, the disadvantaged population must manifest age-specific mortality rates markedly higher than the advantaged population through middle age. It will be presumed that the higher mortality rates of the disadvantaged population are a consequence of the effects of the variables that were used to identify the disadvantaged population. Finally, the age-specific mortality rates of the disadvantaged population, at advanced ages, will rise less rapidly with age than the advantaged population; the rates of the two populations will then converge until at some advanced age the age-specific mortality rates of the disadvantaged population drop below those of the advantaged population. In general, the fact that the age-specific mortality rates are lower for the disadvantaged population is a condition that will be maintained to the most advanced ages. If the age-specific mortality rates of the disadvantaged population approach the age-specific rates of the advantaged population but never actually fall below those rates, we have, instead of a crossover, a mortality convergence. Actually, it is possible to identify two types of convergence. The first is *absolute* convergence. Absolute convergence exists if the absolute difference between the age-specific mortality rates of the advantaged and disadvantaged population, after reaching a maximum at some age, declines monotonically after that age. The second type of convergence is *proportional* convergence. In this case, convergence is said to occur between the two populations if, after the disadvantaged population reaches the highest percentage difference at some age, there is a monotonic decline in the proportional difference of the mortality rates of the two populations after that age. Note that proportional convergence can occur even if there is no absolute convergence.

By defining mortality convergence as well as mortality crossover, our perspective on age-specific mortality differentials is broadened to include other relevant features of the age change of these differentials. First, these concepts indicate that our analysis should be of the entire age pattern or trajectory of the mortality rates of each of the population groups and not just of a single, though significant, feature of the relation between the age-specific mortality rates of each group. By doing so, concepts of biological aging and age increase in the incidence of specific diseases can be used in efforts to investigate the crossover or convergence. Also, by examining the entire age trajectory of the mortality rates, it is possible to evaluate the convergence that initiates at much younger ages than the typical age at crossover. Such an evaluation can be conducted on data for a much broader age range and one for which the Coale and Zelnick (1963) and Coale and Rives (1973) adjustment methodology is thought to work well. Thus, there should be much less controversy over whether the convergence is real as opposed to whether the eventual crossover is real. Second, as a complement to the concept of crossover, attention should be paid to the concept of a peak relative (or absolute) mortality differential, that is, the age at which the greatest proportional (or absolute) difference exists between the age-specific mortality rates for the two populations. Indeed, if a crossover exists, a peak relative mortality differential must exist, and it is quite possible that an explanation of the peak differential may serve to explain mortality convergence or crossover. That is, once it is understood why the peak differential occurs at that point in the age range, the later convergence and crossover of the two mortality curves may turn out to be a natural consequence of the mortality dynamics involved in the explanation. For example, the theory of mortality proposed by Strehler and Mildvan (1960) predicts a negative correlation between the mortality rates at younger ages and the rate of increase of the mortality curve at later ages so that convergence is expected under that model. Third, it will be important to examine the relative status of age-specific life-table functions other than the mortality rate because these reflect different aspects of survival. For example, an examination of the U.S. period life tables for 1969 presented in Chapter 5 shows that the crossover is manifest for males at age 75 for the probability of death (75 for females), at 65 for the average number of remaining years of life expectancy (70 for females), and at 95 for the proportion of the initial population alive (90 for females). Perhaps the most interesting of these other age-specific statistics is the proportion of the initial population surviving to a given age, that is, $_xp_0$ or the ratio $l_x/l_0$, because this statistic represents the cumulative mortality experience of the population. Crossovers in these statistics, which typically do not occur until extremely advanced ages (i.e., about age 90), suggest that eventually even the cumulative effects of black mortality disadvantages at earlier ages are eliminated. If the cumulative mortality advantage were eliminated, then a mortality selection model cannot be a complete explanation of the mortality differentials. However, the crossover in the survival proportion occurs so late in the life span for the U.S. population that adjustment for enumeration error at advanced ages may eliminate this type of crossover. For example, Bayo (1972) presented results that suggest that the mortality rates for nonwhites 85 years and over in 1968 produced by the NCHS were about 20% too low. If the crossover in the survival proportion above age 90 were eliminated through such an adjustment, this would suggest that the cumulative effect of the early mortality disadvantage for blacks, although decreasing with age, was never actually eliminated. The survival proportion thus may be the best overall measure of the relative mortality status of the U.S. black and white population because it is a cumulative measure.

The preceding points suggest that a comparison of the relative mortality status of the two populations should not be summarized by a single phenomenon such as a crossover. Rather, a variety of comparisons should be made so that the mortality differentials of the two groups can be more adequately described.

### The Nature of the Evidence for the Crossover

Although perhaps the definitive evidence for a mortality crossover has not yet been produced, there does exist a broad range of evidence.

## Cross-Species Evidence

The first type of evidence that can be adduced for the crossover has to do with the observation of similar types of phenomena in other animal species. This type of evidence is directed toward establishing the plausibility of mortality selection, altered rates of aging, or environmental shocks as biological mechanisms affecting the aging dynamics of human populations. Such mechanisms have been noted in a variety of animal studies, although it would seem difficult to distinguish, for example, a selection mechanism from a model in which the organism's rate of aging is altered by environmental stress (Comfort, 1979; Economos, 1982).

## Observed Population Heterogeneity

The second type of evidence to be adduced for the mortality crossover as due to mortality selection is simply the observation that human populations are generally quite heterogeneous in their morbidity and mortality risks. If one accepts that there are significant sources of individual variation in the potential for longevity, then, in the face of differential early mortality risks, a mortality convergence or crossover would have to occur because the surviving members of the disadvantaged group would be more highly selected than the surviving members of the advantaged group. Such a phenomenon is well known in the insurance industry where the mortality risks of new policy holders are initially substantially lower than comparable long-term policy holders but where the risks converge over time so that after about 15 years the difference is negligible (Lew and Seltzer, 1970). Similarly, persons who convert from group to individual coverage are initially at substantially higher mortality risks than comparable long-term individual coverage policy holders, but the mortality risks again converge after several years. In each case, the effect of differential mortality selection is to produce a convergence of the average mortality rates in the surviving subgroups, so that the observation of such a convergence in the mortality rates for blacks and whites is to be expected. Indeed, the lack of such a convergence or crossover in the mortality rates under the condition of differential early mortality selection might be more difficult to explain than its occurrence.

## Observed Pervasiveness of Crossover Phenomena

The third type of evidence supporting the existence of mortality crossover and convergence is its consistent observation in many human populations. The following are some examples.

(1)   Crossovers have been observed in many cross-national comparisons of the mortality experience of human populations. These crossovers have been observed in populations with broadly different characteristics and sometimes at relatively early ages in populations with reasonably good vital statistics systems (Nam *et al.,* 1978).

(2)   Crossovers and convergences have been observed in black–white cohort mortality data. Specifically, the NCHS conducted a study of cohort mortality for the period 1900 to 1968. Although there were a number of technical difficulties with the study (the death registration system was not complete until Texas entered in 1933; consequently, early mortality is based on a changing population), there were a number of interesting convergences and crossovers for different cohorts in the same population groups, that is, a crossover of death rates for the white male cohorts of 1896–1900 and 1906–1910 at about age 50. Indeed, one of the pervasive phenomena that was found in the cohort data was that for cohorts in the same demographic category, as early mortality decreased in successive cohorts, there was a steeper rate of increase in mortality rates for older persons—an increase that began at increasingly earlier ages. This phenomenon is consistent with the notion of mortality selection, that is, that death of frail persons averted at earlier ages increased mortality at later ages. This phenomenon is also observed for persons with certain chronic diseases such as diabetes, for which successful management of the acute phase of the disease decreases mortality at early ages but increases it at somewhat more advanced ages because diabetics, even when treated, have a lower life expectancy than the general population.

(3)   Crossovers between blacks and whites have been observed in most official U.S. vital statistics mortality data and life tables even when adjustments for enumeration error are made or when Medicare data have been spliced into the life tables at advanced ages (Rives, 1977; NCHS, 1975).

(4)   A black–white mortality crossover has been observed to exist at different ages for different underlying causes of death (e.g., see Fig. 12, Chapter 5), thus requiring that attempts to explain away the crossover solely as enumeration error involve the assumption that the pattern of enumeration error be correlated with the eventual causes of death.

(5)   A black–white mortality crossover has been observed at different ages for different diseases reported anywhere on the death certificate, that is, in multiple-cause data, as shown in Fig. 13, Chapter 5.

(6)   The proportion of deaths among whites at advanced ages with associated chronic conditions is higher than for blacks (e.g., see Table 1, Chapter 3)—an observation consistent with the notion that differentials in medical care have allowed whites to survive longer than blacks with

certain chronic degenerative diseases, which apparently enhance mortality risks for whites at ages past 70. This finding was also consistent with the fact that blacks had higher mortality rates for various chronic diseases (e.g., diabetes and hypertensive disease) and a smaller proportion of the total mention of the chronic diseases as associated rather than as underlying causes of death (suggesting the greater lethality of these diseases for blacks).

(7)  Mortality crossover and convergence have been found to be consistent with biologically motivated models of total and cause-specific mortality. This implies that there is a logically consistent continuation of mortality patterns observed at early ages through advanced ages. Hence, for a crossover or convergence not to exist, the substantive basis of these models (e.g., biological theory or epidemiological observations of specific study populations) would have to be challenged.

(8)  Various types of mortality and morbidity selection effects have been noted in numerous epidemiological studies. Examples of such effects are geographic selection of migrants for greater longevity; occupational selection, that is, the "healthy worker effect"; and various effects of morbidity selection such as the effect of smoking on lung cancer. This latter phenomenon has been studied in great detail in the study of uranium miners and seems consistent with detailed studies of disease pathology.

(9)  There is clinical evidence that certain degenerative aging processes (i.e., hypertension and atherosclerosis) occur at different rates in blacks and whites, so that the ages at which the aging processes produce peak mortality rates are consistent with the crossover (Phillips and Burch, 1960).

(10)  There is a tendency for a convergence of mortality rates between white males and females in the U.S. population. An analysis of the age trajectory of factors known to be associated with circulatory disease mortality risk (e.g., blood pressure and serum cholesterol) in the Framingham population shows that although females at early ages have significantly lower mean levels on these risk factors, the rate of age increase of these risk factors is faster for females than for males, indicating a convergence of the sex-specific levels of important physiological factors with age and potentially a crossover at more advanced ages (Woodbury et al., 1981).

(11)  There is the logical difficulty that if peak proportional (or possibly absolute) mortality differentials were maintained throughout the life span, the proportion of blacks surviving to advanced ages would have to be extremely small. Indeed, there is some merit to the argument that in comparing two groups, one of which is highly disadvantaged vis-à-vis the other, a peak mortality differential must occur at some age and there seems to be little reason to argue that it should occur at the most advanced ages.

(12)  A cause-specific mortality crossover has been observed over a recent 14-year period (1962–1975) on the basis of population estimates from two censuses, each adjusted for census–enumeration error (Manton *et al.*, 1979).

(13)  Finally, a black–white mortality crossover has been observed in a closed cohort longitudinal community in Evans County, Georgia. This finding is of interest because initial age and age at death were obtained through the study protocol and *not* from either census records or death certificates. Furthermore, studies of risk factors in this population suggest that the crossover can be related to the effects of various physiological and socioeconomic risk factors (Wing *et al.*, 1983).

### *Failure of Enumeration Error Models to Explain Crossover Phenomena*

The fourth type of evidence suggesting that the crossover is more than enumeration error is produced by those researchers who have tried to explain away the crossover as due simply to enumeration error (and age misreporting) (e.g., Kitagawa and Hauser, 1973; Bayo, 1972). In such studies, extreme assumptions are made about enumeration errors, age-specific mortality rates recalculated, and the black–white mortality rates investigated for a crossover. No such attempts at eliminating the crossover have been successful—they have only succeeded in increasing the age at which the crossover is observed and in narrowing its extent beyond this age. It should be strongly emphasized in this regard that successfully eliminating the crossover does not address the more general issues of either the absolute or proportional convergence of black–white mortality rates at advanced ages or the reason for the peak mortality differentials occurring at some age prior to the age at which the convergence begins. The basic concerns about the age variation of the relative health status of the black–white populations exist even if there is only a strong tendency for black rates to converge to white mortality rates.

### **Explanations of Mortality Crossovers and Convergence**

One of the most serious problems with the way crossovers have been investigated is the tendency to attribute the crossover to a single cause. It is almost certain that the observation of a mortality crossover or convergence in demographic data is a product of a variety of factors. In the following section we present certain possible causes of the crossover. Each will be discussed as an independent phenomenon, although an adequate analysis of the crossover would have to take into account the possible simultaneous effect of all these factors.

*Mortality Selection on a Heterogeneous Population*

One mechanism that could operate to produce a mortality crossover or convergence is the population dynamics due to systematic mortality selection. Specifically, if one assumes that the individuals in each of two population groups are differently endowed for longevity at birth, then if one of the populations is subjected to a harsher environment and, consequently, a greater force of mortality before any given age, a smaller and more highly selected proportion of that population is likely to survive to that age. Specifically, the persons who are more likely to survive are those who are constitutionally endowed for a longer survival. Although the basic logic of this model is simple, there are a number of implications of this model that are often misunderstood.

First, *constitutional endowment* is a term that is often interpreted as implying only genetic determinants of longevity. Although these may be important, they are *not* the only source of population heterogeneity that may result in a crossover or convergence. For example, it is known that differences in prenatal care, general maternal health status, smoking, and nutrition can affect the birth weight and other health characteristics of the neonate. Consequently, such effects of the prenatal environment may also help determine individual differences in survival, possibly even at advanced ages. Indeed, there are a number of different types of life experiences and exposures that may induce heterogeneity in longevity potential and hence contribute to the effect of mortality selection.

Second, any factor producing differentials in an individual's potential for survival may be included in a "frailty" model of mortality selection, such as developed in Section 2, as long as that attribute is fixed before significant mortality selection occurs. If such factors are operational after significant mortality selection occurs, then their effects will be more difficult to predict. If these factors are consistent with a diffusion process, however, then they will tend to increase the heterogeneity of the residual group of survivors, thereby increasing the rate of mortality selection and accelerating the rate of convergence and crossover of the mortality rates among the survivors in the two groups.

Third, it should be stressed in discussing the effects of mortality selection that human aging and mortality are not unidimensional. As a consequence, a person who has great susceptibility to one type of disease process (e.g., heart disease) may not have great susceptibility to another disease process (e.g., cancer). Thus, models of total mortality are limited in explaining crossover–convergence phenomena. Further insight can be gained into the effects of mortality selection on mortality crossover–convergence behavior if individual causes of death, which can be related to specific disease mechanisms and risk factors, are studied.

Fourth, the effects of mortality selection will be manifest on age-specific mortality rates regardless of the way in which the determinants of longevity are distributed in the population. Specifically, the differences due to the effects of selection on a heterogeneous population between the age trajectory of mortality rates for an individual and the age trajectory of mortality rates for an individual. Thus, mortality selection can produce a cohort mortality rate will rise relatively less rapidly with age than the mortality rates for an individual. Thus mortality selection can produce a mortality crossover regardless of the shape of the distribution of factors determining longevity in either population as long as there is adequate heterogeneity in the longevity potential of individuals and the early mortality differentials are extreme enough. Consequently, a mortality crossover can be manifest owing to mortality selection even if the individual potential for longevity is identically distributed in the two populations.

Fifth, to explain the mortality crossover by a mortality selection model, it is necessary that the survival proportions of the disadvantaged group not cross over. Otherwise, it could not be argued that the disadvantaged group was more highly selected than the advantaged group. It is possible for a mortality selection model to explain a crossover in the age-specific mortality rates and a convergence in the proportion surviving to a given age. In this regard, it should be noted that efforts to explain the mortality crossover as the result of census enumeration error have actually strengthened the argument that it is a real phenomenon because by narrowing the crossover and raising the mortality rates for blacks at ages 85 and over by about 20% (e.g., Bayo, 1972), they have successfully eliminated the crossover of the survival proportions at these ages. Once the crossover of these survival proportions is eliminated, the disadvantaged group is then unambiguously identified so that a mortality selection model can then be used to explain the convergence–crossover of the two groups' mortality rates.

Finally, the point should be emphasized that an explanation of the mortality crossover by selection does not imply that the social, economic, and health differentials of the two populations have also crossed over. Rather, it suggests that the differentials between the two populations are much greater than is suggested by the ratio of their age-specific mortality rates. For example, if early mortality selection were high for a given population (i.e., the proportion surviving to a given age is small), then the average endowment for longevity of the survivors would be high. If the mortality rates of this group were equal to those for a much less selected group in the advantaged population (whose individuals would have a poorer average intrinsic capacity for longevity), this would suggest that harsher environmental conditions were operating for the disadvantaged group at the advanced age in order to raise its age-specific mortality rates to the level of the advantaged group.

### Census Enumeration Error

The second common explanation of the crossover phenomenon simply states that it does not exist. Rather, it is asserted that there is a particular combination of measurement errors that produces a crossover as an artifact of measurement error. In particular, this argument suggests that at advanced ages there is a bias toward overenumeration of the black population. This overenumeration of the black elderly population implies that the denominators for age-specific mortality rates [e.g., Eq. (6.1.1)] are too large, with the consequence that the mortality rates for the black elderly population are too low.

Actually, the fact that mortality rates for blacks and whites still cross over even when adjusted for estimates of race-, sex-, and age-specific enumeration errors, as was done in Chapter 5, or when based on Medicare data (Bayo, 1972), indicates that the proponents of this argument believe that there are hitherto unidentified factors that contribute to enumeration error being much larger than any of our present estimates indicate (e.g., Rosenwaike et al., 1980). Implied in the enumeration explanation is that mortality rates at early ages for blacks (especially males) are overestimated due to underenumeration at those ages. Underenumeration at early ages and overenumeration at later ages would affect our perception of the degree of either absolute or proportional mortality convergence and our estimate of the peak mortality differential and the age at which it occurred.

### Different Rates of Aging for Blacks and Whites

Another possible explanation of the crossover is that blacks have a different age pattern of mortality from chronic degenerative conditions than whites—owing either to intrinsic differences or to environmental factors. To distinguish this effect clearly from the effect of mortality selection, it should be pointed out that under the most simple selection model, all individuals are assumed to have the same shape curve describing their age-related increase in mortality rates—the standard force of mortality function $\mu(x|1)$—although each individual would be at a different risk level depending on the conditions determining his potential for longevity. Thus, the mortality selection model is primarily a model of the initial distribution of longevity characteristics in the population and of how mortality selection operates to change the characteristics of that distribution over age. In postulating a different aging pattern for blacks and whites, it is being suggested that the two groups have different curves (standard force of mortality functions) describing the age change of mortality rates without necessarily focusing on the initial differentials in average risk levels between the two groups or between-individual variation in mortality risk factors for the two groups. In actuality, it is likely that both mortality selection and different aging rates contribute to black–white mortality differentials. For example, an examination of the official U.S. life tables for 1969 to 1971 shows crossovers in both the mortality rates and the proportion surviving to a given age. If adjustment for enumeration effects did not eliminate the crossover in the survival proportion, then the fact of the crossover of *both* life table functions would require a model that involved some other mechanism, such as race-specific rates of aging, in addition to mortality selection effects.

The first set of factors that might contribute to the observation of differential aging rates is the determinants of the biological rate of aging. For example, it could be hypothesized that blacks age more rapidly in the middle ages than whites. Thus, their aggregate risk of death rises more rapidly in middle age, whereas whites, whose aging processes would be hypothesized to rise more rapidly at advanced ages, would experience rapid mortality increases at those ages. To illustrate, suppose blacks' greater risk of hypertension-related mortality in the middle ages was a property of basic biomedical processes. Also suppose that whites' greater, but later, risk of atherosclerotic changes was a basic property of intrinsic aging processes in that population group. In this case, the crossover could be due to differences in race-specific aging processes, which are manifest as differences in the age trajectory of mortality rates between the two groups.

The second way that race-specific differences in the rate of aging processes might be induced is through environmental differences. For example, there are many animal studies that indicate that various types of stress, such as caloric deprivation, can either slow the rate of aging or somehow strengthen the individual (Economos, 1982). This type of phenomenon has been postulated to explain the different age patterns and types of circulatory disease affecting blacks and whites. Briefly, blacks are proportionately more involved in manual occupations, a situation that reduces their rate of atherosclerotic change. Whites, who are proportionately less involved in manual occupations, do not have the early elevation of rates of hypertensive diseases but do have later increases in mortality rates due to atherosclerotic circulatory disease (Cassel *et al.,* 1971). Similarly, poor nutrition might decrease the ability to respond to infectious disease and increase early mortality rates, whereas it might also slow degenerative circulatory disease and decrease mortality rates at advanced ages. Also, differential occupational exposure to carcinogens could lead to different rates of cancer mortality for blacks and whites. The basic fact that has to be kept in mind in postulating environmentally changed rates of aging is that the environmental factor must induce a permanent change in the age trajectory of mortality rates.

### External Forces of Mortality

A fourth way in which the mortality crossover might arise is simply through differences in environmental stress (Jones, 1962). This explanation would suggest that blacks have high mortality rates in middle age because that is the age range at which they are subjected to the most hazardous environmental conditions. The difference between this effect and environmentally induced changes in aging as just described is that in the altered aging model, the age trajectory of mortality rates for an individual is permanently altered by exposure. The external forces of mortality model, on the other hand, suggests that the individual is unaffected by environmental stress except that the organism's mortality rates are raised over a short period of time. In this way, the environmental stress functions as a series of "shocks" whose distribution over the life span follows different patterns for blacks and whites. If this were the explanation, then the crossover would result from a lessening of the environmental stress, with the implication being that the black elderly would actually have a better environment, relative to whites, at advanced ages. Although some lessening of socioeconomic differentials might be expected at advanced ages, an actual crossover in the relative status of these groups seems unlikely.

### Cohort Differentials

A fifth way in which the crossover might result is through very different mortality conditions for corresponding black–white birth cohorts. For the cohort explanation to work, it would have to be the case that the birth cohorts of elderly blacks have exceptionally low mortality at advanced ages, both with respect to the corresponding white birth cohorts and compared to younger black birth cohorts. Actually, a cohort explanation would be more of a descriptive than an explanatory model because several of the effects listed in the preceding discussion of possible causes could be indexed by the identity of cohorts.

The preceding five possible causes of a mortality crossover represent a broad range of phenomena, each of which may contribute (to some degree) to the observed age patterns of mortality rates in the two populations. Any strategy that purports to attribute these differentials solely to one of the factors discussed, such as enumeration error, ignores other phenomena that are very likely elements of the aging and mortality dynamics of human populations.

## 4 A Model of the Black–White Crossover: Application of a Model of Mortality Selection to Data Adjusted for Enumeration Error

### *Data*

Application of the model developed in Section 2 is premised on the availability of a historical series of population and mortality data from which the cohort life tables for successive cohorts in each population can be generated. Additionally, with our concern over the possible confounding effects of census enumeration errors, we shall need the cohort life tables to be adjusted for enumeration error. Although complete cohort life tables adjusted for enumeration error are not generally available, it is possible to obtain abridged period life tables that are adjusted for enumeration error for the calendar years 1850, 1901, 1910, 1920, 1930, 1940, and 1950 from published sources; for example, for whites, see Jacobson (1957) and Coale and Zelnick (1963); for blacks, see Evans (1962) and Coale and Rives (1973). It is important to note that the Coale and Zelnick (1963) and the Coale and Rives (1973) methodology for adjusting the effects of enumeration error was also employed by Siegel (1974) in developing the two sets of adjustments for the 1960 and 1970 census data, the latter of which is applicable to the 1975 census population projections.

For the present analysis, complete cohort life tables were derived from these published data by linear interpolation, over calendar years, of the age-specific observed cumulative forces of mortality $h_x$'s. The $h_x$'s for each calendar year for which the published abridged life tables were available were themselves obtained by linear interpolation of the $_nh_x$'s derived from the appropriate $_nq_x$ values via formula (6.4.1):

$$_nh_x = -\ln(1 - _nq_x). \tag{6.4.1}$$

The linear interpolation to obtain the single year of age cumulative force of mortality was conducted with the constraint that the interpolated $h_x$'s sum to $_nh_x$; that is,

$$_nh_x = \sum_{i=x}^{x+(n-1)} h_i, \tag{6.4.2}$$

which for $n = 5$ is simply Eq. (5.2.18). Thus, the abbreviated life tables computed from the interpolated period life tables will exactly reproduce the published abridged life tables.

These interpolation procedures lead to estimates of $h_x^y$ for each age $x$ for each year $y$ in the interval 1850–1975. The $h_x$ column for each cohort life table may then be obtained for each cohort birth year $(y - x)$ for ages up to the value $\omega$, where

$$\omega = 1975 - (y - x), \qquad (y - x) \geq 1890,$$
$$\omega = 85, \qquad\qquad\quad (y - x) < 1890. \tag{6.4.3}$$

Although it is unlikely that significant improvement in the quality of these data could be obtained by employing another methodology in their construction, there still remains a number of serious concerns over the data quality. First, there is the issue that the death registration system in the United States was not complete until 1933. Thus, the data prior to 1933 represent a changing definition of the "at risk" population. Second, there is the lengthy interpolation from 1850 to 1901. Third, the extent of census underenumeration is substantially greater for blacks than for whites, so that there are likely to be significant differences in the reliability of the adjusted cohort life tables across the two racial groups. Finally, the fact that interpolation techniques were used at all suggests that even given the constraint (6.4.2), there will be some unknown degree of unreliability introduced.

The first two issues admit to direct response by concentrating the analysis on the latter portion of the mortality time series. Specifically, we shall deal with the black–white crossover as manifest in the mortality data for the calendar year 1969. The year 1969 was chosen primarily because we have analyzed these data in great detail in Chapter 5 and because the black–white crossover persisted in these data even after adjustment for census enumeration error (Siegel, 1974). Actually, to achieve direct comparability between the two types of data, we modified the preceding interpolation procedure to use the 1969 period life table $h_x$ column instead of the 1970 period life table $h_x$ column (see Tables 1–5, Chapter 5).

### Results

We first assess the plausibility of the explanation that the black–white mortality crossover in total mortality is an artifact of the historical occurrence of the differential rates of mortality selection in the two population groups. To do this it is first necessary to demonstrate that these differentials do, in fact, exist in the cohort data after adjustment for census enumeration effects. In Tables 1–4 we present the abbreviated cohort life tables for white males, white females, black males, and black females born in the years 1870, 1880, and 1890.

**Table 1**

White Male Abbreviated Cohort Life Tables

| Age at start of interval $(x, x + 5)$, $x$ | Probability of dying in interval $(x, x + 5)$, $_5q_x$ | Number living at age $x$, $l_x$ | Number dying in interval $(x, x + 5)$, $_5d_x$ | Observed life expectancy at age $x$, $\overset{\circ}{e}_x$ | Cumulative force of mortality over interval $(x, x + 5)$, $_5h_x$ |
|---|---|---|---|---|---|
| | | 1870 birth cohort | | | |
| 0 | 0.2398565 | 100,000 | 23,986 | 45.91 | 0.2742481 |
| 5 | 0.0377145 | 76,014 | 2,867 | 55.09 | 0.0384441 |
| 10 | 0.0170851 | 73,148 | 1,250 | 52.17 | 0.0172327 |
| 15 | 0.0232628 | 71,898 | 1,673 | 48.04 | 0.0235377 |
| 20 | 0.0338798 | 70,225 | 2,379 | 44.12 | 0.0344670 |
| 25 | 0.0360921 | 67,846 | 2,449 | 40.58 | 0.0367595 |
| 30 | 0.0372367 | 65,397 | 2,435 | 37.00 | 0.0379477 |
| 35 | 0.0440762 | 62,962 | 2,775 | 33.34 | 0.0450771 |
| 40 | 0.0486304 | 60,187 | 2,927 | 29.76 | 0.0498526 |
| 45 | 0.0528236 | 57,260 | 3,025 | 26.15 | 0.0542699 |
| 50 | 0.0657548 | 54,235 | 3,566 | 22.47 | 0.0680163 |
| 55 | 0.0915352 | 50,669 | 4,638 | 18.86 | 0.0959991 |
| 60 | 0.1371712 | 46,031 | 6,314 | 15.50 | 0.1475390 |
| 65 | 0.1972544 | 39,717 | 7,834 | 12.55 | 0.2197175 |
| 70 | 0.2840272 | 31,883 | 9,056 | 10.00 | 0.3341131 |
| 75 | 0.3854561 | 22,827 | 8,799 | 7.96 | 0.4868748 |
| 80 | 0.5208685 | 14,028 | 7,307 | 6.41 | 0.7357802 |
| 85 | 1.0000000 | 6,721 | 6,721 | 5.81 | |
| | | 1880 birth cohort | | | |
| 0 | 0.2239456 | 100,000 | 22,395 | 48.36 | 0.2535327 |
| 5 | 0.0306491 | 77,605 | 2,379 | 57.04 | 0.0311286 |
| 10 | 0.0147590 | 75,227 | 1,110 | 53.79 | 0.0148690 |
| 15 | 0.0211846 | 74,117 | 1,570 | 49.56 | 0.0214122 |
| 20 | 0.0305061 | 72,546 | 2,213 | 45.57 | 0.0309811 |
| 25 | 0.0298343 | 70,333 | 2,098 | 41.93 | 0.0302884 |
| 30 | 0.0319024 | 68,235 | 2,177 | 38.14 | 0.0324224 |
| 35 | 0.0365130 | 66,058 | 2,412 | 34.31 | 0.0371963 |
| 40 | 0.0365461 | 63,646 | 2,326 | 30.52 | 0.0372306 |
| 45 | 0.0493835 | 61,320 | 3,028 | 26.58 | 0.0506446 |
| 50 | 0.0693887 | 58,292 | 4,045 | 22.82 | 0.0719136 |
| 55 | 0.0930829 | 54,247 | 5,049 | 19.33 | 0.0977043 |
| 60 | 0.1347465 | 49,198 | 6,629 | 16.05 | 0.1447328 |
| 65 | 0.1896660 | 42,568 | 8,074 | 13.14 | 0.2103087 |
| 70 | 0.2638121 | 34,495 | 9,100 | 10.61 | 0.3062698 |
| 75 | 0.3609871 | 25,395 | 9,167 | 8.51 | 0.4478306 |
| 80 | 0.4921405 | 16,227 | 7,986 | 6.91 | 0.6775504 |
| 85 | 1.0000000 | 8,241 | 8,241 | 6.29 | |

**Table 1** (*Continued*)

| Age at start of interval $(x, x + 5)$, $x$ | Probability of dying in interval $(x, x + 5)$, ${}_5q_x$ | Number living at age $x$, $l_x$ | Number dying in interval $(x, x + 5)$, ${}_5d_x$ | Observed life expectancy at age $x$, $\mathring{e}_x$ | Cumulative force of mortality over interval $(x, x + 5)$, ${}_5h_x$ |
|---|---|---|---|---|---|
| | | 1890 birth cohort | | | |
| 0 | 0.2077017 | 100,000 | 20,770 | 51.11 | 0.2328174 |
| 5 | 0.0235317 | 79,230 | 1,864 | 59.27 | 0.0238130 |
| 10 | 0.0124610 | 77,365 | 964 | 55.65 | 0.0125393 |
| 15 | 0.0182847 | 76,401 | 1,397 | 51.33 | 0.0184540 |
| 20 | 0.0243455 | 75,004 | 1,826 | 47.23 | 0.0246468 |
| 25 | 0.0249147 | 73,178 | 1,823 | 43.35 | 0.0252304 |
| 30 | 0.0258146 | 71,355 | 1,842 | 39.39 | 0.0261537 |
| 35 | 0.0294633 | 69,513 | 2,048 | 35.37 | 0.0299061 |
| 40 | 0.0342955 | 67,465 | 2,314 | 31.36 | 0.0348974 |
| 45 | 0.0445823 | 65,151 | 2,905 | 27.39 | 0.0456067 |
| 50 | 0.0628501 | 62,247 | 3,912 | 23.54 | 0.0649120 |
| 55 | 0.0839640 | 58,334 | 4,898 | 19.95 | 0.0876996 |
| 60 | 0.1311153 | 53,436 | 7,006 | 16.53 | 0.1405448 |
| 65 | 0.1816042 | 46,430 | 8,432 | 13.64 | 0.2004092 |
| 70 | 0.2538875 | 37,998 | 9,647 | 11.09 | 0.2928789 |
| 75 | 0.3490696 | 28,351 | 9,896 | 9.00 | 0.4293525 |
| 80 | 0.4636407 | 18,455 | 8,556 | 7.51 | 0.6229509 |
| 85 | 1.0000000 | 9,898 | 9,898 | 6.93 | |

Examination of the 1870 birth cohort in Tables 1–4 reveals that for males the crossover in ${}_5q_x$ occurs at age 75. For the 1880 and 1890 birth cohorts, the crossover also occurs at age 75. For females the crossover in ${}_5q_x$ occurs at ages 70, 75, and 75, respectively, for the 1870, 1880, and 1890 birth cohorts. In contrast, comparison of the $l_x$ values reveals that there are no cohorts for which the black population has a higher proportion of survivors at age 85 than does the white population.

Although not shown here, similar results are obtained from comparison of the race-specific life tables for other birth cohorts. Thus, we may conclude that adjustments for census enumeration error are not sufficient to eliminate the convergence and crossover of the mortality rates in these data, although because the $l_x$ values do not cross, the blacks can be unambiguously identified as the disadvantaged group.

**Table 2**

White Female Abbreviated Cohort Life Tables

| Age at start of interval $(x, x + 5)$, $x$ | Probability of dying in interval $(x, x + 5)$, $_5q_x$ | Number living at age $x$, $l_x$ | Number dying in interval $(x, x + 5)$, $_5d_x$ | Observed life expectancy at age $x$, $\overset{\circ}{e}_x$ | Cumulative force of mortality over interval $(x, x + 5)$, $_5h_x$ |
|---|---|---|---|---|---|
| | | | 1870 birth cohort | | |
| 0 | 0.2105976 | 100,000 | 21,060 | 50.24 | 0.2364791 |
| 5 | 0.0337236 | 78,940 | 2,662 | 58.36 | 0.0343053 |
| 10 | 0.0190600 | 76,278 | 1,454 | 55.32 | 0.0192440 |
| 15 | 0.0257918 | 74,824 | 1,930 | 51.35 | 0.0261302 |
| 20 | 0.0337661 | 72,894 | 2,461 | 47.64 | 0.0343493 |
| 25 | 0.0355237 | 70,433 | 2,502 | 44.22 | 0.0361700 |
| 30 | 0.0343330 | 67,931 | 2,332 | 40.75 | 0.0349362 |
| 35 | 0.0369646 | 65,599 | 2,425 | 37.11 | 0.0376652 |
| 40 | 0.0359798 | 63,174 | 2,273 | 33.44 | 0.0366430 |
| 45 | 0.0418374 | 60,901 | 2,548 | 29.60 | 0.0427378 |
| 50 | 0.0509571 | 58,353 | 2,973 | 25.78 | 0.0523013 |
| 55 | 0.0667762 | 55,379 | 3,698 | 22.02 | 0.0691103 |
| 60 | 0.0978353 | 51,681 | 5,056 | 18.41 | 0.1029582 |
| 65 | 0.1441711 | 46,625 | 6,722 | 15.12 | 0.1556849 |
| 70 | 0.2121340 | 39,903 | 8,465 | 12.23 | 0.2384272 |
| 75 | 0.3030810 | 31,438 | 9,528 | 9.83 | 0.3610860 |
| 80 | 0.4342120 | 21,910 | 9,514 | 8.00 | 0.5695358 |
| 85 | 1.0000000 | 12,396 | 12,396 | 7.25 | |
| | | | 1880 birth cohort | | |
| 0 | 0.1957846 | 100,000 | 19,578 | 53.51 | 0.2178882 |
| 5 | 0.0278124 | 80,422 | 2,237 | 61.28 | 0.0282065 |
| 10 | 0.0154574 | 78,185 | 1,209 | 57.98 | 0.0155781 |
| 15 | 0.0223676 | 76,976 | 1,722 | 53.85 | 0.0226215 |
| 20 | 0.0294613 | 75,255 | 2,217 | 50.02 | 0.0299040 |
| 25 | 0.0296441 | 73,037 | 2,165 | 46.46 | 0.0300923 |
| 30 | 0.0283216 | 70,872 | 2,007 | 42.81 | 0.0287304 |
| 35 | 0.0323154 | 68,865 | 2,225 | 38.98 | 0.0328490 |
| 40 | 0.0311605 | 66,640 | 2,077 | 35.20 | 0.0316564 |
| 45 | 0.0376026 | 64,563 | 2,428 | 31.25 | 0.0383278 |
| 50 | 0.0487218 | 62,135 | 3,027 | 27.37 | 0.0499487 |
| 55 | 0.0618075 | 59,108 | 3,653 | 23.64 | 0.0638002 |
| 60 | 0.0859294 | 55,455 | 4,765 | 20.02 | 0.0898474 |
| 65 | 0.1239670 | 50,690 | 6,284 | 16.66 | 0.1323515 |
| 70 | 0.1811957 | 44,406 | 8,046 | 13.65 | 0.1999102 |
| 75 | 0.2634911 | 36,360 | 9,580 | 11.09 | 0.3058340 |
| 80 | 0.3933184 | 26,779 | 10,533 | 9.14 | 0.4997512 |
| 85 | 1.0000000 | 16,246 | 16,246 | 8.47 | |

**Table 2** (*Continued*)

| Age at start of interval $(x, x + 5)$, $x$ | Probability of dying in interval $(x, x + 5)$, $_5q_x$ | Number living at age $x$, $l_x$ | Number dying in interval $(x, x + 5)$, $_5d_x$ | Observed life expectancy at age $x$, $\overset{\circ}{e}_x$ | Cumulative force of mortality over interval $(x, x + 5)$, $_5h_x$ |
|---|---|---|---|---|---|
| | | 1890 birth cohort | | | |
| 0 | 0.1806937 | 100,000 | 18,069 | 57.53 | 0.1992973 |
| 5 | 0.0218651 | 81,931 | 1,791 | 65.00 | 0.0221077 |
| 10 | 0.0118804 | 80,139 | 952 | 61.41 | 0.0119515 |
| 15 | 0.0173326 | 79,187 | 1,373 | 57.12 | 0.0174845 |
| 20 | 0.0233512 | 77,815 | 1,817 | 53.08 | 0.0236282 |
| 25 | 0.0271209 | 75,998 | 2,061 | 49.29 | 0.0274954 |
| 30 | 0.0270499 | 73,936 | 2,000 | 45.59 | 0.0274224 |
| 35 | 0.0256311 | 71,936 | 1,844 | 41.79 | 0.0259653 |
| 40 | 0.0260479 | 70,093 | 1,826 | 37.82 | 0.0263932 |
| 45 | 0.0307944 | 68,267 | 2,102 | 33.77 | 0.0312785 |
| 50 | 0.0390119 | 66,165 | 2,581 | 29.76 | 0.0397933 |
| 55 | 0.0504288 | 63,583 | 3,206 | 25.86 | 0.0517448 |
| 60 | 0.0705338 | 60,377 | 4,259 | 22.10 | 0.0731449 |
| 65 | 0.1036657 | 56,118 | 5,818 | 18.57 | 0.1094418 |
| 70 | 0.1584208 | 50,301 | 7,969 | 15.41 | 0.1724752 |
| 75 | 0.2330813 | 42,332 | 9,867 | 12.82 | 0.2653745 |
| 80 | 0.3411152 | 32,465 | 11,074 | 10.94 | 0.4172065 |
| 85 | 1.0000000 | 21,391 | 21,391 | 10.31 | |

When combined with the results presented in Chapter 5, the preceding results show that the black–white mortality crossovers consistently occur in both cohort and period data when these data are adjusted for census enumeration error. As a consequence, if it is to be argued that the crossover of the mortality rates in the adjusted data is an artifact of additional enumeration error beyond that accounted for by Coale and Rives (1973), Coale and Zelnick (1963), and Siegel (1974), then it is important to ascertain the amount of error that needs to be explained in formulating these additional adjustments. For this purpose, we shall deal with the 1969 population estimates, previously described in Chapter 5, in considering three types of crossover elimination procedures.

In considering these three crossover elimination procedures, the reader may find it helpful to examine Fig. 2 of Chapter 5. In the first procedure we identify the age at which the black male mortality hazards

## Table 3

### Black Male Abbreviated Cohort Life Tables

| Age at start of interval $(x, x + 5)$, $x$ | Probability of dying in interval $(x, x + 5)$, $_5q_x$ | Number living at age $x$, $l_x$ | Number dying in interval $(x, x + 5)$, $_5d_x$ | Observed life expectancy at age $x$, $\overset{\circ}{e}_x$ | Cumulative force of mortality over interval $(x, x + 5)$, $_5h_x$ |
|---|---|---|---|---|---|
| | | 1870 birth cohort | | | |
| 0 | 0.2862981 | 100,000 | 28,630 | 37.72 | 0.3372899 |
| 5 | 0.0467800 | 71,370 | 3,339 | 47.44 | 0.0479095 |
| 10 | 0.0324804 | 68,031 | 2,210 | 44.68 | 0.0330196 |
| 15 | 0.0440215 | 65,822 | 2,898 | 41.10 | 0.0450199 |
| 20 | 0.0559104 | 62,924 | 3,518 | 37.87 | 0.0575342 |
| 25 | 0.0590111 | 59,406 | 3,506 | 34.96 | 0.0608239 |
| 30 | 0.0531633 | 55,900 | 2,972 | 32.00 | 0.0546287 |
| 35 | 0.0808875 | 52,929 | 4,281 | 28.65 | 0.0843467 |
| 40 | 0.0834245 | 48,647 | 4,058 | 25.95 | 0.0871109 |
| 45 | 0.1044099 | 44,589 | 4,656 | 23.08 | 0.1102724 |
| 50 | 0.1117055 | 39,933 | 4,461 | 20.48 | 0.1184519 |
| 55 | 0.1373700 | 35,473 | 4,873 | 17.74 | 0.1477694 |
| 60 | 0.1733223 | 30,600 | 5,304 | 15.15 | 0.1903403 |
| 65 | 0.2479174 | 25,296 | 6,271 | 12.81 | 0.2849092 |
| 70 | 0.2851350 | 19,025 | 5,425 | 11.19 | 0.3356616 |
| 75 | 0.3459239 | 13,600 | 4,705 | 9.68 | 0.4245316 |
| 80 | 0.4220588 | 8,896 | 3,754 | 8.52 | 0.5482832 |
| 85 | 1.0000000 | 5,141 | 5,141 | 7.97 | |
| | | 1880 birth cohort | | | |
| 0 | 0.2898855 | 100,000 | 28,989 | 37.88 | 0.3423291 |
| 5 | 0.0434854 | 71,011 | 3,088 | 47.94 | 0.0444593 |
| 10 | 0.0317702 | 67,923 | 2,158 | 45.04 | 0.0322859 |
| 15 | 0.0431775 | 65,766 | 2,840 | 41.43 | 0.0441374 |
| 20 | 0.0567328 | 62,926 | 3,570 | 38.18 | 0.0584057 |
| 25 | 0.0575364 | 59,356 | 3,415 | 35.33 | 0.0592580 |
| 30 | 0.0583044 | 55,941 | 3,262 | 32.33 | 0.0600732 |
| 35 | 0.0708296 | 52,679 | 3,731 | 29.18 | 0.0734632 |
| 40 | 0.0647610 | 48,948 | 3,170 | 26.22 | 0.0669532 |
| 45 | 0.1064248 | 45,778 | 4,872 | 22.85 | 0.1125247 |
| 50 | 0.1340747 | 40,906 | 5,484 | 20.26 | 0.1439566 |
| 55 | 0.1346490 | 35,422 | 4,769 | 18.02 | 0.1446201 |
| 60 | 0.1472688 | 30,652 | 4,514 | 15.44 | 0.1593109 |
| 65 | 0.2450640 | 26,138 | 6,405 | 12.65 | 0.2811223 |
| 70 | 0.2739016 | 19,733 | 5,405 | 10.95 | 0.3200697 |
| 75 | 0.3451108 | 14,328 | 4,945 | 9.14 | 0.4232891 |
| 80 | 0.4576042 | 9,383 | 4,294 | 7.66 | 0.6117593 |
| 85 | 1.0000000 | 5,089 | 5,089 | 7.12 | |

**Table 3** (*Continued*)

| Age at start of interval $(x, x + 5)$, $x$ | Probability of dying in interval $(x, x + 5)$, $_5q_x$ | Number living at age $x$, $l_x$ | Number dying in interval $(x, x + 5)$, $_5d_x$ | Observed life expectancy at age $x$, $\overset{\circ}{e}_x$ | Cumulative force of mortality over interval $(x, x + 5)$, $_5h_x$ |
|---|---|---|---|---|---|
| | | 1890 birth cohort | | | |
| 0 | 0.2934549 | 100,000 | 29,345 | 38.69 | 0.3473682 |
| 5 | 0.0401795 | 70,655 | 2,839 | 49.38 | 0.0410090 |
| 10 | 0.0306877 | 67,816 | 2,081 | 46.37 | 0.0311684 |
| 15 | 0.0418276 | 65,735 | 2,750 | 42.76 | 0.0427276 |
| 20 | 0.0536074 | 62,985 | 3,376 | 39.51 | 0.0550978 |
| 25 | 0.0491767 | 59,609 | 2,931 | 36.61 | 0.0504271 |
| 30 | 0.0477407 | 56,677 | 2,706 | 33.37 | 0.0489179 |
| 35 | 0.0707898 | 53,971 | 3,821 | 29.92 | 0.0734203 |
| 40 | 0.0807411 | 50,151 | 4,049 | 27.00 | 0.0841874 |
| 45 | 0.0960207 | 46,102 | 4,427 | 24.15 | 0.1009488 |
| 50 | 0.1113591 | 41,675 | 4,641 | 21.45 | 0.1180620 |
| 55 | 0.1260877 | 37,034 | 4,670 | 18.82 | 0.1347753 |
| 60 | 0.1491210 | 32,364 | 4,826 | 16.17 | 0.1614853 |
| 65 | 0.2289096 | 27,538 | 6,304 | 13.55 | 0.2599496 |
| 70 | 0.2910875 | 21,234 | 6,181 | 11.83 | 0.3440232 |
| 75 | 0.3361177 | 15,053 | 5,060 | 10.67 | 0.4096504 |
| 80 | 0.4027405 | 9,994 | 4,025 | 9.89 | 0.5154036 |
| 85 | 1.0000000 | 5,969 | 5,969 | 10.02 | |

first drop below the white male mortality hazards. This is age 77. We then adjust the black male population counts at age 77 and above such that the adjusted mortality hazards are at least as large for black males as for white males. In Table 5 we present the results of this adjustment procedure. A similar procedure was followed for the black female data, except that the crossover occurred at age 76. From Table 5 we see that to eliminate the crossover it is necessary to reduce the Siegel (1974) corrected population counts for black males age 77 and over by 25,991 persons (15.5%) and for black females age 76 and over by 61,001 persons (19.2%). Even when preliminary estimates from the 1980 census are used (Passel *et al.*, 1982), the changes in the 75+ black population in 1970 do not exceed 1.8% (males) and 9.1% (females); hence, further reductions of about 14% and 10% would still be required.

## Table 4

### Black Female Abbreviated Cohort Life Tables

| Age at start of interval $(x, x + 5)$, $x$ | Probability of dying in interval $(x, x + 5)$, $_5q_x$ | Number living at age $x$, $l_x$ | Number dying in interval $(x, x + 5)$, $_5d_x$ | Observed life expectancy at age $x$, $\overset{\circ}{e}_x$ | Cumulative force of mortality over interval $(x, x + 5)$, $_5h_x$ |
|---|---|---|---|---|---|
| | | 1870 birth cohort | | | |
| 0 | 0.2568808 | 100,000 | 25,688 | 41.69 | 0.2968989 |
| 5 | 0.0457116 | 74,312 | 3,397 | 50.72 | 0.0467893 |
| 10 | 0.0406349 | 70,915 | 2,882 | 48.05 | 0.0414835 |
| 15 | 0.0514994 | 68,033 | 3,504 | 44.98 | 0.0528728 |
| 20 | 0.0567669 | 64,530 | 3,663 | 42.28 | 0.0584418 |
| 25 | 0.0523364 | 60,867 | 3,186 | 39.68 | 0.0537557 |
| 30 | 0.0470769 | 57,681 | 2,715 | 36.74 | 0.0482211 |
| 35 | 0.0664747 | 54,966 | 3,654 | 33.43 | 0.0687873 |
| 40 | 0.0698395 | 51,312 | 3,584 | 30.62 | 0.0723981 |
| 45 | 0.0837724 | 47,728 | 3,998 | 27.74 | 0.0874905 |
| 50 | 0.0920212 | 43,730 | 4,024 | 25.04 | 0.0965343 |
| 55 | 0.1069840 | 39,706 | 4,248 | 22.32 | 0.1131508 |
| 60 | 0.1327204 | 35,458 | 4,706 | 19.69 | 0.1423939 |
| 65 | 0.1857764 | 30,752 | 5,713 | 17.32 | 0.2055203 |
| 70 | 0.2039866 | 25,039 | 5,108 | 15.69 | 0.2281392 |
| 75 | 0.2460354 | 19,931 | 4,904 | 14.08 | 0.2824099 |
| 80 | 0.3020586 | 15,028 | 4,539 | 12.87 | 0.3596201 |
| 85 | 1.0000000 | 10,488 | 10,488 | 12.36 | |
| | | 1880 birth cohort | | | |
| 0 | 0.2594833 | 100,000 | 25,948 | 41.71 | 0.3004071 |
| 5 | 0.0434947 | 74,052 | 3,221 | 50.96 | 0.0444689 |
| 10 | 0.0394180 | 70,831 | 2,792 | 48.19 | 0.0402159 |
| 15 | 0.0502191 | 68,039 | 3,417 | 45.06 | 0.0515240 |
| 20 | 0.0562971 | 64,622 | 3,638 | 42.31 | 0.0579439 |
| 25 | 0.0498554 | 60,984 | 3,040 | 39.69 | 0.0511411 |
| 30 | 0.0498622 | 57,944 | 2,889 | 36.64 | 0.0511482 |
| 35 | 0.0671641 | 55,054 | 3,698 | 33.43 | 0.0695259 |
| 40 | 0.0652343 | 51,357 | 3,350 | 30.66 | 0.0674593 |
| 45 | 0.0887034 | 48,006 | 4,258 | 27.62 | 0.0928869 |
| 50 | 0.1063257 | 43,748 | 4,652 | 25.06 | 0.1124139 |
| 55 | 0.1030373 | 39,097 | 4,028 | 22.75 | 0.1087410 |
| 60 | 0.1092720 | 35,068 | 3,832 | 20.08 | 0.1157162 |
| 65 | 0.1922238 | 31,236 | 6,004 | 17.21 | 0.2134702 |
| 70 | 0.1927170 | 25,232 | 4,863 | 15.71 | 0.2140810 |
| 75 | 0.2348518 | 20,369 | 4,784 | 13.87 | 0.2676858 |
| 80 | 0.3157274 | 15,585 | 4,921 | 12.36 | 0.3793988 |
| 85 | 1.0000000 | 10,665 | 10,665 | 11.93 | |

**Table 4** (*Continued*)

| Age at start of interval $(x, x + 5)$, $x$ | Probability of dying in interval $(x, x + 5)$, ${}_5q_x$ | Number living at age $x$, $l_x$ | Number dying in interval $(x, x + 5)$, ${}_5d_x$ | Observed life expectancy at age $x$, $\overset{\circ}{e}_x$ | Cumulative force of mortality over interval $(x, x + 5)$, ${}_5h_x$ |
|---|---|---|---|---|---|
| | | | 1890 birth cohort | | |
| 0 | 0.2620767 | 100,000 | 26,208 | 42.51 | 0.3039154 |
| 5 | 0.0412726 | 73,792 | 3,046 | 52.25 | 0.0421485 |
| 10 | 0.0375097 | 70,747 | 2,654 | 49.42 | 0.0382313 |
| 15 | 0.0484200 | 68,093 | 3,297 | 46.25 | 0.0496315 |
| 20 | 0.0542020 | 64,796 | 3,512 | 43.47 | 0.0557263 |
| 25 | 0.0557546 | 61,284 | 3,417 | 40.82 | 0.0573692 |
| 30 | 0.0534631 | 57,867 | 3,094 | 38.08 | 0.0549454 |
| 35 | 0.0687000 | 54,773 | 3,763 | 35.09 | 0.0711739 |
| 40 | 0.0731586 | 51,010 | 3,732 | 32.49 | 0.0759728 |
| 45 | 0.0804733 | 47,279 | 3,805 | 29.86 | 0.0838962 |
| 50 | 0.0885161 | 43,474 | 3,848 | 27.26 | 0.0926813 |
| 55 | 0.0931397 | 39,626 | 3,691 | 24.66 | 0.0977669 |
| 60 | 0.1070099 | 35,935 | 3,845 | 21.94 | 0.1131798 |
| 65 | 0.1633041 | 32,090 | 5,240 | 19.25 | 0.1782946 |
| 70 | 0.1924020 | 26,849 | 5,166 | 17.52 | 0.2136909 |
| 75 | 0.2184511 | 21,683 | 4,737 | 16.09 | 0.2464776 |
| 80 | 0.2822860 | 16,947 | 4,784 | 14.91 | 0.3316842 |
| 85 | 1.0000000 | 12,163 | 12,163 | 14.83 | |

The second and third procedures are concerned with eliminating not just the crossover but the two types of convergence in the mortality hazards that lead to the crossover at ages 77 and 76. In the second procedure, we identify the age at which the maximum difference in the mortality hazards occurs. For males, this is age 72; for females, age 65. We then adjust the black male and female population counts at and above ages 73 or 66 such that the adjusted mortality hazards maintain this absolute difference. From Table 5 we see that in order to eliminate this absolute convergence it is necessary to reduce Siegel's (1974) corrected population counts for black males age 73 and over by 60,439 persons (18.5%) and for black females age 66 and over by 176,977 (20.7%).

In the third procedure, we identify the age at which the ratio of black to white mortality hazards is largest. For males, this is age 35; for females, also age 35. We then adjust the black male and female population counts

Table 5

Adjustments to Black Population Counts Required to Eliminate the
Black–White Crossover and Convergence

| Type of elimination | Crossover | Absolute convergence | Proportional convergence |
|---|---|---|---|
| | Black males | | |
| Affected ages | 77–109+ | 73–109+ | 36–109+ |
| Corrected population | 167,793 | 325,973 | 2,792,420 |
| Adjusted population | 141,802 | 265,534 | 2,340,877 |
| Net population change | 25,991 | 60,439 | 1,451,543 |
| Percentage change | 15.5 | 18.5 | 38.3 |
| | Black females | | |
| Affected ages | 76–109+ | 66–109+ | 36–109+ |
| Corrected population | 317,120 | 856,674 | 4,265,683 |
| Adjusted population | 256,119 | 679,697 | 3,019,973 |
| Net population change | 61,001 | 176,977 | 1,245,710 |
| Percentage change | 19.2 | 20.7 | 29.2 |

at and beyond age 36 such that the adjusted mortality hazards maintain this proportional difference. From Table 5 we see that in order to eliminate this proportional convergence it is necessary to reduce Siegel's (1974) corrected population counts for black males age 36 and over by 1,451,543 persons (38.3%) and for black females age 36 and over by 1,245,710 persons (29.2%). It is important to note that these adjustments represent 12.2 and 10.0% of the total black population at all ages, which implies that Siegel's (1974) corrections were in the wrong direction (9.9% males and 5.5% females).

From the preceding demonstration, it is seen that although it might be argued that the crossover is the result of additional enumeration factors at advanced ages (i.e., above age 75), the proportional convergence that begins at age 36 will be much more difficult to explain as enumeration error. In contrast, if the black population is, in fact, disadvantaged with respect to whites, then a mechanism such as differential mortality selection would appear to be a much more plausible explanation of the proportional convergence in the black versus white mortality hazards. Note that the peak differences at age 36 are even less likely to be an artifact of enumeration error because they would imply about a 200% net overcount if this were true.

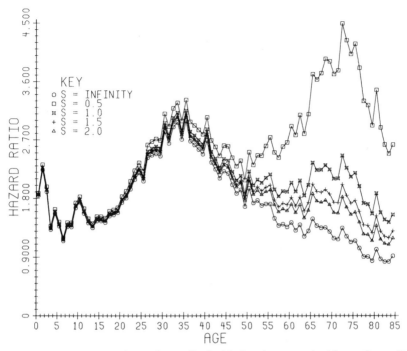

**Fig. 1.** Ratio of standard force of mortality for black males to standard force of mortality for white males for four values of the parameter $s$ and as observed for $s$ = infinity, in 1969 complete standard individual life table.

Under the model developed in Section 2, if each racial group can be assumed to have the same shape parameter $s$ of the initial gamma distribution of the frailty variate $Z$, then it is possible by using Eq. (6.2.11) to determine the value of $s$ in the standard individual life table that just eliminates the crossover of the standard force of mortality $\mu(x|1)$. In Fig. 1 we present ratios of the standard forces of mortality, for black and white males, under four selected values of $s$ (0.5, 1.0, 1.5, and 2.0) derived from the 1969 complete standard individual life tables for black and white males via the approximation

$$\mu(x + \tfrac{1}{2}|1) = h_{x|1}, \tag{6.4.4}$$

where $h_{x|1}$ is obtained from the appropriate cohort life table by using (6.2.12b).

From Fig. 1 it can be seen that all four values of $s$ are sufficient to effect a crossover elimination. Figure 2 presents the corresponding comparisons derived from the 1969 standard individual life tables for black and white females.

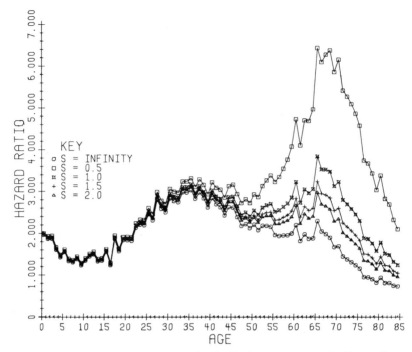

**Fig. 2.** Ratio of standard force of mortality for black females to standard force of mortality for white females for four values of the parameter $s$ and as observed for $s$ = infinity, in 1969 complete standard individual life table.

From Fig. 2 it can be seen that $s$ values of 1.5 and 2.0 are too large. The plots for $s$ = 0.5 appear to be somewhat better than for $s$ = 1.0, so that it is possible that $s$ = 1.0 is too large. However, given that $s$ = 1.0 appears to be an appropriate value for males and just eliminates the crossover for females, we shall examine the implications of population heterogeneity under the assumption that $s$ = 1.0.

To assess the implications of population heterogeneity, we have computed the adjusted abbreviated 1969 period life tables for the four race–sex-groups. These are presented in Tables 6–9.

Tables 6–9 can be directly compared with the corresponding, unadjusted abbreviated 1969 period life tables presented in Tables 2–5 of Chapter 5. For all four race–sex-groups, this comparison shows that with increasing age, $q_x$ and $d_x$ are downwardly biased if the adjusted $\tilde{q}_x$ and $\tilde{d}_x$ are correct. In contrast, $l_x$ and $\overset{\circ}{e}_x$ are upwardly biased if the adjusted $\tilde{l}_x$ and $\overset{\circ}{\tilde{e}}_x$ are correct. For example, the comparison of the life expectancy at birth in the two types of tables reveals differences (i.e., $\overset{\circ}{e}_0 - \overset{\circ}{\tilde{e}}_0$) of 1.42, 1.37, 2.08, and 3.21 years, respectively, for white males, white females, black

## Table 6

White Male Abbreviated Adjusted ($s$ = 1.0) Life Table for 1969

| Age at start of interval $(x, x + 5)$, $x$ | Probability of dying in interval $(x, x + 5)$, $_5\bar{q}_x$ | Number living at age $x$, $\bar{l}_x$ | Number dying in interval $(x, x + 5)$, $_5\bar{d}_x$ | Observed life expectancy at age $x$, $\bar{\overset{\circ}{e}}_x$ | Cumulative force of mortality over interval $(x, x + 5)$, $_5\bar{h}_x$ |
|---|---|---|---|---|---|
| 0 | 0.0241725 | 100,000 | 2,417 | 66.60 | 0.0244695 |
| 5 | 0.0023818 | 97,583 | 232 | 63.24 | 0.0023846 |
| 10 | 0.0023696 | 97,350 | 231 | 58.39 | 0.0023724 |
| 15 | 0.0077552 | 97,120 | 753 | 53.52 | 0.0077855 |
| 20 | 0.0097643 | 96,366 | 941 | 48.92 | 0.0098123 |
| 25 | 0.0083908 | 95,426 | 801 | 44.37 | 0.0084262 |
| 30 | 0.0091698 | 94,625 | 868 | 39.73 | 0.0092121 |
| 35 | 0.0132105 | 93,757 | 1,239 | 35.07 | 0.0132985 |
| 40 | 0.0219326 | 92,519 | 2,029 | 30.51 | 0.0221767 |
| 45 | 0.0359711 | 90,489 | 3,255 | 26.13 | 0.0366340 |
| 50 | 0.0601654 | 87,234 | 5,248 | 22.01 | 0.0620514 |
| 55 | 0.0982819 | 81,986 | 8,058 | 18.24 | 0.1034533 |
| 60 | 0.1503330 | 73,928 | 11,114 | 14.94 | 0.1629108 |
| 65 | 0.2198098 | 62,814 | 13,807 | 12.12 | 0.2482176 |
| 70 | 0.2956678 | 49,007 | 14,490 | 9.82 | 0.3505052 |
| 75 | 0.3916605 | 34,517 | 13,519 | 7.90 | 0.4970221 |
| 80 | 0.5174933 | 20,998 | 10,866 | 6.43 | 0.7287605 |
| 85 | 1.0000000 | 10,132 | 10,132 | 5.77 | |

males and black females. Actually, for these life expectancy comparisons to be appropriate, it is necessary to recompute Tables 2–5 of Chapter 5 in order to close out the life table at age 85. When this is done, the differences in life expectancy are even larger—1.65, 2.46, 2.09, and 4.14 years, respectively, for the four race–sex-groups. The other life-table columns are not affected by this recomputation. It might be noted that differences of these magnitudes are on a level comparable with the cause-elimination life expectancy gains observed in Chapter 5 for the elimination of major causes of death. It should also be emphasized that although the magnitude of these biases is clearly dependent on the selected value of $s$ [see Eq. (6.2.25)], the direction of these biases is empirically established by the historical reality of declining mortality rates for successive cohorts. Furthermore, the direction of these biases does not change even if the assumption of fixed frailty is wrong, so that frailty is dynamically altered under a diffusion process.

**Table 7**

White Female Abbreviated Adjusted ($s = 1.0$) Life Table for 1969

| Age at start of interval $(x, x + 5)$, $x$ | Probability of dying in interval $(x, x + 5)$, $_5\bar{q}_x$ | Number living at age $x$, $\bar{l}_x$ | Number dying in interval $(x, x + 5)$, $_5\bar{d}_x$ | Observed life expectancy at age $x$, $\bar{\mathring{e}}_x$ | Cumulative force of mortality over interval $(x, x + 5)$, $_5\bar{h}_x$ |
|---|---|---|---|---|---|
| 0 | 0.0186905 | 100,000 | 1,869 | 74.23 | 0.0188674 |
| 5 | 0.0016504 | 98,131 | 162 | 70.64 | 0.0016518 |
| 10 | 0.0014559 | 97,969 | 143 | 65.75 | 0.0014570 |
| 15 | 0.0029032 | 97,826 | 284 | 60.84 | 0.0029074 |
| 20 | 0.0033034 | 97,542 | 322 | 56.01 | 0.0033089 |
| 25 | 0.0035485 | 97,220 | 345 | 51.19 | 0.0035548 |
| 30 | 0.0050294 | 96,875 | 487 | 46.36 | 0.0050421 |
| 35 | 0.0078261 | 96,388 | 754 | 41.58 | 0.0078569 |
| 40 | 0.0127406 | 95,634 | 1,218 | 36.89 | 0.0128225 |
| 45 | 0.0198399 | 94,415 | 1,873 | 32.33 | 0.0200394 |
| 50 | 0.0308095 | 92,542 | 2,851 | 27.93 | 0.0312941 |
| 55 | 0.0463941 | 89,691 | 4,161 | 23.73 | 0.0475048 |
| 60 | 0.0704779 | 85,530 | 6,028 | 19.76 | 0.0730847 |
| 65 | 0.1155438 | 79,502 | 9,186 | 16.05 | 0.1227823 |
| 70 | 0.1833354 | 70,316 | 12,891 | 12.81 | 0.2025268 |
| 75 | 0.2832928 | 57,424 | 16,268 | 10.09 | 0.3330879 |
| 80 | 0.4309359 | 41,156 | 17,736 | 8.06 | 0.5637621 |
| 85 | 1.0000000 | 23,421 | 23,421 | 7.28 | |

A second method for assessing the implications of population heterogeneity involves examination of the effects of mortality selection on the distribution of frailty. Here we need to point out that the gamma distribution with $s = 1$ is the well-known exponential distribution. To see this, set $s = 1$ in (6.2.4) with $\zeta = 1$ to obtain

$$f_{Z|(0)}(z|(0)) = \exp(-z), \qquad (6.4.5)$$

which is an exponential distribution with mean $\zeta = 1$.

To examine the effects of mortality selection on the distribution of frailty, let $g_{Z|(x)}(z|(x))$ represent the unnormalized density of $Z$ among the group of persons who survive to at least age $x$. This definition implies two conditions:

$$g_{Z|(0)}(z|(0)) = f_{Z|(0)}(z|(0)) \qquad (6.4.6)$$

**Table 8**

Black Male Abbreviated Adjusted ($s$ = 1.0) Life Table for 1969

| Age at start of interval $(x, x + 5)$, $x$ | Probability of dying in interval $(x, x + 5)$, $_5\bar{q}_x$ | Number living at age $x$, $\bar{l}_x$ | Number dying in interval $(x, x + 5)$, $_5\bar{d}_x$ | Observed life expectancy at age $x$, $\overset{\circ}{\bar{e}}_x$ | Cumulative force of mortality over interval $(x, x + 5)$, $_5\bar{h}_x$ |
|---|---|---|---|---|---|
| 0 | 0.0440924 | 100,000 | 4,409 | 59.12 | 0.0450940 |
| 5 | 0.0032770 | 95,591 | 313 | 56.83 | 0.0032824 |
| 10 | 0.0035390 | 95,278 | 337 | 52.01 | 0.0035453 |
| 15 | 0.0118112 | 94,940 | 1,121 | 47.18 | 0.0118815 |
| 20 | 0.0189413 | 93,819 | 1,777 | 42.71 | 0.0191229 |
| 25 | 0.0198446 | 92,042 | 1,827 | 38.49 | 0.0200441 |
| 30 | 0.0253578 | 90,215 | 2,288 | 34.21 | 0.0256848 |
| 35 | 0.0339098 | 87,928 | 2,982 | 30.04 | 0.0344981 |
| 40 | 0.0484862 | 84,946 | 4,119 | 26.00 | 0.0497010 |
| 45 | 0.0659055 | 80,827 | 5,327 | 22.19 | 0.0681777 |
| 50 | 0.1038562 | 75,500 | 7,841 | 18.58 | 0.1096544 |
| 55 | 0.1486758 | 67,659 | 10,059 | 15.43 | 0.1609622 |
| 60 | 0.2140874 | 57,600 | 12,331 | 12.68 | 0.2409097 |
| 65 | 0.3163122 | 45,269 | 14,319 | 10.44 | 0.3802539 |
| 70 | 0.3707735 | 30,950 | 11,475 | 9.14 | 0.4632640 |
| 75 | 0.3943947 | 19,474 | 7,681 | 8.11 | 0.5015269 |
| 80 | 0.4845426 | 11,794 | 5,715 | 6.92 | 0.6627005 |
| 85 | 1.0000000 | 6,079 | 6,079 | 6.22 | |

and

$$S_X(x) = \int_0^\infty g_{Z|(X)}(z|(x)) \, dz. \qquad (6.4.7)$$

From (4.6.15) it can also be established that

$$g_{Z|(x)}(z|(x)) = f_{Z|(0)}(z|(0)) S_{X|Z}(x|z) \qquad (6.4.8a)$$

$$= \frac{(zs)^s \exp\{-z[s + \int_0^x \mu(a|1) \, da]\}}{z\Gamma(s)}, \qquad (6.4.8b)$$

which is the same as the gamma density in (6.2.8) except for the scale factor

$$[s + \int_0^x \mu(a|1) \, da]^s = s^s / S_X(x), \qquad (6.4.9)$$

as defined in (6.2.10b).

**Table 9**

Black Female Abbreviated Adjusted ($s = 1.0$) Life Table for 1969

| Age at start of interval $(x, x + 5)$, $x$ | Probability of dying in interval $(x, x + 5)$, $_5\tilde{q}_x$ | Number living at age $x$, $\tilde{l}_x$ | Number dying in interval $(x, x + 5)$, $_5\tilde{d}_x$ | Observed life expectancy at age $x$, $\overset{\circ}{\tilde{e}}_x$ | Cumulative force of mortality over interval $(x, x + 5)$, $_5\tilde{h}_x$ |
|---|---|---|---|---|---|
| 0  | 0.0358902 | 100,000 | 3,589  | 65.85 | 0.0365501 |
| 5  | 0.0022672 | 96,411  | 219    | 63.28 | 0.0022698 |
| 10 | 0.0020242 | 96,192  | 195    | 58.42 | 0.0020262 |
| 15 | 0.0047190 | 95,998  | 453    | 53.54 | 0.0047302 |
| 20 | 0.0067526 | 95,545  | 645    | 48.78 | 0.0067755 |
| 25 | 0.0090181 | 94,899  | 856    | 44.09 | 0.0090591 |
| 30 | 0.0144438 | 94,044  | 1,358  | 39.47 | 0.0145491 |
| 35 | 0.0221670 | 92,685  | 2,055  | 35.01 | 0.0224164 |
| 40 | 0.0334993 | 90,631  | 3,036  | 30.74 | 0.0340733 |
| 45 | 0.0457640 | 87,595  | 4,009  | 26.71 | 0.0468442 |
| 50 | 0.0695826 | 83,586  | 5,816  | 22.87 | 0.0721220 |
| 55 | 0.1011130 | 77,770  | 7,864  | 19.38 | 0.1065979 |
| 60 | 0.1569707 | 69,906  | 10,973 | 16.26 | 0.1707536 |
| 65 | 0.2513471 | 58,933  | 14,813 | 13.81 | 0.2894798 |
| 70 | 0.2754700 | 44,120  | 12,154 | 12.63 | 0.3222321 |
| 75 | 0.2866373 | 31,967  | 9,163  | 11.51 | 0.3377652 |
| 80 | 0.3718321 | 22,804  | 8,479  | 10.18 | 0.4649478 |
| 85 | 1.0000000 | 14,325  | 14,325 | 9.78  |           |

In Fig. 3 we compare the effects of mortality selection on the frailty distributions of black males and white males under the assumption that $s = 1$ for the range of $z$, $0 < Z < 3$, for four selected ages: 0, 45, 65, and 85. The approximation to the continuous function $g_{Z|(x)}(z|(x))$ in (6.4.10) was obtained by computing the function values at increments of 0.03 in the values of $z$, where (6.4.10) is (6.4.8b) modified to reflect the standard force of mortality in a synthetic cohort defined for the year $y = 1969$; that is,

$$g_{Z|(x)}(z|(x)) = (zs)^s \frac{\exp\{-z[s + _x\tilde{h}_{0|1}^{1969}]\}}{z\Gamma(s)}. \tag{6.4.10}$$

The top plot in Fig. 3 represents the initial exponential density for both white males and black males. The six plots below this top plot represent the successive decay of this density for white males (circles) and black males (plus signs) at ages 45, 65, and 85 years of age. Examination of Fig. 3 shows that, as expected, the effects of differential mortality selection

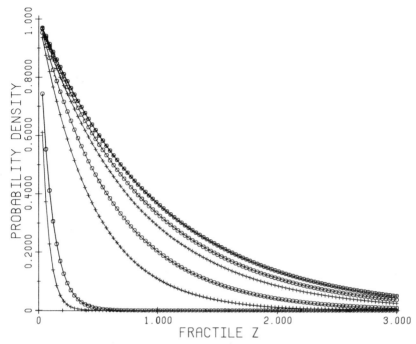

**Fig. 3.** Decay of frailty distributions for white males (o) and for black males (+) due to the effects of mortality selection. The top plot (which is the same) for each group is the initial distribution at age 0. The bottom plot for each group is the distribution at age 85. The intermediate plots for each group indicate the distributions at ages 45 and 65.

produce a more rapid selection of black males. The corresponding comparisons of black females and white females are presented in Fig. 4.

Examination of Fig. 4 again shows that the effects of differential mortality selection produce a more rapid selection of black females. Also, it can be seen from both Figs. 3 and 4 that whereas all four densities have a mean of one ($\zeta = 1$) at birth, by age 85 virtually all individuals with a frailty value greater than 1 ($z > \zeta$) will have been removed from the population through mortality. In effect, the population of survivors at age 85 represents an extremely biased sample of the initial birth population.

# 5  Discussion

In this chapter we have studied the black–white mortality crossover from a broad perspective in which the crossover was but one aspect of a larger convergence phenomenon. Our purpose in doing so was twofold.

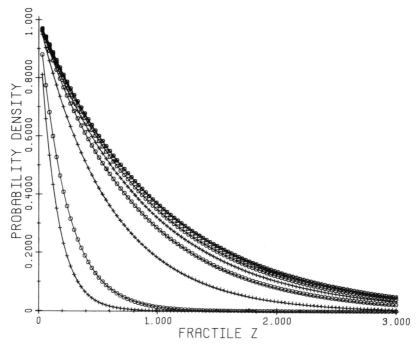

**Fig. 4.** Decay of frailty distributions for white females (o) and for black females (+) due to the effects of mortality selection. The top plot (which is the same) for each group is the initial distribution at age 0. The bottom plot for each group is the distribution at age 85. The intermediate plots for each group indicate the distributions at ages 45 and 65.

First, by focusing on an issue that is still wide open to debate, we hoped to sensitize the reader to the difficulties inherent in interpreting what are ostensibly just some very simple ratios of mortality rates. In many analytic situations, the analysis of mortality data is primarily concerned with performing comparisons of mortality rates between different populations or population subgroups. Thus, the issues involved in explaining the black–white convergence or crossover are pervasive in the comparative analysis of mortality rates. Second, by developing a simple life table model for representing the effects of mortality selection and applying it in a situation that other investigators in the area had suggested was appropriate, we hoped to develop some estimate of the potential level of bias present in the unadjusted period life table calculations. The basic element of this model was the assumption of gamma-distributed fixed frailty, which incorporates the effects of individual differences in longevity potential. The black–white mortality crossover in total mortality was postulated to be an artifact of prior differential mortality selection between whites and blacks in order to estimate the parameter $s$ of the distribution.

From a methodological perspective, this approach indicated that $s$ may be at or below 1.0, an $s$ value that implies an exponential distribution of frailty. Comparisons of the $s$ values estimated for males and females indicated that there was a reasonable concurrence between the obtained values. Naturally, because we are dealing with unobservable parameters, this analysis must be viewed as illustrative. Nonetheless, the model does a good job of accounting for the convergence of the mortality rates from age 36 onward and seemed to be reasonably consistent when applied to data for both males and females. Thus, the analysis does lend support to the role of mortality selection as a factor in shaping the observed age-specific mortality probabilities. For the values of $s = 1.0$, it was found that the unadjusted 1969 life tables overestimated life expectancy by 1.65 and 2.46 years for white males and females, respectively.

The effect of heterogeneity levels of the magnitude we have observed will be to systematically bias the parameter estimates obtained in analyses of period data (although we concede the magnitude of this bias is not well established; it is hoped that it is not as large as our illustrative calculations indicate). One appropriate response would be to perform mortality analyses in a "cohort mode." That is, if cohort cause-specific mortality data were available, then bioactuarial models that specify functional forms for individual level transitions [e.g., as discussed in Section 6, Chapter 4, in the form $\lambda(x|z_\lambda)$] could properly represent the effects of these transitions on the individuals in a cohort. The effects of mortality selection could then be unconfounded from the effects of individual age-specific increases in the standard hazard rate $\lambda(x|\zeta_\lambda)$. With such a model, and given appropriately detailed data, one could estimate additional period effects that might be attributed to such factors as environmental stress or to external forces of mortality. Thus, our analysis of the effects of population heterogeneity, in addition to suggesting the levels of potential biases that might arise if some method were not explicitly employed to account for the mortality selection effects, also provides a biologically plausible rationale for dealing with the analysis of age–cohort–period mortality differentials in a specific hierarchical order.

On a substantive level, the broad programmatic implications of the crossover can be grouped into one of two types: implications if the crossover is real and implications if the crossover is due to enumeration error.

If the crossover is real, there are a variety of areas with important implications. We shall briefly review three broad areas.

## Racial Differentials in Health Status

The existence of a mortality crossover or convergence implies that the relative health status of blacks and whites is highly variable with age. This suggests that we need to learn more of the different pattern of age changes in health status in each population. Specifically, we want to know what contributes to the relative disadvantage of each of the populations at particular intervals of the age range, that is, for blacks during middle ages and for whites during advanced ages. By considering the various types of factors we have proposed as possibly causing the crossover, we might be able to focus on whether the critical factors were "local" age effects (i.e., the shocks under the environmental model) or were due to "historical" effects as under, for example, the selection model in which prior differentials in health status have continuing implications for health status at later ages. In particular, it would seem to be important to examine the differential aspects of the long-term management of a broad range of chronic degenerative disorders. Simply stated, blacks seem to succumb directly to a variety of degenerative conditions, whereas whites with those conditions survive considerably longer; however, the degenerative conditions eventually, but indirectly, contribute to death for whites. The analysis of such effects would involve consideration of the differential availability and accessibility of medical care among blacks and whites. It should also be stressed that even if the crossover were real, there would be no reason to interpret the fact of lower black mortality rates at advanced ages as a sign that individual black persons are not disadvantaged at those advanced ages. It may simply imply the existence of markedly worse mortality conditions for blacks at early ages that contribute to a more highly selected population at advanced ages.

## Health Status Intervention Strategies

Given that further understanding of the pattern of age changes in the relative health status of blacks and whites could be obtained from the study of mortality crossover–convergences, the next question that arises is how one designs various programs to intervene and meet the greatest areas of need for medical and social services. To the extent that mortality crossover–convergence is determined to represent differences in health status, the age pattern of the relative mortality status of the two populations could be a very sensitive monitoring device to assess the population impact of various programs. Again, it should be stressed that several of the explanations of crossover–convergence suggest that early health differentials produce long-term health consequences for the populations, so that interventions might be targeted to different ages than those at which the mortality effects will be manifest. This might be particularly true in prevention programs in which alteration of life-style (i.e., quitting smoking and instituting a program of proper nutrition, exercise, and preventative medical care) is a part of the planned intervention.

### Implication of Survival Differentials for Entitlement Programs and Income Deductions

Apart from what the crossover effect might imply about the requirements for services in the two populations, the mortality schedules implied by the crossover will have implications for the length of payment into various federal programs and duration of entitlement to the benefits of such programs. Naturally, an analysis of such factors requires the evaluation of a number of economic variables such as labor-force participation and income level.

If the crossover were a simple artifact of census enumeration error, there will be an entirely different set of programmatic implications—some of which may have more dramatic implications for federal programs because they would call into question the direction of many existing programs and policies for the elderly minority.

### Programmatic Funding Levels: The Implications of the Overenumeration of Black Elderly

To invalidate the existence of a population mechanism underlying a crossover, or a substantial convergence of mortality rates, the argument would have to be made that the black elderly population is substantially overenumerated (see Table 5). The implications of a considerable over-enumeration are manifold and presumably would affect the status of any program whose magnitude and funding level are related to the size of that minority elderly group.

### Efficiency of Federal Programs' Data Collection Procedures: The Implications of Overenumeration for the Vital Statistics System and the Census

If the overenumeration of the black elderly were substantial enough to explain the crossover–convergence, then there would have to be major implications for the way federal programs gather data. Specifically, given the range and consistency of the demographic data cited in the preceding discussion in which mortality crossovers and convergences were observed, it would appear that the majority of the federal effort at collecting demographic data would have to be reviewed. This would imply a major response in research of census data collection methods and the implementation of improved procedures. Indeed, the recent work by Rosenwaike *et al.* (1980) suggests that Medicare and other administrative record data may play an increasing role in such efforts.

## References

Bayo, F. 1972. Mortality of the aged. *Transactions of the Society of Actuaries* **24**:1–24.

Cassel, J. C., Heyden, S., Bartel, A. G., Kaplan, B. H., Tyroler, H. A., Cornoni, J. C., and Hames, C. G. 1971. Occupational and physical activity and coronary heart disease. *Archives of Internal Medicine* **128**:920–928.

Coale, A. J., and Rives, N. W. 1973. A statistical reconstruction of the black population of the United States, 1880–1970. *Population Index* **39**:3–36.

Coale, A. J., and Zelnick, M. 1963. *New estimates of fertility and population in the United States.* Princeton, New Jersey: Princeton University Press.

Comfort, A. 1979. *The biology of senescence.* New York: Elsevier.

Cox, D. R. 1972. Regression models and life tables. *Journal of the Royal Statistical Society B* **34**:187–202.

Cox, D. R. 1975. Partial likelihood. *Biometrika* **62**:269–276.

Economos, A. C. 1982. Rate of aging, rate of dying and the mechanisms of mortality. *Archives of Gerontology and Geriatrics* **1**:3–27.

Evans, E. 1962. The economics of American Negro slavery, 1830–1860. In *Aspects of labor economics,* pp. 185–243. Princeton, New Jersey: Princeton University Press.

Heckman, J. J., and Singer, B. 1982. Population heterogeneity in demographic models. In *Multidimensional mathematical demography* (K. Land and A. Rogers, eds.), pp. 567–599. New York: Academic Press.

Hougaard, P. 1982. Life table methods for heterogeneous populations: Distributions describing the heterogeneity. Research Rep. 82/5, Statistical Research Unit, Danish Medical Research Council, Danish Social Science Research Council.

Keyfitz, N., and Littman, G. 1979. Mortality in heterogeneous populations. *Population Studies* **33**:333–342.

Kitagawa, E. M., and Hauser, P. M. 1973. *Differential mortality in the United States: A study in socioeconomic epidemiology.* Cambridge, Massachusetts: Harvard University Press.

Jacobson, P. H. 1957. An estimate of the expectation of life in the United States in 1850. *Milbank Memorial Fund Quarterly* **35**:197–201.

Jones, H. B. 1962. Mechanisms of aging suggested from study of altered death risks. In *Proceedings of the Fourth Berkeley Symposium on Mathematical Statistics and Probability,* Vol. 4, *Biology and problems of health* (J. Neyman, ed.), pp. 267–292. Berkeley: University of California Press.

Kalbfleisch, J. D., and Prentice, R. L. 1980. *The statistical analysis of failure time data.* New York: Wiley.

Lew, E. A., and Seltzer, F. 1970. Uses of the life table in public health. *Milbank Memorial Fund Quarterly* **48**:15–37.

Manton, K. G., Poss, S. S., and Wing, S. 1979. The black/white mortality crossover: Investigation from the perspectives of the components of aging. *Gerontologist* **19**:291–299.

Nam, C. B., Weatherby, N. L., and Ockay, K. A. 1978. Causes of death which contribute to the mortality crossover effect. *Social Biology* **25**:306–314.

NCHS (National Center for Health Statistics). 1975. United States life tables: 1969–71. Department of Health, Education and Welfare Pub. No. (HRA) 75-1150. *U.S. decennial life tables for 1969–71*, Vol. 1, No. 1. Rockville, Maryland: Public Health Service.

Passel, J. S., Siegel, J. S., and Robinson, J. G. 1982. Coverage of the national population by age, sex and race: Preliminary estimates by demographic analysis. *Current Population Reports* Series P-23, No. 115. Washington, D.C.: U.S. Bureau of the Census.

Phillips, J. H., and Burch, G. E. 1960. A review of cardiovascular diseases in the white and Negro races. *Medicine* **39**:241–288.

Rives, N. W. 1977. The effect of census errors on life table estimates of black mortality. *American Journal of Public Health* **67**:867–868.

Rosenwaike, I., Yaffee, N., and Sagi, P. C. 1980. The recent decline in mortality of the extreme aged: An analysis of statistical data. *American Journal of Public Health* **70**:1074–1081.

Siegel, J. S. 1974. Estimates of coverage of the population by sex, race and age in the 1970 census. *Demography* **11**:1–23.

Strehler, B. L., and Mildvan, A. S. 1960. General theory of mortality and aging. *Science* **132**:14–21.

Trussell, J., and Hammerslough, C. 1983. A hazards-model analysis of the covariates of infant and child mortality in Sri Lanka. *Demography* **20**:1–26.

Vaupel, J. W., Manton, K. G., and Stallard, E. 1979. The impact of heterogeneity in individual frailty on the dynamics of mortality. *Demography* **16**:439–454.

Wing, S., Manton, K. G., Stallard, E., Hames, C., and Tyroler, H. A. 1983. The black/white mortality crossover: An investigation in a community-based cohort. [In review at the *Journal of Gerontology*.]

Woodbury, M. A., Manton, K. G., and Stallard, E. 1981. A dynamic analysis of chronic disease development: A study of sex specific changes in coronary heart disease incidence and risk factors in Framingham. *International Journal of Epidemiology* **10**:355–366.

# Chapter 7 | Ecological Models of Cause-Specific Mortality Differentials

## 1 Introduction

Recently there has been increasing interest in methods for the covariate analysis of cause-specific mortality data and of survival distributions in general. Examples of such work are the papers by Cox (1972, 1975), Menken *et al.* (1981), Trussell and Hammerslough (1983), as well as the books by Kalbfleisch and Prentice (1980) and by Lee (1980). The common perspective that is evident throughout these and other works is the development of strategies for utilizing covariate information in analyses when available. Furthermore, it is noted that the use of a proportional hazards model simplifies the statistical model so that the causes of death and the time to death are statistically independent (see Kalbfleisch and Prentice, 1980, p. 171). If the loss to follow-up of patients in clinical trials is viewed as an additional independent risk, then this independence property of proportional hazard models greatly facilitates the analysis of clinical trial data with random "censoring."

In applications of the proportional hazard assumption, it has been customary to express the cause-specific force of mortality as an exponential function of the vector $\mathbf{Z}$ of $K$ covariates. This yields the general form

$$\lambda(x|\mathbf{z}) = \lambda(x|\mathbf{0}) \exp(\mathbf{b}^T\mathbf{z}), \qquad (7.1.1)$$

where $\mathbf{b}^T$ is the row vector of exponential regression coefficients. That is, by definition we obtain the expansion

$$\mathbf{b}^T\mathbf{z} = \sum_{k=1}^{K} b_k z_k. \qquad (7.1.2)$$

An important property of (7.1.1) that facilitates parameter estimation is that no restrictions need to be placed on the range of elements of $b$ or $z$. Hence, negative values of parameters or of covariates introduce no special difficulties.

The exponential regression function in (7.1.1) is a form of log-linear models; however, it is somewhat more general than the usual form of log-linear models in that both categorical and continuous variates can be included as components of **Z**. By defining the constant $b_0(x)$ as

$$b_0(x) = \ln[\lambda(x|\mathbf{0})], \tag{7.1.3}$$

one obtains from (7.1.1)

$$\ln[\lambda(x|\mathbf{z})] = b_0(x) + b_1 z_1 + \cdots + b_k z_k, \tag{7.1.4}$$

which expresses the logarithmic transform of the age-specific hazard rate $\lambda(x|\mathbf{z})$ as a linear function of the covariates.

Let us suppose that (7.1.1) or (7.1.4) is used to obtain estimates of individual hazard rates among a group of individuals at the same age $x$ and either this group is homogeneous on other demographic characteristics such as sex, race, and region of residence, or else these variables are included as components of **Z**. In this case, we can use (7.1.1) to obtain the empirical distribution of the individual hazard rates in that population component, so that the need for postulating additional risk variability in this group in the form of fixed frailty or of relative susceptibility does not exist.

In contrast, let us consider the same group of individuals, but now we obtain only information on the number of deaths and the size of the group, not on the individual covariate vectors or on the outcomes (survived versus died). Hence, this second scenario corresponds to the usual data analytic situation faced in using vital statistics data from the NCHS and the U.S. Bureau of the Census. The question that arises is what do we do about the "missing" information provided by the covariate vector **Z**. In other words, does it make any difference that the mortality rates in this group correspond to a heterogeneous population group rather than to a homogeneous group, as is frequently assumed (e.g., see Trussell and Hammerslough, 1983)? As we shall see in the following, this is an empirical question that can best be answered by conducting the analysis with and without inclusion of provisions for the effects of heterogeneity.

In the rest of this chapter, we shall focus on the issues identified previously by formulating a model for analyzing death rates using a covariate regression model of the form (7.1.1), where the effects of missing covariates have representation in the model as components of the unobserved within-cell heterogeneity. We shall illustrate application of this model and interpretation of the various test statistics involved in hierarchical model fitting by an example based on lung cancer mortality in North Carolina. It is stressed that development of models of this type is an area requiring considerable further research so that the results presented here are intended only to be illustrative [also, see Manton *et al.* (1981)].

## 2 Model

### *Preliminaries*

Let $h_{x\lambda}^y$ denote the cause-specific cumulative force of mortality for cause $\lambda$ for the age interval $(x, x + 1)$ in year $y$ in a demographically homogeneous group. That is,

$$h_{x\lambda}^y = \int_x^{x+1} \lambda(a)\, da, \tag{7.2.1}$$

where $\lambda(x)$ is defined for the cohort born on average on January 1 of the year $y - x$. In the following, it will be convenient to assume that $\lambda(x)$ is constant over the age interval $(x, x + 1)$ so that we can simplify our notation by writing $\lambda_x$ in place of $\lambda(x)$. Actually, because we wish to consider data for more than one calendar year in our model, we shall use $\lambda_x^y$ to denote the value $\lambda_x$ in year $y$. With these conventions established, we use $D_{x\lambda}^y$ to denote the number of deaths due to cause $\lambda$ in year $y$ in the age interval $(x, x + 1)$ and $P_x^y$ to denote the corresponding number of person-years of exposure, which is assumed to be the midyear population size. The age- and cause-specific death rate can then be defined as

$$M_{x\lambda}^y = D_{x\lambda}^y / P_x^y. \tag{7.2.2}$$

If $P_x^y$ in (7.2.2) is replaced with $N_x^y$ as defined in Eq. (5.2.5), then one obtains the cause-specific mortality rate $q_{x\lambda}^y$ as used in the multiple-decrement life table model. Hence, whereas $q_{x\lambda}^y$ is a bona fide probability that is restricted to the unit range $(0, 1)$, $M_{x\lambda}^y$ is a rate that may take on values larger than 1.0 because it is not a probability. In practical situations, however, both $q_{x\lambda}^y$ and $M_{x\lambda}^y$ are small. Whereas $q_{x\lambda}^y$ is frequently modeled as a binomial probability, $M_{x\lambda}^y$ is modeled as a Poisson rate. In this case, it follows that the probability of $D_{x\lambda}^y$ is given by the Poisson probability function

$$f(D_{x\lambda}^y) = (P_x^y \lambda_x^y)^{D_{x\lambda}^y} \exp\{-P_x^y \lambda_x^y\}/(D_{x\lambda}^y)\,!. \tag{7.2.3}$$

From (7.2.3) it can be shown that the maximum likelihood estimator $\hat{\lambda}_x^y$ of

$\lambda_x^y$ is

$$\hat{\lambda}_x^y = D_{x\lambda}^y/P_x^y = M_{x\lambda}^y. \qquad (7.2.4)$$

Hence, the death rate $M_{x\lambda}^y$ is the Poisson estimator of the hazard rate $\lambda_x^y$.

The accuracy of the Poisson approximation is an issue of obvious concern in the development of the present model. From (7.2.3) it may be shown that the mean and variance of $M_{x\lambda}^y$ are

$$\mathscr{E}(M_{x\lambda}^y) = \lambda_x^y \qquad (7.2.5)$$

and

$$\mathrm{var}(M_{x\lambda}^y) = \lambda_x^y/P_x^y. \qquad (7.2.6)$$

Replacing $\lambda_x^y$ in (7.2.5) with the estimator $\hat{\lambda}_x^y$ in (7.2.4) yields

$$\hat{\mathscr{E}}(M_{x\lambda}^y) = M_{x\lambda}^y, \qquad (7.2.7)$$

so that $\hat{\lambda}_x^y$ is a reasonable estimator. The estimated variance is similarly obtained as

$$\hat{\mathrm{var}}(M_{x\lambda}^y) = M_{x\lambda}^y/P_x^y \qquad (7.2.8a)$$

$$= D_{x\lambda}^y/(P_x^y)^2. \qquad (7.2.8b)$$

Because we are particularly interested in the effects of population heterogeneity, it is important to evaluate the adequacy of the estimator in (7.2.8b).

To conduct this evaluation, it is convenient to consider that $\lambda$ is the only cause operating on the population. In this case, we can drop the subscript $\lambda$ in the preceding equations and consider the distribution of $D_x^y$ deaths in a population of size $N_x^y$. This is, of course, the binomial distribution. Hence,

$$f(D_x^y) = \binom{N_x^y}{D_x^y} (1 - q_x^y)^{(N_x^y - D_x^y)} (q_x^y)^{D_x^y}, \qquad (7.2.9)$$

with maximum likelihood estimator $\hat{q}_x^y$ of $q_x^y$

$$\hat{q}_x^y = D_x^y/N_x^y. \qquad (7.2.10)$$

The estimator $\hat{q}_x^y$ is precisely the definition used for $q_x^y$ in life table computations, although the carat is conventionally not used. Also, the mean and variance of $D_x^y$ are

$$\mathscr{E}(D_x^y) = N_x^y q_x^y \qquad (7.2.11)$$

and

$$\mathrm{var}(D_x^y) = N_x^y q_x^y(1 - q_x^y). \qquad (7.2.12)$$

Replacing $q_x^y$ in (7.2.11) with the estimator $\hat{q}_x^y$ in (7.2.10) yields

$$\hat{\mathcal{E}}(D_x^y) = D_x^y, \qquad (7.2.13)$$

so that $\hat{q}_x^y$ is a reasonable estimator. Similarly, (7.2.12) can be manipulated to yield

$$\text{var}(D_x^y) = D_x^y(1 - D_x^y/N_x^y). \qquad (7.2.14)$$

With our temporary deletion of the subscript $\lambda$, (7.2.8b) can be rewritten to

$$\text{var}(M_x^y) = D_x^y/(P_x^y)^2, \qquad (7.2.15)$$

where $P_x^y$ is the midyear population estimate that is obtained from $N_x^y$ as

$$P_x^y = N_x^y - \tfrac{1}{2}D_x^y. \qquad (7.2.16)$$

Because we regard $N_x^y$ as "fixed," we rewrite the expression for $M_x^y$ as

$$M_x^y = D_x^y/(N_x^y - \tfrac{1}{2}D_x^y), \qquad (7.2.17)$$

and the adequacy of (7.2.15) as an approximation can be assessed by assessing the variance of the expression on the right of (7.2.17). To do this, we employ the standard Taylor series formula for the variance of an arbitrary function of a random variable $Z$, that is,

$$\text{var}(g(z)) \doteq \left[ \frac{d}{dz}\, g(z) \Big|_{z=\mathcal{E}(z)} \right]^2 \text{var}(z). \qquad (7.2.18)$$

Replacing $g(z)$ with $M_x^y$, one obtains

$$\text{var}(M_x^y) \doteq \left[ \frac{N_x^y}{(P_x^y)^2} \right]^2 \text{var}(D_x^y) \qquad (7.2.19a)$$

$$= \left[ \frac{D_x^y}{(P_x^y)^2} \right] \left[ \left( \frac{N_x^y}{P_x^y} \right)^2 \left( 1 - \frac{D_x^y}{N_x} \right) \right]. \qquad (7.2.19b)$$

By comparing (7.2.15) and (7.2.19b), it is apparent that the approximation is good only if the second bracketed term in (7.2.19b) is close to unity, that is, if

$$(P_x^y/N_x^y)^2 \doteq (1 - D_x^y/N_x^y). \qquad (7.2.20)$$

In the following tabulation, we compare these two values for a range of $\hat{q}_x^y$ from 0.001 to 0.300, a range that spans the observed values of the mortality rate $q_x^y$. One can see that the ratios of the two values are close to 1.0. It is apparent from these calculations that the second factor in (7.2.19b) will not destroy the validity of the Taylor series approximation in (7.2.15). Hence, the variance formula (7.2.15) derived from the assumption that $D_x^y$

| $\hat{q}_x^y$ | $(P_x^y/N_x^y)^2$ | $1 - D_x^y/N_x^y$ | Ratio |
|-------|----------|----------|----------|
| 0.001 | 0.999000 | 0.999000 | 1.000000 |
| 0.010 | 0.990025 | 0.990000 | 1.000025 |
| 0.050 | 0.950625 | 0.950000 | 1.000658 |
| 0.100 | 0.902500 | 0.900000 | 1.002778 |
| 0.200 | 0.810000 | 0.800000 | 1.012500 |
| 0.300 | 0.722500 | 0.700000 | 1.032143 |

is Poisson distributed with parameter $(P_x^y\lambda_x^y)$ is consistent with the assumption that $D_x^y$ is binomially distributed with parameter $q_x^y$ in a population of size $N_x^y$.

The above demonstration justifies the use of the Poisson distribution even though it appears to permit individuals to die more than once. In fact, as seen previously, the tendency for such "excess" deaths is just large enough to compensate the variance estimates for the difference between the two types of population counts, that is, between $N_x^y$ and $P_x^y$.

Note that in other modeling situations in which events are subject to repetition, such as in certain health episode models (e.g., Chiang, 1965), the binomial distribution model would be inappropriate whereas the Poisson model would not be. Hence, the development of our model using the Poisson distribution as the basic distributional form imparts a degree of generality beyond its application to mortality data (see Manton and Stallard, 1981).

### Model Development

When we stratify our data on deaths and population counts according to locality, we can denote the hazard rates in the $i$th locality as $\lambda_x^{yi}$, where the superscript $i$ is used to reference quantities that are specific to a given locality. In particular, using $D_{x\lambda}^{yi}$ and $P_x^{yi}$ to denote deaths and person-years of exposure, we can in analogy to (7.2.3) obtain the Poisson distribution model of $D_{x\lambda}^{yi}$, which is

$$f(D_{x\lambda}^{yi}) = (P_x^{yi}\lambda_x^{yi})^{D_{x\lambda}^{yi}} \exp(-P_x^{yi}\lambda_x^{yi})/(D_{x\lambda}^{yi})!. \qquad (7.2.21)$$

As in (7.2.4), the maximum likelihood estimator $\hat{\lambda}_x^{yi}$ of $\lambda_x^{yi}$ is

$$\hat{\lambda}_x^{yi} = D_{x\lambda}^{yi}/P_x^{yi} = M_{x\lambda}^{yi}, \qquad (7.2.22)$$

which is the age- and cause-specific death rate in the given locality.

In order to permit representation of environmental factors and other potentially relevant covariate effects, we assume that $\lambda_x^{yi}$ is gamma distributed with mean value $\mathcal{E}(\lambda_x^{yi})$ given by

$$\mathcal{E}(\lambda_x^{yi}) = \lambda_x^y \exp(b_{0x}^y + b_{1x}^y c_{1x}^{yi} + \ldots + b_{kx}^y c_{kx}^{yi}), \qquad (7.2.23)$$

where $c_{1x}^{yi}$, $c_{2x}^{yi}$, ..., $c_{kx}^{yi}$ are a set of $K$ predictors that include the locality-specific risk factors and all relevant covariates and where $b_{1x}^y$, $b_{2x}^y$, ..., $b_{kx}^y$ are a set of loglinear coefficients that indicate the linear response in the logarithm of (7.2.23) to a unit change in the corresponding predictor variable. Note that this model is quite general in that any type of polynomial regression effects, interaction effects, or dummy variable effects, which are normally associated with linear regression analysis, can also be specified, if appropriate, in an exponential regression model such as (7.2.23).

A substantive rationale for selecting the functional form in (7.2.23) is based on the choice of localities as the basic unit of observation in the analysis. Because we are dealing with groups of persons rather than with individuals, it is likely that the range of our dose–response relationship will be substantially less than that observed in microlevel data. In this case, any function that is approximately linear in the macrolevel range will be satisfactory, although because it admits negative values of $\mathcal{E}(\lambda_x^{yi})$, an exact linear function is generally unacceptable. Similarly, because the normal distribution also admits negative values, it too is generally unacceptable as a probability model of $\lambda_x^{yi}$, and in cases in which its mass is acceptably far from zero, it is well approximated by the gamma distribution.

In this chapter, as in the preceding chapter, we shall use the gamma distribution as our basic model of distributed mortality hazards. As before, the use of the gamma distribution is motivated by the fact that it is convenient to use. Other distributional forms could also have been employed. It should, however, be stressed that whereas in the life table model of Chapter 6 we were concerned about the effects of diffusion, in this chapter in which we deal with only 1 year of follow-up, the effects of diffusion will be much less severe. This means that the concerns of Hougaard (1982) over the effect of mortality selection on the coefficient of variation of the susceptibility distribution will be much less of an issue because the primary effect we are dealing with is the effect on the covariate parameters of the increased variance of the death rates, not the bias of mortality selection.

To study the effect of population heterogeneity on a quantitative covariate regression model such as (7.2.23), we can start with the simplest form of this model in which all $b$'s are zero, or

$$\mathcal{E}\{\lambda_x^{yi}\} = \lambda_x^y. \qquad (7.2.24)$$

In this model the expected value of $\lambda_x^{yi}$ in the $i$th locality is the cohort hazard rate $\lambda_x^y$, which in view of (7.2.4) is best estimated as the observed death rate $M_{x\lambda}^y$.

If individual members of the cohort exhibit heterogeneity in their cause-specific hazard rates, for example, $\lambda(x|z_\lambda)$ as in Chapter 4, then aggregates of such individuals will also exhibit heterogeneity, but now in their average hazard rates, that is, in the $\lambda_x^{yi}$. With (7.2.24) giving the mean value of $\lambda_x^{yi}$, the gamma density of $\lambda_x^{yi}$ can be written as

$$f(\lambda_x^{yi}) = \left(\frac{P_x^{yi}s_x^y\lambda_x^{yi}}{\lambda_x^y}\right)^{P_x^{yi}s_x^y} \frac{\exp[-P_x^{yi}s_x^y(\lambda_x^{yi}/\lambda_x^y)]}{\lambda_x^{yi}\Gamma(P_x^{yi}s_x^y)}, \tag{7.2.25}$$

which is a gamma density with shape parameter denoted by the product $P_x^{yi}s_x^y$ and scale parameter by the ratio $\lambda_x^y/(P_x^{yi}s_x^y)$. Clearly, the product of the shape and scale parameters yields the value $\lambda_x^y$, the mean of the distribution. We have chosen to include the population size $P_x^{yi}$ in the parameterization of this function because this form of parameterization is invariant with respect to arbitrary definitions of localities in the analysis. If two localities $i'$ and $i''$ are combined to form the locality $i$, then the observed death rate in the combined locality can be obtained as the weighted average of the two component death rates, that is,

$$M_{x\lambda}^{yi} = (D_{x\lambda}^{yi'} + D_{x\lambda}^{yi''})/(P_x^{yi'} + P_x^{yi''}) \tag{7.2.26a}$$

$$= \left(\frac{P_x^{yi'}}{P_x^{yi}}\right) M_{x\lambda}^{yi'} + \left(\frac{P_x^{yi''}}{P_x^{yi}}\right) M_{x\lambda}^{yi''}, \tag{7.2.26b}$$

where the weights are the ratios $(P_x^{yi'}/P_x^{yi})$ and $(P_x^{yi''}/P_x^{yi})$ and where

$$P_x^{yi} = P_x^{yi'} + P_x^{yi''}. \tag{7.2.27}$$

Similarly, it can be shown that if the $\lambda_x^{yi}$ are all distributed as in (7.2.25), then the distribution of the weighted average of any pair, such as $\lambda_x^{yi'}$ and $\lambda_x^{yi''}$, is also of the same form (7.2.25), with $P_x^{yi}$ obtained as the sum in (7.2.27).

Given the selected functional form of the density of $\lambda_x^{yi}$ in (7.2.25), it is obvious that by setting $P_x^{yi} = 1$ we can obtain the implied density for an individual in this cohort. This is a gamma density with mean value $\lambda_x^y$, shape parameter $s_x^y$, and scale parameter $\beta_x^y = \lambda_x^y/s_x^y$. Hence, we can employ the structural characteristics of the model developed in Chapter 6 for heterogeneous cohorts to guide in the imposition of constraints in application of the present model.

The assumption that $\lambda_x^{yi}$ is gamma distributed as in (7.2.25) does not immediately lead to an estimation strategy because $\lambda_x^{yi}$ is an unobserved quantity. However, the fact that it is now assumed to be a distributed quantity changes the interpretation given to (7.2.21) because $\lambda_x^{yi}$ must now be treated as a random parameter. Hence, we rewrite (7.2.21) as

$$f(D_{x\lambda}^{yi}|\lambda_x^{yi}) = (P_x^{yi}\lambda_x^{yi})^{D_{x\lambda}^{yi}} \exp(-P_x^{yi}\lambda_x^{yi})/(D_{x\lambda}^{yi})!, \qquad (7.2.28)$$

where the conditioning on $\lambda_x^{yi}$ in the density symbol on the left indicates that $D_{x\lambda}^{yi}$ is now only a conditional Poisson variable.

Unfortunately, because it is a conditional density in which the conditioning variable $\lambda_x^{yi}$ is unobserved, the expression in (7.2.28) is not directly useful in developing estimation procedures. As noted in discussion of (7.2.21) and (7.2.22), we can develop estimation procedures such as maximum likelihood when the density is specified in terms of *observable* quantities. Because only $D_{x\lambda}^{yi}$ is observable in (7.2.28), this means that we need to specify the marginal density of $D_{x\lambda}^{yi}$. This marginal density is obtained by integrating the product of (7.2.28) and (7.2.25) over the range of $\lambda_x^{yi}$, yielding the result

$$f(D_{x\lambda}^{yi}) = \left(\frac{1}{1+\lambda_x^y/s_x^y}\right)^{P_x^{yi}s_x^y} \frac{\Gamma[P_x^{yi}s_x^y + D_{x\lambda}^{yi}]}{\Gamma(P_x^{yi}s_x^y)(D_{x\lambda}^{yi})!}\left(\frac{\lambda_x^y/s_x^y}{1 + \lambda_x^y/s_x^y}\right)^{D_{x\lambda}^{yi}}, \qquad (7.2.29)$$

which is a negative binomial density with mean and variance

$$\mathscr{E}(D_{x\lambda}^{yi}) = P_x^{yi}\lambda_x^y, \qquad (7.2.30)$$

$$\mathrm{var}(D_{x\lambda}^{yi}) = (1 + \lambda_x^y/s_x^y)P_x^{yi}\lambda_x^y \qquad (7.2.31a)$$

$$= \mathscr{E}(D_{x\lambda}^{yi}) + P_x^{yi}(\lambda_x^y)^2/s_x^y. \qquad (7.2.31b)$$

From (7.2.31b) one can see that a basic property of the negative binomial distribution is that its variance is always larger than its mean. This differs from the Poisson distribution in which the mean and variance are equal. In the negative binomial regression model, this additional variance reflects the heterogeneity associated with missing covariates.

With the simple model specification of equal expected hazard rates across all localities in (7.2.24), the marginal density of $D_{x\lambda}^{yi}$ is given in (7.2.29). For more complex models with covariate effects and environmental factor effects as in (7.2.23), the marginal density of $D_{x\lambda}^{yi}$ is obtained by replacing $\lambda_x^y$ in (7.2.29) with the specific desired parametric form of (7.2.23). Hence, each possible model that can be specified leads to a new specification of the density of $D_{x\lambda}^{yi}$, so that there are an infinite number of possible specifications of $f(D_{x\lambda}^{yi})$. Practical considerations dictate that we consider a limited number of models and hence a limited number of specifications of $f(D_{x\lambda}^{yi})$. Estimation is conducted via maximum likelihood, where

$$\mathscr{L} = \prod_{i=1}^{I} f(D_{x\lambda}^{yi}) \qquad (7.2.32)$$

is the likelihood function if each of $I$ localities is independent. In the models estimated below, we replace $s_x^y$ or $\lambda_x^y$ in (7.2.29) with $s_x^y = \lambda_x^y/\beta_x^y$ or with $\lambda_x^y = \beta_x^y s_x^y$ in order to impose constraints on the scale parameter $\beta_x^y$ [see Manton and Stallard (1981) for further details].

Maximum likelihood estimation allows for easy testing of nested, or hierarchical, models in which one model (A) is "embedded" in a more complex model (B), because a chi-squared variate can be approximated as twice the negative logarithm of the likelihood ratio $\mathscr{L}_A/\mathscr{L}_B$, that is,

$$\chi_{df}^2 \doteq -2 \ln(\mathscr{L}_A/\mathscr{L}_B) = -2[\ln \mathscr{L}_A - \ln \mathscr{L}_B], \qquad (7.2.33)$$

where

$$df = df_A - df_B. \qquad (7.2.34)$$

In (7.2.34) the degrees of freedom are most easily calculated as the difference between the number of parameters estimated in models A and B. The approximation (7.2.33) is based on the assumption that model A is the true model.


## 3  Data

As indicated in the introduction, we shall illustrate the model by application to an analysis of lung cancer mortality in the 100 North Carolina counties over the period 1970–1975. Mortality counts were obtained from tabulations of individual record mortality tapes provided by the state of North Carolina for each of the 6 years 1970–1975. These data were stratified into 24 demographic groups for county for each of 6 years, for a total of 14,400 (= 24 × 100 × 6) "cells." The 24 demographic groups represented stratification into six age categories (35–44, 45–54, 55–64, 65–74, 75–84, and 85 and over) and four race–sex-groups (white males, white females, nonwhite males, and nonwhite females). Hence, each $\lambda_x^y$ actually references a 10-year age-group so that $x$ may be taken as approximately the midpoint of the age interval (e.g., 40, 50, and 60).

Population counts that were similarly stratified by age, race, sex, year, and county to match the structure of the mortality counts were obtained from the U.S. Bureau of the Census's special small area population estimates for North Carolina.

Longitudinal data that were employed as spatial covariates were obtained from the longitudinal coordinates for the county seat indicated on maps obtained from the state of North Carolina.

In Table 1 we present summary statistics by demographic group on the distributions of lung cancer deaths in the 100 counties over the 6 years.

**Table 1**

North Carolina Lung Cancer Data, 1970–1975 Summary Statistics,
by Demographic Group

| Age | Number of cells with $D_i > 0$ | Total lung cancer mortality | Total person-years at risk | State death rate per 100,000 persons | Maximum cell death rate per 100,000 persons |
|---|---|---|---|---|---|
| White males | | | | | |
| 35–44 | 132 | 181 | 1,415,217 | 12.8 | 552.5 |
| 45–54 | 380 | 1,005 | 1,360,002 | 73.9 | 549.5 |
| 55–64 | 512 | 2,055 | 1,025,668 | 200.4 | 937.5 |
| 65–74 | 489 | 1,929 | 588,450 | 327.8 | 3,157.9 |
| 75–84 | 338 | 748 | 235,355 | 317.8 | 2,985.1 |
| 85+ | 535 | 73 | 45,791 | 159.4 | 4,255.3 |
| White females | | | | | |
| 35–44 | 59 | 66 | 1,471,763 | 4.5 | 625.0 |
| 45–54 | 176 | 269 | 1,442,023 | 18.7 | 617.3 |
| 55–64 | 206 | 337 | 1,177,930 | 28.6 | 295.9 |
| 65–74 | 199 | 304 | 813,097 | 37.4 | 503.8 |
| 75–84 | 123 | 170 | 397,762 | 42.7 | 687.3 |
| 85+ | 46 | 50 | 98,489 | 50.8 | 4,545.5 |
| Nonwhite males | | | | | |
| 35–44 | 50 | 63 | 306,207 | 20.6 | 657.9 |
| 45–54 | 197 | 331 | 312,248 | 106.0 | 4,255.3 |
| 55–64 | 268 | 535 | 249,324 | 214.6 | 2,898.6 |
| 65–74 | 247 | 432 | 153,968 | 280.6 | 12,500.0 |
| 75–84 | 108 | 141 | 55,406 | 254.5 | 14,285.7 |
| 85+ | 17 | 17 | 12,998 | 130.8 | 7,142.9 |
| Nonwhite females | | | | | |
| 35–44 | 11 | 11 | 376,054 | 2.9 | 156.0 |
| 45–54 | 40 | 47 | 364,814 | 12.9 | 1,298.7 |
| 55–64 | 59 | 71 | 295,651 | 24.0 | 12,500.0 |
| 65–74 | 61 | 71 | 202,377 | 35.1 | 1,315.8 |
| 75–84 | 35 | 38 | 80,703 | 47.1 | 3,030.3 |
| 85+ | 11 | 11 | 23,634 | 46.5 | 3,448.3 |

This table illustrates characteristics of these data that are likely to be present in most county-level mortality data that are finely stratified by demographic characteristics, that is, the presence of a high percentage of cells in which no deaths occur.

Also included in Table 1 are the total lung cancer mortality counts, the total number of person-years at risk, and the implied average state death rate (per 100,000) for each demographic category. Each of these is based on 600 cells. The column labeled "maximum cell death rate per 100,000 persons" represents the largest of the 600 cell-specific death rates. Comparison of these maximum cell death rates with the average state death rates indicates the high level of instability that necessitates the use of probability functions appropriate for discrete counts such as the Poisson distribution or, in the case of regression models with missing covariates, the negative binomial distribution.

## 4  Results

The analysis was performed in three stages, with each stage involving the introduction of additional parameters into the model. Statistical testing of the effects of each set of additional parameters was accomplished via the likelihood ratio $\chi^2$ approximation, which is defined as twice the negative logarithmic transformation of the likelihood ratio, that is, as in (7.2.32)

$$\chi^2_{df} \doteq -2[\ln \mathcal{L}_A - \ln \mathcal{L}_B],  \tag{7.4.1}$$

where $\mathcal{L}_A$ is the likelihood function value for the model A with fewer parameters and $\mathcal{L}_B$ represents the more complex model B with additional parameters. For this test to be meaningful, it is necessary for models A and B to be hierarchically related; that is, model A can be obtained from model B by imposition of some number of constraints. The number of constraints required to retrieve model A is the degrees of freedom for the test.

In order to conduct the analysis in this fashion, it is necessary to start with some baseline model that serves the role of a "null hypothesis" and against which alternative models can be tested. Because we are dealing with a proportional hazards model, we shall evaluate a hierarchy of nested models in which the entire set of life table hazards is proportional across the four race–sex groups of the analysis. With only six age-groups, such a model can be represented with only 10 parameters in the form

$$\mathscr{E}\{\lambda_x^{yi}\}_{\text{race–sex}} = \beta_{\text{age}} s_{\text{race–sex}},  \tag{7.4.2}$$

**Table 2**

Parameter Estimates for Baseline Model

| Age | $\beta_{age}$[a] | Race–sex | $\ln(s_{race-sex})$[a] | $s_{race-sex}$ |
|-----|------|----------|-----------|-----------|
| 35–44 | 0.0033785 | White males | −3.05532 | 0.04711 |
|       | (0.0012495) |           | (0.36639) |         |
| 45–54 | 0.0178758 | White females | −4.90357 | 0.00742 |
|       | (0.0065496) |           | (0.36473) |         |
| 55–64 | 0.0421202 | Nonwhite males | −3.01422 | 0.04908 |
|       | (0.0154156) |           | (0.36490) |         |
| 65–74 | 0.0642260 | Nonwhite females | −5.05690 | 0.00637 |
|       | (0.0235049) |           | (0.36807) |         |
| 75–84 | 0.0635140 |           |           |         |
|       | (0.0232928) |           |           |         |
| 85+ | 0.0410731 |           |           |         |
|       | (0.0153852) |           |           |         |

[a] Standard errors in parentheses.

where (7.4.2) replaces $\lambda_x^y$ in (7.2.29) to define the marginal density $f(D_{x\lambda}^{yi})$ and where the subscripts age and race–sex specify the categorical dimensions over which the subscripted parameter is allowed to vary. For example, $\beta_{age}$ is a scale parameter that is assumed to vary only over the six age categories but to be constant over race, sex, county, and year. In contrast, $s_{race-sex}$ is a shape parameter, which is assumed to vary only over race and sex but to be constant over age, county, and year. In Table 2 we present the parameter estimates obtained for this baseline model.

Examination of Table 2 reveals that the six scale parameters $\beta_{age}$ were estimated with reasonably good precision ($t \geq 2.67$) despite the presence of a high percentage of cells with zero mortality counts. In view of (7.2.31) and (7.4.2), it also follows that the scale parameters can be interpreted as the proportional increase in Poisson variance that results from the effects of population heterogeneity. The $\beta_{age}$'s in Table 2 thus imply an increase of from 0.3 to 6.4% in Poisson variance due to missing covariates.

Table 2 also reports the shape parameter values. Actually, for computational convenience we conducted estimation in terms of $\ln(s)$ and used an exponential transformation to retrieve the value of $s$ subsequent to the analysis. This explains why the standard errors are in terms of $\ln(s)$.

With a baseline model established we were then in a position to evaluate the three alternative models of substantive interest. The first model was intended to test for the effects of cohort differentials and can be represented with 30 parameters as

$$\mathcal{E}\{\lambda_x^{yi}\}_{race-sex} = \beta_{age} s_{age-race-sex} . \tag{7.4.3}$$

### Table 3

Cohort-Specific Logarithmically Transformed Shape
Parameter Estimates[a]

| Age | White males | White females | Nonwhite males | Nonwhite females |
|---|---|---|---|---|
| 35–44 | −3.27421 | −4.32138 | −2.79864 | −4.74759 |
| | (0.07447) | (0.12323) | (0.12621) | (0.30151) |
| | 0.03785 | 0.01328 | 0.06089 | 0.00867 |
| 45–54 | −3.18568 | −4.56220 | −2.82547 | −4.93212 |
| | (0.03182) | (0.06149) | (0.05546) | (0.14705) |
| | 0.04135 | 0.01044 | 0.05928 | 0.00721 |
| 55–64 | −3.04564 | −4.99120 | −2.97563 | −5.16339 |
| | (0.02252) | (0.05554) | (0.04406) | (0.12061) |
| | 0.04757 | 0.00680 | 0.05102 | 0.00572 |
| 65–74 | −2.97673 | −5.14426 | −3.12629 | −5.20672 |
| | (0.02352) | (0.05897) | (0.04938) | (0.12165) |
| | 0.05096 | 0.00583 | 0.04388 | 0.00548 |
| 75–84 | −2.99429 | −5.00211 | −3.21642 | −4.89684 |
| | (0.03766) | (0.07898) | (0.08654) | (0.16545) |
| | 0.05007 | 0.00672 | 0.04010 | 0.00747 |
| 85+ | −3.24964 | −4.38417 | −3.42674 | −4.45976 |
| | (0.11923) | (0.14288) | (0.24254) | (0.30148) |
| | 0.03879 | 0.01247 | 0.03249 | 0.01157 |

[a] Standard errors in parentheses, with implied $s$ values beneath.

In permitting the shape parameter to vary over age we are, in effect, using age simply as a label to identify different cohorts; that is, because the mortality selection model in Chapter 6 suggests that, within a given cohort the shape parameter will not change with age. We constrained the six $\beta_{age}$ parameters to the values reported in Table 2. This was done because under the alternative with the scale and shape parameters both varying over age, the changes in the shape parameters could not be attributed solely to cohort differences because these changes could be confounded with changes in the scale parameters [e.g., see Manton and Stallard (1981)]. With the scale parameters constrained, however, the age variation in the shape parameters has the direct interpretation as cohort differentials. Table 3 contains the parameter estimates obtained for the model with cohort-specific shape parameters.

The likelihood ratio $\chi^2$ value for this model was 159.96 (20 degrees of freedom), indicating the presence of substantial cohort differences. Examination of the age pattern of the shape parameters suggests that white male cohorts in the age ranges 65–74 and 75–84 have higher shape parameter values than do either the younger or older cohorts. White females exhibit a reverse pattern, with cohorts in the age ranges 65–74 and 75–84 having the lowest shape parameter values. Nonwhite females exhibit a similar pattern except that the cohort aged 55–64 has the lowest shape parameter estimate. For nonwhite males there is a monotonic decrease in the shape parameter estimates over cohort age.

The second stage of analysis involved the introduction of 24 additional coefficients to represent temporal increases in lung cancer mortality over the period 1970–1975. This was of substantive interest because lung cancer mortality rates in the total U.S. data had exhibited substantial increases over this same period, so that a similar increase in the North Carolina data appeared to be likely. This model can be represented as

$$\mathscr{E}\{\lambda_x^{yi}\}_{\text{race-sex}} = \beta_{\text{age}} s_{\text{age-race-sex}} \exp[b_{\text{age-race-sex}}(y - 1972.5)], \quad (7.4.4)$$

where $y$ represents the calendar year and where the origin shift (1972.5, which is the midpoint of the 6 years 1970–1975) is employed to ensure comparability between the shape parameter estimates in this model and the prior model (7.4.3). As before, the six scale parameters were constrained to the values reported in Table 2. The likelihood $\chi^2$ value for this model versus the prior model was 76.24 (24 degrees of freedom), indicating significant temporal trends.

The final stage of analysis involved the introduction of 24 additional coefficients to represent spatial variation in lung cancer mortality over the west-to-east longitudinal axis of the state. The rationale for including these effects in the final stage of the analysis is that the original observation of a spatial gradient was based on examination of the distribution of age-standardized mortality rates over counties in maps developed by the state of North Carolina—measures that were accompanied by warnings that they could be heavily biased by the small population and mortality counts in these data (see Table 1). It was our reasoning that if a better assessment of the reality of such a gradient were to be conducted, then it was necessary to demonstrate that the gradient persisted *after* controlling for the potentially confounding effects of population heterogeneity and any temporal increases that might be present. This model can be represented as

$$\mathscr{E}\{\lambda_x^{yi}\}_{\text{race-sex}} = \beta_{\text{age}} s_{\text{age-race-sex}} \exp[b_{\text{age-race-sex}}(y - 1972.5)]$$
$$\times \exp[c_{\text{age-race-sex}}(80° - \text{longitude}_{\text{county}})], \quad (7.4.5)$$

where the origin shift to 80° longitude approximates the geographic center of the state so that it provides comparability between the shape parameter estimates in this model and the previous two models (7.4.4) and (7.4.3). Again, the six scale parameters were constrained to the values reported in Table 2.

The likelihood $\chi^2$ value for the model (7.4.5) versus the prior model (7.4.4) was 149.32 (24 df), indicating significant spatial gradients. The parameter estimates for the $24b_{\text{age-race-sex}}$ and $24c_{\text{age-race-sex}}$ coefficients in (7.4.5) are presented in Table 4.

Table 4 shows that there are eight significant ($t \geq 1.96$) time coefficients but only four significant spatial coefficients. Significant time coefficients are observed for white males (ages 55–64, 65–74, and 75–84), white females (ages 45–54 and 55–64), and nonwhite males (ages 55–64, 65–74, and 85+). Significant space coefficients are observed for white males (ages 55–64, 65–74, and 75–84) and for white females (ages 65–74). Thus,

**Table 4**

Parameter Estimates for Time and Space Gradients[a]

| Age | White males | White females | Nonwhite males | Nonwhite females |
|---|---|---|---|---|
| | Time coefficients (per year) | | | |
| 35–44 | −0.07876 | 0.04409 | −0.03313 | 0.02031 |
| | (−1.79604) | (0.60929) | (−0.44716) | (0.11482) |
| 45–54 | −0.00138 | 0.08782 | 0.00450 | −0.00938 |
| | (−0.07424) | (2.41920) | (0.13828) | (−0.10896) |
| 55–64 | 0.02976 | 0.11199 | 0.07023 | 0.08853 |
| | (2.25154) | (3.39332) | (2.70328) | (1.23417) |
| 65–74 | 0.04815 | 0.05423 | 0.07875 | 0.04992 |
| | (3.48265) | (1.56101) | (2.70289) | (0.69698) |
| 75–84 | 0.05383 | 0.04547 | 0.00441 | 0.13043 |
| | (2.43318) | (0.97651) | (0.08687) | (1.31142) |
| 85+ | 0.11785 | 0.08760 | 0.32283 | 0.21709 |
| | (1.65856) | (1.03049) | (2.03830) | (1.14654) |
| | Space coefficients (per longitude ° $\doteq$ 60 mi) | | | |
| 35–44 | −0.00462 | −0.04635 | 0.02812 | −0.21593 |
| | (−0.09924) | (−0.60239) | (0.31343) | (−1.05636) |
| 45–55 | 0.01840 | 0.03775 | −0.04665 | −0.05794 |
| | (0.93612) | (0.99647) | (−1.21283) | (−0.57357) |
| 55–64 | 0.09823 | 0.04702 | −0.00995 | −0.10607 |
| | (7.29281) | (1.41227) | (−0.32720) | (−1.29774) |
| 65–74 | 0.09745 | 0.08286 | −0.01166 | −0.10480 |
| | (7.18215) | (2.39104) | (−0.34913) | (−1.28590) |
| 75–84 | 0.09824 | 0.08321 | −0.02798 | −0.09369 |
| | (4.61179) | (1.79216) | (−0.48689) | (−0.86181) |
| 85+ | −0.02683 | −0.01457 | −0.24035 | 0.00806 |
| | (−0.40200) | (−0.17490) | (−1.61643) | (0.03987) |

[a] $t$ values in parentheses.

only the three white male groups in the age range 55–84 exhibited both space and time gradients. Interestingly, nonwhite females exhibited no significant coefficients in either space or time.

## 5   Summary

Several issues involved in the use of covariate information in the analysis of cause-specific mortality data were addressed in this chapter. In particular, it was observed that a certain degree of inconsistency occurs if covariate information is used in assessing risk levels for individuals in a given population group, but the group is then treated as homogeneous when the covariate information is unavailable. To avoid such inconsistency, however, one must be willing to make some assumptions about the extent of heterogeneity in the various groups. This may be, to some extent, arbitrary and leaves the analysis open to the critique that some alternative set of assumptions might be more realistic. One possibility for resolving this issue involves the empirical assessment in various groups of the individual risks. In this manner, one could determine whether the various parametric distributions commonly in use provided a satisfactory representation of the empirical distributions or whether nonparametric methods of adjusting for population heterogeneity are to be preferred.

As we noted in the introduction, the treatment of heterogeneity is an active research topic. In this chapter, we developed a model for covariate analyses of mortality data that explicitly dealt with the issue of heterogeneity and that permitted the complete utilization of whatever covariate information one had available. The model was illustrated by an example based on an analysis of a spatial gradient in North Carolina lung cancer mortality for the period 1970–1975. This example was selected because it is of both methodological and substantive interest. Methodologically, the example illustrated the determination of cohort effects, period effects, and finally spatial effects, the latter of which can easily be generalized to include additional covariates as available. Substantively, the cohort pattern of shape parameters derived from the model suggests that successive cohorts in the North Carolina population have important lung cancer risk-level differentials in either the cohort mean susceptibilities or the cohort variance in susceptibility or, possibly, in both the mean and variance. Additionally, and after controlling for these cohort differentials, it was found that significant gradients in both time and space were present but that these gradients were manifest in very specific demographic groups. Interestingly, white males aged 55–84 were the only groups for which gradients in both space and time were manifest.

Although not reported here, we repeated the same analysis by using a similarly structured Poisson model that is the limiting form of the negative binomial model, under the assumption that the model predicted the true value of $\lambda_x^y$, not its expectation. The results of this analysis indicated that the temporal and spatial gradient coefficients estimated earlier were quite stable, although due to the differences in treatment of the heterogeneity variance, the statistical significance levels were slightly higher.

This similarity of the estimated coefficients was expected because the scale parameters in our baseline model indicated no more than 0.3 to 6.4% excess variance beyond the Poisson variance. In other applications we have found that the use of the Poisson model leads to very different coefficients when the amount of excess variance is large.

## References

Chiang, C. L. 1965. An Index of health: Mathematical models. Vital and Health Statistics, Data Evaluation and Methods Research. Department of Health, Education, and Welfare Pub. No. 1000, Series 2, No. 5. Washington, D.C.: Public Health Service.

Cox, D. R. 1972. Regression models and life tables. *Journal of the Royal Statistical Society B* **34**:187–202.

Cox, D. R. 1975. Partial likelihood. *Biometrika* **62**:269–276.

Hougaard, P. 1982. Life table methods for heterogeneous populations: Distributions describing the heterogeneity. Research Report 82/5, Statistical Research Unit, Danish Medical Research Council, Danish Social Science Research Council.

Kalbfleisch, J. D., and Prentice, R. L. 1980. *The statistical analysis of failure time data.* New York: Wiley.

Lee, E. T. 1980. *Statistical methods for survival data analysis.* Belmont, California: Lifetime Learning.

Manton, K. G., and Stallard, E. 1981. Methods for the analysis of mortality risks across heterogeneous small populations: Examination of space–time gradients in cancer mortality in North Carolina counties 1970–75. *Demography* **18**:217–230.

Manton, K. G., Woodbury, M. A., and Stallard, E. 1981. A variance components approach to categorical data models with heterogeneous cell populations: Analysis of spatial gradients in lung cancer mortality rates in North Carolina counties. *Biometrics* **37**:259–269.

Menken, J., Trussell, J., Stempel, D., and Babakol, O. 1981. Proportional hazards life table models: An illustrative analysis of socio-demographic influences on marriage dissolution in the United States. *Demography* **18**:181–200.

Trussell, J., and Hammerslough, C. 1983. A hazards-model analysis of the covariates of infant and child mortality in Sri Lanka. *Demography* **20**:1–26.

# Chapter 8

## Projection and Estimates of the National State of Health: Disease-Specific Compartment Models of Mortality Time Series

## 1 Introduction

In previous chapters we presented a broad range of demographic methods for analyzing mortality data of various types. In this chapter we shall focus on a class of models that incorporate information from a variety of disciplines to extend the nature of conclusions that can be inferred from a mortality time series. Specifically, information from clinical, epidemiological, and biological studies can be used to specify the elements of a disease-specific compartment model that will permit us to estimate transition rates to morbid states by using mortality time series data. With these estimates of the transition rates to various morbid states, we can produce estimates, specific to race, age, and sex, of the time spent in certain chronic degenerative disease states.

The importance of such prevalence distributions is that they represent detailed planning information for assessing public health policy at a national level in ways not possible with other data. For example, the estimates are derived from mortality data that cover the entire U.S. population for a reasonably lengthy time. This means that analyses can be conducted for any selected geographic unit in the United States down to the county level. This also means that by using a common model and data source temporal changes in population health characteristics can be assessed. This seems to be superior, or at least an important adjunct, to disease incidence and prevalence estimates made from data limited in time and scope. To illustrate, in 1980 a debate emerged over whether cancer incidence had started to increase in the United States (Smith, 1980). It was suggested that cancer incidence had started to increase on the basis of the comparison of fairly extensive data from the Third National Cancer Survey (TNCS) (1969–1971) and the results for the period 1973–1976 of the Surveillance, Epidemiology, and End Results (SEER) program of the NCI. One major difficulty cited with the use of these two major data sets is that they cover only partially overlapping sets of cities with variable population characteristics, so that it is not possible to be certain that increases are due simply to temporal changes. With national mortality data, however, one can select comparable geographic units for cross-temporal analyses in such ways that one can be more confident that increases in mortality rates are due solely to temporal changes. Hence, if the morbidity process that links incidence with mortality is stable over time, one can use the temporal trends in mortality to infer the temporal trends in incidence. In this case, data from surveys such as the TNCS and SEER need only be used to establish the stability of the morbidity process at the patient level over time so that the noncomparability of the survey cities becomes much less problematic. Indeed, even if the morbidity process is changing so that, for example, cancer patient survival is improving, such information can potentially be used in conjunction with the mortality data to infer the temporal trajectory of incidence, at least at the time of each survey, and by interpolation at intermediate times. A further benefit of the use of the national mortality data time series is that cohort-specific effects can be controlled. For cancer mortality the computerized time series files of underlying-cause-of-death data dates back to 1950; for noncancer mortality the computerized time series dates back to 1962. Hence, with 1980 data being released by the NCHS at the time of this writing, up to either 19 or 31 years of follow-up data on each cohort are available to control for cohort effects. Failure to control cohort-specific effects can be a serious problem for certain sets of chronic degenerative diseases for which cohort differences are known to exist—as for many diseases affecting the respiratory system.

Although the temporal and geographic scope of the mortality time series offers a variety of advantages, one important criticism made is that they do not directly reflect the effects of less lethal conditions nor do they give direct information on an important aspect of health service requirements for the elderly, namely, functional disability. It will be seen, however, that the selection of an appropriate bioactuarial model to represent the mortality time series makes it possible to provide useful insights into these two issues. For example, the U.S. Center for Disease Control (CDC) presently uses temporal analyses of weekly mortality rates to monitor influenza epidemic activity in the United States. The rationale for the use of the temporal variation in mortality rates to measure influenza activity is that influenza can induce mortality in high-susceptibility groups in the population, such as the elderly. Consequently, prolonged upswings in total mortality rates are presumed to represent more extensive influenza activity in the general population. Similarly, the analysis of the health effects of various environmental pollutants conducted by Lave and Seskin (1977) used mortality data because it covered a large population and because it was presumed that a linkage between mortality rates and selected environmental pollutants would also strongly imply a linkage between those pollutants and more subtle health effects in the population. An appropriately constructed bioactuarial model may begin to detect some of those effects.

Inferring disability from mortality is a more difficult task because the linkage may not be as direct; that is, fairly severe functional disability may not be strongly related to increased mortality risks. For example, various types of sensory impairment (e.g., poor eyesight or hearing) may prove to be very incapacitating but not indicative of a life-threatening underlying disease. On the other hand, diabetes and hypertension are major disease states whose associated disability may be responsive to medical therapy even though there is increased mortality risk. Thus, it is necessary to investigate the linkage between disability behavior and the mortality time series. This can be done by obtaining community-based assessments of the linkage of primary morbid states with disability and then using the derived linkage to infer disability distributions from the population profile of chronic degenerative diseases. This simply reflects an attempt to link the broad-scope mortality data with intensive, but select, community study data.

Clearly, our suggestion for the use of the mortality time series as the core of a strategy to evaluate and monitor various details of population health characteristics is reliant on a variety of modeling assumptions. If direct information were available on each of the dimensions of population health that we would wish to monitor, then we would directly analyze that information. However, such direct population information is not available, and we are forced to use the indirect modeling strategy we propose. As a consequence, one of the important properties to be sought in the indirect modeling strategy we will use is the capacity to provide a clear statement of the model assumptions so that they are open to scientific review. Actually, scientific reviewability is a multifaceted issue. For example, one criterion for review is that the proposed model can be fitted to empirical data for statistical evaluation. Our proposed bioactuarial models have that characteristic. In contrast, subjective probability models, which are decision models whose only input is the opinions of a selected group of experts, do not possess this trait. However, statistical review is not sufficient. As Murphy (1978) has argued, it will often be necessary to go beyond statistical review and assess the biological and substantive implications of models of chronic diseases if one wishes not only to describe the data, but also to develop the capacity to make accurate and detailed projections. The bioactuarial models we present can be reviewed in three additional ways. First, the elements of the model can be reviewed for substantive meaning. Second, the implied behavior of various internal aspects of the model can be reviewed for reasonableness. To illustrate, if an estimate of the amount of time between disease initiation and death is derived from the model, it may be contrasted to available data on the length of clinical survival. Clearly, the total period should be greater than the clinical period. Third, the sensitivity of the model can be reviewed through the use of simulation experiments. Thus, it is possible to assess how sensitive the outcome of the model is to uncertainty in various of its component elements. High sensitivity would suggest that the model results should be interpreted with appropriate caution and that there is need for specific types of data collection.

In the remainder of this chapter, we (1) present a bioactuarial model of lung cancer mortality in the U.S. population, (2) estimate its parameters from a U.S. mortality time series, and (3) generate the prevalence distribution of lung cancer estimated for 1977 and projected for 1997. This chapter will provide a concrete illustration of the detailed steps involved in bioactuarial modeling efforts.

## 2   A Bioactuarial Model of U.S. Lung Cancer Morbidity and Mortality

The core concept of a bioactuarial model of lung cancer mortality is a stochastic compartmental system representation of a simple illness–death process for an individual. We represent this process schematically in Fig. 1.

In Fig. 1 we identify four compartments, or discrete health states, and four types of transitions between those health states. There are three analytic stages necessary to apply this model to a mortality time series and generate morbidity prevalence. The first stage involves an evaluation of the substantive assumptions that can be made that will allow structural identification of the parameters of the transition functions in Fig. 1 so that they can be estimated from mortality time series data. The second stage involves technical considerations in statistical estimation of parameters. The third stage considers how the prevalence distribution can be generated from the transition parameters.

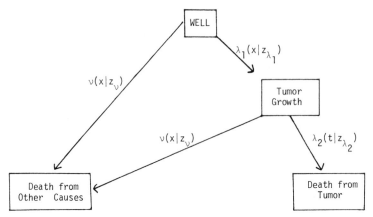

**Fig. 1.** A stochastic compartment model of a lung cancer morbidity–mortality process.

## Model Specification

Given that we shall attempt to generate estimates of the illness–death process described in Fig. 1 from mortality data, it is clear that we have to utilize substantively based restrictions on those functions because the mortality time series will only describe the rate of entry to the well state (i.e., birth) and the rate of exit to the death states. The four transition functions for the individual-level processes described in Fig. 1 will be derived by making assumptions in three general areas.

### Independence of the Forces of Mortality

An assumption that is often made in the analysis of cause-specific mortality data is that the forces of mortality are independent. In the specific model in which we are interested, we make several assumptions about independence of risks. First, we assume that the fundamental conditional independence condition (4.6.43) applies to each pair of exit risks indicated in Fig. 1. As discussed in Chapter 4, this assumption simply states that the model is properly specified in the sense that elimination of any transition rate leaves the remaining transition rates unaltered. This form of independence is at the level of an individual because it is conditional on the risk factors $Z_\nu$, $Z_{\lambda_1}$, and $Z_{\lambda_2}$. Second, we assume that the three risk factors $Z_\nu$, $Z_{\lambda_1}$, and $Z_{\lambda_2}$ are pairwise uncorrelated. This satisfies an analogous condition to (4.6.58) in which case the marginal transition rates $\nu(x)$ and $\lambda_1(x)$ are independent in the sense of condition (4.4.24). Also, conditional on $t$, $\nu(x)$ and $\lambda_2(t)$ are also independent. Third, we assume that the transition rate $\nu(x|z_\nu)$ is unchanged by the presence of a growing tumor. This is analogous to condition (4.5.31) except that it is specified at the level of an individual. With the other assumptions, however, it implies condition (4.5.34), so that the methods of that section become applicable to our present analysis.

The assumption that $\nu(x)$ and $\lambda(x)$ are independent might be questionable in view of the association of cigarette smoking with both lung cancer and heart disease. However, it appears that the risk of heart disease mortality is related to current smoking behavior (Manton and Woodbury, 1983) whereas the risk of lung cancer mortality is related to prior smoking behavior (20 or more years in the past; $\bar{t}$ estimate in Table 2), so that the association depends on the persistence of the smoking habit. If the risks are dependent, then our estimates of the number of persons with a tumor at some stage of development will tend to underestimate the true number, although we shall not know the extent of the bias. It will, however, be less than the cumulative total number of heart disease deaths in the cohort at each age, so that for the younger ages, at least, it must be very small.

With these assumptions we have the following marginal transition rates:

$$\nu(x) = \mathscr{E}_{Z_\nu|(x)}\{\nu(x|z_\nu)\}, \tag{8.2.1}$$

$$\lambda_1(x) = \mathscr{E}_{Z_{\lambda_1}|(x)}\{\lambda_1(x|z_{\lambda_1})\}, \tag{8.2.2}$$

$$\lambda_2(t) = \mathscr{E}_{Z_{\lambda_2}|(t)}\{\lambda_2(t|z_{\lambda_2})\}, \tag{8.2.3}$$

These equations are analogous to (4.6.22b). It also follows from (4.5.34) and (4.5.40) that the total transition from the well state to the tumor death state is governed by $\lambda(x)$, where

$$\lambda(x) = -\frac{d}{dx} \ln \int_x^\infty \lambda_1(a) \exp\left[- \int_0^u \lambda_1(w) \, dw\right]$$

$$\times \lambda_2(u - a) \exp\left[- \int_0^{u-a} \lambda_2(t) \, dt\right] da \, du. \tag{8.2.4}$$

With $\lambda(x)$ defined in (8.2.4), we obtain the total force of mortality as the sum

$$\mu(x) = \lambda(x) + \nu(x). \tag{8.2.5}$$

Note that estimates of the terms in (8.2.5) can be made by using the multiple-decrement life table methods of Chapter 5 because condition (5.4.2) is a consequence of our independence assumptions in the preceding discussion. This permits us to focus our efforts on specification of the components of $\lambda(x)$ in (8.2.2)–(8.2.4).

### The Process of Carcinogenesis

The force of mortality due to cancer is the result of two component processes, that is, the process of cancer onset (carcinogenesis) and the process of cancer death. In order to estimate the parameters of the functions describing these transitions, it is necessary to make substantively based assumptions. In the case of the cancer onset process, there are several theories of human carcinogenesis that can be drawn upon to develop substantive constraints (Armitage and Doll, 1961). Currently, the most widely accepted theory is the multistage theory of human carcinogenesis attributed to Armitage and Doll (1954). This theory was developed to explain the observation that the plot of the natural logarithm of age against the natural logarithm of the stomach cancer mortality rate was linear. Armitage and Doll suggested that this could be explained by assuming that cancer was monoclonal in origin (i.e., stemmed from a single cell) and that a tumor initiated when $m$ nonlethal mutations occurred in that cell. This leads to the specification that the age increase in the rate of tumor onset could be described as a simple Weibull function of age, or

$$\lambda_1(x) = \alpha x^{m-1}, \tag{8.2.6}$$

where $m$ represents the number of mutations and $\alpha$ is proportional to the cumulative product of the probability of each of the $m$ mutations. This function has been found to be a good predictor of the mortality rates of a broad range of cancers for a number of national populations up to age 70 or 75 (Cook et al., 1969). This function has the desirable property in that it is the hazard function for a Type III extreme value distribution (Watson, 1977). Under the theory of failure processes involved in extreme value distributions, this means that the cellular level event of carcinogenesis may be related to the incidence of tumor onset in individuals.

Unfortunately, this functional representation of human carcinogenesis has two problems with it—one theoretical and the other empirical. The theoretical problem is that the function is intended to describe the age of onset of the initiation of the tumor from a single cell. Clearly, our observations are limited to tumors that have progressed far beyond a single cell. There are two solutions to this problem. First, it could be realized that the process describing cancer death is actually the realization of two stochastic processes—one for tumor onset and one for tumor death—so that the parameters of both processes could be estimated. Second, instead of estimating the parameters of the second process directly, one could estimate a "guarantee time" that would represent the temporal offset of tumor onset from tumor death. We have tried both strategies (Tolley et al., 1978) and found, given that the most plausible model of tumor growth is exponential or slightly subexponential (Archambeau *et al.*, 1970), that the effects of the rate of growth of the tumor on the hazard rate $\lambda(x)$ could be well represented by the point estimate $\bar{t}$.

The second problem is an empirical one in that the function describing $\lambda(x)$ is often found to overpredict cancer risks at advanced (i.e., 75+) ages. This raises the question as to how the function describing $\lambda(x)$ might be misspecified. One possibility is that the Armitage and Doll model is not biologically appropriate. However, given that it provides a good fit for a wide variety of tumor types for most younger ages and that it derives from a plausible biological model, this possibility does not suggest a useful alternative. A second possibility is that the functional description of $\lambda(x)$ mistakenly assumes that every individual in the population has the identical cancer risk. This seems more plausible because there are a variety of risk factors (e.g., smoking) that are known to alter individual risks. As a consequence, it was decided that the function describing $\lambda(x)$ needed to be modified to represent the effects of population heterogeneity.

The first step in developing such a modification is to realize that if individuals have different risks to cancer incidence, then the individual with the highest risk level will develop the cancer at the earliest ages and will be selected from the population at risk. This suggests that the age trajectory of individual cancer risks will be different from the age trajectory of cancer risks for a cohort because the cohort will represent a group of individuals with different cancer risks that is being systematically changed.

In order to unconfound the effects of population heterogeneity and selection, we must do two things. First, we must develop a model relating individual cancer risks to the average risks among the cohort survivors to any given age. Second, we must respecify the functional description of $\lambda(x)$ to a form that recognizes the effects of heterogeneity and is estimable.

One of the simplest models of the relation of individual to aggregate risks is based on two assumptions: (1) that an individual's risk level is fixed from some age and (2) that the risk level for individual $i$ is proportional to some standard risk level. This leads to the following expression for $\lambda_1(x|z_{\lambda_1})$:

$$\lambda_1(x|z_{\lambda_1}) = z_{\lambda_1}\alpha x^{m-1}, \tag{8.2.7}$$

where the susceptibility variate $Z_{\lambda_1}$ has an initial average value of unity

$$\mathscr{E}_{Z_{\lambda_1}|(0)}(z_{\lambda_1}) = 1. \tag{8.2.8}$$

With (8.2.8) it is obvious that (8.2.6) must be reinterpreted as a standard force of morbidity rather than as a cohort force of morbidity. Hence,

(8.2.6) is replaced with (8.2.9):

$$\lambda_1(x|1) = \alpha x^{m-1}. \tag{8.2.9}$$

Using the definition

$$\alpha_i = z_{\lambda_1}^i \alpha, \tag{8.2.10}$$

we have the scaled susceptibility factor $\alpha_i$ for the $i$th individual. Whereas $Z_{\lambda_1}$ represents a measure of relative risk for the $i$th individual, the quantity $\alpha_i$ is an absolute measure that is proportional to the cumulative products of the probability of each of the $m$ mutations in a 1-year time interval. Actually, if $N$ is the number of cells at risk to tumor onset and $\rho$ the average interstage transition rate (per cell per annum), then it can be shown that the multistage model implies

$$\alpha_i = N[\rho_i^m/(m-1)!], \tag{8.2.11}$$

so that $\alpha_i$ has a direct biological interpretation.

The next task was to select a distribution for $\alpha_i$. We decided that the $\alpha_i$ should be gamma distributed because (1) the gamma distribution was extremely flexible, thus not requiring that we possess a priori knowledge of the shape of the distribution of susceptibility $Z_{\lambda_1}$ (or, in the respecified model, $\alpha_i$); (2) the gamma distribution only required the estimation of one additional parameter, $s$, the shape parameter of the gamma distribution; and (3) the Laplace transform of the gamma density can be solved analytically to obtain $\lambda_1(x)$ [see Eq. (6.2.5)]. In reality, the assumption of fixed susceptibility is an oversimplification because we know that both initiation of cigarette consumption and its cessation can modify individual susceptibility to lung cancer (Peto, 1977). However, prior to the issue of the warnings by the U.S. surgeon general in 1964, the persistence of the smoking habit and the higher tar and nicotine content of those cigarettes may have led to a susceptibility distribution that was reasonably well approximated by assuming that the values were fixed. At least this appears to be the case if we restrict our analysis to lung cancer mortality in the year 1977 or earlier (implying that the mutagenic events occurred on average in 1957 or earlier, with only a small proportion as late as 1962; see Table 5). There is some indication in our preliminary analyses that the assumption of fixed susceptibility is *not* valid for very young cohorts or for data extending much beyond 1977. We are currently investigating this issue and will report our findings and update our projections in subsequent articles. Substantively, the need for dynamic modeling of susceptibility is consistent with the major changes in cohort smoking habits as well as in the type of cigarette products on the market (low tar and nicotine) since 1964.

Mathematically, the assumption of a gamma distribution leads to

$$\lambda_1(x) = \lambda_1(x|1)\Big/\Big[1 + (1/s) \int_0^x \lambda_1(a|1)\, da\Big], \tag{8.2.12}$$

which shows that the age-specific cohort risk of cancer onset $\lambda_1(x)$ is a function of the individual transition function modified by the two factors in the denominator: the integral of individual transition intensity function and the reciprocal of the gamma shape parameter. Clearly, as $s \to \infty$, the right-hand side of this equation reduces to $\lambda_1(x|1)$; that is, as $s$ increases, the effects of heterogeneity decrease and the standard individual age trajectory of cancer risks becomes more like the cohort age trajectory of cancer risks. When we substitute in the expression (8.2.9) for $\lambda_1(x|1)$, we obtain

$$\lambda_1(x) = \alpha x^{m-1}/\{1 + \alpha[x^m/(ms)]\}, \tag{8.2.13}$$

which shows that the age-specific increase in cancer mortality risks in a cohort can be related to a model of the individual-level trajectory of risks by estimating the one additional parameter $s$. If we include the parameter $\bar{t}$, representing the average amount of time it takes for a tumor to become lethal, then we obtain the prediction equation for our observable quantity, the age-specific cancer mortality rates for the cohort $\lambda(x)$, or

$$\lambda(x) = \alpha(x - \bar{t})^{m-1}/[1 + \alpha(x - \bar{t})^m/(ms)]. \tag{8.2.14}$$

We use (8.2.14) in place of (8.2.4) for purposes of estimating parameter values.

### A Model of the Rate of Progression of the Tumor

In the preceding section the effects of the transition rate to the tumor growth state were modeled by using the simple point estimate $\bar{t}$. The rationale for doing so is computational; that is, that estimation of the parameters of a function $\lambda_2(t)$ describing the cancer force of mortality as a function of time $t$ in the tumor growth state involves the evaluation of the convolution of the waiting-time distributions describing total time spent in the well state and in the tumor growth state. As is obvious from inspection of Eq. (8.2.4), evaluating such a convolution is numerically difficult [see Manton and Stallard (1982a) for discussion of estimation technique], so that the approximation (8.2.14) was employed. For the purpose of evaluating population health characteristics, however, the use of a point estimate is not wholly adequate. As a consequence we need to make certain assumptions that will allow us to relate the point estimate $\bar{t}$ to a tumor growth time distribution by employing auxiliary information. A basic assumption, expressed as

$$\lambda_2(t) \propto g(t), \tag{8.2.15}$$

is that the risk of dying from the tumor is proportional to the size of the tumor, where $g(t)$ is the tumor growth function that indicates the size of the tumor $t$ years after its onset. With this assumption we can examine models of tumor growth, and empirical studies of the rate of tumor growth, to establish an appropriate functional form for $g$. The basic concept behind various models of tumor growth is doubling time, that is, the amount of time it takes for the tumor to double its mass. Archambeau *et al.* (1970) developed three alternative models of tumor growth, and Steel and Lamerton (1966) examined a range of clinical studies of the rate of growth of lung tumors. The conclusion from those two reviews suggested that tumor growth was faster than linear but not quite exponential. As a consequence, we shall assume that the function $g(t)$ is well approximated by a Weibull function, or

$$\lambda_2(t) = \beta t^{n-1}. \tag{8.2.16}$$

To use this assumption, one must equate the parameter $\bar{t}$ to some measure of location of the distribution implied by this Weibull tumor growth function. This can be done by using methods described in Manton and Stallard (1982b), where it is assumed that $\bar{t}$ is the mean of the distribution of waiting times in the tumor growth state determined by the Weibull function with the parameter $n$ prespecified [see Eq. (8.2.37)]. The selection of $n$ must be based both on empirical criteria (i.e., how well the specification of $n$ allows the distribution of time to tumor death to be determined) and on theoretical grounds (i.e., how well the distribution generated from the function produces doubling times consistent with expectations about the physiological mechanisms governing growth and available observations).

One further aspect of the growth function that should be recognized is that individual differences occur in the rate of development of tumors as well as in the rate of tumor onset. Indeed, the empirical evidence suggests that individuals vary widely in terms of the doubling times of tumor development. For example, Steel and Lamerton (1966) observed tumor doubling times from 11 to 745 days in a variety of studies of clinically detectable tumors. Even the range of median doubling times for these studies varied from 32 to 96 days, with an overall median of 53 days. Thus, the effects of $Z_{\lambda_2}$, the factor indicating individual differences in the rate of tumor growth, are important. The distribution of time to death from the tumor generated by the Weibull function can be adjusted through change in the parameter $n$ to represent these individual differences in the rates of tumor growth.

The substantive significance of generating estimates of the distribution of the times to cancer death is that these estimates can be related to the concept of disease severity, at least insofar as increased severity of disease is correlated with an increase in the probability of death. That is, it is generally accepted that a tumor is not clinically detectable until it has undergone 30 doublings and that it is lethal after 40 doublings. Thus, the distribution of the time to death $T$ from lung cancer for those persons who enter the tumor growth state closely approximates the distribution of the time to clinical manifestation of the disease, because for such a highly lethal disease the median survival time after diagnosis is on the order of 6 months (Axtell *et al.*, 1976), whereas the median survival time after onset of tumor growth is about 20 years (see Table 2). This suggests the possibility of combining information on the clinical course of the disease with projections of the distribution of patient cases to make inferences about the type of health services likely to be required in the future.

### The Reviewability of Model Specification

To estimate parameters of the distribution of disease characteristics in the population from the mortality time series, it was necessary to specify a bioactuarial model using auxiliary data and theory. One important feature of this modeling strategy is that we have provided a clear statement of the model assumptions in a form in which they can be reviewed. Three main assumptions were made to develop an estimable model: (1) that there are independent cancer and noncancer forces of mortality; (2) that cancer incidence could be described via the Armitage–Doll model of carcinogenesis, modified to reflect population heterogeneity with fixed susceptibility in cancer risks; and (3) that the distribution of the time from tumor onset to death could be generated by a Weibull hazard function. Naturally, as in any modeling effort, selection of illness-specific functional forms involves some simplifying assumptions. However, the selection of these specific functional forms makes the selections reviewable and helps to focus any criticisms on the specification of better alternatives. The essential point is that the structure of this population model is designed to be substantively meaningful, which is the only avenue through which a meaningful projection strategy can be developed.

### Statistical Estimation

With the specification and review of a substantively derived bioactuarial model of lung cancer mortality risks in the national population, the issue of the statistical estimation of the parameters of that model arises.

We can identify three issues in statistical estimation: (1) data, (2) the statistical model, and (3) inference.

## Data

We have specified the model for specific population cohorts. In general, cause-specific mortality data for the completed mortality experience of a cohort are rare. What was available to us were the partial cohort experiences of a series of cohorts defined for a common time interval. Specifically, we had a 28-year time series on cancer mortality for the U.S. population for the period 1950–1977. This time series contained the records of individual cancer deaths containing the cancer diagnosis, age at death, race, sex, and county of residence. With this time series we focused on nine cohorts, aged 30, 35, 40, 45, 50, 55, 60, 65, and 70 years in 1950. We had a 28-year series of the total and lung cancer mortality rates for these nine cohorts available as well as a corresponding population series, which was adjusted for census enumeration error by using the Siegel (1974) and the Coale and Zelnick (1963) adjustments. In addition, we had available total population and mortality time series data for each of the roughly 3100 U.S. counties, so that it was possible to conduct analyses for specific geographic areas as well as for the nation.

## The Statistical Model

Values of the parameters $\alpha$, $s$, $m$, and $\bar{\imath}$ were estimated by maximum likelihood procedures. The maximum likelihood estimates were produced by assuming that the $D_{x\lambda}$ cancer deaths among the $D_x$ total deaths at age $x$ were binomially distributed. Thus the likelihood function could be written as

$$\mathscr{L} = \prod_x \binom{D_x}{D_{x\lambda}} \left(1 - \frac{h_{x\lambda}}{h_x}\right)^{(D_x - D_{x\lambda})} \left(\frac{h_{x\lambda}}{h_x}\right)^{D_{x\lambda}}, \qquad (8.2.17)$$

where $D_x$ and $D_{x\lambda}$ are the observed age-specific mortality counts for all causes of death and for cause $\lambda$ and where $h_x$ and $h_{x\lambda}$ are the corresponding cumulative hazard functions for the 1-year age interval $(x, x + 1)$:

$$h_x = \int_x^{x+1} \mu(a)\, da, \qquad (8.2.18)$$

$$h_{x\lambda} = \int_x^{x+1} \lambda(a)\, da, \qquad (8.2.19)$$

which are the same as Eqs. (5.2.8) and (5.3.9). The difference between the present methods and those of Chapter 5 is that although $h_x$ is estimated by using Eq. (5.2.7), $h_{x\lambda}$ is estimated from (8.2.14) with a midpoint approximation to the integral (8.2.19); that is,

$$h_{x\lambda} \doteq \frac{\alpha(x + 0.5 - \bar{\iota})^{m-1}}{[1 + \alpha(x + 0.5 - \bar{\iota})^m/(ms)]}. \tag{8.2.20}$$

With (8.2.20) used to introduce the parameters in (8.2.17), the parameter estimates can then be generated by taking the first-order partial derivatives of $\mathscr{L}$ with respect to each parameter $\alpha$, $s$, $m$, and $\bar{\iota}$. The parameter estimates can be obtained with iterative procedures that use these partial derivatives to determine the values of the parameters that maximize $\mathscr{L}$. The variances and covariances of the parameter estimates can be obtained from the negative inverse matrix of the second-order partial derivatives of $\mathscr{L}$ with respect to each pair of parameters. The details of these computations are presented in Manton and Stallard (1979).

### Statistical Inference

In this section we shall deal both with the structuring of analyses to represent specific hypotheses to be evaluated and with the types of statistical tests to be performed. As indicated, there are four parameters—$\alpha$, $m$, $s$, and $\bar{\iota}$—to be estimated for each cohort, and we have identified a basic data structure where nine cohorts are identified and followed for 28 years. This suggests that in the most general case we are interested in models with up to 36 parameters and 252 degrees of freedom. Because of substantive concerns however, we shall not deal with the 36-parameter model. Specifically, the theoretical basis on which the model was specified suggested that the parameter $m$ was an integer value that was a basic characteristic of the disease process. As a consequence, we shall assume that $m$ does not change over cohorts. Second, the parameter $\bar{\iota}$ represents the average time from tumor onset to tumor death, a substantial portion of which is preclinical tumor growth that is not amenable to medical intervention. Furthermore, in the specific case of lung cancer, the median clinical survival time has changed very little over the 28-year period. As a consequence, $\bar{\iota}$ will also be assumed fixed across period and cohort but allowed to vary over race and sex. This suggests that the most complex model we shall wish to deal with for lung cancer has 20 parameters: nine cohort-specific values of $\alpha$, nine cohort-specific values of $s$, and a common $\bar{\iota}$ and $m$. For other tumor types, such as breast cancer, observed changes in the clinical survival time might lead us to modify the model structure by allowing cohort- or period-specific values of $\bar{\iota}$. With the 20-parameter model representing our most general model, our primary analytic interest is the change in lung cancer incidence over cohorts. To investigate this we can generate a series of models that increases in complexity:

Model I:    Common $\alpha$'s, $m$'s, $\bar{\imath}$'s; and $s$ fixed at $\infty$.
Model II:   Cohort-specific $\alpha$'s; common $m$'s and $\bar{\imath}$'s; $s$ fixed at $\infty$.
Model III:  Cohort-specific $\alpha$'s; common $s$'s, $m$'s, and $\bar{\imath}$'s.
Model IV:   Cohort-specific $\alpha$'s and $s$'s; common $m$'s and $\bar{\imath}$'s.

These four models represent a set of nested hierarchical models. For example, the difference between models I and II is that in model II we allow each cohort to have a different average risk for individuals (i.e., $\alpha$'s), although it is still assumed that there is no difference in risk levels for individuals within each cohort. In model III we introduce the assumption that individuals within each cohort have different risks, although the distribution of individual risks over cohorts remains the same shape. Finally, model IV allows for total generality in the distribution of individual risks for cohorts.

Testing the appropriateness of these models involves a two-step procedure. First, the goodness of fit of each of the four models to the data for the nine cohorts is evaluated by using the standard large-sample approximation to the $\chi^2$ distribution:

$$\chi^2_{df_B} \doteq -2[\ln \mathscr{L}_B - \ln \mathscr{L}_C], \qquad (8.2.21)$$

where $\mathscr{L}_B$ is the likelihood function value for the model being tested and $\mathscr{L}_C$ the likelihood function value for the completely saturated model. For the computation of $\mathscr{L}_C$, we estimate $h_{x\lambda}$ in (8.2.17) by using the multiple-decrement equation (5.3.7):

$$h_{x\lambda} = h_x(D_{x\lambda}/D_x). \qquad (8.2.22)$$

One can readily verify that (8.2.22) is the maximum likelihood estimator of $h_{x\lambda}$ in (8.2.17), so that its use yields a completely saturated model.

The goodness-of-fit $\chi^2$ in (8.2.21) has degrees of freedom equal to 252 minus the number of parameters in the model being tested. That is,

$$df = df_B - df_C = df_B, \qquad (8.2.23)$$

because $df_C = 0$ by construction. The likelihood ratio $\chi^2$ approximation for the hierarchically structured pair of models A and B was defined in Chapter 7 as

$$\chi^2_{df} = -2[\ln \mathscr{L}_A - \ln \mathscr{L}_B], \qquad (8.2.24)$$

where

$$df = df_A - df_B. \qquad (8.2.25)$$

In view of (8.2.21), it is obvious that (8.2.24) can be obtained as the difference in the two goodness-of-fit $\chi^2$ values for models A and B; that is,

$$\chi^2_{df} = \chi^2_{df_A} - \chi^2_{df_B}. \tag{8.2.26}$$

One difficulty encountered with direct use of (8.2.26) is that our time series of cause-specific death rates exhibit a certain degree of local unsmoothness (see Fig. 2), which may be due to data error and to period effects such as influenza activity. Because our intent is to estimate cohort risk levels and trends in order to project mortality trends, test statistics are necessary that are not sensitive to the error due to such bias. The likelihood ratio $\chi^2$ statistic based on the absolute difference between the $\chi^2$'s for each model in (8.2.26) will be affected by such biases. However, if we divide the $\chi^2$ difference between models $\chi^2_{df}$ by its degrees of freedom and if we divide the $\chi^2$ goodness of fit associated with the more complex model $\chi^2_{df_B}$ by its degrees of freedom, we can form a variance ratio test that is approximately distributed as an $F$ statistic with the appropriate degrees of freedom; that is,

$$F_{df, df_B} = (\chi^2_{df}/df)/(\chi^2_{df_B}/df_B). \tag{8.2.27}$$

This test is useful because the simpler model A is not so severely penalized for what is, in effect, an irreducible minimum $\chi^2$ contribution due to data error or period effects that we would not wish to represent in our model. Thus, we shall test between the four models by a series of three $F$ tests. The simplest model whose fit is not significantly worse than a more complex model will be the model chosen to project the morbidity distributions.

### Generation of National Morbidity Distribution

With the maximum likelihood estimates of the parameters for the nine cohorts, we can calculate the transition functions identified in Fig. 1. Thus, we have a fully specified model of cancer *incidence*. However, an analysis of national morbidity distributions implies the cross-sectional analysis of population prevalence distributions. In order to compute these prevalence distributions, it is necessary that the cohort-specific estimates of $\alpha$, $s$, $m$, and $\bar{\iota}$ be used to generate the parameters of a two-dimensional life table with a primary transition to the morbid state and a secondary transition from the morbid to the death state. An examination of Fig. 1 shows that the primary force of decrement may be simply modeled as

$$l^{y+1}_{W,(x+1)} = l^y_{W,x} \exp\left\{-\int_x^{x+1} [\nu^y(a) + \lambda^y_1(a)] \, da\right\}, \tag{8.2.28}$$

where $l^{y+1}_{W,(x+1)}$ is the cohort subgroup that survives to age $x + 1$ in year $y + 1$ in the well state. The equation shows that this is simply the number in the well state at age $x$ in year $y$ times the probability of surviving both the transition to death from other causes $\nu^y(a)$ and the transition to the tumor growth state $\lambda^y_1(a)$. In fact, because we need only the cumulative force of mortality for other causes of death, we replace (8.2.28) with

$$l^{y+1}_{W,(x+1)} = l^y_{W,x} \exp(-h^y_{x\nu} - h^y_{x\lambda_1}),  \qquad (8.2.29)$$

where $h^y_{x\nu}$ is obtained by using the multiple-decrement Eq. (5.3.7); that is,

$$h^y_{x\nu} = h^y_x(D^y_{x\nu}/D^y_x),  \qquad (8.2.30)$$

and where $h^y_{x\lambda_1}$ is obtained by integration of (8.2.13) with the cohort-specific parameter estimates:

$$h^y_{x\lambda_1} = \ln\{1 + \alpha_{y-x}[(x + 1)^m/(ms_{y-x})]\}^{s_{y-x}}$$
$$- \ln[1 + \alpha_{y-x}x^m/(ms_{y-x})]^{s_{y-x}}  \qquad (8.2.31)$$

where $\alpha_{y-x}$ and $s_{y-x}$ are specific to the cohort born in year $y - x$ and $m$ is constant over cohort. In case the year $y - x$ corresponds to a cohort that was excluded from the parameter estimation phase of the analysis, we employed linear interpolation to estimate its value. Hence, after using (8.2.31) for the basic set of nine cohorts, we interpolated between each $h^y_{x\lambda_1}$ and $h^{y+5}_{x\lambda_1}$ to obtain estimates for the four intermediate excluded cohorts, who reach age $x$ in years $y + 1$, $y + 2$, $y + 3$, and $y + 4$.

The second life table function that we need to define is the morbidity survivorship function $l^y_{M,x,t}$, which is modeled as

$$l^{y+1}_{M,(x+1),(t+1)} = l^y_{M,x,t} \exp\left\{ - \int_x^{x+1} [\nu^y(a) + \lambda_2(a - x + t)] \, da \right\},  \qquad (8.2.32)$$

which is the density of persons in the cohort surviving to age $x + 1$, given that they have been in the tumor growth state for $t$ years at age $x$ in year $y$. This is the product of the density alive at age $x$ with a tumor growing for $t$ years and the probability of surviving the forces of transition to both cancer and noncancer death states over the interval $x$ to $x + 1$. The evaluation of $\lambda_2$ (which is constant over cohort) is dependent on both the value of $n$ selected for the Weibull hazard function and the estimate of $\bar{t}$. Actually, there is a problem in defining this second force of decrement because the initial starting population $l_{M,x,0}$ is determined by

$$l_{M,x,0} = l_{W,x}\lambda_1(x),  \qquad (8.2.33)$$

which is continuous in $x$. In Chapter 4 we used the term *risk set* to refer to a cohort subgroup whose recorded transition times and ages were identical. We can generate an approximate risk set by defining the integral

$$L_{M,x,0} = \int_0^1 l_{M,x,t}\, dt,$$    (8.2.34)

so that $L_{M,x,0}$ represents the number of persons in the cohort alive at age $x$ whose morbidity duration $t$ is in the range $0 < t < 1$. In general, we use $L_{M,x,t}$ to denote successive values of the survivorship function for this risk set. This revises (8.2.32) to the form

$$L_{M,(x+1),(t+1)}^{y+1} = L_{M,x,t}^y \exp(-h_{xv}^y - h_{t\lambda_2}),$$    (8.2.35)

where $h_{xv}^y$ is computed as in (8.2.30) and $h_{t\lambda_2}$ is obtained by integration of (8.2.16) over the range $(t + 0.5, t + 1.5)$; that is,

$$h_{t\lambda_2} = \int_{t+0.5}^{t+1.5} \beta w^{n-1}\, dw$$    (8.2.36a)

$$= \frac{\beta}{n}\,[(t + 1.5)^n - (t + 0.5)^n].$$    (8.2.36b)

Actually, because we have estimated the mean value $\bar{t}$, (8.2.36b) is revised for use in computation to the form

$$h_{t\lambda_2} = \left[\left(\frac{1}{\bar{t}}\right)\Gamma\left(\frac{n+1}{n}\right)\right]^n [(t + 1.5)^n - (t + 0.5)^n].$$    (8.2.37)

The initial morbid risk set in (8.2.34) can be approximated as

$$L_{M,(x+1),0}^{y+1} = l_{W,x}^y \exp(-h_{xv}^y) - l_{W,(x+1)}^{y+1}.$$    (8.2.38)

This equation requires that $\lambda_2(t)$ be negligible in the range $0 \le t \le 1$, as might be expected with microscopic tumors less than 1 year beyond onset of growth. Specifically, the equation suggests that the number of persons with a tumor starting beyond age $x$ who survive to age $x + 1$ is equal to the number of persons in the well state at age $x$ who survive the force of mortality due to other causes of death minus the number in the well state at age $x + 1$ (Manton and Stallard, 1982b).

The total number of persons in the morbid state at age $x$ is obtained as shown in (4.5.2); that is,

$$l_{M,x}^y = \int_0^x l_{M,x,t}^y\, dt$$    (8.2.39a)

$$= L_{M,x,0}^y + L_{M,x,1}^y + \cdots + L_{M,x,(x-1)}^y,$$    (8.2.39b)

where (8.2.39b) follows from (8.2.34) when $x$ is an integer. Alternatively, the number of persons whose disease duration $t$ is in the interval $(m,$

$m + 1$) is obtained as shown in (4.5.4); that is,

$$L_{M,\cdot,m}^y = \int_m^{m+1} \int_t^\infty l_{M,a,t}^y \, da \, dt \qquad (8.2.40a)$$

$$= \int_m^\infty \int_m^{m+1} l_{M,a,t} \, dt \, da \qquad (8.2.40b)$$

$$= L_{M,(m+1),m}^y + L_{M,(m+2),m}^y + \cdots + L_{M,\omega,m}^y, \qquad (8.2.40c)$$

where (8.2.40c) separates into the age-specific morbidity estimates under the assumption that all cohort birthdays occur on January 1 of each year. This means that all morbidity estimates will also correspond to the January 1 date. Estimates for other dates, such as July 1, can be obtained by interpolation between two successive January 1 estimates, but we shall not deal with that additional issue. Hence, the $l_x^y$'s in these life tables correspond to the $N_x^y$'s defined in Eq. (5.2.5). In the next section we shall normalize the $l_x^{1977}$ values to the $N_x^{1977}$ values to convert the $L_{M,x,t}^{1977}$'s to actual morbidity counts.

With the $l_{W,x}$ and $l_{M,x}$ life table functions calculated from (1) maximum likelihood estimates of $\alpha$, $s$, $m$, and $\bar{i}$ and (2) $v(a)$ estimated from auxiliary data by using (8.2.30), and (3) $n$ selected on the basis of clinical data, we can generate the prevalence distributions for a given period. This is done by normalizing the values of $l_{M,x}$ to the appropriate population figures. Specifically, estimates of the incidence parameters for the nine cohorts are used to produce estimates of the $L_{M,x,0}$ and $l_{W,x}$. The incidence parameters for intermediate cohorts were derived by linear interpolation except for the youngest cohorts, for which the estimate for the cohort aged 30 years in 1950 is assumed to hold.

The prevalence distribution reflects the history of disease incidence in the population. As a consequence, to build a satisfactory prevalence distribution the mortality time series should be long enough to include the hypothesized time of incidence corresponding to the longest time that a person can spend in the morbid state. For example, we shall estimate $\bar{i}$ to be 20.3 years for white males. When $n = 9$, this means that few persons survive more than 25 years with the disease. As a consequence, our 28-year mortality time series is adequate to describe the incidence patterns that determine the 1977 prevalence distribution. If one wished to estimate a prevalence distribution from a mortality time series shorter than the likely maximum survival time in the morbid state, then assumptions would have to be made about how the incidence parameters behaved outside (i.e., prior to) the mortality time series. For example, if one had only a 15-year time series to generate the lung cancer distribution, then the change in the cohort incidence for the 10 years prior to the time series would have to be assumed.

## 3 U.S. Lung Cancer Morbidity and Mortality, 1950–1977

To illustrate the application of the proposed procedures, we examined cohort-specific patterns of lung cancer mortality for white males over the period 1950–1977. Selected results will be presented for nonwhite males for comparison. As we have indicated, there are several stages in the generation of the morbidity distributions. First, there are the cohort-specific analyses of the mortality data and the generation of the maximum likelihood estimates of the incidence parameters $\alpha$, $m$, $s$, and $\bar{t}$. Second, there is the calculation of the morbidity distributions for the last year of the mortality series. Third, we shall project the white male morbidity distributions 20 years into the future. Finally, we shall illustrate how the national data can be used with local area data to provide better estimates of morbidity distributions for specific geographic units.

### *Analysis of the Mortality Time Series*

The parameters for the four different models designated earlier were estimated by maximum likelihood procedures separately for whites and nonwhites and the fits of the four models tested sequentially. The results of these tests are presented in Table 1 for white males.

From the table we see that the most complicated incidence model, with nine different $\alpha$'s and $s$'s, had to be used. The fit of these models can be visually evaluated in Fig. 2, in which the predicted and observed lung cancer mortality rates for the nine white male cohorts are plotted.

From Table 2 we see that for both white and nonwhite males there is an increase in the average incidence parameters from the older cohorts to the younger cohorts. For example, the incidence parameters for the oldest white male cohort ($\alpha_{1880}$) is only 18% of the youngest cohort. This suggests that individuals in the youngest cohort have a relative risk at each

**Table 1**

F Statistics for Tests of the Fit of a
Hierarchical Sequence of Models
for White Males

| Comparisons | F statistic |
|---|---|
| Model I versus model II | |
| $F_{8,241}$ | 259.96 |
| Model II versus model III | |
| $F_{1,240}$ | 750.73 |
| Model III versus model IV | |
| $F_{8,232}$ | 86.77 |

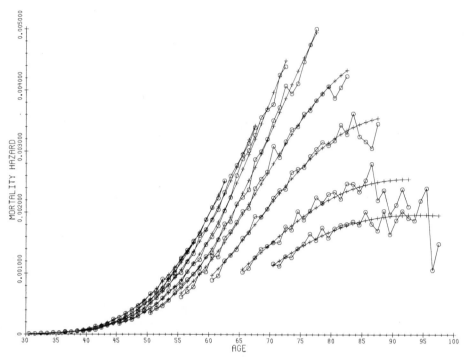

**Fig. 2.** White males observed (○) versus predicted (+) lung cancer for nine cohorts, 1950–1977.

age (because $m$ is the same for all cohorts) that is 5.4 times that of the oldest cohort. For nonwhites the oldest cohort incidence parameter is only 5.2% of the youngest cohort's, suggesting a relative risk of individual nonwhite males of 19.2. An examination of the cohort-specific ratios of the $\alpha$ shows that whereas the oldest white male cohorts have a risk level 2.47 times that of the oldest nonwhite cohorts, the youngest nonwhite cohorts have a higher risk level than that of the youngest white male cohorts. This suggests that as the population ages, nonwhite males will tend to have greater prevalence of lung cancer than do white males as the younger cohorts reach the ages at which their risk reaches high absolute levels.

The $s$ parameters govern the shape of the distribution of susceptibility and for all except the youngest and oldest cohorts (i.e., $s_{1920}$ and $s_{1880}$), the nonwhites have lower $s$ values suggesting greater heterogeneity of risk in those cohorts. These parameters are of interest because these will determine the shape of the age trajectory of the observed cohort mortality rates. Specifically, the smaller the $s$, the greater the heterogeneity and the

Table 2

Stochastic Compartment Model Parameters for Male Cohort
Lung Cancer Mortality, 1950–1977

| Cohort birth year | $\alpha$ | $s$ | $m$ | $\bar{i}$ |
|---|---|---|---|---|
| White males | | | | |
| 1920 | $2.894 \times 10^{-11}$ | $3.395 \times 10^{-2}$ | $6.0^a$ | $20.3^a$ |
| 1915 | $2.381 \times 10^{-11}$ | $8.218 \times 10^{-2}$ | | |
| 1910 | $2.121 \times 10^{-11}$ | $8.621 \times 10^{-2}$ | | |
| 1905 | $1.746 \times 10^{-11}$ | $1.160 \times 10^{-1}$ | | |
| 1900 | $1.473 \times 10^{-11}$ | $1.046 \times 10^{-1}$ | | |
| 1895 | $1.332 \times 10^{-11}$ | $6.906 \times 10^{-2}$ | | |
| 1890 | $1.054 \times 10^{-11}$ | $5.262 \times 10^{-2}$ | | |
| 1885 | $7.261 \times 10^{-12}$ | $3.738 \times 10^{-2}$ | | |
| 1880 | $5.320 \times 10^{-12}$ | $2.907 \times 10^{-2}$ | | |
| Nonwhite males | | | | |
| 1920 | $4.135 \times 10^{-11}$ | $5.368 \times 10^{-2}$ | $6.0^a$ | $19.4^a$ |
| 1915 | $2.858 \times 10^{-11}$ | $8.982 \times 10^{-2}$ | | |
| 1910 | $2.106 \times 10^{-11}$ | $1.086 \times 10^{-1}$ | | |
| 1905 | $1.513 \times 10^{-11}$ | $1.746 \times 10^{-1}$ | | |
| 1900 | $1.241 \times 10^{-11}$ | $1.382 \times 10^{-1}$ | | |
| 1895 | $1.004 \times 10^{-11}$ | $5.769 \times 10^{-2}$ | | |
| 1890 | $6.638 \times 10^{-12}$ | $4.482 \times 10^{-2}$ | | |
| 1885 | $4.359 \times 10^{-12}$ | $2.993 \times 10^{-2}$ | | |
| 1880 | $2.155 \times 10^{-12}$ | $5.347 \times 10^{-2}$ | | |

Source: Mantor and Stallard (1982c).
[a] Parameter assumed equal for all nine cohorts.

earlier the downturn in the cohort mortality rate due to the removal of the most highly susceptible cohort members. A measure of the divergence of the individual age trajectory of risk from the cohort trajectory of risk is the scale parameter $\beta = \alpha/s$, which is presented for males in Table 3.

In Table 3 we see that for eight of the nine cohorts whites have a higher $\beta$ value; this indicates that the force of selection and heterogeneity is greater for whites than for nonwhites and so leads to a greater downturn at advanced ages for these white male cohorts.

The value of the parameter $m$ has been fixed to 6.0 for all cohorts, both white and nonwhite, because this is argued to be a disease-invariant parameter. It is of interest that prior attempts to estimate this parameter from period data tended to yield much lower estimates (e.g., $m = 4.0$). This was because the older males have lower risk levels, which cause the

**Table 3**

Cohort-Specific Divergence Parameters for Lung Cancer
Susceptibility Distributions

| Cohort birth year | White males | Nonwhite males |
|---|---|---|
| 1920 | $8.52 \times 10^{-10}$ | $8.04 \times 10^{-10}$ |
| 1915 | $2.90 \times 10^{-10}$ | $3.18 \times 10^{-10}$ |
| 1910 | $2.46 \times 10^{-10}$ | $1.94 \times 10^{-10}$ |
| 1905 | $1.51 \times 10^{-10}$ | $8.67 \times 10^{-11}$ |
| 1900 | $1.41 \times 10^{-10}$ | $8.98 \times 10^{-11}$ |
| 1895 | $1.93 \times 10^{-10}$ | $1.74 \times 10^{-10}$ |
| 1890 | $2.00 \times 10^{-10}$ | $1.48 \times 10^{-10}$ |
| 1885 | $1.94 \times 10^{-10}$ | $1.46 \times 10^{-10}$ |
| 1880 | $1.83 \times 10^{-10}$ | $4.03 \times 10^{-11}$ |

period rates to rise less rapidly over age and to give the appearance of a
flatter curve. For diseases with decreasing cohort risks (i.e., younger
cohorts having lower risk levels than older cohorts), the bias in the period
estimates of $m$ would be in the opposite direction. The estimates of $\bar{t}$ (i.e.,
20.3 years for white males and 19.4 years for nonwhite males) are consistent with the available auxiliary data on the rate of development of lung
tumors.

### National Morbidity Prevalence Estimates and Projections

With the maximum likelihood estimates of $\alpha$, $s$, $m$, and $\bar{t}$, multiple-
decrement estimates of $h_{xv}^{y}$, and specification of the value 9 for the fixed
parameter $n$, it is possible to calculate the life table parameters $l_{W,x}$ and
$L_{M,x,t}$ to produce national morbidity estimates. In Table 4 we present the
total age-specific populations for both white and nonwhite males in 1977
(i.e., the $N_{x}^{1977}$'s), which are used to normalize the $l_{W,x}$ and $L_{M,x,t}$ life table
parameters to represent the well and morbid population counts. Addition-
ally, the three mortality decrements in Fig. 1 are presented in Table 4 for
comparison. More deaths in the tumor growth state are due to nontumor
causes than to the tumor because of the 20-year latency.

One can see that the nonwhite age-specific prevalence rates are higher
at earlier ages due to the higher incidence parameters at these ages. Also,
the death rates from causes other than cancer but with a tumor growing
are higher at earlier ages for nonwhites.

One other dimension of the lung cancer morbidity distribution we shall
examine is the length of the time spent in the tumor growth state. This is

important because the length of time in the tumor growth state will be related to the level of progression or growth of the tumor and, consequently, to the probable need for medical services. In Table 5 we present the distribution of white males in the tumor growth state for 5-year intervals for 1977.

It will be of interest to assess how the morbidity measures provided in Table 4 will change in the future. As a consequence, we projected the morbidity distributions 20 years into the future. Under the model we can see that this projection involved making certain assumptions for several parameters that guided the morbidity and mortality dynamics. For example, a projection of the change of $\nu(x)$ would determine how competing risk effects will shape future morbidity and mortality distributions. Changes in $\alpha$ over cohorts will determine basic incidence-level changes, and the value of $s$ will determine the overall shape of the observed cohort mortality curves (because $m$ is fixed). The parameter $\bar{t}$ will govern our perception of survivability to the disease process. The illustrative projections in Table 6 were derived with simple assumptions of stability, that is, $\nu(x)$ and $\bar{t}$ unchanged, $\alpha$ and $s$ for younger cohorts fixed to the $\alpha_{1920}$ and $s_{1920}$ values, and a constant number of births per year.

From Table 6 it can be seen that there might be a substantial shift of the population distribution to the older ages. The projected total number of persons with a tumor growing decreases slightly from 2,073,955 to 2,041,352—a change of 32,603 persons. Note however that because of the change in age structure, the number of persons dying from lung cancer increases by 4919, from 60,616 to 65,535—an 8.1% increase. Naturally, because the 1920 birth cohort will be age 77 in 1997, the projections for younger cohorts will be dominated by the assumption of stable mortality parameters. From Table 2 it can be seen that there are significant cohort trends in these parameters so that without an accounting for such trends, the projections in Table 6 should be regarded only as illustrative.

### Small Area Estimates of Lung Cancer Morbidity Distributions

The national mortality time series data are useful because their tremendous amount of information permits us to estimate very detailed cohort-specific incidence models. However, when one wishes to focus on smaller geographic areas, such as state or county, information is more limited — particularly for nonwhites or for less common diseases. The modeling strategy we have presented offers an analytical approach to this local-area estimation problem. First, we suggest that for any area that has extremely limited information, our best parameter estimates are derived from the

**Table 4**

Predicted Lung Cancer Morbidity and Mortality Conditions in 1977

| Age | Observed population | Number of persons in well-state compartment at ages $x$ to $x+5$ | Number of persons in tumor growth compartment at ages $x$ to $x+5$ | Total number of persons dying in age interval $(x, x+5)$ | Number of persons in well state dying in age interval $(x, x+5)$ | Number of persons in tumor growth state dying of nontumor cause in age interval $(x, x+5)$ | Number of persons in tumor growth state dying of tumor in age interval $(x, x+5)$ |
|---|---|---|---|---|---|---|---|
| | | | | White males | | | |
| 0 | 6,578,500 | 6,578,500 | 0 | 22,770 | 22,770 | 0 | 0 |
| 5 | 7,472,793 | 7,472,786 | 7 | 2,796 | 2,796 | 0 | 0 |
| 10 | 8,295,061 | 8,294,910 | 150 | 3,486 | 3,486 | 0 | 0 |
| 15 | 9,193,130 | 9,191,949 | 1,180 | 13,203 | 13,201 | 2 | 0 |
| 20 | 8,787,712 | 8,782,730 | 4,982 | 16,249 | 16,239 | 9 | 1 |
| 25 | 8,043,217 | 8,028,156 | 15,061 | 12,786 | 12,745 | 24 | 17 |
| 30 | 6,994,122 | 6,960,567 | 33,554 | 10,992 | 10,846 | 53 | 93 |
| 35 | 5,514,716 | 5,457,568 | 57,148 | 11,558 | 11,123 | 118 | 317 |
| 40 | 4,969,989 | 4,876,481 | 93,508 | 16,343 | 15,149 | 295 | 899 |
| 45 | 5,164,363 | 5,013,973 | 150,389 | 28,034 | 24,983 | 757 | 2,294 |
| 50 | 5,234,510 | 5,027,697 | 206,813 | 47,214 | 40,876 | 1,677 | 4,660 |
| 55 | 4,904,591 | 4,654,921 | 249,670 | 68,596 | 58,139 | 3,103 | 7,354 |
| 60 | 4,118,206 | 3,783,425 | 334,781 | 92,952 | 76,212 | 6,725 | 10,016 |
| 65 | 3,387,797 | 3,055,655 | 332,143 | 114,659 | 93,326 | 10,008 | 11,325 |
| 70 | 2,420,557 | 2,138,067 | 282,491 | 123,724 | 100,361 | 13,041 | 10,322 |
| 75 | 1,560,768 | 1,380,782 | 179,985 | 117,336 | 97,653 | 12,403 | 7,280 |
| 80 | 979,411 | 889,364 | 90,047 | 104,148 | 91,173 | 8,914 | 4,061 |
| 85 | 471,559 | 438,084 | 33,475 | 68,261 | 62,107 | 4,580 | 1,575 |
| 90 | 148,381 | 140,702 | 7,679 | 29,226 | 27,422 | 1,443 | 361 |
| 95 | 22,252 | 21,361 | 890 | 5,613 | 5,355 | 217 | 41 |
| | 94,261,634 | 92,187,679 | 2,073,955 | 909,948 | 785,963 | 63,369 | 60,616 |

## Nonwhite males

| | | | | | | | |
|---|---|---|---|---|---|---|---|
| 0 | 1,502,632 | 1,502,632 | 0 | 8,823 | 8,823 | 0 | 0 |
| 5 | 1,585,129 | 1,585,127 | 2 | 756 | 756 | 0 | 0 |
| 10 | 1,647,978 | 1,647,936 | 42 | 856 | 857 | 0 | 0 |
| 15 | 1,686,303 | 1,685,998 | 305 | 2,364 | 2,363 | 1 | 0 |
| 20 | 1,505,621 | 1,504,423 | 1,198 | 3,787 | 3,783 | 4 | 0 |
| 25 | 1,289,888 | 1,286,469 | 3,419 | 4,132 | 4,116 | 11 | 5 |
| 30 | 1,026,277 | 1,019,205 | 7,072 | 3,634 | 3,584 | 26 | 25 |
| 35 | 858,360 | 845,577 | 12,783 | 3,963 | 3,818 | 58 | 86 |
| 40 | 769,523 | 748,508 | 21,015 | 5,104 | 4,734 | 133 | 236 |
| 45 | 737,011 | 705,813 | 31,199 | 6,995 | 6,185 | 274 | 536 |
| 50 | 668,880 | 630,315 | 38,565 | 9,694 | 8,239 | 501 | 954 |
| 55 | 575,201 | 534,092 | 41,109 | 11,840 | 9,773 | 743 | 1,324 |
| 60 | 439,284 | 398,771 | 40,513 | 13,479 | 11,019 | 1,108 | 1,352 |
| 65 | 377,684 | 337,046 | 40,638 | 15,054 | 12,181 | 1,446 | 1,427 |
| 70 | 238,552 | 207,528 | 31,024 | 14,412 | 11,611 | 1,707 | 1,095 |
| 75 | 146,510 | 128,463 | 18,047 | 12,267 | 10,157 | 1,400 | 710 |
| 80 | 95,445 | 87,985 | 7,459 | 8,415 | 7,456 | 615 | 344 |
| 85 | 48,392 | 45,705 | 2,687 | 4,916 | 4,528 | 257 | 131 |
| 90 | 18,165 | 17,430 | 735 | 2,183 | 2,062 | 84 | 36 |
| 95 | 4,148 | 3,952 | 197 | 564 | 529 | 26 | 9 |
| | 15,220,982 | 14,922,976 | 298,006 | 133,238 | 116,574 | 8,394 | 8,270 |

Source: Manton and Stallard (1982c).

**Table 5**

White Male Lung Cancer Prevalence in 1977

| Age | Total | Time in tumor growth state (years) | | | | | |
|---|---|---|---|---|---|---|---|
| | | 0–4 | 5–9 | 10–14 | 15–19 | 20–24 | 25–29 |
| 0 | 0 | 0 | 0 | 0 | 0 | 0 | 0 |
| 5 | 7 | 7 | 0 | 0 | 0 | 0 | 0 |
| 10 | 150 | 142 | 8 | 0 | 0 | 0 | 0 |
| 15 | 1,180 | 1,020 | 152 | 9 | 0 | 0 | 0 |
| 20 | 4,982 | 3,875 | 958 | 141 | 7 | 0 | 0 |
| 25 | 15,061 | 10,490 | 3,573 | 879 | 117 | 3 | 0 |
| 30 | 33,554 | 20,860 | 8,978 | 3,023 | 654 | 39 | 0 |
| 35 | 57,148 | 31,253 | 16,551 | 7,068 | 2,084 | 192 | 0 |
| 40 | 93,508 | 44,057 | 28,342 | 14,900 | 5,538 | 670 | 2 |
| 45 | 150,389 | 60,076 | 45,860 | 29,221 | 13,265 | 1,961 | 7 |
| 50 | 206,813 | 69,973 | 61,049 | 46,114 | 25,215 | 4,443 | 18 |
| 55 | 249,670 | 75,142 | 70,302 | 59,240 | 37,336 | 7,613 | 37 |
| 60 | 334,781 | 101,664 | 93,832 | 78,529 | 50,109 | 10,592 | 54 |
| 65 | 332,143 | 94,352 | 90,431 | 79,976 | 54,812 | 12,502 | 70 |
| 70 | 282,491 | 77,477 | 75,489 | 68,645 | 49,050 | 11,760 | 70 |
| 75 | 179,985 | 46,489 | 46,656 | 44,396 | 33,736 | 8,653 | 56 |
| 80 | 90,047 | 21,745 | 22,476 | 22,443 | 18,274 | 5,073 | 36 |
| 85 | 33,475 | 7,835 | 8,188 | 8,353 | 7,041 | 2,043 | 15 |
| 90 | 7,679 | 1,778 | 1,862 | 1,913 | 1,637 | 485 | 4 |
| 95 | 890 | 205 | 215 | 222 | 191 | 57 | 0 |
| | 2,073,955 | 668,440 | 574,922 | 465,071 | 299,067 | 66,086 | 369 |

Source: Manton and Stallard (1982c).

national data. That is, we only estimate parameters specific to local areas if there is sufficient information to estimate parameters that are different than the national estimates. Thus, we can proceed by

(1) fitting the national parameter estimates to the data for the local area;

(2) selecting those parameters that we believe will represent differences between the local area and the national data, leaving other parameters fixed at the values derived for the national population;

(3) assessing the improvement in fit due to the free parameters; and

(4) using the mixture of local area and national parameters to estimate the morbidity distributions.

We conducted such a local-area evaluation for white males in North Carolina. We assumed that local environmental factors (see Chapter 7)

**Table 6**

Illustrative Projection of White Male Lung Cancer Morbidity Distribution for 1997

| Age at start of interval (x, x + 5) | Number of persons in well state compartment at ages x to x + 5 | Number of persons in tumor growth compartment at ages x to x + 5 | Total number of persons dying in age interval (x, x + 5) | Number of persons in well state dying in age interval (x, x + 5) | Number of persons in tumor growth state dying of nontumor cause in age interval (x, x + 5) | Number of persons in tumor growth state dying of tumor in age interval (x, x + 5) |
|---|---|---|---|---|---|---|
| 0 | 6,735,312 | 0 | 22,877 | 22,877 | 0 | 0 |
| 5 | 6,699,044 | 6 | 2,512 | 2,512 | 0 | 0 |
| 10 | 6,687,217 | 117 | 2,770 | 2,770 | 0 | 0 |
| 15 | 6,662,024 | 854 | 9,563 | 9,561 | 1 | 0 |
| 20 | 6,447,598 | 3,698 | 11,924 | 11,916 | 7 | 1 |
| 25 | 7,290,202 | 13,762 | 11,605 | 11,568 | 22 | 15 |
| 30 | 8,018,506 | 39,927 | 12,823 | 12,645 | 64 | 114 |
| 35 | 8,792,875 | 92,956 | 18,717 | 18,005 | 193 | 519 |
| 40 | 8,303,091 | 158,498 | 27,694 | 25,679 | 498 | 1,518 |
| 45 | 7,435,391 | 222,602 | 41,450 | 36,943 | 1,118 | 3,389 |
| 50 | 6,234,673 | 254,830 | 57,840 | 50,096 | 2,045 | 5,698 |
| 55 | 4,650,274 | 234,646 | 67,957 | 57,864 | 2,884 | 7,209 |
| 60 | 3,868,962 | 220,049 | 90,828 | 77,941 | 4,353 | 8,534 |
| 65 | 3,566,255 | 213,357 | 125,023 | 109,025 | 6,368 | 9,629 |
| 70 | 3,043,251 | 182,833 | 160,418 | 143,055 | 8,362 | 9,001 |
| 75 | 2,199,024 | 144,212 | 172,678 | 155,382 | 10,027 | 7,269 |
| 80 | 1,221,964 | 142,690 | 146,471 | 125,133 | 14,366 | 6,972 |
| 85 | 596,020 | 78,303 | 99,562 | 84,840 | 10,878 | 3,844 |
| 90 | 207,053 | 32,193 | 48,339 | 40,632 | 6,159 | 1,548 |
| 95 | 39,570 | 5,818 | 11,657 | 9,959 | 1,423 | 275 |
| | 98,698,306 | 2,041,352 | 1,142,708 | 1,008,405 | 68,768 | 65,535 |

would change the cohort specific $\alpha$'s from the national estimates. The modified estimates of $\alpha$ are presented in Table 7.

From Table 7 we see that the modified $\alpha$'s yielded a $134.77\chi^2$ improvement (9 degrees of freedom) and an absolute fit to the data with $\chi^2 = 277.45$ (241 degrees of freedom).

With the national estimates of $m$, $s$, and $\bar{\iota}$ combined with the estimates of $\alpha$ in Table 7, we generated morbidity distributions for white males in 1977 and 1997 from North Carolina by following the procedures used with the national morbidity estimates. These are presented in Tables 8 and 9.

The projected total number of persons with a tumor growing increases slightly from 43,383 to 46,349, a change of 2966 in the direction opposite to the national estimate. Perhaps more important is the projected increase in lung cancer mortality of 255 from 1201 to 1456, a 21.2% increase, which is 13.1% more than in the illustrative projection for the total United States.

## 4  Summary

We have shown in detail how a bioactuarial modeling strategy and mortality time series data can be applied to the generation of national prevalence distributions for selected chronic degenerative diseases. These distributions can be important inputs into policy analyses requiring population estimates of health service needs. The strategy provides quantitative measures of such needs that are especially appropriate to detailed economic analyses. The strategy is quite general because the mortality time series contains information on a wide variety of chronic degenerative diseases for detailed race–sex-groups and ages, permits cohort-specific analyses, and allows the analysis of local-area health variations.

**Table 7**

Modified Estimates of $\alpha$ for White Males from North Carolina[a]

| | |
|---|---|
| $\alpha_{1920}$ | $3.05 \times 10^{-11}$ |
| $\alpha_{1915}$ | $2.54 \times 10^{-11}$ |
| $\alpha_{1910}$ | $2.04 \times 10^{-11}$ |
| $\alpha_{1905}$ | $1.44 \times 10^{-11}$ |
| $\alpha_{1900}$ | $1.19 \times 10^{-11}$ |
| $\alpha_{1895}$ | $1.03 \times 10^{-11}$ |
| $\alpha_{1890}$ | $6.25 \times 10^{-12}$ |
| $\alpha_{1885}$ | $3.39 \times 10^{-12}$ |
| $\alpha_{1880}$ | $1.74 \times 10^{-12}$ |

[a] $\chi_9^2 = 134.77$; $\chi_{241}^2 = 277.45$.

**Table 8**

Estimated Lung Cancer Morbidity Distribution for 1977 for White Males from North Carolina

| Age at start of interval (x, x + 5) | Number of persons in well state compartment at ages x to x + 5 | Number of persons in tumor growth compartment at ages x to x + 5 | Total number of persons dying in age interval (x, x + 5) | Number of persons in well state dying in age interval (x, x + 5) | Number of persons in tumor growth state dying of nontumor cause in age interval (x, x + 5) | Number of persons in tumor growth state dying of tumor in age interval (x, x + 5) |
|---|---|---|---|---|---|---|
| 0  | 148,815 | 0 | 489 | 489 | 0 | 0 |
| 5  | 165,427 | 0 | 75 | 75 | 0 | 0 |
| 10 | 178,692 | 3 | 82 | 82 | 0 | 0 |
| 15 | 209,177 | 28 | 298 | 298 | 0 | 0 |
| 20 | 217,143 | 130 | 386 | 386 | 0 | 0 |
| 25 | 183,948 | 363 | 282 | 281 | 1 | 0 |
| 30 | 164,990 | 835 | 280 | 277 | 1 | 2 |
| 35 | 132,264 | 1,448 | 322 | 311 | 3 | 8 |
| 40 | 116,520 | 2,324 | 489 | 457 | 9 | 23 |
| 45 | 116,015 | 3,597 | 760 | 683 | 21 | 56 |
| 50 | 112,635 | 4,759 | 1,252 | 1,097 | 46 | 109 |
| 55 | 100,985 | 5,545 | 1,881 | 1,626 | 89 | 166 |
| 60 | 79,392 | 7,196 | 2,315 | 1,923 | 174 | 218 |
| 65 | 64,784 | 6,892 | 2,656 | 2,195 | 230 | 232 |
| 70 | 41,577 | 5,072 | 2,521 | 2,093 | 251 | 177 |
| 75 | 25,240 | 3,041 | 2,211 | 1,873 | 221 | 117 |
| 80 | 16,157 | 1,533 | 1,833 | 1,619 | 148 | 66 |
| 85 | 7,065 | 494 | 1,079 | 990 | 67 | 22 |
| 90 | 2,254 | 110 | 433 | 409 | 19 | 5 |
| 95 | 344 | 12 | 88 | 84 | 3 | 1 |
|    | 2,083,425 | 43,383 | 19,732 | 17,247 | 1,285 | 1,201 |

**Table 9**

Illustrative Projected Lung Cancer Morbidity Distribution for 1997 for White Males from North Carolina

| Age at start of interval $(x, x+5)$ | Number of persons in well state compartment at ages $x$ to $x+5$ | Number of persons in tumor growth compartment at ages $x$ to $x+5$ | Total number of persons dying in age interval $(x, x+5)$ | Number of persons in well state dying in age interval $(x, x+5)$ | Number of persons in tumor growth state dying of nontumor cause in age interval $(x, x+5)$ | Number of persons in tumor growth state dying of tumor in age interval $(x, x+5)$ |
|---|---|---|---|---|---|---|
| 0  | 152,417   | 0     | 491    | 491    | 0     | 0     |
| 5  | 151,588   | 0     | 69     | 69     | 0     | 0     |
| 10 | 151,297   | 3     | 68     | 68     | 0     | 0     |
| 15 | 150,707   | 20    | 215    | 215    | 0     | 0     |
| 20 | 145,807   | 88    | 259    | 258    | 0     | 0     |
| 25 | 161,419   | 321   | 248    | 247    | 0     | 0     |
| 30 | 172,739   | 903   | 296    | 292    | 2     | 3     |
| 35 | 199,853   | 2,209 | 488    | 470    | 5     | 12    |
| 40 | 204,556   | 4,061 | 852    | 796    | 16    | 39    |
| 45 | 168,855   | 5,225 | 1,103  | 991    | 31    | 81    |
| 50 | 145,528   | 6,109 | 1,599  | 1,401  | 59    | 139   |
| 55 | 109,766   | 5,653 | 2,026  | 1,760  | 89    | 176   |
| 60 | 88,561    | 5,113 | 2,466  | 2,144  | 122   | 201   |
| 65 | 77,664    | 4,695 | 3,000  | 2,631  | 155   | 214   |
| 70 | 63,499    | 3,842 | 3,578  | 3,200  | 188   | 190   |
| 75 | 44,187    | 2,915 | 3,637  | 3,278  | 211   | 147   |
| 80 | 24,116    | 2,840 | 2,836  | 2,417  | 280   | 140   |
| 85 | 12,309    | 1,607 | 2,033  | 1,734  | 221   | 79    |
| 90 | 4,158     | 630   | 906    | 764    | 113   | 30    |
| 95 | 789       | 113   | 226    | 193    | 27    | 5     |
|    | 2,229,815 | 46,349 | 26,395 | 23,420 | 1,519 | 1,456 |

Archambeau, J. O., Heller, M. B., Akanuma, A., and Lubell, D. 1970. Biologic and clinical

# References

Archambeau, J. O., Heller, M. B., Akanuma, A., and Lubell, D. 1970. Biologic and clinical implications obtained from the analysis of cancer growth curves. *Clinical Obstetrics and Gynecology* **13**:831–856.

Armitage, P., and Doll, R. 1954. The age distribution of cancer and a multi-stage theory of carcinogenesis. *British Journal of Cancer* **8**:1–12.

Armitage, P., and Doll, R. 1961. Stochastic models for carcinogenesis. In *Proceedings of the Fourth Berkeley Symposium on Mathematical Statistics and Probability*, Vol. 4, *Biology and Problems of Health* (J. Neyman, ed.), pp. 19–38. Berkeley: University of California Press.

Axtell, L. M., Asire, A. J., and Myers, M. H. 1976. Cancer patient survival. Report No. 5, Department of Health, Education and Welfare Pub. No. (NIH) 77-992, Bethesda, Maryland.

Coale, A. J., and Zelnick, M. 1963. *New estimates of fertility and population in the United States*. Princeton, New Jersey: Princeton University Press.

Cook, P. J., Doll, R., and Fellingham, S. A. 1969. A mathematical model for the age distribution of cancer in man. *International Journal of Cancer* **4**:93–112.

Lave, L. B., and Seskin, E. P. 1977. *Air pollution and human health*. Baltimore, Maryland: Johns Hopkins University Press.

Manton, K. G., and Stallard, E. 1979. Maximum likelihood estimation of a stochastic compartment model of cancer latency. *Computers and Biomedical Research* **12**:313–325.

Manton, K. G., and Stallard E. 1982a. A population-based model of respiratory cancer incidence, progression, diagnosis, treatment and mortality. *Computers and Biomedical Research* **15**:342–360.

Manton, K. G., and Stallard, E. 1982b. The use of mortality time series data to produce hypothetical morbidity distributions and project mortality trends. *Demography* **19**:223–240.

Manton, K. G., and Stallard, E. 1982c. Bioactuarial models of national mortality time series data. *Health Care Financing Review* **3**(3):89–106.

Manton, K. G., and Woodbury, M. A. 1983. *Models of the processes of risk factor change and risk selection for multiple disease endpoints in the Kaunas study population*. Geneva: World Health Organization, Development of an Integrated Programme for Noncommunicable Disease Prevention and Control.

Murphy, E. A. 1978. Epidemiological strategies and genetic factors. *International Journal of Epidemiology* **7**:7–14.

Peto, R. 1977. Epidemiology, multistage models, and short-term mutagenicity tests. In *Origins of human cancer* (H. H. Hiatt, J. D. Watson, and J. A. Winston, eds.), pp. 1403–1428. Cold Spring Harbor, New York: Cold Spring Harbor Laboratory.

Siegel, J. S. 1974. Estimates of coverage of the population by sex, race, and age in the 1970 census. *Demography* **11**:1–23.

Smith, R. J. 1980. Government says cancer rate is increasing. *Science* **209**:998–1002.

Steel, G. G., and Lamerton, L. F. 1966. The growth rate of human tumors. *British Journal of Cancer* **20**:74–86.

Tolley, H. D., Burdick, D., Manton, K. G., and Stallard, E. 1978. A compartment model approach to the estimation of tumor increase and growth: Investigation of a model of cancer latency. *Biometrics* **34**:377–389.

Watson, G. 1977. Age incidence curves for cancer. *Proceedings of the National Academy of Sciences* **74**:1341–1342.

# Index

# STUDIES IN POPULATION

*Under the Editorship of:* H. H. Winsborough

Department of Sociology
University of Wisconsin
Madison, Wisconsin

*Doreen S. Goyer.* International Population Census Bibliography: *Revision and Update,* 1945-1977.

*David L. Brown and John M. Wardwell (Eds.).* New Directions in Urban–Rural Migration: *The Population Turnaround in Rural America.*

*A. J. Jaffe, Ruth M. Cullen, and Thomas D. Boswell.* The Changing Demography of Spanish Americans.

*Robert Alan Johnson.* Religious Assortative Marriage in the United States.

*Hilary J. Page and Ron Lesthaeghe.* Child-Spacing in Tropical Africa.

*Dennis P. Hogan.* Transitions and Social Change: *The Early Lives of American Men.*

*F. Thomas Juster and Kenneth C. Land (Eds.).* Social Accounting Systems: *Essays on the State of the Art.*

*M. Sivamurthy.* Growth and Structure of Human Population in the Presence of Migration.

*Robert M. Hauser, David Mechanic, Archibald O. Haller, and Taissa O. Hauser (Eds.).* Social Structure and Behavior: *Essays in Honor of William Hamilton Sewell.*

*Valerie Kincade Oppenheimer.* Work and the Family: *A Study in Social Demography.*

*Kenneth C. Land and Andrei Rogers (Eds.). Multidimensional Mathematical Demography.*

*John Bongaarts and Robert G. Potter.* Fertility, Biology, and Behavior: *An Analysis of the Proximate Determinants.*

*Randy Hodson.* Workers' Earnings and Corporate Economic Structure.

*Ansley J. Coale and Paul Demeny.* Regional Model Life Tables and Stable Populations, Second Edition.

*Mary B. Breckenridge.* Age, Time, and Fertility: *Applications of Exploratory Data Analysis.*

*Neil G. Bennett (Ed.).* Sex Selection of Children.

*Rodolfo A. Bulatao and Ronald D. Lee (Eds.).* Determinants of Fertility in Developing Countries. Volume 1: *Supply and Demand for Children;* Volume 2: *Fertility Regulation and Institutional Influences.*

*Joseph A. McFalls, Jr., and Marguerite Harvey McFalls.* Disease and Fertility.

*Kenneth G. Manton and Eric Stallard.* Recent Trends in Mortality Analysis.